Basic Business Mat
and
Electronic Calculators

Basic Business Math
and
Electronic Calculators

SIXTH EDITION

RONALD MERCHANT
University of Phoenix

RENEE C. GOFFINET
Spokane Community College

VIRGINIA E. KOEHLER
Spokane Falls Community College

Star
PUBLISHING COMPANY, INC.

PUBLISHING COMPANY, INC.

Star Publishing Company, Inc.
Belmont, CA 94002
www.starpublishing.com

Managing Editor: Stuart Hoffman
Chapter opening cartoons: Barry Geller

2011 Printing
Revised Printing 2008

ISBN: 978-0-89863-249-1

Printed in the United States of America

10 09 08 · 10 9 8 7 6 5 4 3

Contents

Chapter 2   Multiplication and Division   79

Chapter 4   Special Functions and Operations With an Electronic Calculator   143

Chapter 5   Introducing the Metric System   181

Preface

In our continuing commitment to help teach number skills for jobs, the Sixth Edition of *Basic Business Math and Electronic Calculators* has several significant changes. It has been extensively expanded, however, it retains the best of the previous editions and the built-in flexibility that helped revolutionize the way business math and calculator courses are taught in the United States. The idea that combining basic math with the use of calculators allows students to learn both skills better in less time is now an accepted fact. We express our sincere thanks to each of you using *Basic Business Math and Electronic Calculators* for granting us a modest role in your efforts to teach or learn these vitally important subjects.

The *Sixth Edition* has been revised, polished, and updated. We have been aided in preparing this volume by my teaching, visiting schools nationwide, participating in national, regional and state business and vocational conferences, and reviewing the suggestions of many people who used the fifth edition.

The *Sixth Edition* is even easier to read. We have added more color, more practice problems, additional real business examples and applications.

We have provided you with a self-contained package focusing on skills that are useful on the job and in other classes. Surveys of the people who hire our students and also of vocational advisory committee members told us that if students take only one quantitative class it should be *Basic Business Math and Electronic Calculators*. The *Instructor's Manual* and *Test Bank* show you how to use segments of the *Sixth Edition* to teach this class. We offer the most complete "turn-key" package available for any business math or calculator course. The *Instructor's Manual* contains the answers to the pretests, numerous supplemental work sheets, and many suggestions for use including tutor guidelines, a sample course outline, chapter hints and grading suggestions for each of the tests in the *Test Bank* which contains at least three ready to use versions of each chapter test.

The fundamental premise of this book is that all vocational students, those with "math anxiety," as well as those with strong backgrounds in algebra or calculus, should have a basic proficiency with numbers as applied to business. Students should be able to add, subtract, multiply, divide, and estimate without the aid of a calculator; they should be able to operate a desk calculator by "touch control"; they should be aware of the special features found on most business calculators; and they should be able to "think metric." This text meets students where they are. Students *without* basic skills have material designed to meet their needs. Students *with* basic number skills can be branched around what they already know.

The publication of this the *Sixth Edition* will extend the life of *Basic Business Math and Electronic Calculators* well into its third decade. The expansion and acceptance of each edition has no doubt been fostered by the many teachers and students who have been kind enough to provide their suggestions and criticisms. I wish to thank the many faculty and students who have contributed to this text, especially Denise Dahmen, Russ Denniston, Terry Engleman, Carol Graham, Jim Lawrence, Mariner Manchester, Sharon Niblock, Margaret Ross, Shirley Schimanski, Charlotte Sullivan, Jim Snook, and Barbara White. We are especially indebted to Stuart A. Hoffman of Star Publishing Company for his support and guidance.

All corrections and suggestions are welcome and will be responded to in writing.

Ron Merchant
Renee Goffinet
Virginia Koehler

To The Student

This text is meant to give you two very important skills: (1) the ability to work with numbers, and (2) the ability to operate an business desk calculator. Since the book branches you around subject matter you already know, you will find the material more challenging and be able to use your time more efficiently. These skills will benefit you in other classes, in a business career, and even in the everyday business of living.

The arithmetic section of this book makes a stimulating refresher course for those already skilled in arithmetic. It also will help beginners to build fundamental skills with fractions, decimals, and percents. Even in the areas of addition, subtraction, multiplication, and division, this section offers a stimulating review and some novel methods for estimating answers, increasing speed, and improving accuracy.

Nowadays we find business calculators not only in many homes, but in almost all businesses. As a business student you should become proficient on a 10-key calculator and gain awareness of just what they can do for you. Employers have come to expect such skill and knowledge.

This text does not assume, however, that business calculators have eliminated altogether the need for basic arithmetic skills. Rather, it assumes that the calculator is truly a learning tool which, along with a knowledge of basic mathematics, will help you solve complex real-life problems without becoming bogged down in time-consuming calculations. Skill with a calculator will not only give beginning students more confidence in tackling difficult problems, but it will allow those of you who are more advanced the time to probe deeper into meanings and relationships.

Business calculators are easy to operate, yet most people learn to use them just to solve a particular problem. In other words, they are more concerned with getting the answer to that problem than in developing skill in machine operation. It takes a concentrated effort to develop touch control and fully utilize the capabilities of the business calculator. This book offers you the opportunity to concentrate on using a calculator efficiently.

You need not think like a mathematician to use the tools and language of business mathematics. You can best learn the tools and develop skill with a calculator not through abstract numbers, theorems, rules, and proofs but by association with everyday experience and general knowledge.

The book's format also allows you to work at your own pace. You will not be just a passive reader; you will respond actively to each unit of material. As a self-directed learner you will achieve more, retain more, and learn 20 to 50 percent faster.

The course will enable you to:

- Work with numbers and solve business problems.
- Estimate answers and thereby improve your accuracy and self-confidence.
- Operate a 10-key calculator using "touch control."
- Use the special features found on most modern business electronic desk calculators.
- Use basic business math formulas.
- "Think metric."

How To Use This Text

This text is meant to help you develop two essential skills: (1) the ability to solve business problems involving mathematics and (2) the ability to use electronic calculators efficiently. To accomplish its purpose, the book uses an integrated approach. It provides a thorough review of basic arithmetic; careful introductions to principles; *Self-Assessments* and branching instructions; guidelines for operating calculators; numerous application problems to work; and *Pretests* to check performance.

Each chapter begins with a list of **learning goals** and a description of the content and its importance. Be sure to read these introductory materials—they let you know where you are going and why.

For each of the four sections in Chapters 1 and 2 that review arithmetic skills, you will find a *Self-Assessment*. These *Self-Assessments* will tell you how much you already know of each subject and will guide you in designing your own individual program of review. Using small units of material and the discovery method of learning, your individualized program will introduce you to basic mathematical principles, definitions, and sample solutions, and provide practice problems that suit your particular needs.

Every section within a chapter contains a series of **sample problems** plus instructions for solving them. Follow the instructions carefully before attempting the unanswered problems. When you have worked the problems as directed and recorded your answers in the space provided in your text, compare them with the correct answers, which follow each set of problems. If any of your answers are incorrect, determine why before proceeding to the next section. This will give you greater confidence in your mathematical ability.

To maximize your learning efficiency follow these guidelines:

- Work the sections of this book in sequence unless directed otherwise by your instructor or the *Self-Assessments.*
- Record each answer in the space provided in the text. Deciding on a definite answer and finishing all the problems in a section before checking your work against the answers provided, greatly improves your learning effectiveness. So that you won't be tempted to peek, you may want to cover the correct answers with an index card or piece of scratch paper while you work the problems.
- Pay careful attention to the hints given in enclosed boxes throughout the text. These hints will help you work more efficiently and give you a better understanding of what you are doing.

- Don't try to go too fast, even when the material seems easy. Concentrate on getting the correct response the first time. Each correct answer reinforces your knowledge and helps you learn the material.
- Don't spend too much time on any one concept. If, after a few minutes, you have made no progress, look at the answer and use it to help solve the problem. If you don't understand why a given answer is correct, note the problem and ask someone. If you are in class, discuss the concept with the instructor. Working several additional sets of problems will sometimes make the answer obvious. You may want to ask for a supplemental work sheet from the *Instructor's Manual.* In any event, be certain you understand each section before completing a chapter.
- Be sure to take the *Pretests* at the end of each major topic, tear them out and give them to your instructor or tutor to grade. The answers are in the *Instructors Manual.* These *Pretests* not only review the content of the chapter but are part of your learning package. If you have difficulty on a *Pretest,* return to the appropriate place in your text or ask your instructor for assistance. Be certain you understand each Pretest question before attempting an examination.

Remember: to solve problems in business you must be able to use numbers. As with learning to ski or play the piano, you will learn to solve numerical problems only through imitation and practice. There are no magic formulas. If you want to be a problem solver, you must solve problems.

GENERAL RULES FOR ROUNDING

Rounding: If the portion to be dropped begins with 5 or more, add 1 to the last figure retained. If the portion to be dropped is less than 5, discard it.

Intermediate calculations: Don't round off too soon. Carry intermediate answer to at least one place more than is needed in the final answer.

Recording final answers: Round money answers to the nearest cent ($.01) Round percentages to the nearest tenth (.1%). Round decimal answers to the nearest thousandth (.001).

A more complete discussion of rounding is given in Chapter 1.

Hint

Refer back to "How To Use This Text" several times during your course.

To Students Who Are Using A
Hand Held Calculator Only

The book can easily be used with a hand held calculator. Simply skip the following:

Addition with a calculator, pages 12–19.

Subtraction with a calculator, pages 40–42.

Developing touch control, speed, and accuracy with a calculator, pages 125–128.

Pretest IB, pages 61–62.

Timed practice drills, pages 63–77.

Developing touch control, speed, and accuracy with a calculator, pages 125–128.

Pretest IIB, pages 129–130.

Additional practice for developing touch control, speed, and accuracy with a calculator, pages 177–180.

If you are using the book with a hand held calculator you may want to mark these sections now.

Fundamental Operations: Numbers, Addition, and Subtraction

LEARNING GOALS

After completing this chapter you should be proficient with:

- Numbers
- Addition
- Subtraction
- Touch control on a 10-key keyboard

You also will be able to pass Pretest 1A, a test on addition, subtraction, and certain properties of numbers, *without* the aid of a calculator. You will also have developed touch control giving adequate speed and accuracy to pass Pretest 1B, a 10-minute timed test on addition and subtraction, using a calculator.

To pass these tests you must complete 30 problems correctly and the number correct must be at least 90 percent of the number of problems you attempt (a minimum of 60 strokes per minute plus recording answers).

Hint

For best results, be certain you have read "HOW TO USE THIS TEXT," at the beginning of the book.

All students need the ability to obtain meaning from the numbers they encounter and make sound decisions based on them. This book offers you the opportunity to enhance your number skills and to effectively use a business calculator. These skills are needed in many college classes and are essential for employment. Since you are able to learn both number skills and calculator skills better when they are taught together, some of the exercises in this chapter are to be worked without a calculator and some with a calculator.

Some of the practice in this book may have an element of drudgery to it, but it has been demonstrated that people who are not willing to practice fundamentals often find success very elusive. Ask any athletic coach about the necessity of practice and the importance of fundamental skills.

Calculators are widely used in business, and the ability to operate them with speed and accuracy is a necessity in many jobs and useful in many other jobs. While electronic calculators are easy to use and all have a standardized 10-key keyboard, many people unfortunately operate them without touch control; still fewer utilize their full capabilities. This chapter will help you develop a touch control and learn the fundamental operations of addition and subtraction. It will help you learn to utilize more fully the electronic calculator and apply it in the solutions of business problems.

Numbers

To communicate well with numbers, it is essential that you understand certain fundamental concepts of our number system.

Number Competencies

You need to understand certain fundamental concepts of our number system before you can use them to solve problems with business mathematics.

When you have completed this section on numbers you will be able to:

- Read numbers
- Write numbers
- Distinguish whole numbers from decimal numbers
- Round numbers
- Recognize significant digits

If you have not yet read "HOW TO USE THIS TEXT," read it now.

Hint

This text is designed to be used as a workbook. Most instructors will require you to tear out the Pretests and turn them in before taking a test. WRITE IN THE BOOK. Make notes to yourself in the book. Be an active learner. Active learners learn up to 60 percent faster, and with better retention. Decide on a definite answer before checking it.

OUR NUMBER SYSTEM

1. The number system we use today is called the **Hindu-Arabic number system.** It is a decimal place system because it is based on 10 symbols or digits. A **digit** is a one-place number. The digits or symbols our regular system uses are: 0, 1, 2, 3, 4, 5, 6, 7, 8, 9. The number 23 contains _____ digits; they are _____ and _____.

   Answers: Two; 2; 3

PLACE VALUE

2. Digits obtain their value according to the place they hold. In the decimal system it takes ten in one place to equal 1 in the next higher place. It takes 10 ones to equal 10, _____ tens to equal 100, and _____ hundreds to equal 1,000.

   Answers: 10; 10

3. The following example shows the place name of each digit.

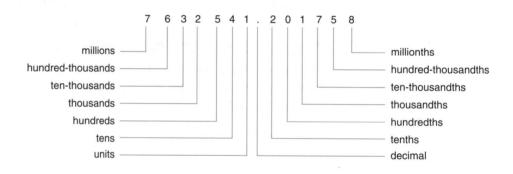

   In the above example there are 4 tens, _____ hundreds, and _____ thousands.

   Answers: 5; 2

4. The value of a digit *increases/decreases* ten times with each position it is moved to the left of the decimal and the value of a digit *increases/decreases* ten times with each position it is moved to the right of the decimal.

   Answers: increases; decreases

5. 732 means two units, three tens, seven hundreds or
   $(2 \times 1) + (3 \times 10) + (7 \times 100)$, or $2 + 30 + 700$.

   859 means nine units, five tens, eight hundreds or
   $(9 \times 1) + (5 \times \_\_\_\_) + (8 \times \_\_\_\_)$, or $9 + 50 + 800$.

   Answers: 10; 100

6. A **whole number** consists of one or more digits all to the left of the decimal point. A **decimal number** has one or more numbers to the right of a decimal point.
.31 is a _____ number, 64 is a _____ number.

Answers: decimal; whole

7. A decimal number is *less than/greater than* a whole number.

Answer: less than

8. When a decimal point separates a whole number and a decimal number, it is called a **mixed number.** 13.71 is a _____ number because it consists of a whole number (13) and a decimal number (.71)

Answer: mixed

READING AND WRITING NUMBERS

9. Notice that in the number 4,123,478,123, commas break up the number into **groups** of _____ digits. Each group of digits has a name: units, thousands, millions, or billions. Reading numbers is easy when you read each group of three as a three-place number followed by the name of that group. That is, each group of _____ is read separately and then the name of that group is _____.

Answers: 3; 3; read or added

10. When writing numbers in words be sure that compound numbers like 34 have a hyphen separating the digits; thirty-four. The following numbers are written:
37 (thirty-seven);

52 _____

29 _____ .

Answers: fifty-two; twenty-nine

11. The number 3,451,002 is read; three million, four hundred fifty-one thousand, two. (Say "two," not "two units.") The number 4,850,000 is read: four _____, eight hundred fifty _____. Since there are no units, there is nothing to read for them.

Answers: million; thousand

12. How would you write in words 6,452,338? _____
_____

Answer: Six million, four hundred fifty-two thousand, three hundred thirty-eight

13. Never say "and" when reading whole numbers. Use the word "and" to indicate the decimal point when reading _____ numbers. For example: read 2.7 as "two and seven tenths." Read 31.045 as "thirty-one and forty-five thousandths." Read 6,025.002138 as "six thousand, twenty-five and two thousand, one hundred thirty-eight millionths."

Answer: mixed

14. The following numbers are read:

    37 _____

    31.02 _____

    1,432.00311 _____

    _____

    23,907.011 _____

    Answers: thirty-seven; thirty-one and two hundredths; one thousand, four hundred thirty-two and three hundred eleven hundred-thousandths; twenty-three thousand, nine hundred seven and eleven thousandths

15. You may add zeros after the decimal point without changing a number's value. The additional zeros, however, mean increased accuracy. That is, 7.4 equals 7.400, but 7.400 shows accuracy to the nearest _____ while 7.4 shows accuracy only to the nearest _____.

    Answers: thousandth; tenth

16. Using the digits 0 through 9 write the following numbers.

    twenty-seven thousand _____
    eight thousand twenty-two _____
    seven and fifty thousandths _____

    Answers: 27,000; 8,022; 7.050

    Even though you have only ten digits or symbols to work with, there is no limit to the size of the number you can write.

17. The monetary value of the total output of goods and services in the United States exceeded 10 trillion dollars in 2004. That is 10 followed by 12 zeros. The full number is written _____. An even larger number is a googol, 1 followed by 100 zeros.

    Answer: 10,000,000,000,000

    Numbers above a trillion are seldom used but if you are interested in all their names, consult a number table in a dictionary such as Webster's New Collegiate Dictionary.

ROUNDING NUMBERS

Rail car shipments increased from 1.97 million to 2.26 million tons. In the same time period cargo trucks increased from 10.12 million to 11.19 million tons, sea containers increased from 4.46 million to 5.71 million tons and aircraft shipments increased from .93 to .96 million tons.

Newspapers often use figures that are only approximations, other examples are "damages exceeded $3.8 million," "consumers have piled up $5.6 billion on new debt in May" and "earnings jumped $211 billion." These are instances when you do not need to know the exact amount. Often a business-person uses approximation rather than exact figures.

18. If the Chairman of the Board reported two million dollars at a stockholder's meeting as an increase in sales, it would be easier to remember (and perhaps even more meaningful) than $1,983,187.28. Numbers used this way are called **round** or _____ numbers.

   Answer: approximate

19. When we change $1,983,187.28 to two million dollars, we have _____.

   Answer: rounded

20. Many situations can be simplified by rounding numbers. Money amounts on federal tax returns can be _____ to the nearest dollar. Figures in the text of a business report are often _____. Most news releases use _____ figures.

   Answers: rounded; rounded; rounded

Rounding is an easy technique; it is also an essential one, since it has so many business applications—estimating, percentages, accounting forms, graphs, tables, reports, etc. How many digits or decimal places to round is determined by the degree of accuracy required, which usually differs from situation to situation.

21. In manufacturing a part for a precision instrument, its measurement would be *exact/rounded*. In a news release, government expenditures would be an *exact/rounded* dollar figure.

Answers: exact; rounded

22. The most commonly used rule for rounding numbers in business is: Add 1 to the last figure to be retained if the following digit is 5 or more. If the number to be dropped is less than 5, drop it and record the preceding digits unchanged. For example: rounded to the nearest hundred, 471 equals 500, 5,359 equals 5,400 and 1,295 equals _____. Rounded to the nearest dollar, $5.98 equals $6.00, $2.19 equals $2.00, and $167.49 equals _____. Rounded to the nearest thousandth, 5.3219 equals 5.322, 14.89412 equals 14.894, and 181.187634 equals _____.

Answers: 1,300; $167; 181.188

23. In Problem 22, the number 1,295 rounded to the nearest hundred is 1,300 because the digit following the hundreds position (9) is 5 or greater. Therefore, the 2 in the hundreds position is raised to 3. Round the following numbers to the nearest hundred.

413 rounds to _____   1,749 rounds to _____

3,456 rounds to _____   681.9 rounds to _____

Answers: 400; 1,700; 3,500; 700

24. In Problem 22, $167.49 rounded to the nearest dollar was $167 because the digit following the units position (4) was less than 5. Therefore, the 49 cents was dropped. Round the following numbers to the nearest dollar.

$5.17 rounds to _____ $18.94 rounds to _____

$132.54 rounds to _____ $49.49 rounds to _____

Answers: $5; $19; $133; $49

25. Round the following numbers to the nearest tenth.

35.478 _____   48.7321 _____   325.78 _____

Answers: 35.5; 48.7; 325.8

26. Round the following numbers to the nearest thousandth.

0.112493 _____   809.18765 _____   9.32187 _____

Answers: .112; 809.188; 9.322

27. Rounded to the nearest hundredth, 3.0015 is 3.00, not 3, because 3.00 tells us the number is correct to the nearest _____ and 3 designates accuracy only to the nearest _____.

Answers: hundredth; unit or whole number

28. When you read "Total sales for Mer-Mag was $159 million," you may assume that the number is _____. A sales figure of $15,978,935 from Summit Corp is probably exact to the nearest_____.

Answers: approximated or rounded; dollar

SIGNIFICANT DIGITS

If you have trouble with rounding, you may need a better understanding of Significant Digits. **Significant Digit** is an important concept in business mathematics, especially when rounding numbers. Basically, a significant digit is one that is exact or measurable. Since zeros often simply fill out a numeral, they are not considered significant unless they are both preceded and followed by nonzero digits. In other words, zeros are not significant when they function as place holders only.

29. 542 has _____ significant digits since all digits are nonzero.

3,508 has _____ significant digits since the zero is preceded and followed by nonzero digits.

12,000 has _____ significant digits because the zeros function only as place holders and, therefore, are not significant.

1.600 has _____ significant digits because the two zeros following the 6 show accuracy to the nearest thousandth, whereas 1.6 would only show accuracy to the nearest tenth.

Answers: 3; 4; 2; 4

30. How many significant digits do the following numbers have?

1.0034 has _____ (1) $1.05 has _____ (2)

520 has _____ (3)   80.0312 has _____ (4)

22.300 has _____ (5) $1,000.01 has _____ (6)

Answers: (1) 5; (2) 3; (3) 2; (4) 6; (5) 5; (6) 6

31. Round the following numbers to three significant digits.

320,946 _____ (1) $375.37 _____ (2)

5.0149 _____ (3)   81.094 _____ (4)

487,917 _____ (5) $25,297.32 _____ (6)

$698.3872 _____ (7)   1,109.87793 _____ (8)

1.00384 _____ (9)   492,223 _____ (10)

Answers: (1) 321,000; (2) $375 (We don't write the zeros after the decimal because they would show unwarranted accuracy.); (3) 5.01; (4) 81.1; (5) 488,000; (6) $25,300; (7) $698; (8) 1,110; (9) 1.00; (10) 492,000

32. Name four situations or areas where rounded numbers are used: _____, _____, _____, _____.

Answer: Newspaper, radio, TV, magazines, population figures, mileage, calorie measurements for diets, and many other areas

General Rules for Rounding

Rounding: If the portion to be dropped begins with 5 or more, add 1 to the last figure retained. If the portion to be dropped is less than 5, leave unchanged the last figure retained.

Intermediate Calculations: Be careful not to round off too soon! Carry intermediate answers to at least one place more than is needed in the final answer.

Recording Final Answers: Unless instructed otherwise in the text, round money answers to the nearest cent ($.01), round percentages to the nearest tenth (.1%), and round decimal answers to the nearest thousandth (0.001).

33. Round the following numbers according to the rules for rounding final answers.

$9.3245 _____ (1)   150.87% _____ (2)

.04328 _____ (3) $17.3456 _____ (4)

.791% _____ (5)   31.87645 _____ (6)

$17.3457 _____ (7)   .679% _____ (8)

4.37865 _____ (9) $.185437 _____ (10)

Answers: (1) $9.32; (2) 150.9%; (3) .043; (4) $17.35; (5) .8%; (6) 31.876; (7) $17.35; (8) .7%; (9) 4.379; (10) $.19

Operating a Business Calculator

Some calculators have a lighted number system to display answers; others print the answers on a paper tape; most do both. Though there are many different makes and models of electronic calculators, their operation is fundamentally the same. They differ in the location of function keys, key and tape symbols, display mechanisms, and special features. Review the operating manual of your particular machine to find the *add* and *subtract* bars; if you are in class, ask your instructor to acquaint you with the machine you will be using.

To achieve the operating proficiency of an office employee, you will need to operate a business desk calculator without looking at it, while concentrating on the material being computed. Most skilled operators look only to find a few of the function keys.

As in typing your posture is important. Sit erect but relaxed. Place the machine to the right of center of your desk or work table so that it is in line with your forearm when you reach for it—close enough so you don't have to stretch but not so close as to crowd. This position leaves the space in front of you and to your left free for the work you are doing. Your right hand can now run the machine while your left follows the list of numbers or turns pages. Left-handed people have a real advantage because they can also write with the left hand as they operate the machine with the right.

Left-handed people shift gears with their right hand. Right-handed people roll car windows up and down with their left hand. Most left-handed people are more ambidextrous, able to use either hand with ease. Once a left-handed person has tried operating a calculator with their right hand for more than a few hours, they will almost always continue to operate it with their right hand.

You should not strive for speed at this point. Rather, direct your attention to learning the correct finger operation even though it may seem slow. Speed comes later.

The keys are arranged so that the 4, 5, 6 become **home keys**, as in Figure 1-1. On most 10-key keyboards, the 5 key or the 4,5,6 keys have a different surface from the others so that you know when you are on the home keys. After you have practiced, your fingers will not really rest on the 4, 5, 6 keys but will be over them and will return to home position after reaching for another key. Each finger in home position reaches up for the key above it or down for the one directly below. The thumb operates the zero and the little finger operates the *add, subtract,* and *total* bars.

Be careful to clear the calculator before each problem so that no figures from the previous problem remain in it. The add mode of most machines is cleared by depressing the *total* key, not the *clear* key, which usually clears the *multiply* and *divide* modes. In addition to a *clear* key, most machines have a *clear entry* key. When entering numbers (indexing), you may push a wrong key; the *clear entry* key clears that number only.

Addition With a Calculator

Addition is the process by which two or more numbers are combined to form a single quantity known as a **sum** or **total**. The 10-key keyboard readily performs this function. Again, remember to place your hand on the machine as shown in Figure 1-1. Your objective is to operate the machine efficiently, not just get answers.

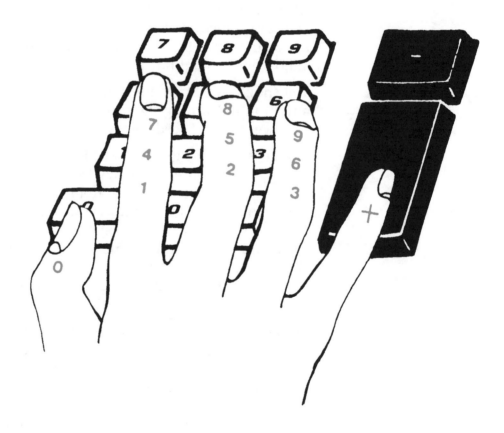

Figure 1-1. Keyboard arrangement and hand position for any 10-key calculator

Preventing Repetitive Motion Problems

Your wrist aches, your fingers feel numb, you have difficulty doing even the most simple tasks like opening a door. What's going on? It may be that you suffer from a repetitive motion problem such as carpal tunnel syndrome—a hand disorder resulting from repetitious motion of the hands and wrists. The carpal tunnel is the bony cavity in your wrist through which your nerves and tendons extend to your hand. When you repeat the same hand and wrist movements day in and day out, the excess strain causes tendons to swell and press on the main nerve in your hand. This persistent irritation of the nerve can result in pain, numbness, and dysfunction not only in the hands and wrists, but may extend up to the forearm or even the elbow. Repetitive motion problems are common and affect those who use the same hand motions over and over again—painters, textile workers, electronics assemblers, word processors, cashiers, and even those who use desk calculators. Fortunately, you don't need to "grin and bear it." Repetitive motion problems are often preventable through proper posture, hand positioning and hand exercises.

Sit Up Straight Your posture at your work station affects the position of your wrist and hand. If you lean your body forward or backward, or if you slouch, your wrist and hand adapts by becoming flexed or extended. This means that the nerves, muscles, and tendons that support your wrists and hands become tense and strained.

Keep Your Wrist and Hand Straight Each time you touch a key, nerves tell muscles and tendons in your wrist and hand that they are needed to help you move your fingers. When you work with a straight wrist and fingers, these nerves, muscles and tendons stay more relaxed and comfortable. So, they're less likely to develop the strains and pains that may be associated with using a calculator.

Exercise Your Wrist and Hand The following exercises, when done regularly, can help strengthen wrist and hand muscles. They can help relieve strain caused by tasks requiring repetitive motions such as operating a desk calculator.

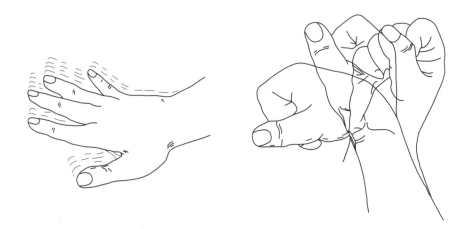

ADDING: 4, 5, 6 KEYS
Here are some exercises for learning the basic operation of the home keys.

1. Find the machine diagram in your machine manual and locate these keys:

   ■ 1 through 9
   ■ zero

- total
- clear entry
- add

2. Set the decimal setting at *zero.*

3. Position your fingers over the 4, 5, 6 keys.

4. Clear the *add* mode by depressing the *total* key, usually with the little finger.

5. Using the 4, 5, 6 keys, index the following numbers, depressing the *add* bar after each. Be sure to use the proper finger according to Figure 1-1. Operate the keys without looking.

   456   455   654

6. You now have listed three numbers. **Press the total bar to print the sum and clear the add mode of your machine.** It is not necessary to clear the display before starting the next problem. If the calculator displays or prints 1,565, you have understood the procedure and should go to Exercise 7. If not, go back to Exercise 1.

7. To check what you have learned, do these sample problems. Are your answers the same as ours?

(a)	4	(b)	45	(c)	456
	5		54		654
	6		65		546
	15		164		1,656

Now proceed to the following problems. Remember, your objective is to build skill in machine operation, not just to get correct answers to specific problems. Do the following problems on the 4, 5, 6 keys. Write down your answers as you go. When you have completed all the problems, compare your answers with the ones that follow.

(1)	4	(2)	5	(3)	6	(4)	45	(5)	54
	5		4		5		56		65
	6		4		6		45		54
	5		6		4		46		65
	6		5		5		45		54

(6)	64	(7)	54	(8)	56	(9)	456	(10)	444
	56		64		46		664		555
	65		56		64		555		544
	54		56		45		455		654
	46		65		64		666		546
	55		46		44		656		654
	44		65		66		565		655
	66		64		55		544		545

(11)	656	(12)	666	(13)	654	(14)	456	(15)	644
	565		444		654		555		646
	464		555		456		564		646
	565		444		654		555		545
	545		555		456		645		546
	456		444		654		444		655
	654		666		456		645		565
	645		444		654		654		645

Answers: (1) 26; (2) 24; (3) 26; (4) 237; (5) 292; (6) 450; (7) 470; (8) 440; (9) 4,561; (10) 4,597; (11) 4,550; (12) 4,218; (13) 4,638; (14) 4,518; (15) 4,892

ADDING: 7, 8, 9 KEYS

Be sure to reach for the higher number from the home key directly below it. For example, reach for the 7 with the same finger that was "at home" on the 4 key.

Do the following problems without watching the keys. Write down your answers. After you have completed all the problems, compare your answers with the ones following this frame.

(1)	7	(2)	8	(3)	9	(4)	74	(5)	85
	4		5		6		47		58
	7		8		9		74		85
	7		5		6		47		58
	7		8		9		47		58
	4		8		9		47		58

(6)	96	(7)	89	(8)	75	(9)	474	(10)	474
	69		45		49		474		477
	96		78		57		585		744
	69		79		84		585		745
	69		98		75		969		458
	69		59		76		478		698

(11)	4,747	(12)	7,485	(13)	7,659	(14)	9,876
	4,585		5,986		8,758		5,874
	5,469		9,674		8,689		9,649
	5,849		6,958		7,984		8,567
	4,568		4,785		6,459		8,459
	5,945		7,894		8,844		8,977

Answers: (1) 36; (2) 42; (3) 48; (4) 336; (5) 402; (6) 468; (7) 448; (8) 416; (9) 3,565; (10) 3,596; (11) 31,163; (12) 42,782; (13) 48,393; (14) 51,402

ADDING: 1, 2, 3 KEYS

(1)	1	(2)	2	(3)	3	(4)	36	(5)	25
	4		5		6		39		28
	1		2		3		63		25
	7		8		9		93		82
	1		2		3		63		52
	7		8		9		93		28

(6)	14	(7)	17	(8)	19	(9)	141	(10)	171
	17		28		73		171		144
	14		39		82		252		411
	71		71		91		232		541
	41		82		37		343		251
	17		39		82		313		258

(11)	1,144	(12)	1,234	(13)	9,336	(14)	7,381
	2,255		5,678		8,225		8,343
	3,366		9,363		7,115		7,673
	3,613		8,252		9,581		9,185
	2,582		7,141		8,473		6,782
	4,711		8,921		1,639		5,956

Answers: (1) 21; (2) 27; (3) 33; (4) 387; (5) 240; (6) 174; (7) 276; (8) 384; (9) 1,452; (10) 1,776; (11) 17,671; (12) 40,589; (13) 44,369; (14) 45,320

ZERO KEY

For the problems in this section, use the nine numbered keys and the zero key. Use your thumb to operate the *zero* key. Work without watching the keys. Don't try for speed; concentrate on the correct finger and thumb positions.

(1)	10	(2)	40	(3)	600	(4)	700	(5)	630
	20		90		300		800		700
	40		50		500		100		50
	30		80		700		400		60
	50		70		900		400		800
	60		60		200		700		300

(6)	902	(7)	404	(8)	470	(9)	4,170	(10)	4,011
	611		400		500		5,280		5,080
	50		50		80		830		60
	506		460		600		5,802		2,003
	300		406		503		7,401		4,201
	259		405		407		1,030		1,006

(11)	6,086	(12)	3,075	(13)	205	(14)	3,447	(15)	1,530
	7,085		9,230		9,527		2,480		680
	550		8,033		6,780		2,320		4,055
	7,065		410		734		831		880
	5,200		1,255		7,320		6,403		2,870
	8,086		6,630		1,881		1,669		5,072

(16)	3,929	(17)	7,234	(18)	8,708	(19)	6,018	(20)	1,008
	982		1,862		1,042		8,004		3,900
	3,508		4,021		5,055		7,576		7,350
	443		9,628		2,200		5,301		2,002
	1,217		944		2,780		835		3,000
	1,119		543		4,072		2,330		7,006

Answers: (1) 210; (2) 390; (3) 3,200; (4) 3,100; (5) 2,540; (6) 2,628; (7) 2,125; (8) 2,560; (9) 24,513; (10) 16,361; (11) 34,072; (12) 28,633; (13) 26,447; (14) 17,150; (15) 15,087; (16) 11,198; (17) 24,232; (18) 23,857; (19) 30,064; (20) 24,266

DECIMAL KEY

Electronic calculators have a **decimal key** (.) for entering decimals. This section will help you develop your touch control of the *decimal* key.

The ring finger is usually used to depress the *decimal* key. When entering decimals you must depress the decimal key on the keyboard, then electronic circuits automatically and correctly place the decimal point in your answer. Most electronic calculators are equipped with a **decimal selector** that allows the operator to preset the number of decimal digits wanted in the final answer.

The following tapes, from a machine set to round at 4 decimals, show how problems would be rounded using our rules for rounding.

97.23	97.2300 +
7.428	7.4280 +
943.1	943.1000 +
.0817	0.0817 +
	1,047.8397 *

Rounded 1,047.840

1.049%	1.0490 +
.9376%	0.9376 +
23.78%	23.7800 +
241.9%	241.9000 +
	267.6666 *

Rounded 267.7%

If your machine is so equipped, use it to round at 4 and do these problems without watching the keys. The machine will place the decimal point automatically in your answer.

Hint

Remember the rounding rules given on page 10 for all final answers ($.01, .001, and .1%). To match the answers furnished, round to four decimal digits for all intermediate answers.

(1)   .913 + 3.07 + .69 + .091 + 1.9 = _____

(2)   4.285 + .013 + 9.1 + 17.97 + 2.02 = _____

(3)   .0088 + 19.07 + 22.4 + .021 + 36.69 = _____

(4)   11.01 + 88.3 + .0095 + 28.36 + .0001 = _____

(5)   2.177 + .0976 + .38 + .0873 + 6.9 = _____

(6)   .075 + .0038 + 9.2 + .53 + 6.29 = _____

(7)   53.8 + .0034 + .013 + 7.7 + .06 = _____

(8)   74.38 + 93.2 + .425 + 6.23 + .092 = _____

(9)   44.99 + .908 + 0.889 + 63.9 + .0947 = _____

(10) .07 + 3.5 + 144 + 13.18 + 8.08 = _____

(11) $.0545 + 56.14 + .0278 + .1985 + 9.1 =$ _____

(12) $.0449 + 352.4 + 7.5 + 24.6 + 63.82 =$ _____

(13) $45.86 + 35.1 + 6.19 + .972 + 7.93 =$ _____

(14) $7.85 + 65.1 + .565 + 2.016 + 33.93 =$ _____

(15) $.0015 + 4.03 + 54.56 + 145.6 + 7.6 =$ _____

Answers: (1) 6.664; (2) 33.388; (3) 78.190 (rounded correctly); (4) 127.680; (5) 9.642; (6) 16.099; (7) 61.576; (8) 174.327; (9) 110.782; (10) 168.830; (11) 65.521; (12) 448.365; (13) 96.052; (14) 109.461; (15) 211.792

Addition Without a Calculator

Every day, numerous questions confront us when we don't have a calculator handy. For example: Did the clerk add the bill correctly? Will the five dollars in my pocket cover the cost of a hamburger, fries, and a milkshake? **Addition**, the process by which two or more numbers of the same kind are combined to form a single quantity known as a **sum** or **total**, is a relatively simple process, one you should be able to do without the aid of calculator. Being able to add with accuracy and speed is an important skill that can be enhanced with a little practice using the proper technique. This section reviews your mental addition skills and shows some methods to improve your speed and accuracy. The following self-assessment will tell you if you need this section.

Hint

If you do not understand several of the problems on a self-assessment, simply skip the self-assessment and work the section. If there are only one or two problems on the self assessment you do not fully comprehend, you may want to look up those types of problems in the unit that follows.

Self-Assessment I—Addition (Without a Calculator)

(1) Recopy and add the following numbers: 431, 8.31, .03, 1.3564, .078

(2)		(3)		(4)	
	8		5		3
	9		4		7
	7		8		4
	6		8		5
	1		1		5
	6		4		7
	5		9		5
	3		2		3

(5) 59	(6) 997	(7) $303.52
25	6,145	743.78
22	4,637	27.31
17	2,682	885.85
25	8,711	54.66

(8) Add using Angular Addition:

3,749
5,718
7,269
8,631
2,451
4,309
―――

―

―

―

―

―――

(9) Add using Subtotal Addition:

374
431
571 _____
358
561
670 _____
729
825
290 _____
565
672
474 _____
_____

(10) Use horizontal addition (add without recopying):

$5.27 + $43.21 + $587.45 + $150.89 + $3.42 = _____

Answers: (1) 440.774; (2) 45; (3) 41; (4) 39; (5) 148; (6) 23,172; (7) $2,015.12; (8) (37, 19, 29, 29) 32,127; (9) (1,376, 1,589, 1,844, 1,711) 6,520; (10) $790.24

If you missed no more than two of the Self-Assessment problems, turn to PAGE 30, Subtraction. If you missed more than two problems or would like to review addition competencies, continue with this section.

Addition Competencies

When you have completed this section you will be able to:

- Add while thinking subtotals only
- Use combinations or groupings of 10 to increase your speed
- Use reverse-order addition to check your work
- Use angular and subtotal addition to increase accuracy
- Add horizontally

To improve accuracy and speed in adding, always write clearly and neatly. Line up the digits of each place value directly under each other—units under units, tens under tens, and so on. For example, to add seven and twenty-three hundredths; three hundred twenty-four; and five hundred and three tenths, we write:

```
       7.23                        7.23
     324.          or           324.00
     500.3                      500.30
     ------                     -------
     831.53                     831.53
```

As shown above, align the digits so that whole numbers and decimals are in the same column. You may wish to add zeros as place holders, as shown on the right; however, the example on the left is sufficient.

1. Copy and add the following numbers: 523, 8.1, .031, 2.65, 123.018

```
Answer:        523.                    523.000
                 8.1                     8.100
                  .031        or          .031
                 2.65                     2.650
               123.018                  123.018
               -------                  -------
               656.799                  656.799
```

2. Write in a column and add the following: sixteen and three tenths; seven hundred four; five hundred and thirty-three thousandths; four and eight tenths.

```
Answer:         16.3                     16.300
               704.                     704.000
               500.033      or          500.033
                 4.8                       4.800
              --------                 ---------
              1,225.133                1,225.133
```

THINKING SUBTOTALS ONLY

3. One of the easiest and most important ways to increase your speed and accuracy when adding a column of numbers is to think subtotals only, without thinking the individual intermediate summations. For example:

When adding:	think:	don't think:
5	7	$5 + 2 = 7$
2	11	$7 + 4 = 11$
4	18	$11 + 7 = 18$
7	26	$18 + 8 = 26$
8	35	$26 + 9 = 35$
9		
35		

4. Fill in the blanks while adding the following numbers using the subtotal-only method. That is, don't think about the intermediate summations.

7 think		5		2		9	
8 15		6	11	5	___(9)	2	___(14)
9	___(1)	2	___(5)	3	___(10)	3	___(15)
3	___(2)	1	___(6)	7 17		8	___(16)
2	___(3)	8	___(7)	8	___(11)	5	___(17)
1 30		9	31	6	___(12)	4	___(18)
_5_	___(4)	_6_	___(8)	_4_	___(13)	_1_	___(19)
35		37		35		32	

Answers: (1) 24; (2) 27; (3) 29; (4) 35; (5) 13; (6) 14; (7) 22; (8) 37; (9) 7; (10) 10; (11) 25; (12) 31; (13) 35; (14) 11; (15) 14; (16) 22; (17) 27; (18) 31; (19) 32

5. Using the same techniques, add the following columns of numbers.

(1)	8	(2)	4	(3)	7	(4)	8	(5)	2
	2		5		4		7		7
	3		2		2		6		8
	5		8		8		2		8
	6		9		8		5		3
	9		8		7		5		4
	5		5		8		7		2
	4		9		5		8		4
	6		9		8		3		5
	4		6		2		6		6
	2		5		5		7		7
	_8_		_9_		_8_		_9_		_7_

Answers: (1) 62; (2) 79; (3) 72; (4) 73; (5) 63

GROUPING IN TENS

Another method to increase speed and accuracy in adding, especially speed, is **grouping in tens.** This means combining two or more digits that total 10.

6. Using the method of grouping in tens, solve the following problems:

(1)	5	(2)	8	(3)	6
	7		4		3
	5		6		2
	3		2		1
	_4_		_7_		_8_

Answers: (1) 24; (2) 27; (3) 20

Grouping in tens may not appear to be a shortcut at first, but with practice it does work. Two-digit combinations that yield ten are (1 + 9), (8 + 2), (3 + 7), (6 + 4), (5 + 5). There are also three-digit combinations like: (3 + 4 + 3), (2 + 3 + 5), (3 + 6 + l), (7 + 1 + 2), and so on.

7. Find the following sums using combinations of 10. Mark the combinations as illustrated in frame 6.

(1)	(2)	(3)	(4)	(5)
9	8	7	3	7
1	7	6	2	9
9	2	4	5	3
6	3	6	1	1
3	5	8	9	5
2	4	9	4	4
1	3	4	7	5
8	2	2	6	6

Answers:

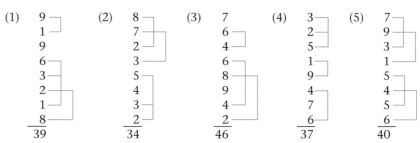

(1)	(2)	(3)	(4)	(5)
9	8	7	3	7
1	7	6	2	9
9	2	4	5	3
6	3	6	1	1
3	5	8	9	5
2	4	9	4	4
1	3	4	7	5
8	2	2	6	6
39	34	46	37	40

REVERSE-ORDER ADDITION

An easy way to check your addition is the **reverse-order** method: add the column of numbers from the top down, then add the numbers from the bottom up. This reduces the chance of making the same mistake twice, which often happens when you check by re-adding in the same direction.

8. Calculate the following sum and check your answer using reverse-order addition.

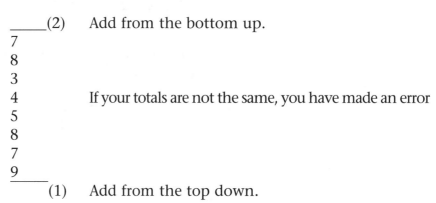

_____(2)   Add from the bottom up.

7
8
3
4   If your totals are not the same, you have made an error
5
8
7
9
_____
(1)   Add from the top down.

Answers: (1) 51; (2) 51

9. Using the technique of thinking subtotals only or groupings in tens, add the following columns of numbers and check by reverse-order addition.

(2)_____	(4)_____	(6)_____	(8)_____	(10)_____	(12)_____	(14)_____	(16)_____
7	5	9	5	1	3	9	3
1	2	1	5	2	2	3	7
2	7	1	8	1	8	5	9
5	1	9	4	7	4	6	6
9	3	3	5	5	9	6	8
3	7	5	7	1	3	4	8
8	5	4	2	7	4	8	6
8	2	6	1	3	3	8	9
5	6	5	7	3	2	1	6
6	8	7	1	3	8	5	6
(1)	(3)	(5)	(7)	(9)	(11)	(13)	(15)

Answers: (1) 54; (2) 54; (3) 46; (4) 46; (5) 50; (6) 50; (7) 45; (8) 45; (9) 33; (10) 33; (11) 46; (12) 46; (13) 55; (14) 55; (15) 68; (16) 68

ANGULAR ADDITION

10. Problem (a) below is the same as problem (b); however, problem (b) seems more difficult than the three simple problems in (a) because problem (b) involves _____.

(a)	8	9	1	(b)	891
	7	7	5		775
	6	3	4		634
	3	1	1		311
	2	8	5		285
	7	5	2		752
	33	33	18		3,648

Answer: "carrying"

11. When you add numbers with more than one digit, you can increase your accuracy by adding each column separately and setting the sum one place further to the left each time, as shown below. Because the sums of each column form an angle, this is known as _____ addition.

Answer: angular

```
  891
  775
  634
  311
  285
  752
   18
   33
   33
3,648
```

Angular addition eliminates errors made by "carrying" and lends itself well to checking by reverse-order addition.

12. Add the following problems by angular addition, showing the details of your work. Check by reverse-order addition.

```
  861        8,095        98,851
  735        2,063        74,392
  689        1,595        47,186
  971        8,867        19,834
  832        9,895        44,352
  576        6,581        33,505
  325        8,679        10,687
  ___         ___          ___
   __          __           __
   __          __           __
  ____         __           __
              ____         ____
```

Answer: 29   35   27
             36   54   38
             46   32   34
          4,989   42   35
                         45,775   29
                                      328,807

13. Civil service employees have been encouraged to use this method of adding columns separately. Therefore, as well as being called _____ addition, this method is sometimes referred to as **civil service addition.**

   Answer: angular

14. Adding by thinking subtotals only or grouping in _____ increases both speed and accuracy.

An often used and very effective way to insure accuracy in addition is to check your answers by _____ addition.

A method for increasing accuracy when adding numbers with more than one digit is the civil service or _____ method.

Answers: tens; reverse-order; angular

SUBTOTAL ADDITION

When adding a long column of figures, another way to improve accuracy is to divide the column into two or more parts, get a subtotal for each part, and then add up the subtotals.

15. The monthly sales of Sunset West are shown in the following table, with a subtotal for each quarter. To find annual sales, it is easier to add quarterly sales than monthly sales. This is called _____ addition. Use this method to find annual sales: $ _____, or rounded to the nearest thousand, $_____.

Sunset West
Monthly Sales

Jan.	$43,281		
Feb.	81,721		
Mar.	93,812	$218,814	1st quarter
Apr.	78,546		
May	68,981		
June	21,131	168,658	2nd quarter
July	82,345		
Aug.	78,956		
Sept.	87,654	248,955	3rd quarter
Oct.	88,543		
Nov.	18,987		
Dec.	23,871	131,401	4th quarter

Answers: subtotal; $767,828; $768,000

16. The 1st-quarter sales of Sunset West are the sum of $43,281, $81,721 and $_____.

Answer: $93,812

17. Find quarterly and annual output of Summer Tone Inc.

Summer Tone Inc.
Monthly Output

Jan.	81		
Feb.	32		
Mar.	54	_____	1st quarter
Apr.	71		
May	81		
June	197	_____	2nd quarter
July	78		
Aug.	91		
Sept.	43	_____	3rd quarter
Oct.	35		
Nov.	42		
Dec.	82	_____	4th quarter
		_____	Total output for year

Answers: 167; 349; 212; 159; 887

18. Like reverse-order addition and _____ addition, the use of subtotals increases accuracy.

Answer: angular

HORIZONTAL ADDITION

It is not uncommon in business to be faced with the task of adding figures across a page instead of vertically, as with payroll forms, inventory forms, and checkbooks. Of course, you could always rewrite such figures in columns on a piece of scratch paper, but it is much quicker and more convenient to add them just as they are.

19. To add a deposit of $252.12 horizontally to a balance of $87.15 in a checkbook, we use the same mental process as in adding numbers in vertical columns.

$252.12 + $87.15 = _____(1)

First add the hundredths. Think $2 + 5 = 7$ and write the 7 on the right of the balance column. Then, $1 + 1 = 2$, and put the 2 just to the left of the 7. Then, $2 + 7 = 9$. Then, $5 + 8 = 13$, placing the 3 just to the left of 9 and mentally carrying forward the 1. Finally, combine the 1 carried forward with the 2 in the hundreds position, to get a new balance of $ _____ . (2)

Answers: (1) $339.27; (2) $339.27

20. Add without recopying:

$2.10 + $3.81 + $5.73 + $3.84 + $6.85 + $7.13 + $3.95

= _____
           Total

Answer: $33.41

21. To check horizontal addition by the procedure of reverse addition, first you add from left to _____, then you add from _____ to _____.

Answers: right; right; left

22. Adding across a line of numbers is known as _____ addition. Skill in adding horizontally can help you avoid making transposition or copying errors. Because the numbers do not need to be rewritten, it also increases your _____.

Answers: horizontal; speed

23. Add by thinking subtotals only and verify by reverse addition.

_____ = 8 + 7 + 9 + 6 + 7 + 8 + 7 + 6 + 4 + 3 = _____

_____ = 7 + 6 + 9 + 5 + 7 + 8 + 6 + 2 + 6 + 8 = _____

Answers: 65; 65; 64; 64

24. Test your ability by adding the following two numbers horizontally without recopying. $2,456,821 + $8,763,452 = _____

Answer: $11,220,273

BUSINESS APPLICATION

25. Complete the restaurant checks in Figure 1-2 on the next page by adding down each column. To get the total check for the Old Stone Barn it is necessary to combine horizontally the subtotals for beverage and food.

Answers: $169.75; $13.25; $81.65; $94.90

26. Sam Clark's daily sales were $217.81 Monday, $389.72 Tuesday, $178.13 Wednesday, $412.50 Thursday, and $781.72 Saturday. His total sales for the week were _____.

Answer: $1,979.88

27. During the last basketball season Paul Long played 12 league games and the points he scored each game were: 14, 24, 37, 8, 31, 7, 14, 15, 31, 9, 5, 32. His total points in league play were _____.

Answer: 227

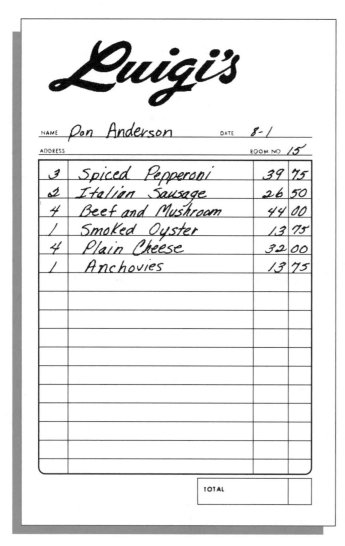

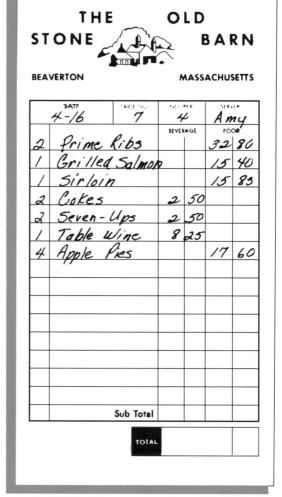

Figure 1-2.

Subtraction Without a Calculator

Did the clerk give you the right change? How much will you have in your checking account after writing a check for $32.18? These and many other subtraction problems are encountered often. Subtraction is the process of finding the difference between two like numbers. It is addition in reverse. In a subtraction problem the number being subtracted is called the **subtrahend**, the number subtracted from is the **minuend**, and the answer is the **difference**. Many errors can occur in subtraction, especially in "borrowing" or regrouping. This section will help you improve your speed and accuracy when performing mental subtraction. The following self-assessment will tell you if you should do this subtraction section.

Self-Assessment II—Subtraction (Without a Calculator)

(1)	20	(2)	34	(3)	45	(4)	65
	−16		−26		−29		−14

(5)	1,143	(6)	9,874	(7)	$14.28	(8)	$294.20
	−752		−1,884		−7.32		−107.22

Combine without recopying:

(9) $8 - 2 + 4 - 9 =$ _____

(10) $2 - 8 - 5 + 4 =$ _____

Answers: (1) 4; (2) 8; (3) 16; (4) 51; (5) 391; (6) 7,990; (7) $6.96; (8) $186.98; (9) 1; (10) −7

If you missed no more than two problems on this self-assessment turn to PAGE 40, Subtraction With a Calculator.

If you missed more than two problems on this self-assessment or would like to review the Subtraction Competencies listed on the next page, continue with this section.

Subtraction Competencies

After completing this section you will be able to:

- ■ Subtract vertically
- ■ Check subtraction by addition
- ■ Subtract horizontally

When subtracting, always write clearly and neatly. Be certain to align all numbers, whole or decimal, in their proper column. For example:

5,728	minuend	$6.25	minuend
−617	subtrahend	−1.03	subtrahend
5,111	difference	$5.22	difference

Subtraction problems can be read in several different ways. Thus, for $7 - 5$ you could read "7 minus 5," "7 take away 5," "7 subtract 5," "5 subtracted from 7," or "the difference between 7 and 5."

1. The difference between 7 and 5 is _____.

Answer: 2

We can diagram the subtraction 7 − 4 by drawing 7 circles, boxing in 4 of the circles, and counting the circles that are not boxed:

2. If we have ten dollars and spend eight, we have _____ dollars left.

   Answer: 2

   Subtraction can also be pictured on a number line. For example, to subtract 17 from 25 on a number line:

   Count 25 spaces to the
   RIGHT
   Count back 17 spaces
   to the LEFT.
   The answer is 25 − 17 = 8.

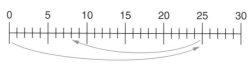

3. To use the number line above to subtract 8 from 21, we count 21 spaces to the *left/right,* then count back ____ spaces to the left. The answer is ____.

   Answers: right; 8; 13

CHECKING BY ADDITION

4. Subtraction is the opposite, or reverse, of addition. We say that addition and subtraction are **inverse operations** because one undoes the other. This principle is used to check subtraction by _____. It can also be a way of thinking about subtraction problems.

   Answer: adding

5. That subtraction is the opposite or reverse of addition allows us to check subtraction by adding. For example:

   $$\begin{array}{r} 5 \\ -3 \\ \hline 2 \end{array}$$ Check: 2 + 3 = 5

   The check is: difference + subtrahend = minuend, or answer + small number = larger number.

Which subtraction checks? _____

(a) 13   (b) 15   (c) 18
     −7   −9   −9
     ——   ——   ——
      5   7   9

Answer: (c) $13 − 7 = 5$ does not check because $7 + 5 = 12$; $15 − 9 = 7$ does not check because $9 + 7 = 16$, $18 − 9 = 9$ does check because $9 + 9 = 18$

6. Do the following subtractions and check with addition.

    13   16   13   11   17
    −7   −8   −5   −4   −9
   ————   ————   ————   ————   ————

Checks   _____   _____   _____   _____   _____

Answers: 6 8 8 7 8; 13 16 13 11 17

Since addition problems are sometimes easier, you may want to think of subtraction as reverse addition.

7. To solve the problem 748 minus 532, we think:

   2 in the units column plus _____ units equals 8 units.

   3 in the tens column plus _____ tens equals 4 tens.

   5 in the hundreds column plus _____ hundreds equals 7 hundreds.

   Answer: 6; 1; 2

8. Always check your answer, at least mentally. We check a subtraction answer by adding the difference to the _____. The sum should be the same as the _____.

   Answers: subtrahend (bottom number or smaller number); minuend (top number or larger number)

REGROUPING OR BORROWING
What is 56 minus 33?

$$56 = 5 \text{ tens} + 6 \text{ units}$$
$$\text{subtract} \quad 33 = 3 \text{ tens} + 3 \text{ units}$$
$$2 \text{ tens} + 3 \text{ units}$$

A shorter method is simply to write the numbers in columns and subtract each column separately:

       56
      −33
      ——
       23

9. Arrange 25,738 – 5,436 in columns and find the difference.

Answer: 25,738
           –5,436
           ─────
           20,302   Check: 25,738

If we subtract 52 – 24, we must **regroup** or **borrow**:

52	5 tens + 2 units		4 tens + 12 units
–24 →	2 tens + 4 units	or	2 tens + 4 units
		Answer:	2 tens + 8 units

Notice that we regrouped 52 to get 4 tens + 12 units. We borrowed ten in order to get enough units to subtract.

10. Now try: 831 – 554 = ?

831	8 hundreds + 3 tens + 1 units		7 hundres + 12 tens + _____
–554 →	5 hundreds + 5 tens + 4 units	or	5 hundreds + 5 tens + 4 units
		Answer:	2 hundreds + _____ + _____

Answers: 11 units; 7 tens; 7 units

11. The problem in frame 10 could have been written:

831		7	12	11
–554	→	–5	5	4
		2	7	7

This is the *short/long* method.

Answer: short

12. To avoid mistakes, always check subtraction problems by _____.

Answer: addition (even if you only do it mentally)

Regrouping is often necessary when we subtract larger numbers. It may also be necessary to borrow several times, as the following example shows using the short form:

6,845		5	17	13	15
–3,948	→	–3	9	4	8
		2	8	9	7

13. In the previous example we borrowed 1 ten to get 15 units. We borrowed 1 hundred to get 13 _____, and we _____ 1 thousand to get 17 hundreds.

Answers: tens; borrowed

DIFFICULTIES WITH ZERO

Remember that in our number system each digit has a place value ten times that of the digit on its right. Therefore, we can borrow from any column if necessary, even in problems such as the following.

14. $\begin{array}{r} 503 \\ -218 \\ \hline \end{array}$

How can we borrow from the zero in the tens column? First let's regroup:

503 = 5 hundreds + 0 tens + 3 units

or

4 hundreds + 10 tens + 3 units

Now we can borrow from the tens.

$$\begin{array}{r} 503 \\ -218 \\ \hline \end{array} \longrightarrow \begin{array}{r} 4\ 10\ 3 \\ -2\ \ \ 1\ 8 \\ \hline \end{array} \longrightarrow \begin{array}{r} 4\ 9\ 13 \\ -2\ 1\ \ 8 \\ \hline \end{array}$$

So the answer is _____.

Answer: 285

15. Subtract 5,962 from 8,001. (Show each step.)

$$\begin{array}{r} 8,001 \\ -5,962 \\ \hline \end{array} \longrightarrow \begin{array}{r} 7\ 10\ 0\ 1 \\ -5\ \ \ 9\ 6\ 2 \\ \hline \end{array} \longrightarrow \begin{array}{r} 7\ 9\ 10\ 1 \\ -5\ 9\ \ \ 6\ 2 \\ \hline \end{array} \longrightarrow \begin{array}{r} 7\ 9\ 9\ 11 \\ -5\ 9\ 6\ \ \ 2 \\ \hline \end{array}$$

The answer is _____. Check _____.

Answers: 2,039; 8,001

16. Finish the following subtraction problem. (Show each step.)

$$\begin{array}{r} 8,030 \\ -6,783 \\ \hline \end{array} \longrightarrow \begin{array}{r} 8\ 0\ 2\ 10 \\ -6\ 7\ 8\ \ \ 3 \\ \hline \end{array}$$

Answer: _____. Check _____.

Answers: $\begin{array}{r} 7\ 9\ 12\ 10 \\ -6\ 7\ 8\ \ \ 3 \\ \hline 1\ 2\ \ 4\ \ 7 \end{array}$ Check: 8,030

SUBTRACTING MONEY OR DECIMALS

17. As shown below, the process of borrowing is used with money as well.

$$\begin{array}{r} \$7.34 \\ -3.63 \\ \hline \end{array} \longrightarrow \begin{array}{r} \$6.\ 13\ 4 \\ -3.\ \ \ 6\ 3 \\ \hline \$3.\ \ 7\ 1 \end{array}$$

$7.34 minus $3.63 means: first take 3 cents away from 4 cents, leaving _____ cent. Then take 6 dimes away from 13 _____ by borrowing 10 dimes or one dollar from the dollars column and adding these to the 3 dimes in the dimes column. This leaves _____ dollars, from which we subtract 3 dollars, leaving _____ dollars.

Answers: 1; dimes; 6; 3

18. Regrouping is also used with decimal numbers. To subtract 59.31 from 68.4, write:

$$\begin{array}{r} 68.40 \\ -59.31 \\ \hline \end{array}$$

Notice that we added a zero after the 4 in the top number so that both top and bottom numbers would have the same number of decimal places. Decimal points are aligned as in addition. Starting from the hundredths column on the right, we must subtract 1 from 0. Since we don't want a negative number, we borrow 1 tenth from the column to the left. And since .40 = .30 + .10, we rewrite this as:

$$\begin{array}{r} 6\ 8.\ 3\ 10 \\ -5\ 9.\ 3\ \ \ 1 \\ \hline .\ 0\ \ 9 \end{array}$$

After completing the subtraction in the first two places, we have another problem: subtracting 9 from 8. Again we _____ from the position to the left because 60 = 50 + 10. Rewriting this problem, we have:

$$\begin{array}{r} 5\ 18.\ 3\ 10 \\ -5\ \ 9.\ 3\ \ \ 1 \\ \hline 9.\ 0\ \ 9 \end{array}$$

Answer: borrow

MENTAL REGROUPING

19. Regrouping or borrowing is often done mentally without writing in the new digits. For example:

$$\begin{array}{r} 617 \\ -238 \\ \hline \end{array}$$

We think:

8 from 17 leaves 9
3 from 10 leaves ___
2 from ___ leaves 3

Answers: 7; 5

20. Work the following problems mentally without writing the new digits. (Show your check.)

315	907	874
−74	−398	−785

Check _____ Check _____ Check _____

Answers: 241 Check: 315; 509 Check: 907; 89 Check: 874

21. Work the following without rewriting and check the answers mentally.

707	897	2,942	$62.81	$540.17
−644	−398	−768	−35.29	−52.28

Answers: 63; 499; 2,174; $27.52; $487.89

HORIZONTAL SUBTRACTION

Most of the subtraction problems we have solved thus far have been rewritten in columns or worked vertically. But notice the following two examples.

(a) 732
    −89
    ‾‾‾
     643

(b) $732 - 89 = 643$

22. In the two examples above, example _____ shows vertical subtraction and example _____ shows horizontal subtraction.

Answers: a; b

Some business forms require horizontal subtraction to be worked efficiently. To subtract horizontally, follow the same steps as in vertical subtraction.

23. In the problem 764 minus 353 = _____, think: first take 3 from 4, then take 5 from 6, then take 3 from 7.

Answer: 411

24. When regrouping is necessary, we make the same notations as in vertical subtraction. For example: $2,058.54 − $79.37.

Think: first take 7 from 14
         then take 3 from 4
         then take 9 from 18
         then take 7 from 14   or
         1 9 14 18 4 14 − 7 9.3 7 = _____

Answer: $1,979.17

25. Mentally work the following horizontal subtraction problems and check your work by addition.

17 – 9 = _____ 637 – 178 = _____ $7.53 – $3.19 = _____

Answers: 8; 459; $4.34

THE MINUS SIGN AND NEGATIVE NUMBERS

The minus sign not only signals subtraction, as in 10 – 15 = –5, it also designates a **negative number.** To understand the meaning of negative numbers, visualize a thermometer (Figure 1-3), which shows that negative numbers fall on the other side of zero and, further, that they run in the opposite direction from positive numbers. In business we find negative numbers in, for instance, bank overdrafts: cash checks for more money than you have in your bank account and you create a negative balance. Overdrafts show that you can add negative numbers: –$10 + –$5 = –$15.

Minus signs also appear in expressions like –x = 3. Negative x or any other unknown may look just like a negative number, but will not be if the unknown x is itself negative. For instance, when x = –3, then –x = 3. The minus sign here is telling us to "change signs," "choose the opposite," or "choose the inverse of."

Adding and subtracting signed numbers really should be thought of as a combining operation in which you move up and down, backward and forward, or side to side as you combine negative and negative, negative and positive, or positive and positive

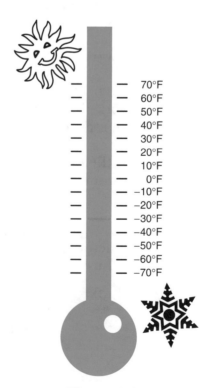

Figure 1-3.

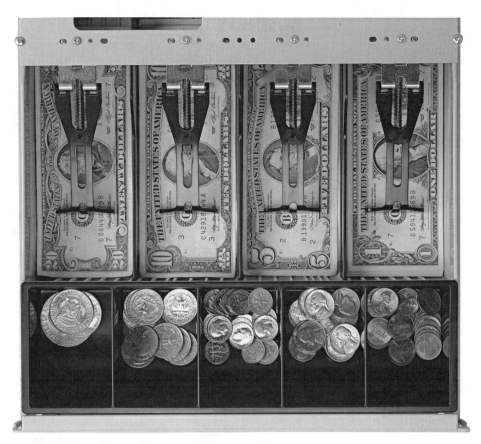

Figure 1-4.

numbers. Seen this way, addition doesn't necessarily mean "increase"; it could also mean "go up" or "go to the right." Similarly, subtraction no longer means simply "remove" or "take away," but also "go down" or "go to the left". Sometimes it is easier to think of combining negative and positive numbers in terms of money. For example if you had $7 and you wanted to buy something for $11 you could borrow $4 from a friend. Then you would be in debt $4. That is $7 - 11 = -4$.

Using money we could reason this way:

Combine $4 - 8 + 5 - 7 = $ _____

If you had $4 and you wanted to spend $8 perhaps you could borrow $4. If you earned $5 and paid back your $4 debt you would have $1 left. If you decided you wanted to spend $7 you would need to borrow $6. You would then be in debt $6 or the answer is –6.

26. Now try the following problems.

(1) $5 + 3 - 4 = $ _____   (2) $7 - 8 - 4 = $ _____

(3) $3 - 6 + 2 = $ _____   (4) $4 - 8 + 4 - 3 = $ _____

(5) $7 - 9 + 3 - 2 = $ _____   (6) $7 - 1 - 5 - 6 = $ _____

Answers: (1) 4; (2) –5; (3) –1; (4) –3; (5) –1; (6) –5

BUSINESS APPLICATION

27. Complete the following money receipts. For each, find the balance due on both the account and note.

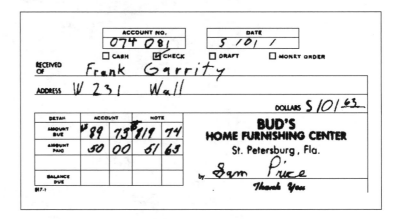

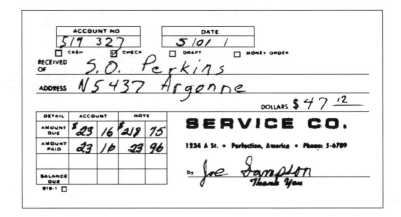

Answers: $39.73; $768.11; 0.00; $194.79

Subtraction With a Calculator

The *subtraction* key enables you to perform simple subtractions and deduct negative amounts. To subtract, enter the number to be added (minuend) with the *plus* bar and the number to be subtracted (subtrahend) with the *minus* bar, or *subtraction* key. Depress *total* and the difference appears automatically in the display register or on a tape.

Hint

While most popular hand-held calculators use algebraic logic, most business electronic desk calculators use arithmetic logic. The difference is mainly in operations involving subtraction. With *algebraic logic*, the *minus* key is depressed *before* the negative number is entered. The instructions in this text correspond to *arithmetic logic*, for which you depress the *minus* key *after* the negative number is entered.

Example:

```
72. +          93. +
12. -          84. -
60. *           9. *
```

We also use the *subtraction* key in business when it is necessary to add some figures and subtract others, for example:

$4.50	$39.62	$263.30
5.80–	18.94–	89.62–
9.25	29.80	478.43
6.38	32.45–	682.52
4.25–	56.98	73.91
$10.08	$75.01	$1,408.54

1. Do the following subtraction problems with debit balances. Operate all keys without looking at them.

(1)	83	(2)	47	(3)	99	(4)	829
	–74		–9		–87		–73

(5)	752	(6)	5,048	(7)	2,782	(8)	5,289
	–66		–382		–834		–722

(9)	$7.94	(10)	$7.57	(11)	$88.93	(12)	$28.82
	4.32–		7.83		60.82		12.84
	9.47		.95–		67.19–		84.82–
	4.78		2.36		49.63		63.01
	8.47–		6.52–		7.47–		88.32–
	4.87		7.87		36.69		17.97
	3.34–		8.35		62.12		63.28
	9.32		6.28–		35.70–		69.57–
	7.47		9.53		11.88		76.46
	5.35		.87		91.34		26.76

(13)	$62.52	(14)	$96.98	(15)	$358.17
	31.46		74.38		71.14
	29.60		32.78		162.32
	3.44–		45.52–		35.60–
	8.83		92.02		985.64
	67.69		67.94		965.58
	74.79–		64.55		540.03–
	15.29		4.98–		715.50
	8.02–		93.62		103.85
	43.44		31.67		664.69

Answers: (1) 9; (2) 38; (3) 12; (4) 756; (5) 686; (6) 4,666; (7) 1,948; (8) 4,567; (9) $33.07; (10) $30.63; (11) $291.05; (12) $46.43; (13) $172.58; (14) $503.44; (15) $3,451.26

CREDIT BALANCES

When the total of the amounts subtracted exceeds the total of the amounts added, the result will be a minus, or negative, amount known as a **credit balance.** Most machines are equipped with a credit-balance feature, such as a negative light, and others print the credit balance in red or identify the answer with a credit-balance symbol such as CR. Credit balances can be shown with the minus sign before or after the number, in red, with CR or shown in parenthesis. For example:

37	538	$67.32
−85	−759	58.49−
−48	221 CR	86.38
		97.25−
		($2.04)

1. Using touch control, do the following problems. Remember to write CR after your answers when a credit balance occurs.

(1) 65	(2) 16	(3) 52	(4) 631
−93	−70	−38	−767

(5) 5,447	(6) 7,305	(7) 5,437	(8) 3,547
−8,120	−8,623	−8,543	−9,713

(9)	(10)	(11)	(12)
31	555	868	$425.09
859	482	558−	83.25
45	65	418	96.45
852−	440	701−	83.89
861−	880−	255	175.81
173	337−	531−	567.72−
87	758	762−	821.71−
430−	682−	285	8.32
258	590	333	87.25
325	532−	722−	963.47−

Answers: (1) 28 CR; (2) 54 CR; (3) 14; (4) 136 CR; (5) 2,673 CR; (6) 1,318 CR; (7) 3,106 CR; (8) 6,166 CR; (9) 365 CR; (10) 459; (11) 1,115 CR; (12) $1,392.84 CR

BUSINESS APPLICATION

Businesses often set up a line of credit with their bank. This credit is similar to overdraft privileges or a preapproved loan and it allows a business to write checks even when it has a negative or credit balance.

1. If Mer-Mac Inc., has a bank balance of $2,747.59, what would the balance be after these following transactions? checks: $2,147.50, $129.16, $345.29, $5,821.47; deposits: $416.89, $48.32.

2. If Southside Wholesale has a bank balance of –$342.14, what would the balance be after the following transactions? Deposits: $417.82, $14.29, $137.18, $28.87; checks: $5.38, $12.41, $49.88, $687.92.

Answers: (1) –$5,230.62; (2) –$499.57

Estimating

To **estimate** an answer, we round off each number in a problem to one or two digits other than zero. This makes the calculations easier.

For example, to estimate 739 + 288:

think: 739 = 700 to 1 digit
           288 = 300 to 1 digit

The sum is about 1,000, therefore the estimate is 739 + 288 = 1,000 approximately. Every time you do a problem you should estimate the answer just as a check.

1. What is your estimate for 9,147 + 9,834? _____

Answer: 9,000 + 10,000 = 19,000

Estimates sometimes are inaccurate. For example, you estimate 448 + 239 as 400 + 200 = 600. The exact answer is 687. Still, your estimate of about 600 is reasonably close to 687.

2. Use estimates and circle the answer below that seems correct.

   627 + 386 = 613   748 + 214 = 962   481 + 195 = 576

Answer: 962

We estimate subtraction in a similar manner. For example, to estimate 18,432 – 11,871, first round off to 2 significant digits.

18,432 = 18,000 to 2 digits
11,871 = 12,000 to 2 digits

The difference is about 6,000. (The answer is exactly 6,561.)

3. Use estimates and circle the answer below that seems correct.

   17,314 – 16,104 = 2,210   51,832 – 48,616 = 2,216

   75,408 – 70,909 = 4,499

Answer: 4,499

Most business people automatically estimate answers both before and after working a problem or when reviewing a problem someone else has worked. The last time you went to a restaurant or drive-in, for instance, you probably estimated the change you would receive after paying your bill.

4. Using estimating techniques, circle the closest estimated answers to the following problems.

		(a)	(b)	(c)	(d)
(1)	$9,637 + 5,119 =$	13,756	12,987	14,756	16,173
(2)	$5,876 + 7,216 =$	14,192	12,092	10,722	13,092
(3)	$5,407 - 3,187 =$	2,220	3,220	3,700	890
(4)	$8,137 - 3,923 =$	5,324	3,294	5,214	4,214
(5)	$2,059 + 8,911 =$	16,070	9,970	10,970	12,070
(6)	$12,597 - 7,059 =$	19,656	5,538	8,528	19,456
(7)	$6,887 + 5,918 =$	12,805	11,605	11,575	14,705
(8)	$2,875 - 995 =$	3,880	1,880	5,880	4,880
(9)	$8,215 + 3,951 =$	14,916	10,706	13,276	12,166
(10)	$19,496 - 11,923 =$	9,573	7,573	8,373	6,413

Answers: (1) c; (2) d; (3) a; (4) d; (5) c; (6) b; (7) a; (8) b; (9) d; (10) b

Practice Problems Without a Calculator

The best way to become proficient at mental addition is the same way you become proficient at baseball; practice the right technique. Work the following problems for practice.

ADD, THINKING SUBTOTALS ONLY

(1)	(2)	(3)	(4)	(5)
7	9	9	4	7
4	1	6	2	6
9	4	5	8	3
9	4	2	5	4
3	2	7	8	9
5	3	3	4	7
1	2	7	7	6
8	8	5	4	8

(6)	(7)	(8)	(9)	(10)
7	4	9	8	9
4	3	4	3	9
2	2	4	6	9
4	5	3	8	2
8	1	1	2	3
3	6	4	6	7
5	7	9	4	4
8	4	2	3	9

(11)	(12)	(13)	(14)	(15)
2	4	9	7	8
8	1	8	4	3
5	6	8	7	5
7	5	3	4	9
4	2	6	2	2
6	2	2	7	5
8	8	8	5	6
5	2	6	4	9
9	2	7	3	4
2	7	2	2	7

Check your work by reverse addition and then with your calculator. (Answers are on page 49.)

ADD, GROUPING IN TENS

(1)	3	(2)	6	(3)	8	(4)	1	(5)	3
	9		4		4		7		8
	1		4		6		9		9
	7		2		2		3		7
	4		8		5		5		2
	6		6		4		4		1
	5		5		5		1		4
	8		4		6		6		6

(6)	4	(7)	2	(8)	8	(9)	7	(10)	8
	7		1		4		7		7
	3		7		4		6		5
	6		4		8		4		3
	3		1		4		1		1
	5		5		2		5		6
	2		8		6		3		9
	8		2		4		7		1

(11)	5	(12)	8	(13)	9	(14)	7	(15)	2
	8		3		1		3		3
	7		2		8		5		5
	3		7		3		5		7
	5		6		2		6		3
	2		4		3		4		5
	9		5		3		6		5
	4		8		1		2		6
	7		7		9		8		4
	8		9		1		5		9

Check your work by reverse addition and then with your calculator. (Answers are on page 49.)

ADD, THINKING SUBTOTALS ONLY
OR GROUPING IN TENS

(1)	1	(2)	5	(3)	9	(4)	6
	3		3		1		3
	9		3		4		3
	4		9		1		5
	4		1		4		2
	7		8		1		7
	5		8		4		7
	3		9		7		1

(5)	(6)	(7)	(8)
6	1	8	1
8	2	4	2
1	4	2	9
6	5	8	6
1	5	2	9
7	1	2	7
2	8	6	4
7	6	4	7
	4	5	6
	2	6	4

(9)	(10)	(11)	(12)
8	6	7	9
4	9	8	7
4	2	1	2
3	3	2	4
6	7	6	8
2	8	7	9
8	6	7	5
1	8	9	7
8	2	3	1
5	4	5	3

Check your work by reverse addition and then with your calculator. (Answers are on page 49.)

ADD WITH ANGULAR ADDITION

(1)	(2)	(3)	(4)
4,985	3,700	7,469	9,093
4,114	8,741	3,104	8,566
4,896	9,474	1,146	6,160
3,928	1,245	867	847
7,395	1,471	6,173	2,754

(5)	(6)	(7)	(8)
77,070	70,481	98,884	29,420
2,902	74,472	89,747	29,651
25,571	11,436	18,059	10,701
90,193	77,535	67,054	25,722
65,704	38,102	77,501	22,751

Check by reverse addition and then with your calculator. (Answers on page 50.)

ADD WITH SUBTOTAL ADDITION

(1) 44,442
     57,070
     16,059 _____
     58,041
     47,803
     80,580 _____
     60,478
     95,043
     54,061 _____

     Total _____

(2) 85,301
     54,066
     98,525 _____
     90,391
     26,629
     37,301 _____
     92,003
     16,453
     99,837 _____

     Total _____

(3) 14,924
     70,312
     90,850 _____
     24,781
     40,902
     72,682 _____
     21,443
     61,176
     80,582 _____

     Total _____

(4) 41,468
     94,559
     41,615 _____
     50,273
     41,396
     25,807 _____
     60,170
     19,516
     60,808 _____

     Total _____

(5) 49,386
     60,312
     60,942 _____
     92,329
     77,936
     38,101 _____
     39,641
     84,054
     47,468 _____

     Total _____

(6) 64,281
     66,847
     72,461 _____
     21,032
     95,362
     49,712 _____
     58,275
     89,514
     15,472 _____

     Total _____

Check by reverse addition and then with your calculator. (Answers on page 50.)

ADD WITH HORIZONTAL ADDITION

(1) $2 + 7 + 7 + 6 + 4 + 3 + 5 + 8 + 4 =$ _____
(2) $1 + 3 + 2 + 5 + 1 + 4 + 3 + 3 + 8 + 9 =$ _____
(3) $80 + 21 + 73 + 62 + 92 =$ _____
(4) $54 + 12 + 75 + 73 + 26 + 62 =$ _____

(5)   497 + 379 + 148 + 492 = _____

(6)   414 + 688 + 514 + 949 + 955 = _____

(7) $4.35 + $6.41 + $4.17 + $9.06 + $7.06 = _____

(8) $70.66 + $.32 + $1.92 + $53.85 + $.99 = _____

(9) $154.71 + $3.47 + $121.20 + $5.61 = _____

(10) $5.12 + $474.43 + $302.60 + $6,085.10 = _____

Check by reverse addition and then with your calculator. (Answers on page 50.)

SUBTRACT AND CHECK BY ADDITION

(1) 73	(2) 795	(3) 2,186	(4) 1,314
−49	−93	−719	−1,181

Check _____   _____   _____   _____

(5) 4,599	(6) 1,492	(7) 7,268	(8) 1,317
−766	−703	−2,419	−928

Check _____   _____   _____   _____

(9) $47.38	(10) $712.09	(11) $247.00	(12) $623.42
−9.57	−85.56	−127.31	−588.51

Check _____   _____   _____   _____

HORIZONTAL SUBTRACTION
Subtract without recopying

(1)   14 − 7 = _____   (2)   281 − 73 = _____

(3)   453 − 87 = _____   (4)   758 − 259 = _____

(5)   184 − 87 = _____   (6)   547 − 431 = _____

(7) $36.18 − $9.21 _____   (8) $453.50 − $174.29 = _____

(9) $25.70 − $6.35 = _____   (10) $706.99 − $193.24 = _____

COMBINATION PROBLEMS

(1) 5 − 3 + 4 = ____   (2) 7 − 8 − 9 = ___   (3) 8 + 9 − 7 = _____

(4) −3 + 2 − 6 = ___   (5) 7 + 2 − 2 = ___   (6) − 7 − 8 − 2 = ____

(7) 8 − 7 − 5 = ____   (8) 4 − 9 + 7 = ___   (9) − 6 + 7 − 9 = ____

(Answers on page 50.)

ROUNDING NUMBERS

Hint
Round percentages to the nearest tenth (.1%).
Round money answers to the nearest cent ($.01).
Round decimal answers to the nearest thousandths (.001).

(1) 3,410.6959 _____   (2) $890,596.05541 _____

(3) $9,901.895 _____   (4) 143.15% _____

(5) 876.765% _____   (6) 4.0678 _____

(7) .05213% _____   (8) $33.8951 _____

(9) .00129 _____   (10) 134.54% _____

SIGNIFICANT DIGITS
Round the following numbers to two significant digits.

(1) 783,178 _____   (2) .22499 _____

(3) 5.99945 _____   (4) .11523 _____

(5) $4,498 _____   (6) 33,369 _____

(7) 1,109.0029 _____   (8) $662.059 _____

(9) .1351 _____   (10) 77,540 _____

Round the following numbers to four significant digits.

(11) 489.546 _____   (12) $76,929.005 _____

(13) 9.4605 _____   (14) 9,011,682 _____

(15) $22,940.99 _____   (16) .11151 _____

(17) 3.50283 _____   (18) .99519 _____

(19) 204.269 _____   (20) 555.29 _____

(Answers on page 50.)

Answers to Practice Groups:

ADD, THINKING SUBTOTALS ONLY: (1) 46; (2) 33; (3) 44; (4) 42; (5) 50; (6) 41; (7) 32; (8) 36; (9) 40; (10) 52; (11) 56; (12) 39; (13) 59; (14) 45; (15) 58

ADD, GROUPING IN TENS: (1) 43; (2) 39; (3) 40; (4) 36; (5) 40; (6) 38; (7) 30; (8) 40; (9) 40; (10) 40; (11) 58; (12) 59; (13) 40; (14) 51; (15) 49

ADD, THINKING SUBTOTALS ONLY or GROUPING IN TENS: (1) 36; (2) 46; (3) 31; (4) 34; (5) 38; (6) 38; (7) 47; (8) 55; (9) 49; (10) 55; (11) 55; (12) 55

ADD WITH ANGULAR ADDITION: (1) 25,318; (2) 24,631; (3) 18,759; (4) 27,420; (5) 261,440; (6) 272,026; (7) 351,245; (8) 118,245

ADD WITH SUBTOTAL ADDITION: (1) 117,571, 186,424, 209,582, 513,577; (2) 237,892, 154,321, 208,293, 600,506; (3) 176,086, 138,365, 163,201, 477,652; (4) 177,642, 117,476, 140,494, 435,612; (5) 170,640, 208,366, 171,163, 550,169; (6) 203,589, 166,106, 163,261, 532,956

ADD WITH HORIZONTAL ADDITION: (1) 46; (2) 39; (3) 328; (4) 302; (5) 1,516; (6) 3,520; (7) $31.05; (8) $127.74; (9) $284.99; (10) $6,867.25

SUBTRACT AND CHECK BY ADDITION: (1) 24; (2) 702; (3) 1,467; (4) 133; (5) 3,833; (6) 789; (7) 4,849; (8) 389; (9) $37.81; (10) $626.53; (11) $119.69; (12) $34.91

HORIZONTAL SUBTRACTION: (1) 7; (2) 208; (3) 366; (4) 499; (5) 97; (6) 116; (7) $26.97; (8) $279.21; (9) $19.35; (10) $513.75

COMBINATION PROBLEMS: (1) 6; (2) –10; (3) 10; (4) –7; (5) 7; (6) –17; (7) –4; (8) 2; (9) –8

ROUNDING NUMBERS: (1) 3,410.696; (2) $890,596.06; (3) $9,901.90; (4) 143.2%; (5) 876.8%; (6) 4.068; (7) .1%; (8) $33.90; (9) .001; (10) 134.5%

SIGNIFICANT DIGITS: (1) 780,000; (2) .22; (3) 6.0; (4) .12; (5) $4,500; (6) 33,000; (7) 1,100; (8) $660; (9) .14; (10) 78,000; (11) 489.5; (12) $76,930; (13) 9.461; (14) 9,012,000; (15) $22,940; (16) .1115; (17) 3.503; (18) .9952; (19) 204.3; (20) 555.3

Stop

You are now ready to take Pretest IA. This is a test of addition, subtraction, and numbers, to be taken *without* the aid of a calculator. Your performance on Pretest IA will tell you if you have developed sufficient skill to proceed to **Test IA.** Unless instructed otherwise, turn in your Pretest for correction and review before taking Test IA. To pass Test IA, you must have no more than 10 percent of your answers incorrect.

On Test IA, if you have overall accuracy of 90 percent or better, continue on to the next section, Developing Touch Control, Speed, and Accuracy With a Calculator.

If you get more than 10 percent of your answers wrong, review the section on Numbers (pages 2–10); Addition (pages 21–30); and Subtraction (pages 31–40).

REMEMBER: It is important to be able to tell whether your answers are reasonable. Many employment tests demand skill with numbers and you won't always have the aid of a calculator.

Pretest IA

NUMBERS, ADDITION, AND SUBTRACTION WITHOUT THE AID OF A CALCULATOR

You need 90 percent accuracy to pass.

Add.

(1)	3	(2)	3	(3)	6	(4)	6
	5		7		9		6
	8		7		1		2
	2		6		3		5
	4		1		2		2

(5)	26	(6)	98	(7)	27	(8)	77
	66		2		10		86
	66		38		65		68
	32		34		26		10
	25		81		47		14

Subtract.

(9)	71	(10)	88	(11)	48	(12)	43
	−63		−51		−29		−27

(13)	351	(14)	819	(15)	693	(16)	766
	−81		−99		−95		−375

Combine. (17) $17 - 18 + 21 =$ _____   (18) $-3 + 4 - 5 =$ _____

Round to the nearest hundred.

(19)   432 _____   (20)   681.7 _____

(21)   5,387 _____   (22)   549.83 _____

Using words, write out the following numbers.

(23) 53 _____   (24) 571.4 _____

(25) 2,007.043 _____

Using the digits 0 through 9, write the following numbers.

(26) thirty-four _____   (27) nine thousand forty-seven _____

(28) eight hundred and seven-tenths _____

Round the following numbers to 2 significant digits.

(29) 843,278 _____   (30) $8,298 _____

(31) 314,972 _____   (32) .3762 _____

Round the following numbers using the general rules for rounding.

(33) 56.8732 _____   (34) .05879 _____

(35) $58.7489 _____   (36) .7825% _____

How many significant digits do the following numbers have?

(37) 540 _____   (38) $3.07 _____

(39) 27,400 _____   (40) 42.630 _____

Using words, write out the following numbers.

(41) 358.004 _____

(42) $5,008.74 _____

Using the digits 0 through 9, write the following numbers.

(43) Seven thousand fifty-eight _____

(44) Two hundred twenty-nine dollars and five cents _____

Combine without recopying.

(45) $2 + 3 - 9 + 3 =$ _____   (46) $9 + 5 - 6 + 7 =$ _____

Add using angular addition.   **Add using subtotal addition.**

(47)	994	(48)	1,490	(49)	97	(50)	7,570
	966		8,734		25		4,735
	600		7,158		18 ____		4,169 ___
	219		6,475		72		3,392
	359		5,979		54		4,614
	409		5,403		86 ____		6,178 ___
					23		4,000
	—		—		54		9,096
					29 ____		1,473 ___
	—		—		Total ____		Total ____
	—		—				
			—				
	____		____				

Developing Touch Control, Speed, and Accuracy With a Calculator

It is essential that a business machine operator work fast and accurately. Time yourself on the following practice groups; they are designed to improve your touch control, speed, and accuracy. Work as fast as possible while maintaining accuracy. When you have completed the practice groups, you should have sufficient touch control to take a timed test on addition and subtraction.

ADDITION WITH 1, 2, 3, 4, 5, AND 6 KEYS

Work the following problems as rapidly as possible while maintaining accuracy. Take care to place your fingers correctly. Operate the keys without looking.

(1)	(2)	(3)	(4)	(5)
45	55	44	456	654
44	54	55	445	554
54	45	66	444	466
46	66	65	654	544
64	44	54	655	455
45	46	46	555	655
66	45	45	666	646
54	64	46	664	455
64	55	54	554	456
46	44	65	446	654

(6)	(7)	(8)	(9)	(10)
12	22	11	123	321
22	21	22	112	221
32	12	33	111	133
13	33	21	321	211
31	11	13	322	122
12	13	12	222	322
33	12	13	333	313
21	31	21	331	122
31	22	22	221	123
13	11	31	113	321

(11)	(12)	(13)	(14)	(15)
42	35	15	426	116
53	36	51	126	225
61	34	52	423	334
35	26	25	153	411
24	62	26	126	422
36	63	62	423	334
41	61	51	513	522
15	35	63	631	633
16	53	36	522	411
24	63	35	336	141

(16) 212	(17) 131	(18) 151	(19) 2,345	(20) 3,232
313	232	252	5,432	3,434
414	434	353	1,524	3,535
515	535	454	3,216	3,636
616	636	656	5,321	4,141
121	141	161	4,215	4,242
323	242	262	4,513	4,343
424	343	363	2,365	4,545
525	545	464	2,563	4,646
626	646	565	6,565	5,656

Answers: (1) 528; (2) 518; (3) 540; (4) 5,539; (5) 5,539; (6) 220; (7) 188; (8) 199; (9) 2,209; (10) 2,209; (11) 347; (12) 468; (13) 416; (14) 3,679; (15) 3,549; (16) 4,089; (17) 3,885; (18) 3,681; (19) 38,059; (20) 41,410

Hint

On most electronic calculators there is an easy way to correct a wrong number entered during addition. First you delete the wrong entry by depressing the minus key. The machine will automatically recall the previous entry so that you may continue adding from there. Thus, in Problem 16 above, had you entered 662 for the last number instead of 626, you could depress the minus key to delete 662, enter 626, and then total. The calculator would sum correctly and you would have avoided re-adding the entire column.

ADDITION WITH THE 4, 5, 6, 7, 8, AND 9 KEYS

(1) 45	(2) 55	(3) 56	(4) 456	(5) 545
65	66	45	445	454
45	64	54	554	565
54	65	65	664	566
65	56	44	544	464
56	64	55	655	646
66	44	56	656	565
44	55	44	444	464
55	54	66	555	646
66	46	45	445	656

(6)	78	(7)	77	(8)	79	(9)	789	(10)	787
	97		88		87		778		898
	78		89		89		887		789
	87		97		97		997		899
	97		79		77		877		797
	78		97		88		788		979
	88		77		89		989		898
	77		88		77		777		797
	99		87		88		888		979
	88		79		78		778		989

(11)	47	(12)	74	(13)	95	(14)	474	(15)	995
	48		84		84		484		884
	49		94		76		494		776
	75		57		67		757		678
	85		58		48		858		945
	95		59		84		959		458
	67		79		47		679		945
	76		67		74		767		749
	86		68		59		868		848
	96		69		95		969		949

(16)	545	(17)	484	(18)	987	(19)	4,848	(20)	8,686
	646		585		468		4,949		8,787
	747		686		459		6,969		8,989
	848		787		646		7,474		9,494
	949		989		987		7,575		9,595
	454		494		749		7,676		9,696
	659		594		947		7,878		9,797
	757		696		578		7,979		9,898
	858		797		968		8,484		5,678
	959		898		849		8,585		9,876

Answers: (1) 561; (2) 569; (3) 530; (4) 5,418; (5) 5,571; (6) 867; (7) 858; (8) 849; (9) 8,548; (10) 8,812; (11) 724; (12) 709; (13) 729; (14) 7,309; (15) 8,227; (16) 7,422; (17) 7,010; (18) 7,638; (19) 72,417; (20) 90,496

ADDITION WITH ALL KEYS, INCLUDING ZERO

Work the following problems as rapidly as possible while maintaining accuracy. Use correct finger placement. Operate the keys without looking.

(1)	(2)	(3)	(4)	(5)
70	58	15	905	707
60	28	46	801	995
80	30	85	700	438
23	15	40	904	800
10	46	69	800	903
46	85	43	708	302
21	40	77	705	800
35	77	60	795	905
44	60	73	200	600
33	40	80	408	208

(6)	(7)	(8)	(9)	(10)
25	53	42	970	300
96	15	92	808	760
13	79	82	876	706
94	18	72	602	696
55	10	47	200	316
92	24	32	202	379
79	31	55	420	690
88	41	59	300	891
10	36	88	524	489
90	75	88	270	222

(11)	(12)	(13)	(14)	(15)
102	429	880	4,080	7,700
968	920	876	9,050	9,095
135	881	616	8,010	4,038
949	723	743	7,021	8,703
814	824	229	9,014	9,830
440	417	402	8,600	3,820
670	286	362	7,068	8,015
158	927	459	6,805	9,040
704	216	608	7,900	6,800
881	596	700	2,040	2,200

Answers: (1) 422; (2) 479; (3) 588; (4) 6,926; (5) 6,658; (6) 642; (7) 382; (8) 657; (9) 5,172; (10) 5,449; (11) 5,821; (12) 6,219; (13) 5,875; (14) 69,588; (15) 69,241

MIXED ADDITION, WITH DOLLARS AND CENTS

Hint

To increase your speed when adding a column of dollars and cents, do not press the decimal key. If your machine is equipped with an "adding machine" decimal setting, use it to set the decimal at 2 places. However, remember to write the decimal in your answer.

(1)	$6.30	(2)	$2.77	(3)	$2.93	(4)	$9.49	(5)	$5.30
	1.99		9.77		1.10		5.67		9.02
	4.46		3.15		5.66		4.72		3.43
	2.27		1.34		1.79		5.78		8.48
	7.37		2.83		6.78		1.34		9.51
	8.87		4.72		8.44		6.07		5.95
	7.89		4.13		8.13		6.97		9.03
	2.70		2.70		6.34		6.26		3.56
	2.12		1.62		8.63		8.48		6.86
	7.64		5.86		7.48		3.63		9.51

(6)	$4.62	(7)	$1.94	(8)	$5.43	(9)	$2.25	(10)	$1.69
	7.58		6.42		6.20		2.24		1.74
	8.40		7.12		9.06		2.68		5.73
	3.38		1.22		7.47		3.79		6.05
	6.66		3.94		1.93		8.43		2.88
	3.94		5.36		5.92		7.83		4.00
	5.98		3.07		5.74		4.34		4.16
	6.38		5.20		8.50		2.19		3.04
	1.11		9.49		7.78		5.58		3.64
	1.06		7.77		5.88		4.05		5.94

(11)	$19.47	(12)	$54.37	(13)	$26.89	(14)	$157.36	(15)	$588.53
	64.23		62.00		37.98		260.55		265.56
	71.28		90.63		84.35		628.81		534.10
	12.29		74.77		78.36		140.02		756.70
	39.40		19.32		43.45		241.60		107.42
	53.65		59.23		21.92		430.43		582.79
	30.75		57.41		55.83		936.46		376.40
	52.04		85.03		40.53		759.40		514.66
	94.90		77.86		16.91		522.52		951.48
	77.72		58.81		17.48		275.22		475.73

Answer: (1) $51.61; (2) $38.89; (3) $57.28; (4) $58.41; (5) $70.65; (6) $49.11; (7) $51.53; (8) $63.91; (9) $43.38; (10) $38.87; (11) $515.73; (12) $639.43; (13) $423.70; (14) $4,352.37; (15) $5,153.37

MIXED ADDITION

(1)		(2)		(3)		(4)		(5)	
	84		12		455		664		428
	75		39		740		274		286
	33		89		317		326		241
	78		74		356		761		895
	61		78		567		163		993
	48		20		436		927		821
	16		19		964		760		171
	53		83		433		927		595
	51		41		828		681		813
	41		31		117		478		281

(6)		(7)		(8)		(9)		(10)	
	43		74		120		208		904
	15		51		893		365		421
	13		56		444		993		141
	85		75		921		324		208
	51		91		400		249		365
	34		14		504		990		795
	42		97		311		130		905
	51		51		306		726		607
	90		39		755		735		207
	30		80		514		717		702

(11)		(12)		(13)		(14)		(15)	
	$9.09		$7.42		$90.43		$77.26		$54.44
	6.69		6.06		42.15		67.35		97.92
	6.16		1.06		14.13		56.25		72.42
	4.74		7.98		20.85		47.17		80.50
	2.75		4.08		36.51		36.84		39.31
	7.70		2.56		99.34		76.09		57.03
	2.33		9.89		32.42		97.20		97.55
	7.76		8.07		52.51		93.52		88.51
	3.79		4.20		29.90		77.83		10.02
	4.09		1.06		89.90		90.02		21.39

Answers: (1) 540; (2) 486; (3) 5,213; (4) 5,961; (5) 5,524; (6) 454; (7) 628; (8) 5,168; (9) 5,437; (10) 5,255; (11) $55.10; (12) $52.38; (13) $508.14; (14) $719.53; (15) $619.09

RANDOM SUBTRACTION

(1) 4,178
   −945

(2) 4,328
   −645

(3) 3,289
   −491

(4) 9,856
   −198

(5) 9,856
   −979

(6) 4,579
   −681

(7) 6,531
   −684

(8) 1,284
   −318

(9) 5,638
   −499

(10) 7,328
   −849

(11)	(12)	(13)	(14)	(15)
232	666	868	642	662
657−	601−	558−	786	827−
405	702	438	865−	806−
732−	726	223−	350	812
961	700	531	658−	643
373−	658	965−	622−	752−
231	682−	395	878−	823−
368−	591−	333−	362	703
424	551−	602−	701	552−
161	553	742	270−	734

(16) $860 + 381 - 562 - 537 + 427 =$ _____

(17) $277 - 532 + 364 - 206 + 549 =$ _____

(18) $76.838 + 2.07 - 125.31 + 5.98 =$ _____

(19) $835 + 72.68 - 4.306 + .2468 =$ _____

(20) $.6838 - 1.923 + .900 - 4,000.1 + 20 =$ _____

Answers: (1) 3,233; (2) 3,683; (3) 2,798; (4) 9,658; (5) 8,877; (6) 3,898; (7) 5,847; (8) 966; (9) 5,139; (10) 6,479; (11) 284; (12) 1,580; (13) 293; (14) 452 CR; (15) 206 CR; (16) 569; (17) 452; (18) 40.422 CR; (19) 903.621; (20) 3,980.439 CR

MATRIX ADDITION

Add the following numbers both horizontally and vertically. Be certain to cross check your answers by adding number 19 both directions.

$89 + 76 + 73 + 456 + 356 + 802 + 7,832 + 8,734 + 2,378 =$ _____ (10)

$32 + 91 + 54 + 718 + 932 + 935 + 9,834 + 8,431 + 8,153 =$ _____ (11)

$53 + 83 + 39 + 318 + 523 + 724 + 7,529 + 8,932 + 9,021 =$ _____ (12)

$92 + 71 + 45 + 329 + 433 + 845 + 3,491 + 9,472 + 2,984 =$ _____ (13)

$85 + 84 + 99 + 298 + 397 + 926 + 7,393 + 7,462 + 3,972 =$ _____ (14)

$19 + 80 + 32 + 337 + 276 + 387 + 4,333 + 3,399 + 8,738 =$ _____ (15)

$82 + 49 + 74 + 555 + 392 + 411 + 8,229 + 3,984 + 3,982 =$ _____ (16)

$22 + 58 + 92 + 388 + 992 + 387 + 2,876 + 2,998 + 3,722 =$ _____ (17)

$49 + 32 + 52 + 873 + 348 + 333 + 4,991 + 3,925 + 5,531 =$ _____ (18)

___(1) __ (2) __ (3) ____ (4) ____ (5) ___ (6) _____ (7) _____ (8) ____ (9) _____ (19)

Answers: (1) 523; (2) 624; (3) 560; (4) 4,272; (5) 4,649; (6) 5,750; (7) 56,508; (8) 57,337; (9) 48,481; (10) 20,796; (11) 29,180; (12) 27,222; (13) 17,762; (14) 20,716; (15) 17,601; (16) 17,758; (17) 11,535; (18) 16,134; (19) 178,704

Stop

You are now ready to take Pretest IB. This is a 10-minute test of addition and subtraction with a calculator. Pretest IB has been used in both classrooms and industry and is similar to many employment screening devices.

Your performance on Pretest IB will tell you if you have developed sufficient touch control to proceed to **Test IB**. Unless instructed otherwise, turn in your Pretest for correction and review before taking Test 1B. On Test IB, if you complete at least 30 problems correctly and also have better than 90 percent accuracy, proceed to Chapter 2. If not, turn to Chapter 11 to find further practice problems that will help build touch control, and confidence. You may want to work selected exercises in Chapter 11 before retaking Test IB.

Hint

Remember, when adding dollars and cents you need not index a decimal; however, if your machine is equipped with a "+" or ADD mode you may want to use it to automatically set the decimal at two places so you won't have to index every decimal.

Pretest IB

ADDITION AND SUBTRACTION WITH A CALCULATOR

10 minutes

This test must be worked in sequence. Problems skipped count as errors. You need 90 percent accuracy and 30 problems correct to pass. (30 problems correct is 60 strokes per minute (spm), 40 is 100 spm, 45 is 124 spm, and a perfect paper is 136 spm.)

Do not start until instructed to do so and be sure to write your answers as you go.

(1)	(2)	(3)	(4)	(5)
44	80	85	27	64
59	46	66	47	68
60	27	18	36	41
78	31	34	82	93
13	78	61	70	07

(6)	(7)	(8)	(9)	(10)
3,122	7,776	2,207	3,470	1,374
−984	−228	−418	−110	−572

(11)	(12)	(13)	(14)	(15)
479	224	205	898	698
840	485	372	457	539
341	751	463	523	492
928	605	561	177	389
539	926	682	211	229
185	559	703	905	893
675	414	837	178	112

(16)	(17)	(18)	(19)	(20)
9,959	9,230	3,102	8,513	5,413
−3,288	−3,951	−1,027	−7,586	−3,640

(21)	(22)	(23)	(24)	(25)
1,748	1,632	2,813	3,504	4,315
2,599	3,134	4,515	5,326	6,247
3,686	5,026	6,007	7,088	8,339
4,927	7,048	8,729	9,001	1,262
5,404	9,991	1,862	2,083	3,354

(26)	$9.18	(27)	$4.27	(28)	$1.36	(29)	$7.63	(30)	$2.89
	3.18		8.47		4.05		3.59		9.81
	5.76		.41		.51		9.82		4.13
	.54		3.61		5.02		6.05		4.97
	4.40		3.82		1.26		.83		.66
	6.99		7.06		6.15		1.08		3.66
	8.62		4.31		8.93		3.98		6.77

(31)	$580.44	(32)	$757.18	(33)	$918.82	(34)	$785.42	(35)	$398.85
	646.59		207.91		731.89		813.33		385.24
	18.27		238.21		757.68		815.94		828.70
	234.31		553.35		540.16		616.36		520.34
	178.13		84.20		28.66		75.83		934.33

(36)	325	(37)	5,270	(38)	296	(39)	8,159	(40)	7,621
	2,619		5,882		3,117		7,124		6,128
	5,177		6,749		4,552		1,385		3,768
	1,109		2,288		2,669		2,663		507
	3,354		2,743		511		3,548		341
	633		4,650		2,344		671		2,470
	9,191		1,744		173		6,183		2,883
	5,708		9,616		4,295		4,748		9,716
	4,113		9,764		3,948		1,325		3,271
	4,780		5,014		9,544		5,780		6,809

(41)	6,353	(42)	6,526	(43)	3,846	(44)	7,694	(45)	2,414
	3,084		8,151		4,068		7,034		5,267
	8,805		224		1,621		6,117		1,593
	6,593		7,429		3,972		2,699		3,021
	7,754		6,209		8,809		4,538		9,932
	12		9,743		8,381		8,994		5,976
	1,991		4,938		1,896		189		4,707
	8,859		8,447		6,842		2,887		3,405
	9,594		1,961		146		1,112		4,286
	8,966		6,187		7,879		3,865		115

(46) $860 + 390 - 427 - 110 + 279 =$ _____

(47) $166 - 421 + 254 - 196 + 438 =$ _____

(48) $76.727 + 208 - 12,421 + 4.87 =$ _____

(49) $8,241 + 61.57 - 3.295 + .1357 =$ _____

(50) $67.45 - 7.314 + 4,723 - 765.2 =$ _____

Speed Test 12

Timed Practice Drill 1

The following *timed practice drills* will help improve your touch control, speed, and accuracy development. Work as fast as possible while maintaining accuracy. Use correct finger placement. Operate the keys without looking. The numbers in parentheses are total strokes. On a 10-minute test you can find strokes per minute by moving the decimal one place to the left on the last problem you completed.

10 minutes

(1)	(2)	(3)	(4)	(5)
54	80	51	71	46
61	64	77	74	81
92	37	81	63	14
87	13	34	28	39
31	29	16	72	78
(16)	(32)	(48)	(64)	(80)

(6)	(7)	(8)	(9)	(10)
568	335	394	909	709
730	596	483	568	640
231	862	574	434	583
827	716	672	205	490
428	837	793	200	209
274	668	813	804	804
564	323	948	286	993
(109)	(138)	(167)	(196)	(225)

(11)	(12)	(13)	(14)	(15)
2,859	2,742	3,924	4,605	5,426
3,600	4,245	5,626	6,437	7,358
4,797	6,037	7,118	8,199	9,440
5,038	8,059	8,930	8,001	1,336
6,505	8,002	2,751	2,003	4,455
(251)	(277)	(303)	(329)	(355)

(16)	(17)	(18)	(19)	(20)
$8.27	$5.36	$2.25	$6.42	$1.98
4.27	8.27	3.04	2.47	8.90
6.67	.30	.42	9.71	4.12
.74	3.81	4.01	5.04	5.87
5.50	4.26	1.16	.72	.55
7.88	8.05	5.14	1.09	4.77
9.51	4.31	7.82	4.71	7.52
(383)	(411)	(439)	(467)	(495)

(21) $490.55	(22) $757.18	(23) $807.82	(24) $786.51	(25) $481.25
545.49	317.92	720.09	803.44	375.20
18.37	387.42	656.86	826.85	721.82
234.81	672.41	541.26	606.41	541.41
179.24	84.20	32.77	74.72	831.67
(565)	(555)	(585)	(615)	(645)

(26) 1,214	(27) 6,380	(28) 2,285	(29) 8,060	(30) 7,532
1,528	4,772	4,226	6,114	5,918
4,066	6,639	4,663	3,174	3,762
1,028	278	3,770	1,352	5,007
2,243	7,234	5,022	2,537	4,041
622	6,450	481	560	2,470
8,101	1,833	1,833	1,174	871
5,697	8,525	4,007	4,647	7,961
4,223	8,655	9,040	3,124	2,342
4,781	4,923	8,433	7,591	6,790
(695)	(745)	(795)	(845)	(895)

(31) 5,464	(32) 6,423	(33) 4,735	(34) 6,585	(35) 3,424
3,184	7,262	3,057	7,024	5,378
8,815	2,031	1,510	6,007	1,682
7,684	5,362	3,861	2,699	2,030
8,843	5,108	708	4,428	9,843
1,002	634	7,270	883	6,087
119	5,827	1,784	8,019	808
9,948	8,336	5,731	3,005	3,605
8,483	1,852	1,052	1,003	4,377
7,855	5,086	8,768	4,974	1,008
(945)	(995)	(1,045)	(1,095)	(1,145)

(36) $620.40	(37) $808.72	(38) $801.72	(39) $798.41	(40) $400.05
454.49	632.78	802.79	804.44	385.34
108.27	68.75	57.58	16.87	27.60
178.13	102.77	208.67	726.25	421.24
34.32	504.17	500.16	704.72	862.22
(1,175)	(1,205)	(1,235)	(1,265)	(1,295)

(41)	$672.42	(42)	$870.45	(43)	$138.50	(44)	$762.11	(45)	$287.75
	532.48		641.87		266.30		456.25		700.00
	108.27		201.37		600.05		320.40		31.27
	130.82		45.72		74.80		385.01		241.32
	88.24		818.43		132.50		91.00		597.60
	(1,325)		(1,355)		(1,385)		(1,415)		(1,445)

(46)	$368.51	(47)	$680.92	(48)	$815.92	(49)	$526.82	(50)	$340.26
	302.22		992.41		712.41		159.33		815.63
	470.70		21.83		38.50		302.12		24.00
	40.50		115.52		266.32		91.42		729.41
	428.62		100.02		354.82		590.07		974.33
	(1,475)		(1,505)		(1,535)		(1,565)		(1,595)

NAME	
DATE	
SECTION	PROBLEMS COMPLETED
ERRORS	NUMBER CORRECT

Timed Practice Drill 2

The following *timed practice drills* will help improve touch control. Work as fast as possible while maintaining accuracy. Use correct finger placement. Operate the keys without looking. The numbers in parentheses are total strokes. On a 10-minute test you can find strokes per minute by moving the decimal one place to the left on the last problem you completed.

10 minutes

(1)	23	(2)	98	(3)	90	(4)	67	(5)	12
	23		54		87		65		43
	33		93		14		32		78
	40		88		22		77		43
	11		66		99		32		65
	(16)		(32)		(48)		(64)		(80)

(6)	123	(7)	297	(8)	666	(9)	900	(10)	444
	654		945		408		976		321
	765		333		905		765		476
	899		100		147		214		111
	423		432		977		800		906
	178		976		258		345		443
	999		555		534		665		831
	(109)		(138)		(167)		(196)		(225)

(11)	2,222	(12)	3,456	(13)	7,890	(14)	2,877	(15)	7,777
	1,234		9,005		1,256		6,400		3,790
	5,868		3,256		2,888		8,999		2,227
	9,998		8,989		9,977		2,229		1,000
	1,267		5,555		4,321		2,478		2,244
	(251)		(277)		(303)		(329)		(355)

(16)	$9.77	(17)	$5.35	(18)	$4.25	(19)	$5.33	(20)	$5.45
	5.77		8.25		8.64		3.00		1.22
	9.09		.50		.46		9.78		5.12
	.34		4.81		4.55		9.66		5.66
	6.30		7.77		9.56		.77		.45
	9.88		3.56		8.13		1.04		3.66
	3.51		1.01		6.82		6.55		7.53
	(383)		(411)		(439)		(467)		(495)

(21)	$590.45	(22)	$675.78	(23)	$705.37	(24)	$746.59	(25)	$125.65
	222.67		987.56		222.89		103.44		995.70
	90.37		111.11		900.86		456.78		456.82
	678.81		897.46		234.67		789.01		900.71
	991.44		24.77		99.77		44.62		567.68
	(525)		(555)		(585)		(615)		(645)

(26)	1,214	(27)	6,380	(28)	2,285	(29)	8,060	(30)	7,532
	1,528		4,772		4,226		6,114		5,918
	4,066		6,639		4,663		3,174		3,762
	1,028		278		3,770		1,352		5,007
	2,243		7,234		5,022		2,537		4,041
	622		6,450		481		560		2,470
	8,101		1,833		1,833		1,174		871
	5,697		8,525		4,007		4,647		7,961
	4,223		8,655		9,040		3,124		2,342
	4,781		4,923		8,433		7,591		6,790
	(695)		(745)		(795)		(845)		(895)

(31)	9,080	(32)	3,674	(33)	4,935	(34)	3,654	(35)	6,578
	3,188		9,806		6,543		9,998		7,678
	2,876		1,234		1,918		3,765		6,756
	3,030		1,029		2,376		1,254		9,444
	4,848		2,039		789		9,845		3,989
	9,876		399		3,674		783		1,000
	666		4,876		2,900		3,765		976
	2,345		1,287		8,975		9,287		9,984
	8,888		9,080		2,222		7,006		2,343
	8,765		4,376		2,787		2,974		7,654
	(945)		(995)		(1,045)		(1,095)		(1,145)

(36)	$920.40	(37)	$898.72	(38)	$243.72	(39)	$432.41	(40)	$563.33
	459.49		222.33		876.79		824.44		900.64
	878.54		98.23		90.48		12.87		27.10
	278.13		102.00		348.57		234.56		421.21
	76.32		287.57		503.16		787.72		892.11
	(1,175)		(1,205)		(1,235)		(1,265)		(1,295)

(41) $672.42	(42) $870.45	(43) $138.50	(44) $762.11	(45) $987.65
532.48	641.87	266.30	456.25	701.00
108.27	201.37	600.05	320.40	31.07
130.82	45.72	74.80	385.01	954.32
88.24	818.43	132.50	91.00	876.90
(1,325)	(1,355)	(1,385)	(1,415)	(1,445)

(46) $898.51	(47) $611.92	(48) $111.11	(49) $443.22	(50) $765.11
992.22	987.41	799.41	999.33	976.33
471.11	23.33	89.50	213.12	28.99
48.50	445.52	288.32	87.42	785.43
428.62	122.02	761.92	945.32	988.88
(1,475)	(1,505)	(1,535)	(1,565)	(1,595)

NAME	
DATE	
SECTION	PROBLEMS COMPLETED
ERRORS	NUMBER CORRECT

Timed Practice Drill 3

(WITH SUBTRACTION)

The following *timed practice drills* will help improve touch control. Work as fast as possible while maintaining accuracy. Use correct finger placement. Operate the keys without looking. The numbers in parentheses are total strokes. On a 10-minute test you can find strokes per minute by moving the decimal one place to the left on the last problem you completed.

10 minutes

(1)	74	(2)	46	(3)	72	(4)	58	(5)	80
	47		68		48		66		64
	85		14		63		81		72
	94		39		28		43		13
	70		70		78		87		87
	(16)		(32)		(48)		(64)		(80)

(6)	6,209	(7)	5,437	(8)	6,349	(9)	8,514	(10)	4,834
	−809		−949		−489		−326		−947
	(90)		(100)		(110)		(120)		(130)

(11)	845	(12)	214	(13)	527	(14)	809	(15)	652
	357		323		603		333		477
	740		282		634		188		416
	253		478		827		765		886
	708		847		416		541		385
	452		521		714		321		222
	849		445		914		914		983
	(159)		(188)		(217)		(246)		(275)

(16)	1,300	(17)	3,920	(18)	4,744	(19)	2,403	(20)	8,360
	5,970		3,044		3,221		3,065		8,035
	808		7,068		762		340		7,560
	5,260		248		3,534		9,775		835
	8,874		8,776		2,760		2,735		1,240
	(300)		(325)		(350)		(375)		(400)

(21)	(22)	(23)	(24)	(25)
242	555	757	543	652
748	591	447–	785–	916
45	615	327	854	705–
843–	521	601–	35	82
872	70–	22	547–	632–
284	446–	421–	791	741
678	647	854–	631–	442
340–	571–	284	767–	812–
259	480	222	352	730–
434	443	631–	160	624
(440)	(480)	(520)	(560)	(600)

(26)	(27)	(28)	(29)	(30)
$511.09	$874.52	$277.07	$991.41	$412.88
47.75	643.98	223.08	82.52	29.61
707.24	309.54	645.36	888.00	467.42
800.01	10.65	52.41	572.45	760.83
223.49	400.07	824.65	300.60	228.54
(630)	(660)	(690)	(720)	(750)

(31)	(32)	(33)	(34)	(35)
$7.30	$6.55	$2.49	$9.21	$1.82
5.41	2.47	6.65	8.48	8.47
2.27	4.09	8.07	7.60	4.99
6.80	.58	.87	3.42	.25
2.95	3.80	5.32	.25	6.02
.85	6.51	5.42	4.42	4.73
4.82	8.72	8.87	7.43	6.76
(778)	(806)	(834)	(862)	(890)

(36)	(37)	(38)	(39)	(40)
3,579	1,234	4,358	6,201	360
6,798	6,707	4,578	1,148	7,241
8,132	2,249	3,949	7,423	8,162
7,851	3,463	1,028	2,558	9,116
122	134	6,632	8,543	1,102
2,321	2,162	721	5,143	752
3,474	5,680	1,170	358	5,502
3,460	8,913	2,460	4,681	1,002
8,821	4,582	2,460	7,702	7,241
(935)	(980)	(1,025)	(1,070)	(1,115)

(41)		(42)		(43)		(44)		(45)	
1,942		6,625		4,521		5,192		6,094	
1,758–		4,008		8,243–		6,845		7,532–	
8,030–		1,954–		2,391		4,562–		6,814	
4,411		9,308		5,281		1,775–		6,912	
255–		7,025–		4,947–		6,782		7,324–	
6,150		3,002		6,281		9,621–		8,271	
5,228–		455–		8,682		3,215–		816	
1,632		1,491–		4,027		8,762		2,011–	
9,141		3,982		831		772		1,947	
2,371		4,071		1,111		4,111		4,592	
(1,165)		(1,215)		(1,265)		(1,315)		(1,365)	

(46) 885 – 763 + 540 – 856 + 172 = _____ (1,386)

(47) 344 + 221 – 467 – 840 – 322 = _____ (1,407)

(48) 24.87 + 107 – .8376 + 472.1 = _____ (1,430)

(49) 6,741 + 63.27 – 435.1 – 576.82 = _____ (1,455)

(50) 64.31 – 7.844 + 87.62 – 372.411 = _____ (1,482)

NAME	
DATE	
SECTION	PROBLEMS COMPLETED
ERRORS	NUMBER CORRECT

Timed Practice Drill 4

(WITH SUBTRACTION)

The following *timed practice drills* will help improve touch control. Work as fast as possible while maintaining accuracy. Use correct finger placement. Operate the keys without looking. The numbers in parentheses are total strokes. On a 10-minute test you can find strokes per minute by moving the decimal one place to the left on the last problem you completed.

10 minutes

(1)	65	(2)	53	(3)	66	(4)	14	(5)	70
	19		98		42		71		33
	82		11		15		89		82
	88		66		70		26		44
	90		32		68		33		81
	(16)		(32)		(48)		(64)		(80)

(6)	6,289	(7)	6,431	(8)	6,621	(9)	1,234	(10)	4,314
	−651		−999		−822		−300		−996
	(90)		(100)		(110)		(120)		(130)

(11)	900	(12)	876	(13)	119	(14)	934	(15)	432
	234		399		188		330		407
	840		567		890		775		117
	654		718		804		799		899
	799		960		777		394		389
	123		111		719		478		333
	777		845		432		665		804
	(159)		(188)		(217)		(246)		(275)

(16)	9,008	(17)	8,765	(18)	9,879	(19)	6,543	(20)	1,227
	1,123		9,044		2,478		9,065		8,999
	900		3,337		999		765		5,432
	9,876		208		3,276		1,116		875
	7,654		3,366		9,876		9,456		9,076
	(300)		(325)		(350)		(375)		(400)

(21)	444	(22)	955	(23)	509	(24)	765	(25)	543
	654		501		876–		654–		234
	40		321		115		987		795–
	987–		987		687–		30		80
	665		77–		90		113–		445
	987		685–		476–		742		432–
	111		977		899–		894–		887–
	854–		106–		200		942–		564–
	876		490		543		453		900
	888		876		900–		243		111
	(440)		(480)		(520)		(560)		(600)

(26)	$566.99	(27)	$267.82	(28)	$765.34	(29)	$906.43	(30)	$999.99
	26.98		543.08		222.88		65.99		14.61
	765.28		309.65		543.90		878.33		967.48
	220.01		19.65		52.49		372.45		112.83
	287.49		444.77		765.00		522.98		855.54
	(630)		(660)		(690)		(720)		(750)

(31)	$3.87	(32)	$9.55	(33)	$9.76	(34)	$1.80	(35)	$9.76
	9.00		1.08		1.23		7.48		1.47
	7.65		8.99		8.54		1.10		6.78
	6.88		.18		.57		9.99		.15
	3.78		9.80		6.00		.55		8.92
	.75		8.51		7.42		9.72		9.88
	9.82		5.02		9.76		1.88		2.98
	(778)		(806)		(834)		(862)		(890)

(36)	8,889	(37)	8,524	(38)	9,876	(39)	6,222	(40)	908
	6,796		7,654		9,623		5,678		4,325
	8,154		9,876		9,000		7,089		8,089
	2,455		7,890		1,876		7,654		1,212
	126		100		5,556		8,070		8,876
	2,327		1,234		111		9,060		543
	3,438		9,432		1,006		555		5,908
	3,269		9,876		5,432		9,807		1,777
	1,820		7,777		9,988		3,456		9,512
	(935)		(980)		(1,025)		(1,070)		(1,115)

(41)	8,765	(42)	1,121	(43)	2,341	(44)	5,976	(45)	4,445
	2,244–		9,876		8,543–		8,685		9,090
	7,879–		9,080–		2,381		9,992–		8,765–
	9,876		9,191		5,289		3,232–		1,910
	276–		7,456–		7,543–		6,909		9,234
	6,543		3,009		8,000		6,543–		7,654–
	8,876–		876–		1,111		9,876–		900
	1,630		7,868–		9,876		1,115		7,654–
	1,876		2,345		765		908		6,543–
	1,978		9,405		3,151		4,765		5,432
	(1,165)		(1,215)		(1,265)		(1,315)		(1,365)

(46) $805 - 766 + 340 - 756 + 179 =$ _____ (1,386)

(47) $144 + 451 - 987 - 654 - 234 =$ _____ (1,407)

(48) $26.77 + 137 - .6376 + 489.7 =$ _____ (1,430)

(49) $7,771 + 33.47 - 735.9 - 173.52 =$ _____ (1,455)

(50) $74.51 - 3.564 + 88.62 - 975.618 =$ _____ (1,482)

DRILL 1: (1) 325; (2) 223; (3) 259; (4) 308; (5) 258; (6) 3,622; (7) 4,337; (8) 4,677; (9) 3,406; (10) 4,428; (11) 22,799; (12) 29,085; (13) 28,349; (14) 29,245; (15) 28,015; (16) $42.84; (17) $34.36; (18) $23.84; (19) $30.16; (20) $33.71; (21) $1,468.46; (22) $2,219.13; (23) $2,758.80; (24) $3,097.93; (25) $2,951.35; (26) 33,503; (27) 55,689; (28) 43,760; (29) 38,333; (30) 46,694; (31) 61,397; (32) 47,921; (33) 38,476; (34) 44,627; (35) 38,242; (36) $1,395.61; (37) $2,117.19; (38) $2,370.92; (39) $3,050.69; (40) $2,096.45; (41) $1,532.23; (42) $2,577.84; (43) $1,212.15; (44) $2,014.77; (45) $1,857.94; (46) $1,610.55; (47) $1,910.70; (48) $2,187.97; (49) $1,669.76; (50) $2,883.63

DRILL 2: (1) 130; (2) 399; (3) 312; (4) 273; (5) 241; (6) 4,041; (7) 3,638; (8) 3,895; (9) 4,665; (10) 3,532; (11) 20,589; (12) 30,261; (13) 26,332; (14) 22,983; (15) 17,038; (16) $44.66; (17) $31.25; (18) $42.41; (19) $36.13; (20) $29.09; (21) $2,573.74; (22) $2,696.68; (23) $2,163.56; (24) $2,140.44; (25) $3,046.56; (26) 33,503; (27) 55,689; (28) 43,760; (29) 38,333; (30) 46,694; (31) 53,562; (32) 37,800; (33) 37,119; (34) 52,331; (35) 56,402; (36) $2,612.88; (37) $1,608.85; (38) $2,062.72; (39) $2,292.00; (40) $2,804.39; (41) $1,532.23; (42) $2,577.84; (43) $1,212.15; (44) $2,014.77; (45) $3,550.94; (46) $2,838.96; (47) $2,190.20; (48) $2,050.26; (49) $2,688.41; (50) $3,544.74

DRILL 3: (1) 370; (2) 237; (3) 289; (4) 335; (5) 316; (6) 5,400; (7) 4,488; (8) 5,860; (9) 8,188; (10) 3,887; (11) 4,204; (12) 3,110; (13) 4,635; (14) 3,871; (15) 4,021; (16) 22,212; (17) 23,056; (18) 15,021; (19) 18,318; (20) 26,030; (21) 2,379; (22) 2,765; (23) 1,342 CR; (24) 5; (25) 578; (26) $2,289.58; (27) $2,238.76; (28) $2,022.57; (29) $2,834.98; (30) $1,899.28; (31) $30.40; (32) $32.72; (33) $37.69; (34) $40.81; (35) $33.04; (36) 44,558; (37) 35,124; (38) 27,356; (39) 43,757; (40) 40,478; (41) 10,376; (42) 20,071; (43) 19,935; (44) 13,291; (45) 18,579; (46) 22 CR; (47) 1,064 CR; (48) 603.132; (49) 5,792.35; (50) 228.325 CR

DRILL 4: (1) 344; (2) 260; (3) 261; (4) 233; (5) 310; (6) 5,638; (7) 5,432; (8) 5,799; (9) 934; (10) 3,318; (11) 4,327; (12) 4,476; (13) 3,929; (14) 4,375; (15) 3,381; (16) 28,561; (17) 24,720; (18) 26,508; (19) 26,945; (20) 25,609; (21) 2,824; (22) 4,239; (23) 2,381 CR; (24) 617; (25) 365 CR; (26) $1,866.75; (27) $1,584.97; (28) $2,349.61; (29) $2,746.18; (30) $2,950.45; (31) $41.75; (32) $43.13; (33) $43.28; (34) $32.52; (35) $39.94; (36) 37,274; (37) 62,363; (38) 52,468; (39) 57,591; (40) 41,150; (41) 11,393; (42) 9,667; (43) 16,828; (44) 1,285 CR; (45) 395; (46) 198 CR; (47) 1,280 CR; (48) 652.832; (49) 6,895.05; (50) 816.052 CR

CHAPTER 2

Multiplication and Division

LEARNING GOALS

After completing Chapter Two you should be proficient at:

- Multiplying without a calculator
- Multiplying with a calculator
- Dividing without a calculator
- Dividing with a calculator
- Estimating products and quotients

You will also be able to pass two timed tests: Pretest IIA on multiplication and division without a calculator, and Pretest IIB, on addition, subtraction, multiplication, and division with a calculator. You should be able to complete correctly at least 30 of the 50 problems while maintaining at least 90 percent accuracy.

N ow that you have completed Chapter One and have developed touch control for addition and subtraction, **you have a job skill.** You should be ready to pass a screening test for employment using a ten-key pad. You have had the opportunity to review certain properties of numbers and should be able to add and subtract without a calculator.

Multiplication Without a Calculator

It isn't difficult to find business problems that require multiplication. What is the total cost of 10 hand-held calculators if they cost $19.44 each? What will 20 liters of gasoline cost at $.59 per liter? What is the total pay for working 13 hours at $8.00 an hour? Multiplication is simply repeated addition, a quick way of adding the same quantity over and over. But, while you might multiply by carrying out repeated addition, it is much easier to memorize multiplication facts and multiply the original number, or **factor**, to arrive at the result, or **product.** Multiplication, like addition and subtraction, is relatively simple if you know your multiplication tables. Even with today's calculators, learning these facts is a must; there just isn't a shortcut. The multiplication techniques presented in this section will enable you to minimize the number of calculations in multiplication problems and thereby reduce the chance for error.

The following self-assessment will tell you if you need this section on multiplication.

Self-Assessment III—Multiplication (Without a Calculator)

(1)	(2)	(3)	(4)	(5)
6	325	879	475	576
× 4	× 7	× 9	× 100	× 608

(6)	(7)	(8)	(9)	(10)
7.34	4.837	$870.05	$24.12	9,348
× .008	× 96.7	× 1,010	× 25	× 999

Answers: (1) 24; (2) 2,275; (3) 7,911; (4) 47,500; (5) 350,208; (6) 0.059; (7) 467.738; (8) $878,750.50; (9) $603.00; (10) 9,338,652

If you missed only one or two problems on Self Assessment III skip to page 94, Multiplication With a Calculator. If you missed more than two problems or would like to review any of the Multiplication Competencies listed on the next page, continue with this section.

Multiplication Competencies

When you have completed this exercise you will be able to:

■ Solve simple and complex multiplication problems
■ Check multiplication
■ Use multiplication shortcuts

SIMPLE MULTIPLICATION

Multiplication means repeated addition. For example: 6×3 means that 6 is added three times. Let us draw 6 sets of 3 objects and count all the objects.

pictures	adding	multiplying
□□□□□□	6	6
□□□□□□	6	× 3
□□□□□□	6	18
	18	

These three methods for multiplying 6×3 require about the same amount of work. But what about this next problem?

1. Which is simpler, (a) or (b)? _____
   (a) $9 \times 9 = 81$ (b) $9 + 9 + 9 + 9 + 9 + 9 + 9 + 9 + 9 = 81$

   Answer: (a), if you know your multiplication facts

2. We read 9×8 as "9 times 8" or "8 multiplied by 9." Since $9 \times 8 = 72$, and $8 \times 9 = 72$, we say that order *does/does not* matter. Mathematicians call this the **commutative property of multiplication.**

   Answer: does not

3. The commutative property of multiplication says that _____ does not matter. That is, $3 \times 4 = 4 \times 3$.

   Answer: order ▢▢▢▢ has the same number of squares as: ▢▢▢
                   ▢▢▢▢   ▢▢▢
                   ▢▢▢▢   ▢▢▢
                                                   ▢▢▢

   Although numbers being multiplied together are often called **factors,** they also are known as **multiplicand** and **multiplier.**

28	Multiplicand
$\times 2$	Multiplier
56	Product

4. The number multiplied (28) is the _____, and the number that denotes the number of times it is multiplied (2) is the _____. The answer (56) is called the _____.

   Answers: multiplicand; multiplier; product

5. $3 \times 0 = 0$. If we add zero 3 times ($0 + 0 + 0 = 0$) or if we add 3 zero times, we get 0. Therefore, if a number is multiplied by 0, the answer is _____.

   Answer: 0

6. The product of 89×0 is _____.

   Answer: 0

7. $5 \times 1 = 5$ (If we add 5 ones ($1 + 1 + 1 + 1 + 1$) or if we add one 5 times, we get 5. Therefore, if a number is multiplied by _____, the answer is that same number. This is called the **identity element for multiplication.**

   Answer: 1

8. The product of 787×1 is _____.

Answer: 787

9. To solve business problems you need to know the multiplication facts. You will need to know them to tell if your answers are reasonable, even if you have a calculator. To review these multiplication facts, let's build a **multiplication table.** Using problems 5 through 8, fill in the first two horizontal rows and the first two vertical columns.

×	0	1	2	3	4	5	6	7	8	9
0										
1										
2										
3										
4										
5										
6										
7										
8										
9										

Answer: See problem 10

10. To fill in the third row and third column, you need to know the multiplication facts for 2. Or you could count by twos or just add _____ to each figure as you move across or down the table. Fill the third row and column.

×	0	1	2	3	4	5	6	7	8	9
0	0	0	0	0	0	0	0	0	0	0
1	0	1	2	3	4	5	6	7	8	9
2	0	2								
3	0	3								
4	0	4								
5	0	5								
6	0	6								
7	0	7								
8	0	8								
9	0	9								

Answer: 2 (See problem 11)

11. The same method can be used to fill in the rest of the table. For example, to fill in the row and column for 5, simply count by fives or just add _____ to each figure as you move across or down the table. Several numbers have

×	0	1	2	3	4	5	6	7	8	9
0	0	0	0	0	0	0	0	0	0	0
1	0	1	2	3	4	5	6	7	8	9
2	0	2	4	6	8	10	12	14	16	18
3	0	3	6							
4	0	4	8							
5	0	5	10							
6	0	6	12		24					
7	0	7	14					49		
8	0	8	16							
9	0	9	18							81

been placed in the table to help you check your work. Now fill in the remainder of the table.

×	0	1	2	3	4	5	6	7	8	9
0	0	0	0	0	0	0	0	0	0	0
1	0	1	2	3	4	5	6	7	8	9
2	0	2	4	6	8	10	12	14	16	18
3	0	3	6	9	12	15	18	21	24	27
4	0	4	8	12	16	20	24	28	32	36
5	0	5	10	15	20	25	30	35	40	45
6	0	6	12	18	24	30	36	42	48	54
7	0	7	14	21	28	35	42	49	56	63
8	0	8	16	24	32	40	48	56	64	72
9	0	9	18	27	36	45	54	63	72	81

The six most frequently forgotten multiplication facts are:

$6 \times 8 = 48$ $7 \times 8 = 56$ $8 \times 9 = 72$
$6 \times 9 = 54$ $7 \times 9 = 63$ $9 \times 9 = 81$

12. The factor that appears most often in the above list is _____.

Answer: 9

13. Multiplying by 9 **should** be easy because of the fact that 9 is 1 less than _____ and because, to multiply a number by 10 you simply **annex** or attach one _____ to that number. Therefore, to multiply a number by 9, simply annex one _____ and *add/subtract* the number once. Thus

$6 \times 9 = (6 \times 10) - 6 = 60 - 6 = 54$
$7 \times 9 = (7 \times 10) - 7 = 70 - 7 = 63$
$8 \times 9 = (8 \times 10) - 8 = 80 - 8 = 72$
$9 \times 9 = (9 \times 10) - 9 = 90 - 9 = 81$

Answers: 10; zero; zero; subtract

14. For each of the previous examples the two digits in the answer (5 and 4, 6 and 3, 7 and 2, 8 and 1) always sum to _____. That is, the sum of the digits in the product of 9 times any number, 1 through 10, is _____.

Answer: 9; 9($1 \times 9 = 9 + 0 = 9$, $2 \times 9 = 18$ and $1 + 8 = 9$, $3 \times 9 = 27$ and $2 + 7 = 9$, etc.)

For any number multiplied by 9, the sum of the digits in the product is always a multiple of 9. For example: $23 \times 9 = 207$, $2 + 0 + 7 = 9$; $576 \times 9 = 5,184$, $5 + 1 + 8 + 4 = 18$; $1 + 8 = 9$.

MULTIPLYING LARGER NUMBERS

Most business multiplication problems involve not only single-digit numbers, but numbers of several digits.

47	Multiplicand	$37.85	Multiplicand
× 34	Multiplier	× 24	Multiplier
188	Partial product	15140	Partial product
141	Partial product	7570	Partial product
1598	Product	$908.40	Product

15. Now let's find the product of 432 × 3.

432 means: 4   hundreds + _____ tens + _____ units

                                                        × 3
_____
        ____ hundreds + 9   tens +   6   units

or in short form:

432
× 3
_____
1,296

The abacus, called a soroban in Japan, can be used to add, subtract, multiply and divide. Skilled users are as quick and accurate as people using calculators.

We started with the units digit and multiplied 2 × 3. Then we moved to the left and multiplied 3 × 3, making it easy to keep each digit in its proper place.

Answers: 3; 2; 12

16. To multiply larger numbers, we usually must **carry.** This operation is much like addition. For example:

583 means   5   hundreds +   8 tens +   3 units

                                                              × 3
_____
583 × 3 =   _____   hundreds +   24 tens +   _____ units

24 tens = 2 hundreds + _____ tens. Therefore, when we carry the 2 hundreds from the 24 tens and add them to 15 hundreds, our answer is 17 hundreds + 4 tens + 9 units, or 1,749.

In short form:

583
× 3
_____
1,749

Answers: 15; 9; 4

To multiply by a two-digit multiplier, obtain the partial product and add them. For example:

```
   514
 × 72
  1028    First partial product, 2 × 514
  3598    Second partial product, 7 × 514
 37008    Product
```

17. The second partial product is 7 *tens/units* times 514, so the second partial product must be moved one place to the left.

    Answer: tens

    Here's another example:

```
    8966
  × 742
   17932
   35864
   62762
 6652772
```

18. Since the 7 in the multiplier is in the *hundreds/tens* position, the product of 7 × 8,966 is moved _____ places to the left. For the same reason, when there are several partial products, each must be moved to the *left/right* one more place.

    Answers: hundreds; 2; left

19. In the problem at the right, 2 × 516 gives the partial product _____. Which partial product contains an error? _____. The correct product, therefore, is _____.

```
    516
  × 352
   1032
   2570
   1548
 181532
```

    Answers: 1,032; 2,570 (it should be 2,580); 181,632

DIFFICULTIES WITH ZERO

Zeros in multiplication can be treated like any other digit. For example:

```
   2,789        2,789        2,789
 ×   10       ×  100       × 1,000
   0000         0000         0000
   2789         0000         0000
  27890         2789         0000
              278900         2789
                          2789000
```

20. From the previous examples, we see that it would be easier and quicker just to transfer the zeros in the multiplier to the _____.

Answer: product or answer

21. Multiply the following numbers by transferring zeros.

$$
\begin{array}{r} 327 \\ \times\,10 \\ \hline \end{array}
\qquad
\begin{array}{r} 4{,}562 \\ \times\,100 \\ \hline \end{array}
\qquad
\begin{array}{r} 89{,}345 \\ \times\,1000 \\ \hline \end{array}
$$

Answers: 3,270; 456,200; 89,345,000

The short method can be extended to multiplying any number that ends in zero or zeros.

300	2 zeros	15,000	3 zeros
× 70	1 zero	× 300	2 zeros
21,000	3 zeros	4,500,000	5 zeros

22. As shown above, the problem of multiplying by numbers that end in zero can be simplified by _____ the number of zeros separately and transferring the zeros to the _____ of the remaining numbers.

Answers: adding or counting; product

23. Solve these problems.

$$
\begin{array}{r} 320 \\ \times\,40 \\ \hline \end{array}
\qquad
\begin{array}{r} 800 \\ \times\,700 \\ \hline \end{array}
\qquad
\begin{array}{r} 2{,}500 \\ \times\,500 \\ \hline \end{array}
\qquad
\begin{array}{r} 9{,}000 \\ \times\,300 \\ \hline \end{array}
$$

Answers: 128 annexing 00 = 12,800; 56 annexing 0,000 = 560,000; 125 annexing 0,000 = 1,250,000; 27 annexing 00,000 = 2,700,000

Now let us multiply when zero is between two other digits in the multiplier.

$$
\begin{array}{r} 459 \\ \times\,302 \\ \hline 918 \\ 000 \\ 1377 \\ \hline 138618 \end{array}
\qquad \text{or shorter:} \qquad
\begin{array}{r} 459 \\ \times\,302 \\ \hline 918 \\ 13770 \\ \hline 138618 \end{array}
$$

24. What we have done above is to replace the row of zeros with a single zero, which shifts the _____ partial product _____ extra place to the *left/right*.

Answers: third; one; left

25. Solve these problems using the shorter method. (Show your work.)

$$
\begin{array}{r}
518 \\
\times\,203 \\
\hline
\end{array}
\qquad
\begin{array}{r}
781 \\
\times\,108 \\
\hline
\end{array}
$$

Answers:
$$
\begin{array}{r}
518 \\
\times\,203 \\
\hline
1554 \\
10360 \\
\hline
105154
\end{array}
\qquad
\begin{array}{r}
781 \\
\times\,108 \\
\hline
6248 \\
7810 \\
\hline
84348
\end{array}
$$

MULTIPLYING DECIMAL NUMBERS

If numbers contain decimals, only a slight variation is necessary. For convenience we may align the numbers on the right. (Remember you may not do this when adding decimals.) For example:

$$
\begin{array}{r}
3.724 \\
\times\,3.22 \\
\hline
7448 \\
7448 \\
11172 \\
\hline
1199128
\end{array}
$$

26. We can now place the decimal by estimating the product. If we ignore the numbers to the right of the decimal, the problem becomes $3 \times 3 = 9$. The answer, then, should be somewhat larger than _____. Thus, the correct answer is 11.99128. This is placing the **decimal point by estimating.**

    Answer: 9

27. In the above example we could also **place the decimal by counting.** There are 3 places to the right of the decimal in 3.724. In the multiplier (3.22), there are _____ places to the right of the decimal. The total number of digits to the right of the decimal in both numbers is $3 + 2 = 5$. Therefore, we put the decimal in the product 5 places to the left.

    Answer: 2

28. What is the number of decimal places in the product of each of the following problems? (Do not multiply the numbers.)

    (a) 63.6×5.8 _____   (b) $6.59 \times .07$ _____

    (c) 9.233×34.7244 _____   (d) $.04286 \times 22.38$ _____

    Answers: (a) 2; (b) 4; (c) 7; (d) 7

29. The rule for multiplying decimal numbers is: Perform the multiplication as if the numbers were whole numbers. Then

estimate your answer or count as many decimals in the product as there are digits to the *right/left* of the decimal in both of the original numbers.

Answer: right

30. Place the decimal in problems (b) and (c).

(a)
```
      76.3   1 decimal place
    × 1.64   2 decimal places
      3052
      4578
       763
   125.132   3 decimal places
```
(b)
```
      .784
    × 22.8
      6272
      1568
      1568
    178752
```
(c)
```
    $14.53
    × .125
      7265
      2906
      1453
  $181625
```

Answers: (b) 3 decimal places + 1 decimal place = 4 decimal places: therefore 17.8752 (c) 2 decimal places + 3 decimal places = 5 decimal places: therefore, $1.81625

CHECKING MULTIPLICATION

31. In the problem $237 \times 15 = 3,555$, the product is _____. The factors are 237 and _____.

Answers: 3,555; 15

To verify or check a multiplication problem simply reverse the factors. For example:

(a)
```
      237
    ×  15
     1185    equals
      237
     3555
```
(b)
```
       15
    × 237
      105
       45
       30
     3555
```

32. The factors in (a) have been _____ in (b).

Answer: reversed (We could also check by dividing 3,555 by 15. The result of the division would be 237.)

33. By reversing the factors, check these multiplication problems.
```
      88   Check:
    × 53
     264
     440
    4664
```
```
      76   Check:
    × 22
     152
     152
    1672
```

Answer:
```
        53        22
      × 88      × 76
       424       132
       424       154
      4664      1672
```

MULTIPLICATION SHORTCUTS (OPTIONAL)

This section on shortcuts is an enrichment exercise. Which your instructor may consider optional. Some people, however, may find it is useful for improving speed, accuracy, and estimating.

34. When a 0 is placed to the right of a number, the zero is annexed to that number. When we multiply 10×37, we place a zero to the right of the 37, which results in 370. Thus, to multiply any number by 10, simply annex one _____.

    Answer: zero

35. $1,000 \times 84 = 84,000$
    84 is changed to 84,000 by _____ three zeros to 84.

    Answer: annexing

36. To multiply any whole number by 10, 100, 1,000, etc., simply _____ one _____ to the number for each zero in the multiplier.

    Answers: annex; zero

37. $853 \times 100 =$ _____

    $789 \times 10,000 =$ _____

    Answers: 85,300; 7,890,000

38. Five is one-half of _____. Therefore, we can multiply 412×5 by annexing one zero and taking one-half of the product.

    Answer: 10

39. Study the following.

Problem	Think
412 $\times 5$	$4,120 \div 2 = 2,060$

    To multiply by 5, annex one _____ and divide by _____.

    Answers: zero; 2

40. Use the shortcut for multiplying mentally by 5.

    $5 \times 846 =$ _____

    $5 \times 4,812 =$ _____

    $5 \times 5,072 =$ _____

    Answers: 4,230; 24,060; 25,360

41. A similar shortcut can be used to multiply by 50, 500, and so on. Fifty is one-half of _____ and 500 is one-half of _____. Therefore, to multiply by 50, annex two zeros and divide by two; to multiply by 500, annex _____ zeros and divide by _____.

Answers: 100; 1,000; 3; 2

42. Using the shortcut method work these problems mentally.

$50 \times 82,504 =$ _____ think: $(8,250,400 \div 2)$
$500 \times 4,862 =$ _____
$5,000 \times 12,804 =$ _____

Answers: 4,125,200; 2,431,000; 64,020,000

43. Moving the decimal point in a number one place to the right is the same as multiplying that number by ten. To multiply 3.1671 by 1,000, move the decimal point _____ places to the _____.

Answers: three; right

44. Solve these problems by moving the decimal point.

(a) $10 \times 57.32 =$ _____   (b) $632.55 \times 100 =$ _____
(c) $1,000 \times .5789 =$ _____   (d) $6.7325 \times 1,000 =$ _____

Answers: (a) 573.2; (b) $63,255.00; (c) 578.9; (d) 6,732.5

45. Extend this invoice by mentally multiplying the unit price by the quantity.

Quantity	Description	Unit Price	Extension
5	#857 Sleepers	$182.24	$ _____
10	#858 Sofas	98.57	_____
50	#831 Tables	218.82	_____
500	#845 Chairs	8.62	_____

Answers: $911.20; $985.70; $10,941.00; $4,310.00

46. Twenty-five is one-fourth of _____; therefore, a shortcut for multiplying by 25 is to annex two zeros and divide by _____.

Answers: 100; 4

47. To multiply 25×816, first annex _____ zeros and divide by _____ $(81,600 \div 4)$. The product is _____.

Answers: two; 4; 20,400

48. What is a shortcut method for multiplying by 250? _____

_____

_____

Answer: Annex three zeros and divide by 4. Note: A similar method works for multiplying by 125, 16 2/3, 33 1/3, etc.

49. Complete the following problems mentally.

Items		Price	
25	@	$1.28 =	_____
50	@	6.32 =	_____
250	@	88.44 =	_____
100	@	7.16 =	_____

Answers: $32.00; $316.00; $22,110.00; $716.00

50. What is the shortcut rule for multiplying by 100? _____
_____

Answer: annex two zeros to the multiplicand or the factor being multiplied

51. What is the shortcut rule for multiplying by 2,500? _____
_____

Answer: annex four zeros and divide by 4

52. Multiplying 99 by 346 is easy when you think: 99 is one less than_____. ($100 \times 346 = 34,600$ and $1 \times 346 = 346$.) Since 99 is one less than 100, $99 \times 346 = 34,600 - 346 = $_____.

Answers: 100; 34,254

53. Use this shortcut to complete the following problems.

$9 \times 56 = 560 - 56 = $_____

$99 \times 378 = 37,800 - 378 = $_____

$9 \times 128 = $_____ $- $_____ $= $_____

$999 \times 785 = $_____ $- $_____ $= $_____

Answers: 504; 37,422; 1,280; 128; 1,152; 785,000; 785; 784,215

54. Does $98 \times 8 = 800 - 16$? Yes/No _____ Why? _____
_____
Does $97 \times 9 = 900 - 27$? Yes/No _____ Why? _____
_____

Answers: Yes, because 98 is 2 less than 100 and 2 times 8 is 16; yes, because 97 is 3 less than 100 and 3 times 9 is 27.

55. A similar procedure is used for multiplying numbers slightly larger than a multiple of 10.

$101 \times 82 = 8,200 + 82 = $_____

$102 \times 33 = 3,300 + 66 = $_____

$1,001 \times 56 = 56,000 + $_____ $= $_____

$103 \times 321 = $_____ $+ 963 = $_____

Answers: 8,282; 3,366; 56; 56,056; 32,100; 33,063

56. Perform the following calculations using shortcut methods.

$$37 \times 9 = 370 - 37 = \underline{\hspace{4cm}} \quad (1)$$

$$28 \times 99 = \underline{\hspace{2cm}} - 28 = \underline{\hspace{3cm}} \quad (2)$$

$$79 \times 90 = \underline{\hspace{2cm}} - 790 = \underline{\hspace{3cm}} \quad (3)$$

$$38 \times 101 = 3,800 + \underline{\hspace{2cm}} = \underline{\hspace{3cm}} \quad (4)$$

$$64 \times 110 = 6,400 + \underline{\hspace{2cm}} = \underline{\hspace{3cm}} \quad (5)$$

$$88 \times 25 = 8,800 \div 4 = \underline{\hspace{3cm}} \quad (6)$$

$$176 \times 50 = 17,600 \div \underline{\hspace{2cm}} = \underline{\hspace{3cm}} \quad (7)$$

$$1,616 \times 250 = \underline{\hspace{2.5cm}} \div 4 = \underline{\hspace{3cm}} \quad (8)$$

Answers: (1) 333; (2) 2,800, 2,772; (3) 7,900, 7,110; (4) 38, 3,838; (5) 640, 7,040; (6) 2,200; (7) 2, 8,800; (8) 1,616,000, 404,000

BUSINESS APPLICATION

57. Complete the following sales slips by **extending** (multiplying quantity by price) and then totaling the amounts.

WILLIAMS 2 SERVICE

1234 A ST. • PERFECTION, AMERICA

PHONE 781-5023   DATE May 4
NAME Joe Smith

QTY.	DESCRIPTION		PRICE	AMOUNT	
22	GALS	GASOLINE	2.59		a
5	QTS.	OIL	2.23		b
1		LUBRICATION	15.50		c
				TOTAL	d

REC'D BY

WESTERN MOTORS inc.

111 BENSON AVENUE

CUSTOMER'S ORDER NO. 220399   DATE Nov. 23
SOLD TO Jim Bryme
ADDRESS W 314 Central
SALESMAN I M   TERMS Cash

QTY.	PART NUMBER	DESCRIPTION	PRICE	AMOUNT	
4	88A 4021	Tune-Up Kits	15 96		a
9	49X8991	Bearings	23 28		b
6	37M6879	Gasket Kits	10 94		c
2	612 7841	Wrenches	14 88		d

All claims and returned goods MUST be accompanied by this bill

RECEIVED BY   TOTAL   e

Answers: Williams 2 Service: (a) $56.98; (b) $11.15; (c) $15.50; (d) $83.63; Western Motors: (a) $63.84; (b) $209.52; (c) $65.64; (d) $29.76; (e) $368.76

58. Smith's Sporting Goods purchased 416 tennis rackets at a net price of $25 each. What was the total net cost of the tennis rackets? _____

Answer: $416 \times 25 = 41,600 \div 4 = \$10,400$

Multiplication With a Calculator

Multiplication is important in many business problems (see the section on **Invoices and Business Forms** in Chapter 7.) On electronic calculators, multiplication is completely automatic. On most machines, you index the numbers and functions into the machine in the same order they are written. However, if this is not so for your calculator, follow the instructions in the operating manual. Work the following sample multiplication problems.

$12 \times 3 = 36$ $12 \times 12 = 144$
$14 \times 10 = 140$ $396 \times 48 = 19,008$
$3,942 \times 153 = 603,126$ $7,143 \times 591 = 4,221,513$

```
        12. ×                       12. ×
         3. =                       12. =
        36.    *                   144.    *

        14. ×                      396. ×
        10. =                       48. =
       140.    *                 19,008.    *

     3,942. ×                    7,143. ×
       153. =                      591. =
   603,126.    *              4,221,513.    *
```

If your answers match these examples, do the following problems. If not, review the instructions or consult your instructor.

Hint

Multiplication and division keys are found in different locations on various calculators. "Touch control," therefore, is not required except for the ten-key pad and the plus, minus and total keys.

Do the following problems.

(1) $54 \times 16 =$ _____ (2) $32 \times 44 =$ _____

(3) $66 \times 67 =$ _____ (4) $74 \times 27 =$ _____

(5) $542 \times 44 =$ _____ (6) $390 \times 497 =$ _____

(7) $924 \times 2{,}658 =$ _____   (8) $948 \times 9{,}966 =$ _____

(9) $8{,}062 \times 9{,}185 =$ _____   (10) $888 \times 485 =$ _____

(11) $888 \times 2{,}747 =$ _____   (12) $2{,}942 \times 940 =$ _____

(13) $669 \times 9{,}324 =$ _____   (14) $6{,}249 \times 990 =$ _____

(15) $550 \times 856 =$ _____   (16) $385 \times 247 =$ _____

(17) $787 \times 939 =$ _____   (18) $4{,}226 \times 2{,}837 =$ _____

(19) $3{,}064 \times 851 =$ _____   (20) $7{,}876 \times 2{,}242 =$ _____

Answers: (1) 864; (2) 1,408; (3) 4,422; (4) 1,998; (5) 23,848; (6) 193,830; (7) 2,455,992; (8) 9,447,768; (9) 74,049,470; (10) 430,680; (11) 2,439,336; (12) 2,765,480; (13) 6,237,756; (14) 6,186,510; (15) 470,800; (16) 95,095; (17) 738,993; (18) 11,989,162; (19) 2,607,464; (20) 17,657,992

MULTIPLYING DECIMAL NUMBERS

Multiplying decimal numbers is very common in business problems. Most electronic calculators have automatic decimal placement. All you do is place the decimal correctly as you enter the number. Here are some examples.

$.32 \times .05 = .0160$ $2.7 \times .3 = .81$
$.45 \times .005 = .0023$ $\$5.58 \times .02 = \$.11$

Hint

Many serious errors result from a misplaced decimal point. You can avoid most of these mistakes if you estimate the answer or ask yourself whether the answer is reasonable. One hundred dollars is quite different from $10 or $1,000, and 25 percent is quite different from 2.5 percent or 250 percent.

Perform the following calculations. Remember the rules for rounding—decimals to three places, dollars and cents to the nearest cent.

(1) $9.4 \times 15 =$ _____   (2) $0.1 \times 88.2 =$ _____

(3) $9.004 \times 58.54 =$ _____   (4) $519.8 \times 15.06 =$ _____

(5) $9.493 \times 881.9 =$ _____   (6) $9.187 \times .076 =$ _____

(7) $.068 \times .766 =$ _____   (8) $.271 \times .06708 =$ _____

(9) $20.714 \times 1.28 =$ _____   (10) $.0770 \times 61.78 =$ _____

(11) $\$23.84 \times .05 =$ _____   (12) $\$77.76 \times 22.07 =$ _____

(13) $\$94.54 \times 137.40 =$ _____   (14) $\$728.93 \times 355.50 =$ _____

(15) $8.00 × 74.54 = _____   (16) $386.07 × 834.49 = _____

(17) .438 × $93.51 = _____   (18) .3102 × $47.31 = _____

(19) .0546 × $269.20 = _____   (20) $973.41 × .0303 = _____

Answers: (1) 141; (2) 8.820; (3) 527.094; (4) 7,828.188; (5) 8,371.877; (6) .698; (7) .052; (8) .018; (9) 26.514; (10) 4.757; (11) $1.19; (12) $1,716.16; (13) $12,989.80; (14) $259,134.62; (15) $596.32; (16) $322,171.55; (17) $40.96; (18) $14.68; (19) $14.70; (20) $29.49

MULTIFACTOR MULTIPLICATION

In many business problems, it is useful to be able to multiply the product of one multiplication without re-entering the product. Check your machine operating manual to find out how your machine performs this function. Some electronic calculators require the first product to be reentered on the keyboard with the times key. However, the following examples show the more typical process.

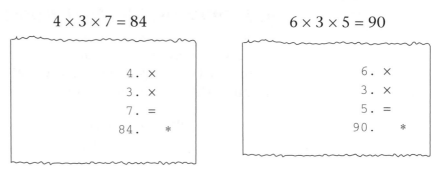

$4 × 3 × 7 = 84$ $6 × 3 × 5 = 90$

Work the following examples without recording or re-entering the intermediate products.

$$6 × 8 × 5 = 240$$
$$17 × 24 × 63 = 25,704$$
$$37 × 25 × 68 × 57 × 19 = 68,120,700$$
$$16.27 × 14.3 × .8 = 186.129$$

If your answers match these examples, work the following problems. If not, consult your operating manual again or ask your instructor to explain the process.

Complete the following problems. If your machine has a decimal setting, set the decimal at four places.

(1) $7 × 4 × 8 =$ _____   (2) $5 × 9 × 8 × 2 × 6 =$ _____

(3) $27 × 76 × 74 =$ _____   (4) $85 × 30 × 18 =$ _____

(5) $294 × 6 × 97 =$ _____   (6) $47 × 43 × 143 =$ _____

(7) $53 × 85.6 × .07 =$ _____   (8) $3.05 × .78 × 8.6 =$ _____

(9) $5.92 × 2.1 × 9.3 =$ _____   (10) $25.57 × 1.7 × .08 =$ _____

Answers: (1) 224; (2) 4,320; (3) 151,848; (4) 45,900; (5) 171,108; (6) 289,003; (7) 317.576; (8) 20.459; (9) 115.618; (10) 3.478

Division Without a Calculator

Many business problems require division: How many gallons of gasoline at $2.99 per gallon can you buy with $19.00? How many hours do you need to work to earn $120 if you are paid $12.00 an hour? How many chairs can you buy for $1,000 if they cost $25 each? Division, the opposite of multiplication, is a quick way of subtracting the same quantity over and over. If you know your multiplication tables, division is quite simple. This section will enable you to solve division problems using techniques similar to those for multiplication.

Division Competencies

After completing this exercise, you will be able to:

- Perform simple division
- Perform long division
- Check division
- Use division shortcuts

The following self-assessment will tell you if you need this section on division.

Self-Assessment IV—Division (Without a Calculator)

Round answers to the nearest thousandth.

(1) $7\overline{)42}$ (2) $12\overline{)144}$ (3) $73\overline{)326}$ (4) $65\overline{)961}$

(5) $8\overline{)11}$ (6) $5\overline{).28}$ (7) $1.04\overline{)20.8}$ (8) $41.1\overline{)9.63}$

(9) $51,000\overline{)153,000}$ (10) $.25\overline{)323}$

Answers: (1) 6; (2) 12; (3) 4.466; (4) 14.785; (5) 1.375; (6) 0.056; (7) 20; (8) 0.234; (9) 3; (10) 1292

If you missed only one or two problems on Self-Assessment IV skip to page 116, Division With a Calculator.

If you missed more than two problems or would like to review any of the Division Competencies listed on the previous page, continue with this section.

SIMPLE DIVISION

Division and multiplication, like addition and subtraction, are inverse operations. That is, what multiplication puts together, division takes apart. For example:

$$3 \times 6 = 18 \qquad 8 \times 5 = 40 \qquad 5 \times 3 = 15$$
$$18 \div 3 = 6 \qquad 40 \div 8 = 5 \qquad 15 \div 3 = 5$$

1. If $5 \times 7 = 35$, then $35 \div 5 = $ _____.

Answer: 7

Division can be represented in picture form. The squares below represent two sample division problems. Arranged in groups of four across, there are 3 rows of 4 squares each. Arranged in groups of 3 coming down, there are 4 columns of 3 squares each.

2. What two division problems can be represented by the circles below?

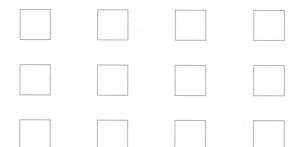

$$30 \div \text{_____} = \text{_____}$$

$$30 \div \text{_____} = \text{_____}$$

Answers: 5 6 (if the circles are arranged in groups of 6 across, there are 5 rows of 6 circles); 6 5 (if the circles are arranged in groups of 5 columns, there are 6 columns of 5 circles)

We can write division in several ways:

$15 \div 3$ is read 15 divided by 3 $\qquad$ $3\overline{)15}$ is read 3 into 15

$15/3$ is read 15 over 3

Each problem asks the same question: "How many 3's are in 15?" The 3 is called the **divisor**; 15, the number being divided, is called the **dividend**; and 5, the result, is called the **quotient.**

$$\text{divisor } 3\overline{)15} \begin{array}{l} 5 \quad \text{quotient} \\ 15 \quad \text{dividend} \end{array}$$

3. In the problem $12/4 = 3$, what are the quotient, the dividend, and the divisor? _____ is the quotient, _____ is the dividend, and _____ is the divisor.

   Answers: 3; 12; 4

4. Write "thirty-six divided by 4" in three ways: _____, _____, _____

   Answer; $\dfrac{36}{4}$; $4\overline{)36}$; $36 \div 4$ (in any order)

5. In the division problem $40 \div 5 = 8$, what is the quotient? _____

   Answer: 8

6. In the division problem $14/7 = 2$, 7 is the _____.

   Answer: divisor

7. In the division problem $63 \div 9 = 7$, 63 is the _____.

   Answer: dividend

Since division is the inverse or opposite of multiplication, you can determine the facts of division from your knowledge of multiplication facts. For example, $18 \div 2$ asks, "How many 2's are in 18?" The answer is nine 2's = 18. And you can check the answer by multiplying $9 \times 2 = 18$.

8. What is $21 \div 3$? _____

   Answer: 7, which can be checked by $7 \times 3 = 21$

9. Division facts are the inverse of multiplication. Circle the four groups below that are entirely correct.

(A)	(B)	(C)	(D)
$35 \div 5 = 7$	$49 \div 7 = 6$	$16 \div 2 = 8$	$36 \div 6 = 5$
$25 \div 5 = 5$	$42 \div 6 = 7$	$45 \div 9 = 5$	$56 \div 8 = 7$
$15 \div 5 = 3$	$48 \div 8 = 6$	$18 \div 3 = 6$	$54 \div 9 = 6$

(E)	(F)	(G)	(H)
$63 \div 7 = 9$	$48 \div 6 = 8$	$20 \div 4 = 5$	$27 \div 9 = 3$
$64 \div 8 = 8$	$81 \div 9 = 8$	$20 \div 5 = 4$	$32 \div 4 = 9$
$54 \div 9 = 7$	$24 \div 6 = 4$	$32 \div 4 = 8$	$54 \div 9 = 5$

(I)	(J)	(K)	(L)
$49 \div 7 = 7$	$72 \div 9 = 8$	$63 \div 9 = 7$	$32 \div 8 = 4$
$21 \div 7 = 3$	$63 \div 9 = 8$	$54 \div 6 = 9$	$54 \div 7 = 8$
$24 \div 6 = 3$	$27 \div 3 = 9$	$72 \div 8 = 9$	$35 \div 7 = 5$

Answers: A; C; G; K

If you had trouble with this exercise, return to page 89 and review your multiplication facts.

DIVISION BY ZERO

Division by zero creates a special problem. For example $5 \div 0 = ?$ Since division is the opposite of multiplication, could we have $0 \times ? = 5$? In any multiplication problem when zero is a factor, the product is zero; therefore, $0 \times ?$ cannot $= 5$ and we conclude that it is not possible to divide 5 by 0.

Using this same reasoning it can be shown that no number can be divided by zero. For example, does $0 \div 0 = 1$ because $0 \times 1 = 0$? Does $0 \div 0 = 2$ because $0 \times 2 = 0$? Does $0 \div 0 = 3$ because $0 \times 3 = 0$? Since a division problem can have only one answer, it is impossible to divide by zero. The rule, then, is that division by zero is undefined or impossible.

10. Find $7 \div 0$._____

Answer: undefined or impossible

11. Find $0/0$._____

Answer: undefined or impossible

It is true that $8 \times 0 = 0$ and $0 \div 8 = 0$, and that $11 \times 0 = 0$ and $0 \div 11 = 0$. In the same manner we can show that if zero is divided by any other number the result is always zero.

12. The rule, then, is that when zero is divided by any number other than zero the result is _____.

Answer: zero

13. Find $72 \div 0$. _____.

Answer: undefined

14. $0 \div 72 =$ _____

Answer: 0

15. $0/0 =$ _____

Answer: undefined

16. $0 \div 8 =$ _____

Answer: 0

REMAINDERS

The division problem $8 \div 4$ asks, "How many 4's are in 8?" The answer is 2 and the check is $2 \times 4 = 8$. We say that 8 is evenly divisible by 4 or that 8 is a multiple of 4.

17. Which number is evenly divisible by 7: 36, 42, or 48?

Answer: 42 Checks: $7 \times 5 = 35$, so 36 is not evenly divisible by 7. $7 \times 6 = 42$, so 42 is evenly divisible by 7. $7 \times 7 = 49$, so 48 is not evenly divisible by 7.

The division problem $53 \div 9$ can be shown as

$$\text{divisor } 9\overline{)\begin{matrix} 5 \\ 53 \\ 45 \\ \hline 8 \end{matrix}} \quad \begin{matrix} \text{quotient} \\ \text{dividend} \\ \\ \text{remainder} \end{matrix}$$

18. If the divisor is 8 and the dividend is 65, the quotient is _____ with remainder _____.

Answers: 8; 1

LONG DIVISION

Long division is used for more difficult division problems. For each, here are the steps for dividing 75 by 3:

(1) Divide 3 into 7; write 2 above the 7 in the dividend.
(2) Multiply 2 times 3; write 6 under the seven.
(3) Subtract 6 from 7; bring down the 5; write 15 under the 6, as shown
(4) Divide 3 into 15; write 5 above the 5 in the dividend.
(5) Multiply 5 times 3; write 15 under the 15.
(6) Subtract 15 from 15; write 0 under the 15.

$$\begin{matrix} & 25 \\ 3\overline{)75} \\ & 6 \\ \hline & 15 \\ & 15 \\ \hline & 0 \end{matrix}$$

The check is $3 \times 25 = 75$.

19. Complete this long division problem.

$$
\begin{array}{r}
1 \\
5\overline{)87} \\
\underline{5} \\
37
\end{array}
$$

Answer:

$$
\begin{array}{r}
17 \\
5\overline{)87} \\
\underline{5} \\
37 \\
\underline{35} \\
2
\end{array}
$$
or
$$
\begin{array}{r}
17\ \text{R2} \\
5\overline{)87} \\
\underline{5} \\
37 \\
\underline{35} \\
2
\end{array}
$$

To avoid errors it is important to place the digits in the quotient neatly above the dividend. For example, when we divide 201 by 6, since $2 \div 6 = 0$ R2, we could place a 0 above the 2. Then $20 \div 6 = 3$ R2 and we write 3 above the 0. Then we proceed as shown:

$$
\begin{array}{r}
033 \\
6\overline{)201} \\
\underline{18} \\
21 \\
\underline{18} \\
3
\end{array}
$$

Remember that even though the first place in this quotient is zero or is left empty, the 3 must be placed above the 0 in the second place.

20. What is $4,572 \div 7$? (Show your work.)

Answer:

$$
\begin{array}{r}
653 \\
7\overline{)4572} \\
\underline{42} \\
37 \\
\underline{35} \\
22 \\
\underline{21} \\
1
\end{array}
$$
or $\quad$ 653 R1

Difficulty may occur when there is a zero in the middle of a quotient. In the example $4,257 \div 7$:

$5 \div 7 = 0$ R5

$$
\begin{array}{r}
608 \\
7\overline{)4257} \\
\underline{42} \\
05 \\
\underline{0} \\
57 \\
\underline{56} \\
1
\end{array}
$$

Here we place the 0 above the 5 in the dividend, multiply 0 times 7, write 0 under the 5, and proceed as before. Notice that only when zero is at the beginning of a quotient may we omit it. Any other zero must appear in the quotient.

21. What is $9\overline{)7,234}$?

Answer: $\begin{array}{r} 803 \\ 9\overline{)7234} \\ 72 \\ \hline 03 \\ 0 \\ \hline 34 \\ 27 \\ \hline 7 \end{array}$ or   803 R7

Since division is the opposite of multiplication, we can check a division problem by multiplying. For example: $9\overline{)7,234} = 803$ R7. To check, first multiply the quotient by the divisor: $803 \times 9 = 7,227$. Then add the remainder: $7,227 + 7 = 7,234$.

22. The process for checking a division problem with a remainder is: quotient × _____ + _____ = dividend.

Answers: divisor; remainder

23. Which one of the following problems does not check?

(a) $345 \div 7 = 49$ R2   (b) $893 \div 9 = 99$ R2   (c) $537 \div 5 = 101$ R2

Answer: (c) since $(101 \times 5) + 2 = 507$ not 537. By the way, $(107 \times 5) + 2 = 537$.

When a divisor has more than one digit, we can increase efficiency by rounding before performing the division. (See page 6, Rounding Numbers.) First we find a **trial divisor**, a **trial dividend**, and a **trial quotient**. For example, in the problem $372 \div 29$, we round 29 to 30 and take the first digit, 3, as the trial divisor. Then we round 372 to 400 to take the first digit, 4, as the trial dividend. The trial quotient then is 1, since $4 \div 3 = 1$ R1.

24. In the problem $7,831 \div 38$, the trial divisor is _____, the trial dividend is _____, the trial quotient is _____.

Answers: 4; 8; 2

25. In the problem $87,459 \div 211$, the trial divisor is _____, the trial dividend is _____, the trial quotient is _____.

Answers: 2; 9; 4

If the trial divisor is larger than the trial dividend, we must modify the procedure for obtaining the trial dividend by rounding the dividend to two digits as in the following problems.

26. For 37,652 ÷ 516, if only one digit were used as the trial dividend, 5 would be larger than 4. Rounding the dividend to two digits gives 38 as a trial dividend. Since the trial divisor is 5, the trial quotient will be _____.

Answer: 7

27. In the problem 507,328 ÷ 69, the trial divisor is _____, the trial dividend is _____, the trial quotient is _____.

Answers: 7; 51; 7

28. In the problem 687,431 ÷ 847, the first trial divisor is _____, the first trial dividend is _____, the first trial quotient is _____.

Answers: 8; 69; 8

In some problems the trial quotient is not the final quotient; however, the adjustments are easy. For example:

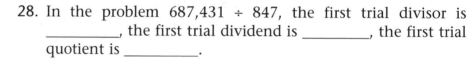

$16\overline{)3,456}$ the trial quotient 1 must be changed to 2

$241\overline{)4,338}$ the trial quotient 2 must be changed to 1

Let's now do some division problems.

29. 832 ÷ 38 =

The trial divisor is 4. The trial dividend is 8. The trial quotient is 2. Since 38 is smaller than 83, the trial quotient is placed over the 3 in the dividend.

$$\begin{array}{r} 2 \\ 38\overline{)832} \end{array}$$

Multiply 2 × 38 = 76. Record the 76 beneath the 83. Subtract 83 − 76 = 7. Bring down the 2.

$$\begin{array}{r} 2 \\ 38\overline{)832} \\ \underline{76} \\ 72 \end{array}$$

Now divide 72 by 38. The second trial dividend is 7. Since 7 ÷ 4 = 1 R3, the second trial quotient is 1. Record the 1 above the 2 in the dividend. Multiply 1 × 38 = 38. Record the 38 beneath the 72. Subtract 72 − 38 = 34.

```
      21
38)832
   76
   ──
    72
    38
   ──
    34
```

Thus, 832 ÷ 38 = _____

Answer: 21 R34   Check   38
                        × 21
                        ────
                          38
                          76
                        ────
                         798
                        + 34
                        ────
                         832

30. In the problem 237,518 ÷ 735, the trial divisor is 7, the trial dividend is 24, the trial quotient is 3. Since 735 is larger than 237, place the trial quotient over the 5 in the dividend.

```
          3
735)237,518
```

Multiply 3 × 735 = 2,205. Record the 2,205 beneath the 2,375. Subtract 2,375 − 2,205 = 170. Bring down the 1.

```
          3
735)237518
    2205
    ────
    1701
```

Now divide 1,701 by 735. The second trial dividend is 17. Since 17 ÷ 7 = 2 R3, the second trial quotient is 2. Record the 2 above the 1 in the dividend. Multiply 2 × 735 = 1,470. Record the 1,470 beneath the 1,701. Subtract 1,701 − 1,470 = 231. Bring down the 8.

```
         32
735)237518
    2205
    ────
    1701
    1470
    ────
    2318
```

Now divide 2,318 by 735. The third trial dividend is 23. Since 23 ÷ 7 = 3 R2, the third trial quotient is 3. Record the 3 above the 8 in the dividend. Multiply 3 × 735 = 2,205. Subtract 2,318 − 2,205 = 113.

```
            323
      735)237518
          2205
          1701
          1470
          2318
          2205
           113
```

Thus, 237,518 ÷ 735 = _____.

Answer: 323 R113   Check   735
                              × 323
                              2205
                              1470
                              2205
                             237405
                             + 113
                             237518

31. Complete the following problems and check your solutions.

$$215\overline{)43,342} \qquad 4,983\overline{)205,874}$$

Answers:

```
         201       Check:     215              41       Check:      4983
   215)43342                 ×201      4983)205874                 × 41
       430                    215          19932                   4983
       342                   4300           6554                  19932
       215                  43215           4983                 204303
       127                  +127            1571                 +1571
                            43342                               205874
```

DIVIDING DECIMAL NUMBERS

Decimal numbers are divided in much the same way as whole numbers are divided, except we have the added task of deciding where to place the decimal point in the answer or quotient. For instance, if three identical items cost a total of $1.50, what should one item cost?

$$\frac{\$.50}{3\overline{)\$1.50}}$$

32. In the above example, the decimal point in the quotient ($.50) is placed _____ the decimal point in the dividend.

Answer: directly above

If a $5.25 bill were shared equally by three students, how much would each student pay?

$$\frac{\$1.75}{3\overline{)\$5.25}}$$

Again, note that the decimal point is placed directly above the decimal point in the dividend.

33. Place the decimal point in the following problems.

$$\begin{array}{r} \$150 \\ 5\overline{)\$7.50} \end{array} \qquad \begin{array}{r} \$12102 \\ 8\overline{)\$968.16} \end{array} \qquad \begin{array}{r} \$53 \\ 9\overline{)\$4.77} \end{array}$$

Answers: $1.50; $121.02; $.53

The same rule holds true whenever a whole number is divided into a decimal number.

34. Place the decimal point in the following problems.

$$\begin{array}{r} 152 \\ 18\overline{)273.6} \end{array} \qquad \begin{array}{r} 456 \\ 23\overline{)104.88} \end{array} \qquad \begin{array}{r} 592 \\ 78\overline{)4.6176} \end{array}$$

Answers: 15.2; 4.56; .0592

35. A rule for dividing a decimal number by a whole number is: Divide as though both numbers were whole numbers and place the decimal point in the _____ directly above the decimal point in the dividend.

Answer: quotient or answer

Take care and work neatly. If the quotient is placed incorrectly over the dividend, the decimal will not be in the correct place in the answer.

Each of the division problems with decimals thus far had a remainder of zero. Now we will solve some problems that result in a remainder of more than zero. For example, let us divide 2.18 by 16.

Place the decimal point of the quotient directly above the decimal point in the dividend.

$$16\overline{)2.18}$$

Divide as though both were whole numbers.

$$\begin{array}{r} .13 \\ 16\overline{)2.18} \\ \underline{1\ 6} \\ 58 \\ \underline{48} \\ 10 \end{array}$$

Because it is sometimes possible to obtain a remainder of zero if division is carried out several more steps, we annex a zero to the dividend. That is, we write a zero to the right of the last digit of the dividend and continue dividing.

```
        .136
   16)2.180
      1 6
       58
       48
      100
       96
        4
```

There is still a remainder, so we annex another zero.

```
        .1362
   16)2.1800
      1 6
       58
       48
      100
       96
        40
        32
         8
```

Again, annex another zero.

```
        .13625
   16)2.18000
      1 6
       58
       48
      100
        96
        40
        32
        80
        80
```

Thus, by annexing zeros, we have eliminated the remainder.

36. Divide 3.92 by 25 and check. Annex sufficient zeros to eliminate any remainder other than zero.

```
Answer:      .1568          .1568
        25)3.9200        ×  25
           2 5            7840
           1 42           3136
           1 25          3.9200
            170
            150
            200
            200
```

When we divide, we can sometimes eliminate the remainder by annexing zeros. But in most cases there will be a remainder no matter how many zeros we annex. Therefore, with most business problems we should decide beforehand how much accuracy we want and round off accordingly. (See the rounding exercises in Chapter One.)

For example, if you want an answer correct to the nearest cent or hundredth, you divide until the quotient is one decimal place more than wanted and then round to the desired accuracy. It may be necessary to annex zeros to the dividend to obtain the desired accuracy.

37. If 24 items cost $37.14, what is the cost per item to the nearest cent?

$$
\begin{array}{r}
1.547 \\
24\overline{)37.140} \\
\underline{24} \\
13\ 1 \\
\underline{12\ 0} \\
1\ 14 \\
\underline{96} \\
180 \\
\underline{168} \\
12
\end{array}
$$

First, carry the division process out to the nearest thousandth. Then round $1.547 to the nearest cent, giving _____.

Answer: $1.55

38. Perform the following divisions and round according to the General Rules for Rounding on page 9, Chapter One.

(a) $52\overline{).163}$ (b)* $213\overline{)4}$ (c) $15\overline{)\$11.24}$ (d) $72\overline{)\$36.98}$

Answers: (a) .003; (b) .019; (c) $.75; (d) $.51

So far we have considered only division of decimal numbers by whole numbers. Now let's consider division of a decimal number by a decimal number.

---

*After every whole number there is an understood decimal, therefore we change the dividend 4 to 4.000 before we begin dividing.

39. $34.5 \div .15 =$

To do this, first convert the divisor to a whole number:

$$34.5 \div .15 = \frac{34.5}{.15}$$

Multiplying .15 by 100 moves the decimal _____ places to the right, making .15 a whole number. Then, if we multiply the numerator (top number) of the fraction by the same number (100), the value of the fraction does not change. Thus,

$$\frac{34.5}{.15} \times \frac{100}{100} = \frac{3,450}{15} = 230$$

Answer: Two

40. To change $5.813 \div 1.8$ into a problem where the divisor is a whole number, we rewrite the problem.

$$5.813 \div 1.8 = \frac{5.813}{1.8}$$

We want to move the decimal point in the divisor, 1.8 one place to the right, so we multiply both sides of the fraction by _____ . Thus, we have:

$$\frac{5.813 \times 10}{1.8 \times 10} = \frac{58.13}{18} \quad \text{or} \quad 18\overline{)58.13}$$

Answer: ten

41. From the previous examples you can see that we can move the decimal point in the divisor to the right to obtain a whole-number divisor if we move the decimal point in the dividend the _____ number of places to the right.

Answer: same

In order to have a whole-number divisor, we move the decimal point of the divisor and the decimal point of the dividend the same number of places to the right. The new position of the decimal is indicated by a triangle (Δ).

$$8.2710 \div .15 = .15 \, \Delta\overline{)8.27 , \Delta 10}$$

The decimal point in the quotient then appears directly over the triangle in the dividend.

$$.15 , \Delta\overline{)8.27 \Delta 10}^{\,55.14}$$

42. Solve the following problems, using a triangle to show the new decimal point position.

$$.17\overline{)\,.102} \qquad 78.3\overline{)\,5.481}$$

Answer:

$$.17\triangle\overline{)\,.10\triangle2}^{\;.6} \qquad 78.3\triangle\overline{)\,5.4\triangle81}^{\;.07}$$
$$\phantom{.17\triangle\overline{)\,}}10\;\;2 \qquad\qquad \phantom{78.3\triangle\overline{)\,}}5\;4\;\;81$$

43. Place the decimal point in the following quotients.

(a) $3.47\overline{)\,10.757}^{\;31}$ (b) $.7\overline{)\,.0217}^{\;31}$

(c) $.576\overline{)\,.051264}^{\;89}$ (d) $8.98\overline{)\,50.3778}^{\;561}$

Answers: (1) 3.1; (b) .031; (c) .089; (d) 5.61

44. Divide and round off to hundredths.

$$1.9\overline{)\,34.58} \qquad .81\overline{)\,5.4}$$

Answers: 18.20; 6.67

45. Divide and round to the nearest whole number.

$$2.11\overline{)\,45.6} \qquad .763\overline{)\,54.81}$$

Answers: 22; 72

DIVISION SHORTCUTS (OPTIONAL)

Like the exercise on multiplication shortcuts, this section is an enrichment exercise and is not required. However, it is useful for improving speed, accuracy, and estimating.

Division by powers of 10 or multiples of powers of 10 is the inverse of multiplying by those numbers; that is, you need only shift the decimal point. For example:

$$
\begin{aligned}
684 \div 10 &= 68.4 \\
684 \div 100 &= 6.84 \\
684 \div 1{,}000 &= .684
\end{aligned}
$$

$$684 \div 20 \quad = \quad 68.4 \quad \div 2 \quad = \quad 34.2$$
$$684 \div 200 \quad = \quad 6.84 \quad \div 2 \quad = \quad 3.42$$
$$684 \div 2{,}000 \quad = \quad .684 \quad \div 2 \quad = \quad .342$$

46. The previous examples show that when we divide a number by an even power of ten, we move the decimal point of the number as many places to the left as there are _____ in the power of ten and then divide by the digit other than zero.

Answer: zeros

47. Complete the following problems.

(a) $67 \div 10$ _____   (b) $231 \div 300 =$ _____

(c) $8{,}583 \div 100$ _____   (d) $5{,}863 \div 1{,}000 =$ _____

(e) $974.3 \div 1{,}000$ _____   (f) $9.428 \div 200 =$ _____

Answers: (a) 6.7; (b) .77; (c) 85.83; (d) 5.863; (e) .9743; (f) .04714

Dividing with powers of 0.1 or multiples of powers of 0.1 also is the inverse of multiplying by these numbers. For example:

$$852 \div .1 \quad = \quad 8{,}520$$
$$852 \div .01 \quad = \quad 85{,}200$$
$$852 \div .001 \quad = \quad 852{,}000$$

$$852 \div .2 \quad = \quad 8{,}520 \quad \div 2 \quad = \quad 4{,}260$$
$$852 \div .02 \quad = \quad 85{,}200 \quad \div 2 \quad = \quad 42{,}600$$
$$852 \div .002 \quad = \quad 852{,}000 \quad \div 2 \quad = \quad 426{,}000$$

48. The examples show that when a number is divided by a decimal power or multiple of ten, the decimal point of the number is shifted to the _____ as many places as there are decimal digits in the divisor. Zeros are added when necessary to accommodate the decimal point shift.

Answer: right

49. Complete the following problems.

(a) $67 \div .1 =$ _____   (b) $231 \div .03 =$ _____

(c) $85.83 \div .01 =$ _____   (d) $5.863 \div .001 =$ _____

(e) $97.43 \div .01 =$ _____   (f) $9.428 \div .002 =$ _____

Answers: (a) 670; (b) 7,700; (c) 8,583; (d) 5,863; (e) 9,743; (f) 4,714

50. Examine the following problems.

(a) $45{,}000 \div 300 = \dfrac{45000}{300} = \dfrac{450}{3} = 150$

(b) $297{,}000 \div 9{,}000 = \dfrac{297000}{9000} = \dfrac{297}{9} = 33$

A shortcut for dividing numbers ending in zeros is to cross off, in both the divisor and dividend, the number of zeros in the *divisor/dividend* and then divide.

Answer: divisor

51. Complete the following problems.

$$3{,}200\overline{)96{,}000} = 320\cancel{0}\overline{)9600\cancel{0}} \;\;{\overset{\displaystyle 30}{}}$$

$$42{,}000\overline{)84{,}000} =$$

Answer:
$$42000\overline{)84000} \;\;{\overset{\displaystyle 2}{}}$$

52. Cross out zeros to solve the following problems.

(a) $51{,}000\overline{)153{,}000}$ (b) $3{,}700\overline{)74{,}000}$

(c) $127{,}000\overline{)2{,}540{,}000}$ (d) $700\overline{)69{,}300}$

Answers: (a) $51000\overline{)153000}\;{\overset{\displaystyle 3}{}}$;   (b) $3700\overline{)74000}\;{\overset{\displaystyle 20}{}}$;

(c) $127000\overline{)2540000}\;{\overset{\displaystyle 20}{}}$;   (d) $700\overline{)69300}\;{\overset{\displaystyle 99}{}}$;

53. We can divide 425 by 5 if we shift the decimal point one place to the left and multiply by _____.

Answer: 2

54. Problem: $425 \div 5$ Think: $42.5 \times 2 = 85$

To divide by 5, shift the decimal one place to the _____ and multiply by _____.

Answer: left; 2

55. Use the shortcut for dividing mentally by 5.

$422 \div 5 =$ _____

$437.5 \div 5 =$ _____

$53.21 \div 5 =$ _____

Answers: 84.4; 87.5; 10.642

56. The same shortcut can be used for dividing by 50, 500, and so on. Fifty is one-half of _____ and 500 is one-half of _____. Therefore, to divide by 50, shift the decimal point two places to the left and multiply by 2; to divide by 500, shift the decimal point _____ places to the left and multiply by _____ .

Answers: 100; 1,000; three; 2

57. Using the shortcut method, work the following problems mentally.

$82,513 \div 50 =$ _____   Think: $(825.13) \times 2$

$4,862 \div 500 =$ _____

$12,333 \div 500 =$ _____

Answers: 1,650.26; 9.724; 24.666

58. Twenty-five times four is _____ . Therefore, a shortcut for dividing by 25 is to shift the decimal place two places to the left and multiply by _____ .

Answers: 100; 4

59. To divide 333 by 25, first shift the decimal point _____ places to the left and multiply times (3.33×4). The product is _____ .

Answers: two; 4; 13.32

60. What is a shortcut method for dividing by 250?_____
_____
_____

Answer: Shift the decimal point three places to the left and multiply by 4. (Note: A similar method works for dividing by 125, 16 2/3, 33 1/3, etc.)

61. Find the unit price of the items on the following invoice by mentally dividing extension price by quantity.

Quantity	Description	Extension	Unit Price
5	#932 Sleeper	$ 1,243.35	_____
25	#852 Sofa	5,831.00	_____
100	#831 Table	7,216.00	_____
500	#833 Chair	11,675.00	_____

Answers: $248.67; $233.24; $72.16; $23.35

62. Perform the following calculations, using shortcut methods.

$37 \div .001 =$ _____ (1)

$32.4 \div 25 = .324 \times$ _____ $=$ _____ (2)

$478 \div 500 =$ _____ $\times 2 =$ _____ (3)

$568,000 \div 25,000 = 5.68\,000 \times 4 =$ _____ (4)

$627,000 \div 3,000 = 627,000 \div 3,000 =$ _____ (5)

$573 \div 1,000 =$ _____ (6)

$565 \div 500 =$ _____ (7)

$16,160 \div 250 =$ _____ (8)

$4,230,000 \div 2,000 =$ _____ (9)

$3,212 \div 25 =$ _____ (10)

Answers: (1) 37,000; (2) 4, 1.296; (3) .478, .956; (4) 22.72; (5) 209; (6) .573; (7) 1.130; (8) 64.64; (9) 2,115; (10) 128.48

If you had difficulty with any of the previous problems, review frames 46 though 60.

BUSINESS APPLICATION

63. The earnings of Trans-National Corp. were $214,000 last year. If they had 25,000 stock-holders, each owning one share, what were earnings per share? _____

Answer: $214\,000 \div 25\,000 = $2.14 \times 4 = 8.56

64. It takes about 133 liters of fuel per passenger to fly a jumbo jet from coast to coast in the U. S. If the average American automobile requires four times that amount of gasoline to drive from coast to coast, how many liters of gasoline does the automobile require? _____

Answer: 532 liters

65. A hardware store paid $1,153.00 for 25 storm doors. If each door costs the same, how much was paid per door?

_____

Answer: $11.53 \times 4 = 46.12 each

66. Sam Pike drove 383 km on 57.5 liters of gasoline. How many kilometers per liter did he get? _____

Answer: 6.661 km per liters (17.5 mpg)

67. Johnson's Men's Store advertises shirts at 3 for $80.00. Colby's, a local competitor, advertises the same shirts for $27.25 each. If you want to buy three shirts, which store offers the better deal per shirt? How much better? _____

Answer: Johnson's, by $.58($80 ÷ 3 = $26.67 and $27.25 − $26.67 = $.58)

68. If you can buy a 13-oz bottle of shampoo for $2.87 or a 25-oz bottle for $5.98, which size bottle has the lower price per ounce? _____

Answer: The 13-oz bottle, which is about $.22 per oz, while the 25-oz bottle is about $.24 per oz.

Division With a Calculator

Most business problems involving division use decimals. Common applications include interest calculations, averages, and percentages. Electronic calculators are efficient for solving problems involving division because they perform automatically, including the placing of the decimal point. Consult your operating manual to find out how to perform division.

Work the following sample problems to be sure that you can place the decimal point correctly. An answer with a misplaced decimal is wrong, even though the figures are correct.

$$32 ÷ 6 = 5.333 \qquad 51 ÷ 7 = 7.286$$
$$.157 ÷ .06 = 2.617 \qquad .071 ÷ 6.5 = .011$$

Go on to the next set of problems if you understand the examples. If not, consult your operating manual or instructor and rework the examples.

1. Calculate the following.

> ## Hint
>
> Remember the Rules for Rounding given in the front of the book for all final answers (.001, .1%, and $.01). Set the decimal to round at three decimal digits for the following problems. If your calculator has no decimal setting for three, set it at four.

(1) 3.37 ÷ 14 = _____	(2) 9.35 ÷ 58 = _____
(3) 47.28 ÷ 6.9 = _____	(4) 51.92 ÷ 6.6 = _____
(5) 58.3 ÷ .032 = _____	(6) 5.159 ÷ .004 = _____
(7) 738.56 ÷ 9.1 = _____	(8) 85.49 ÷ 88.8 = _____

(9) 74.219 ÷ 404.9 = _____ (10) 646.9 ÷ 11.92 = _____

(11) If there are 100 centimeters in a meter, 3,482 cm equals _____ meters.

(12) If there are 10,000 square meters in a hectare, 4,271 sq m = _____ h.

(13) If there are 320 rods in a mile, 75,200 rods = _____miles.

(14) If there are 9 square feet in a square yard, 47,961 sq ft = _____ sq. yds.

(15) If there are 4,840 square yards in an acre, 11,320 sq yds = _____ acres.

(16) If there are 640 acres in a square mile, 56,960 acres = _____ sq mi.

(17) If there are 1,728 cubic inches in a cubic foot, 98,496 cu in. = _____ cu ft.

(18) If there are 12 units in a dozen, 68,376 units = _____ dozen.

(19) If there are 144 units in a gross, 36,864 units = _____ gr.

(20) If there are 60 seconds in a minute, 131,220 sec. _____min.

Answers: (1) .241; (2) .161; (3) 6.852; (4) 7.867; (5) 1,821.875; (6) 1,289.75; (7) 81.160; (8) .963; (9) .183; (10) 54.270; (11) 34.82; (12) .427; (13) 235; (14) 5,329; (15) 2.339; (16) 89; (17) 57; (18) 5,698; (19) 256; (20) 2,187

Estimating

Estimating is a useful method for checking multiplication or division. As with addition and subtraction, you use a simple calculation to get the approximate value of the answer. To do this, round off each number to one digit other than zero. For example, to estimate 715×28, first round both factors to 1 digit:

715 = 700 rounded to 1 digit
28 = 30 rounded to 1 digit

Then estimate the product:

$700 \times 30 = 21,000$ (the correct answer is 20,020)

1. By making your own estimate of the following products, determine which answers are reasonable and which are unreasonable.

(a) $827 \times 638 = 345,926$ _____ (b) $763 \times 87 = 45,281$ _____

(c) $973 \times 421 = 409,633$ _____ (d) $234 \times 197 = 46,098$ _____

Answers: (a) unreasonable ($800 \times 600 = 480,000$); (b) unreasonable ($800 \times 90 = 72,000$); (c) reasonable ($1,000 \times 400 = 400,000$); (d) reasonable ($200 \times 200 = 40,000$)

Estimating division can also be carried out by rounding the divisor and dividend to one digit other than zero. For example, to estimate $8,341 \div 227$, first, round both numbers to 1 digit other than zero.

$$8,341 = 8,000 \text{ rounded to 1 digit}$$
$$227 = 200 \text{ rounded to 1 digit}$$

Then estimate the quotient:

$$8,000 \div 200 = 40 \text{ or } 200\overline{)8000}^{\,40} \quad \text{(the exact answer is 36.744)}$$

2. By making your own estimate of the following quotients, determine which answers are reasonable and which are unreasonable.

(a) $72,834 \div 487 = 149.556$ ___   (b) $5,287 \div 713 = 72.437$ ___

(c) $9,052 \div 288 = 31.431$ _____   (d) $67,217 \div 1,931 = 34.809$ __

Answers: (a) reasonable $(70,000 \div 500 = 140)$; (b) unreasonable $(5,000 \div 700 = 7)$; (c) reasonable $(9,000 \div 300 = 30)$; (d) reasonable $(70,000 \div 2,000 = 35)$

To improve your accuracy, estimate the answer to a problem **before** attempting to solve it. Once you've solved the problem, use the estimate to check if your solution is reasonable.

3. Using estimating techniques, underline the closest estimated answers to the following problems.

		(a)	(b)	(c)	(d)
(1)	$48 \times 53 =$	5,264	2,544	3,014	7,124
(2)	$138 \times 289 =$	18,782	10,574	39,882	52,784
(3)	$1,818 \div 317 =$	5.735	57.350	39.78	4.035
(4)	$2,439 \div 63 =$	80.914	3.871	4.714	38.714
(5)	$17,896 \div 931 =$	2.222	193.012	19.222	9.703
(6)	$2,971 \times 333 =$	98,343	989,343	746,343	9,458
(7)	$9,741 \times 89 =$	866,949	88,794	666,949	83,941
(8)	$13,971 \div 6,813 =$	20.613	2.051	17.891	4.072
(9)	$45 \times 6,848 =$	108,160	509,007	208,160	308,160
(10)	$21,972 \div 4,989 =$	54.044	10.704	4.404	8.971

Answers: (1) b; (2) c; (3) a; (4) d; (5) c; (6) b; (7) a; (8) b; (9) d; (10) c

Practice Problems Without a Calculator

The following practice groups are to help you develop additional proficiency without the aid of a calculator. You may want to work all the problems or only those you feel will improve your ability.

MULTIPLICATION FACTS

(1) $9 \times 4 =$ _____   (2) $7 \times 4 =$ _____   (3) $6 \times 2 =$ _____

(4) $7 \times 9 =$ _____   (5) $6 \times 6 =$ _____   (6) $5 \times 4 =$ _____

(7) $3 \times 9 =$ _____   (8) $6 \times 9 =$ _____   (9) $8 \times 3 =$ _____

(10) $7 \times 7 =$ _____   (11) $3 \times 5 =$ _____   (12) $5 \times 4 =$ _____

(13) $9 \times 5 =$ _____   (14) $6 \times 8 =$ _____   (15) $3 \times 6 =$ _____

(16) $9 \times 8 =$ _____   (17) $5 \times 8 =$ _____   (18) $6 \times 7 =$ _____

(19) $7 \times 8 =$ _____   (20) $5 \times 5 =$ _____

Answers are on page 122, or check your work with your calculator.

MULTIPLICATION PRACTICE

(1) $\begin{array}{r} 37 \\ \times 16 \\ \hline \end{array}$ (2) $\begin{array}{r} 83 \\ \times 45 \\ \hline \end{array}$ (3) $\begin{array}{r} 77 \\ \times 29 \\ \hline \end{array}$

(4) $\begin{array}{r} 55 \\ \times 49 \\ \hline \end{array}$ (5) $\begin{array}{r} 67 \\ \times 11 \\ \hline \end{array}$ (6) $\begin{array}{r} 79 \\ \times 67 \\ \hline \end{array}$

(7) $\begin{array}{r} 474 \\ \times 58 \\ \hline \end{array}$ (8) $\begin{array}{r} 992 \\ \times .61 \\ \hline \end{array}$ (9) $\begin{array}{r} 12.9 \\ \times 67 \\ \hline \end{array}$

(10) $\begin{array}{r} 700.7 \\ \times 15.9 \\ \hline \end{array}$ (11) $\begin{array}{r} 33.33 \\ \times 60.8 \\ \hline \end{array}$ (12) $\begin{array}{r} 10.22 \\ \times .65 \\ \hline \end{array}$

Answers are on page 122, or check your work with your calculator.

DIVISION PRACTICE

(1) $8\overline{)32}$ (2) $12\overline{)132}$ (3) $9\overline{)684}$

(4) $7\overline{)539}$ (5) $11\overline{)957}$ (6) $6\overline{)372}$

(7) $13\overline{)273}$ (8) $5\overline{)625}$ (9) $15\overline{)375}$

(10) $27\overline{)621}$ (11) $16\overline{)336}$ (12) $71\overline{)852}$

Answers are on page 122, or check your work with your calculator.

DIVISION WITH DECIMALS

(1) $7\overline{)1.03}$ (2) $8\overline{)9.4}$ (3) $15\overline{)47.4}$

(4) $9\overline{)1.34}$ (5) $.78\overline{)21.8}$ (6) $1.7\overline{).974}$

(7) $6.9\overline{)57.2}$ (8) $.76\overline{).463}$ (9) $.26\overline{)70.6}$

(10) $12.3\overline{)20.5}$ (11) $.97\overline{).377}$ (12) $8.5\overline{).103}$

Answers are on page 122, or check your work with your calculator.

MIXED DIVISION PRACTICE

(1) $100\overline{)8{,}594}$

(2) $2{,}000\overline{)67.92}$

(3) $.0025\overline{)5{,}050}$

(4) $51{,}000\overline{)255{,}000}$

(5) $700\overline{)453{,}800}$

(6) $500\overline{)243{,}500}$

(7) $250\overline{)22.13}$

(8) $60.79\overline{)90{,}802}$

(9) $16.17\overline{)450.007}$

Answers are on page 122, or check your work with your calculator.

MULTIPLICATION AND DIVISION SHORTCUTS (OPTIONAL)

(1) $22 \times 10 =$ _____

(2) $100 \times 49 =$ _____

(3) $12 \times 50 =$ _____

(4) $56 \times 125 =$ _____

(5) $500 \times 2.085 =$ _____

(6) $\$1.48 \times 250 =$ _____

(7) $.0024 \times 5{,}000 =$ _____

(8) $\$4.92 \times 200 =$ _____

(9) $99 \times \$1.37 =$ _____

(10) $999 \times \$4.98 =$ _____

(11) $\$1.25 \times 48 =$ _____

(12) $\$.25 \times 360 =$ _____

(13) $125 \times \$1.60 =$ _____

(14) $250 \times \$8.44 =$ _____

(15) $98 \times \$7.50 =$ _____

(16) $684 \div 10 =$ _____

(17) $715 \div 1{,}000 =$ _____

(18) $1{,}288 \div 200 =$ _____

(19) $93 \div 30 =$ _____

(20) $3.5347 \div .01 =$ _____

(21) $.933 \div .003 =$ _____

(22) $2{,}540{,}000 \div 127{,}000 =$ ____

(23) $\$2{,}000 \div 125 =$ _____

(24) $\$141.12 \div 500 =$ _____

(25) $\$4.22 \div .25 =$ _____

(26) $\$9{,}000 \div 1{,}600 =$ _____

(27) $\$86.24 \div .02 =$ _____

(28) $\$111.11 \div 1.25 =$ _____

(29) $\$24.32 \div 5 =$ _____

(30) $\$22.22 \div .25 =$ _____

Answers are on the next page, or check your work with a calculator

MULTIPLICATION FACTS: (1) 36; (2) 28; (3) 12; (4) 63; (5) 36; (6) 20; (7) 27; (8) 54; (9) 24; (10) 49; (11) 15; (12) 20; (13) 45; (14) 48; (15) 18; (16) 72; (17) 40; (18) 42; (19) 56; (20) 25

MULTIPLICATION PRACTICE: (1) 592; (2) 3,735; (3) 2,233; (4) 2,695; (5) 737; (6) 5,293; (7) 27,492; (8) 605.12; (9) 864.3; (10) 11,141.13; (11) 2,026.464; (12) 6.643

DIVISION PRACTICE: (1) 4; (2) 11; (3) 76; (4) 77; (5) 87; (6) 62; (7) 21; (8) 125; (9) 25; (10) 23; (11) 21; (12) 12

DIVISION WITH DECIMALS: (1) .147; (2) 1.175; (3) 3.160; (4) .149; (5) 27.949; (6) .573; (7) 8.290; (8) .609; (9) 271.538; (10) 1.667; (11) .389; (12) .012

MIXED DIVISION PRACTICE: (1) 85.940; (2) .034; (3) 2,020,000; (4) 5; (5) 648.286; (6) 487; (7) .089; (8) 1,493.700; (9) 27.830

MULTIPLICATION AND DIVISION SHORTCUTS: (1) 220; (2) 4,900; (3) 600; (4) 7,000; (5) 1,042.500; (6) $370; (7) 12; (8) $984; (9) $135.63; (10) $4,975.02; (11) $60; (12) $90; (13) $200; (14) $2,110; (15) $735; (16) 68.400; (17) .715; (18) 6.440; (19) 3.100; (20) 353.470; (21) 311; (22) 20; (23) $16; (24) $.28; (25) $16.88; (26) $5.63; (27) $4,312; (28) $88.89; (29) $4.86; (30) $88.88

Stop

You are now ready to take Pretest IIA, a 10-minute test of multiplication and division to be taken **without** the aid of a calculator. Your performance on Pretest IIA will tell you if you have sufficient skill to proceed to **Test IIA.** Unless instructed otherwise, turn in your Pretest for correction and review before taking Test IIA. To pass Test IIA, you must work at least 15 problems correctly and have no more than 10 percent of your answers incorrect. Thus, even if you work 20 problems you will not pass if you have more than 2 errors.

On Test IIA, if, in 10 minutes, you have better than 90 percent accuracy and 15 problems correct, continue on to the next section, Developing Touch Control, Speed, and Accuracy With a Calculator. If not, review the multiplication and division exercises on pages 119–121.

Remember, many employment tests demand skill with numbers and you will not always have the aid of a calculator.

Notes

NAME	
DATE	
SECTION	PROBLEMS COMPLETED
ERRORS	NUMBER CORRECT

MULTIPLICATION AND DIVISION WITHOUT A CALCULATOR

10 minutes

This test must be worked in sequence. Any problems skipped are counted as errors. You need 90 percent accuracy and 15 problems correct to pass.

(1) $9 \times 6 =$ _____   (2) $7 \times 8 =$ _____ (3) $6 \times 6 =$ _____

(4) $48 \div 8 =$ _____   (5) $42 \div 7 =$ _____ (6) $28 \div 4 =$ _____

Multiply. (You must show your work on the remaining problems.)

(7) $\begin{array}{r} 708 \\ \underline{37} \end{array}$

(8) $\begin{array}{r} 684 \\ \underline{50} \end{array}$

(9) $\begin{array}{r} 400 \\ \underline{.25} \end{array}$

(10) $\begin{array}{r} 6.07 \\ \underline{306} \end{array}$

(11) $\begin{array}{r} 3.03 \\ \underline{203} \end{array}$

(12) $\begin{array}{r} 40.2 \\ \underline{.18} \end{array}$

Divide. (Round quotients to three decimal places when necessary.)

(13) $200\overline{)4,800}$
(14) $.025\overline{)75}$
(15) $80\overline{)32.24}$

(16) $5.05\overline{)15.15}$
(17) $3.2\overline{).408}$
(18) $250\overline{)1,111}$

(19) $11\overline{)95.6}$
(20) $.98\overline{).735}$
(21) $.07\overline{)50.6}$

Round products to the nearest whole cent.

(22) 225 items @ 25 cents = _____

(23) 448 items @ \$1.25 = _____

(24) 2,500 items @ \$16.16 = _____

(25) 1,250 items @ \$8.80 = _____

Developing Touch Control, Speed, and Accuracy With a Calculator

To improve your ability, you may want to work the following multiplication and division practice problems with a calculator. Remember, touch control applies only to the ten-key pad, the plus, minus and total key.

Multiplying Whole Numbers

(1) $54 \times 68 =$ _____

(2) $74 \times 32 =$ _____

(3) $44 \times 77 =$ _____

(4) $59 \times 82 =$ _____

(5) $90 \times 61 =$ _____

(6) $63 \times 64 =$ _____

(7) $64 \times 654 =$ _____

(8) $42 \times 584 =$ _____

(9) $29 \times 233 =$ _____

(10) $44 \times 701 =$ _____

(11) $28 \times 809 =$ _____

(12) $91 \times 703 =$ _____

(13) $62 \times 977 =$ _____

(14) $76 \times 447 =$ _____

(15) $42 \times 537 =$ _____

(16) $98 \times 5,249 =$ _____

(17) $78 \times 3,165 =$ _____

(18) $65 \times 7,040 =$ _____

(19) $94 \times 5,593 =$ _____

(20) $75 \times 5,949 =$ _____

(21) $49 \times 6,785 =$ _____

(22) $197 \times 312 =$ _____

(23) $205 \times 682 =$ _____

(24) $669 \times 863 =$ _____

(25) $909 \times 744 =$ _____

(26) $742 \times 704 =$ _____

(27) $416 \times 157 =$ _____

(28) $306 \times 6,411 =$ _____

(29) $227 \times 7,066 =$ _____

(30) $193 \times 2,420 =$ _____

Answers: (1) 3,672; (2) 2,368; (3) 3,388; (4) 4,838; (5) 5,490; (6) 4,032; (7) 41,856; (8) 24,528; (9) 6,757; (10) 30,844; (11) 22,652; (12) 63,973; (13) 60,574; (14) 33,972; (15) 22,554; (16) 514,402; (17) 246,870; (18) 457,600; (19) 525,742; (20) 446,175; (21) 332,465; (22) 61,464; (23) 139,810; (24) 577,347; (25) 676,296; (26) 522,368; (27) 65,312; (28) 1,961,766; (29) 1,603,982; (30) 467,060

Multiplying Decimal Numbers

Round answers to the nearest thousandth. Remember, the add mode setting is only for the adding and/or subtracting of dollars and cents; you need to enter the decimal.

(1) $.61 \times 9.5 =$ _____

(2) $1.7 \times .26 =$ _____

(3) $3.5 \times 2.8 =$ _____

(4) $.35 \times 66.3 =$ _____

(5) $5.2 \times .297 =$ _____

(6) $16 \times .818 =$ _____

(7) $6.03 \times 11.6 =$ _____

(8) $8.02 \times .371 =$ _____

(9) $87.4 \times 1.37 =$ _____

(10) $.41 \times 84.98 =$ _____

(11) $.46 \times 3.589 =$ _____

(12) $4.4 \times 8.035 =$ _____

(13) $35.8 \times 4.208 =$ _____

(14) $1.06 \times 22.48 =$ _____

(15) $.497 \times 670.4 =$ _____

Round answers to the nearest cent.

(16) $37 \times \$1.85 =$ _____   (17) $86 \times \$2.25 =$ _____

(18) $508 \times \$16.97 =$ _____   (19) $438 \times \$52.59 =$ _____

(20) $\$689.71 \times .071 =$ _____   (21) $\$184.77 \times .079 =$ _____

(22) $\$2,036.07 \times .125 =$ _____   (23) $\$4,119.96 \times .374 =$ _____

(24) $\$7,998 \times 1.78 =$ _____   (25) $\$1,861.11 \times 9.24 =$ _____

Answers: (1) 5.795; (2) .442; (3) 9.800; (4) 23.205; (5) 1.544; (6) 13.088; (7) 69.948; (8) 2.975; (9) 119.738; (10) 34.842; (11) 1.651; (12) 35.354; (13) 150.646; (14) 23.829; (15) 333.189; (16) $68.45; (17) $193.50; (18) $8,620.76; (19) $23,034.42; (20) $48.97; (21) $14.60; (22) $254.51; (23) $1,540.87; (24) $14,236.44; (25) $17,196.66

Dividing Whole Numbers

Round answers to the nearest thousandth.

(1) $64 \div 5 =$ _____   (2) $27 \div 8 =$ _____

(3) $85 \div 8 =$ _____   (4) $68 \div 47 =$ _____

(5) $66 \div 46 =$ _____   (6) $41 \div 36 =$ _____

(7) $50 \div 70 =$ _____   (8) $61 \div 78 =$ _____

(9) $13 \div 80 =$ _____   (10) $785 \div 43 =$ _____

(11) $242 \div 78 =$ _____   (12) $136 \div 61 =$ _____

(13) $730 \div 46 =$ _____   (14) $326 \div 46 =$ _____

(15) $460 \div 47 =$ _____   (16) $759 \div 411 =$ _____

(17) $901 \div 840 =$ _____   (18) $917 \div 575 =$ _____

(19) $374 \div 161 =$ _____   (20) $613 \div 622 =$ _____

(21) $691 \div 905 =$ _____   (22) $3,800 \div 102 =$ _____

(23) $7,681 \div 719 =$ _____   (24) $9,117 \div 117 =$ _____

(25) $17,160 \div 292 =$ _____   (26) $9,377 \div 421 =$ _____

(27) $9,640 \div 499 =$ _____   (28) $64,584 \div 449 =$ _____

(29) $76,983 \div 740 =$ _____   (30) $29,639 \div 940 =$ _____

Answers: (1) 12.800; (2) 3.375; (3) 10.625; (4) 1.447; (5) 1.435; (6) 1.139; (7) .714; (8) .782; (9) .163; (10) 18.256; (11) 3.103; (12) 2.230; (13) 15.870; (14) 7.087; (15) 9.787; (16) 1.847; (17) 1.073; (18) 1.595; (19) 2.323; (20) .986; (21) .764; (22) 37.255; (23) 10.683; (24) 77.923; (25) 58.767; (26) 22.273; (27) 19.319; (28) 143.840; (29) 104.031; (30) 31.531

Dividing Decimal Numbers

Round to the nearest thousandth.

(1) $3.9 \div 2.9 =$ _____ (2) $27 \div .49 =$ _____

(3) $.45 \div .65 =$ _____ (4) $.08 \div 2.2 =$ _____

(5) $9.1 \div 66 =$ _____ (6) $.35 \div 8.3 =$ _____

(7) $12.1 \div .71 =$ _____ (8) $11.1 \div 9.9 =$ _____

(9) $.234 \div .03 =$ _____ (10) $18.6 \div 2.38 =$ _____

(11) $85.7 \div .983 =$ _____ (12) $.562 \div 4.58 =$ _____

(13) $68.71 \div .011 =$ _____ (14) $2.96 \div .0734 =$ _____

(15) $23.47 \div .841 =$ _____

Round to the nearest cent.

(16) $\$40.21 \div 83 =$ _____ (17) $\$14.38 \div 55 =$ _____

(18) $\$96.28 \div 602 =$ _____ (19) $\$94.40 \div .805 =$ _____

(20) $\$543.82 \div 14.5 =$ _____ (21) $\$207.20 \div 7.31 =$ _____

(22) $\$929.27 \div 5.978 =$ _____ (23) $\$305.52 \div 2.562 =$ _____

(24) $\$6,533.71 \div 901 =$ _____ (25) $\$8,539.41 \div 183 =$ _____

Answers: (1) 1.345; (2) 55.102; (3) .692; (4) .036; (5) .138; (6) .042; (7) 17.042;
(8) 1.121; (9) 7.800; (10) 7.815; (11) 87.182; (12) .123; (13) 6,246.364; (14) 40.327;
(15) 27.907; (16) $.48; (17) $.26; (18) $.16; (19) $117.27; (20) $37.50; (21) $28.34;
(22) $155.45; (23) $119.25; (24) $7.25; (25) $46.66

Hint

You do not need to index zeros at the end of a decimal number;
the machine automatically aligns the decimal.

Problems Where Zero Need Not Be Indexed

(1) $4.700 \times 87.080 =$ _____ (2) $45.00 + 4.700 + .6000 =$ _____

(3) $30.900 \div .0871 =$ _____ (4) $.0890 - .1020 - 7.100 =$ _____

(5) $5007 \div 2.100 =$ _____ (6) $81.10 + 9.100 - .9000 =$ _____

(7) $.8800 \times 78.79 =$ _____ (8) $.8700 + .7811 + 67.00 =$ _____

(9) $.3000 \times 91.70 =$ _____ (10) $370.0 + 87.94 - .0700 =$ _____

Answers: (1) 409.276; (2) 50.300; (3) 354.765; (4) 7.113 CR; (5) 2,384.286; (6) 89.300;
(7) 69.335; (8) 68.651; (9) 27.510; (10) 457.870

Stop

You are now ready to take Pretest IIB, a 10-minute test of addition, subtraction, multiplication and division with a calculator. Your performance on Pretest IIB will tell if you have developed sufficient skill to proceed to **Test IIB.** Unless instructed otherwise, turn in your Pretest for correction and review before taking Test IIB. On Test IIB, if you complete at least 30 problems correctly and also have better than 90 percent accuracy; proceed to Chapter Three. If not, review the practice problems on pages 125 to 127.

Hint

Remember the rules for rounding. Since there are no intermediate calculations on this test, you may want to set your machine to round to two decimal places for dollars and cents and three decimal places for other problems.

Pretest IIB

ADDITION, SUBTRACTION, MULTIPLICATION, AND DIVISION WITH A CALCULATOR

10 minutes

This test must be worked in sequence. Any problems skipped count as errors! You need 90 percent accuracy and 30 problems correct to pass. Write your answers as you go.

(1)
567
823
197
303
265

(2)
390
587
190
708
205

(3)
457
601
404
111
232

(4)
957
181
928
959
363

(5)
$\quad$ 4,233
$-$ 2,592

(6)
$\quad$ 9,149
$-$ 8,089

(7)
$\quad$ 4,428
$-$ 1,846

(8)
$\quad$ 6,360
$-$ 5,719

(9) $507 - 638 + 786 - 297 + 378 =$ _____

(10) $245 + 403 - 153 - 963 + 781 =$ _____

(11) $2.8300 - 7.020 + 6.300 - 5.00 - 15.400 =$ _____

(12) $42.300 - 33.200 - .8740 + 7.40 + 10.200 =$ _____

(13) $83 \times 74 =$ _____ (14) $74 \times 93 =$ _____

(15) $52 \times 707 =$ _____ (16) $746 \times 869 =$ _____

(17) $6.09 \times 0.78 =$ _____ (18) $29.4 \times .052 =$ _____

(19) $18.47 \times 546 =$ _____ (20) $9.037 \times 4.76 =$ _____

(21) $7,303 \div 95 =$ _____ (22) $2,111 \div 57 =$ _____

(23) 4,552 ÷ 164 = _____   (24) 7,662 ÷ 113 = _____

(25) 96.29 ÷ 9.77 = _____   (26) 88.22 ÷ 2.27 = _____

(27) 531.41 ÷ 89.9 = _____   (28) 96.644 ÷ 8.49 = _____

(29) 26,251 × .0831 = _____   (30) 619.621 ÷ 78.4 = _____

(31) $72.89 + $54.49 + $76.54 + $53.07 + $83.91 = _____

(32) $50.97 + $14.30 + $49.38 + $19.47 + $60.72 = _____

(33) $98.08 − $62.48 + $45.24 − $20.84 − $40.44 = _____

(34) $41.94 + $15.09 − $49.89 − $43.54 + $85.81 = _____

(35) 271 items @ $6.75 = _____

(36) 572 items @ $32.30 = _____

(37) 191 items @ $7.54 = _____

(38) 694 items @ $17.39 = _____

(39) If 37 items cost $212.75, one item costs _____.

(40) If 327 items cost $540.73, one item costs _____.

(41) If 53 items cost $1,000.64, one item costs _____.

(42) If 137 items cost $682.26, one item costs _____.

(43) $4,852.47 ÷ 5.312 = _____

(44) $95,765.78 × 13.457 = _____

(45) $37,451,763.00 ÷ 87.842 = _____

(46) $72,694.88 × 98.321 = _____

(47) $849,002 ÷ 5,691 = _____

(48) $628.34 × .0908 = _____

(49) $457,104 ÷ 6,782 = _____

(50) $29.44 × .0076 = _____

3

Estimating

LEARNING GOALS

After completing this chapter, you should be proficient at:

- Estimating decimals
- Estimating sums
- Estimating differences
- Estimating products
- Estimating quotients

You also will be able to pass Pretest III, a 10-minute timed test of your ability to estimate answers. You should be able to estimate accurately at least 30 of the 50 problems on this test with better than 90 percent accuracy.

stimating is the most important skill taught in this text-book—a skill vital in auditing or checking answers, a skill that will improve accuracy, and perhaps most important, a skill that builds confidence. This chapter should be worked without using a calculator.

You have already had some experience estimating with addition and subtraction (page 43–44 of Chapter 1) and with multiplication and division (page 117–118 of Chapter 2).

Why Estimate?

These days we can obtain highly precise answers with a calculator or computer by simply entering data correctly. But what if data is entered incorrectly? To check for such errors, we need to be able to distinguish a reasonable answer from an unreasonable one. This we can do by estimating.

Estimating an answer is one of the best ways to solve a problem. Often, if you determine what answer is reasonable, you will then see how to solve the problem. And estimating again **after** solving a problem helps you check whether the answer you obtained is indeed reasonable.

Make a habit of estimating answers—it will help you solve problems, improve your accuracy, and build your self-confidence. Use your intuition. "Guesstimate." And don't be concerned if your estimate is slightly different from someone else's or from those given in this book. People think differently. There may be many ways to solve a problem, even if there is only one correct answer.

Estimating Decimal Placement

Misplacing the decimal point is the most common mistake when multiplying or dividing with pencil or business machine. It is a major problem even on electronic calculators with automatic decimal placement. There are two key ways you can avoid misplacing a decimal. The first is easy and you should always use it! Follow the rules of programming your machine as outlined in this text and various machine instruction manuals. The second way to check decimal placement is to estimate your answers.

Estimating Products of Whole Numbers

To estimate products, round each factor to just one non-zero digit plus zeros. In the problem 598×327, the 598 would be rounded to 600 and the 327 to 300. (Chapter 1 reviews how to round numbers.) Then simply multiply 6×3 and annex 4 zeros (the two zeros in 600 plus the two zeros in 300). That is, $6 \times 3 = 18$. Annexing four zeros gives 180,000 as your estimated answer.

If you solved this problem with a calculator and your machine were to print out 195,546, you would accept it because it is reasonable. You would reject answers such as 19,544.6 or 1,955,460 because they are unreasonable. Here is another example:

$$329 \times 4{,}896 = 0161078400$$
Estimate $\qquad 300 \times 5{,}000 = (3 \times 5) + 5 \text{ zeros}$
$$= 1{,}500{,}000$$
Exact answer $\qquad = 1{,}610{,}784$

You should be able to spot an answer that is not reasonable. You can do this by estimating your answer **before** you work the problem on your machine. Then you can immediately check to see if you have made any major errors. Most business people do this automatically. Thus, we have the following procedure for estimating products with whole numbers.

1. Round each factor to one digit other than zero.

2. Find the product of these two digits.

3. Annex as many zeros to the product as there are zeros in the two rounded factors.

1. Write the estimated answers and the exact answers to the following problems.

Problem	Estimated Answer	Correct Digits	Exact Answer
(1) 51 × 67	_____	003417000	_____
(2) 731 × 32	_____	002339200	_____
(3) 595 × 40	_____	000238000	_____
(4) 297 × 800	_____	023760000	_____
(5) 91 × 67	_____	006097000	_____

Answers: (1) 3,500; 3,417; (2) 21,000; 23,392; (3) 24,000; 23,800; (4) 240,000; 237,600; (5) 6,300; 6,097

Estimating Products With Decimal Numbers

The procedure for estimating is changed only slightly when the factors being multiplied have decimals. Let's use the problem 42.5 × .0789 as an example. First round both numbers to one digit other than zeros. The 42.5 rounds to 40 and the .0789 rounds to .08. Then multiply 4 by 8, which is 32. Because 40 has one zero, we annex it, giving 320. However, the other rounded factor is .08, which has two decimal places instead of zeros. We then move the decimal one place to the left for each decimal place in the rounded factor, giving the estimated answer of 3.2. To put it another way, since you have one more decimal place than zeros, move the decimal point one place to the left in your estimated answer, giving 3.2. Sometimes you may even want to write by hand the intermediate multiplication to aid in estimating. If the machine reads 0335325000, your correct answer would be 3.353 rounded to three decimal places. Here is another example:

$$74.37 \times .003219 = 0023939703$$

Estimate   70   × .003   = .210 (annex one zero then move the decimal to the left three places)

Exact answer   = .239

1. Even with these guidelines it is sometimes easier to write by hand the simplified intermediate multiplication. Write the estimated answers for the following problems. Round the exact answers to three decimal places.

	Intermediate Multiplication	Estimated Answer	Correct Digits	Exact Answer Rounded to 3 Decimal Places
(1) $5.32 \times 1.8200 =$	$\begin{array}{r} 2 \\ \times\,5 \\ \hline 10 \end{array}$	_____	0968240000	_____
(2) $.489 \times 1.8750 =$	$\begin{array}{r} .5 \\ \times\,2 \\ \hline 1.0 \end{array}$	_____	0091687500	_____
(3) $82.54 \times .0037 =$	$\begin{array}{r} 80 \\ \times\,.004 \\ \hline .320 \end{array}$	_____	0305398000	_____
(4) $1.158 \times .0498 =$	$\begin{array}{r} 1 \\ \times\,.05 \\ \hline .05 \end{array}$	_____	0005766840	_____
(5) $.0871 \times .0823 =$	$\begin{array}{r} .09 \\ \times\,.08 \\ \hline .0072 \end{array}$	_____	7168330000	_____

Answers: (1) 10, 9.682; (2) 1.0, .917; (3) .320, .305; (4) .05, .058; (5) .0072, .007

2. It is often easier to estimate when we think in terms of money.

		Thought Process	Estimated Answer	Correct Digits	Answer
(1)	$.97653 \times 29$	($1 × 30)	_____	0002831937	_____
(2)	$.89329 \times 71$	($1 × 70)	_____	6342359000	_____
(3)	9.87×389	($10 × 400)	_____	0038394300	_____
(4)	$1.376 \times 8.93	(1 × $9)	_____	0001228768	_____
(5)	$3.8976 \times 2.15	(4 × $2)	_____	083798400	_____

Answers: (1) $30, $28.32; (2) $70, $63.42; (3) $4,000, $3,839.43; (4) $9, $12.29; (5) $8, $8.38

3. Write the estimated answers and the exact answers for these problems. Round the exact answer to three decimal places.

		Estimated Answer	Correct Digits	Answer
(1)	3.21 × .051	_____	0016371000	_____
(2)	5.20 × 30.7	_____	0001596400	_____
(3)	77.5 × .0095	_____	0736250000	_____
(4)	111.6 × .085	_____	0000948600	_____
(5)	65.31 × .0048	_____	0313488000	_____

Answers: (1) .15, .164; (2) 150, 159.640; (3) .8, .736; (4) 9, 9.486; (5) .35, .313

Estimating With Division

As with multiplication, estimating with division is simple if you understand certain estimating techniques. In estimating 60,717 ÷ 326, first round both the dividend and the divisor to just one significant digit. So, 60,717 ÷ 326 rounded for estimation is 60,000 ÷ 300 or, canceling two zeros, 60,000 ÷ 300. The problem can now be thought of as 600 ÷ 3, which is 200. If the calculator displays a quotient of 18624846, you know the exact quotient is 186.248, rounded to three decimal places.

Estimating division with decimal numbers is similar. For example, in 27 ÷ .0513, first round both numbers to one digit other than zero, which gives you 30 ÷ .05. Now change the divisor to a whole number by multiplying both sides by 100, that is, by moving the decimal point two places to the right. The problem is now thought of as 3,000 ÷ 5, which is 600. Thus, for the problem 27 ÷ .0513, if the calculator displays 52631578, the exact answer would be 526.316 because it is much closer to the estimate of 600 than is 52 or 5,263. The procedure for estimating quotients, then, is:

1. Round the divisor and dividend to one digit other than zero.
2. Cancel zeros when possible or add zeros as necessary.
3. To estimate a quotient with one non-zero digit, it may be necessary to annex or prefix zeros to place the decimal point correctly.

Even with these guidelines, it is sometimes easier to write out the simplified intermediate division problems with pencil.

1. Write the estimated answers and the exact answers for the following division problems. Round the exact answers to three decimal places. Round answers according to the rules for rounding.

	Intermediate Division	Estimated Answer	Correct Digits	Exact Answer Rounded to 3 Decimal Places
(1) 619 ÷ 283	$\overset{2}{300\overline{)600}}$	_____	21872791	_____
(2) 394 ÷ .053	$\overset{8000}{.05\overline{)400.00}}$	_____	74339622	_____
(3) 78.06 ÷ 7.607	$\overset{10}{8\overline{)80}}$	_____	10261601	_____
(4) .0264 ÷ 36	$\overset{.0007}{40\overline{).0300}}$	_____	73333333	_____
(5) 7.893 ÷ 2.128	$\overset{4}{2\overline{)8}}$	_____	37091165	_____

Answers: (1) 2, 2.187; (2) 8,000, 7,433.962; (3) 10, 10.262; (4) .0007, .001; (5) 4, 3.709

2. Maybe it is easier to estimate when we think in terms of money.

  (1) If 7 items cost $69.18, what would one item cost?

    (a) $9.88   (b) $98.83   (c) $12.87   (d) $493.36

  (2) If 12 items cost $9.88, what would one item cost?

    (a) $8.23   (b) $91.85   (c) $.82   (d) $.09

  (3) If 198 items cost $327.38, what would one item cost?

    (a) $.27   (b) $1.65   (c) $15.92   (d) $3.64

  (4) If 221 items cost $413.98, what would one item cost?

    (a) $19.27   (b) $1.87   (c) $42.53   (d) $.53

  (5) If 485 items cost $1,893.71, what would one item cost?

    (a) $.39   (b) $8.72   (c) $40.35   (d) $3.90

Answers: (1) (Think $70 ÷ 7 = $10) a; (2) (Think $10 ÷ 10 = $1) c; (3) (Think $300 ÷ 200 = $1.50) b; (4) (Think $400 ÷ 200 = $2) b; (5) (Think $2,000 ÷ 500 = $4) d

3. Write the estimated answers and the exact answers for the following division problems. Round the exact answers to three decimal places.

	Estimated Answer	Correct Digits	Answer
(1) 538 ÷ 489	_____	11002044	_____
(2) 237 ÷ .061	_____	38852459	_____
(3) 82.06 ÷ 7.708	_____	10646081	_____
(4) .0374 ÷ 28	_____	13357142	_____
(5) 5.484 ÷ 1.31	_____	41862595	_____

Answers: (1) 1, 1.100; (2) 3,000, 3,885.246; (3) 10, 10.646; (4) .001, .001; (5) 5, 4.186

Review Problems

These techniques for estimating will be some of your most valuable skills. They will help you prevent serious errors and guide you to correct problem solving. As a review of the techniques, do the following problems.

Addition and Subtraction

Use the estimating techniques from page 43, Chapter 1, to select the closest estimated answers to the following problems.

(1) 9,637 + 5,119 =	(a) 13,756	(b) 12,987	(c) 14,756	(d) 16,173
(2) 5,876 + 7,216 =	(a) 14,192	(b) 12,092	(c) 11,772	(d) 13,092
(3) 5,407 − 3,187 =	(a) 2,220	(b) 3,220	(c) 3,700	(d) 1,190
(4) 8,137 − 3,923 =	(a) 3,809	(b) 4,214	(c) 5,495	(d) 2,910
(5) 2,059 + 8,911 =	(a) 7,970	(b) 9,970	(c) 10,970	(d) 12,070
(6) 12,579 − 7,059 =	(a) 3,656	(b) 5,520	(c) 7,528	(d) 9,456
(7) 6,887 + 5,918 =	(a) 12,805	(b) 15,905	(c) 11,575	(d) 14,705
(8) 2,875 − 995 =	(a) 3,880	(b) 1,880	(c) 5,880	(d) 4,880
(9) 8,215 + 3,951 =	(a) 11,216	(b) 10,706	(c) 13,276	(d) 12,166
(10) 19,496 − 11,923 =	(a) 9,573	(b) 7,573	(c) 8,373	(d) 6,413

Answers: (1) c; (2) d; (3) a; (4) b; (5) c; (6) b; (7) a; (8) b; (9) d; (10) b

Multiplication and Division

Select the closest estimated answers to the following problems.

(1) $83 \times 44 =$	(a) 6,472	(b) 11,009	(c) 3,652	(d) 7,432
(2) $324 \times 145 =$	(a) 15,200	(b) 46,980	(c) 95,540	(d) 75,470
(3) $1,575 \div 73 =$	(a) 40.823	(b) 8.991	(c) 1.237	(d) 21.575
(4) $4,272 \div 614 =$	(a) 18.402	(b) 6.958	(c) 3.095	(d) 17.424
(5) $56.421 \div .824 =$	(a) 68.472	(b) 321.497	(c) 123.091	(d) 24.423
(6) $4,231 \times 456 =$	(a) 192,937	(b) 224,301	(c) 1,929,336	(d) 4,645,997
(7) $8,149 \times 74 =$	(a) 6,030	(b) 603,026	(c) 56,071	(d) 442,784
(8) $13,443 \div 514 =$	(a) 202.783	(b) 7.894	(c) 32.147	(d) 26.154
(9) $68 \times 6,332 =$	(a) 361,463	(b) 687,848	(c) 430,576	(d) 42,076
(10) $24,099 \div 5,988 =$	(a) 14.007	(b) 4.025	(c) 5.799	(d) 40.252

Answers: (1) c; (2) b; (3) d; (4) b; (5) a; (6) c; (7) b; (8) d; (9) c; (10) b

Decimals

Estimate the answers to the following problems and find the exact answers, rounded to three decimal places.

		Estimated Answer	Correct Digits	Answer
(1)	517×497	_____	25694900	_____
(2)	3.27×25.1	_____	08207700	_____
(3)	$.4278 \times .389$	_____	16641420	_____
(4)	$721 \div 698$	_____	10329512	_____
(5)	$8.9761 \div 538.4$	_____	16671805	_____
(6)	43.254×1.9078	_____	82519981	_____
(7)	$3.781 \div 1.827$	_____	20695128	_____
(8)	$563.24 \div 490.37$	_____	1148602	_____
(9)	$7.5581 \times .00439$	_____	33180059	_____
(10)	$5.1135 \div 10.0897$	_____	50680396	_____

Answers: (1) 250,000, 256,949; (2) 90, 82.077; (3) .16, .166; (4) 1, 1.033; (5) .01, .017; (6) 80, 82.520; (7) 2, 2.070; (8) 1, 1.149; (9) .032, .033; (10) .5, .507

If you missed more than two of the review questions, redo this section or ask your instructor for help.

Stop

You are now ready to take Pretest III, a 10-minute test of estimating without a calculator. Your performance on Pretest III will tell you if you have developed sufficient skill to proceed to **Test III**. Unless instructed otherwise, turn in your Pretest for correction and review before taking Test III. On Test III, if you complete at least 30 problems correct and get 90 percent of all the problems you attempt, proceed to Chapter 4; if not, review Chapter 3.

You may also want to retake Tests IA, IB, IIA, or IIB, since the skill of estimating will improve your skill at multiplying and dividing with and without a calculator.

Pretest III

ESTIMATING WITHOUT A CALCULATOR

10 minutes

This test must be worked in sequence. Any problems skipped count as errors. To pass, you need to get 90 percent of the problems you try and at least 30 correct answers.

Circle the closest estimated answers.

(1) $8,527 + 3,109 =$	(a) 13,756	(b) 12,987	(c) 11,636	(d) 16,176
(2) $4,765 + 6,105 =$	(a) 13,000	(b) 10,870	(c) 13,870	(d) 9,810
(3) $8,128 - 2,829 =$	(a) 10,957	(b) 9,409	(c) 5,299	(d) 4,299
(4) $6,305 - 4,176 =$	(a) 2,129	(b) 1,029	(c) 5,029	(d) 6,819
(5) $3,171 + 7,822 =$	(a) 4,657	(b) 9,081	(c) 7,238	(d) 10,993
(6) $12,687 - 7,068 =$	(a) 4,521	(b) 5,619	(c) 8,669	(d) 3,521
(7) $211 \times 398 =$	(a) 48,202	(b) 59,302	(c) 39,302	(d) 83,978
(8) $1,819 \div 324 =$	(a) 56.147	(b) 78.071	(c) .561	(d) 5.614
(9) $17,852 \div 911 =$	(a) 193.596	(b) 1.960	(c) 19.596	(d) 203.111
(10) $2,977 \times 44 =$	(a) 1,893	(b) 130,988	(c) 5,984	(d) 145,187
(11) $45 \times 6,772 =$	(a) 509,740	(b) 105,704	(c) 304,740	(d) 804,740
(12) $17,981 \div 5,981 =$	(a) 3.006	(b) 300.651	(c) .301	(d) 9.081
(13) $12,973 \div 6,921 =$	(a) 18.745	(b) .1874	(c) 5.791	(d) 1.874
(14) $6,892 + 7,109 =$	(a) 14,001	(b) 1,400	(c) 140,001	(d) 8,231
(15) $7,843 - 954 =$	(a) 9,889	(b) 9,081	(c) 8,171	(d) 6,889
(16) $.9588 \times .7067 =$	(a) .678	(b) 677.580	(c) 677.581	(d) 7.758
(17) $8,556 + 1,296 =$	(a) 9,852	(b) 5,752	(c) 6,342	(d) 4,455
(18) $7,120 - 902 =$	(a) 4,228	(b) 5,176	(c) 8,022	(d) 6,218
(19) $8.556 \times .4756 =$	(a) 3.069	(b) 11.018	(c) 4.069	(d) 2.183
(20) $926.1 \div 321.8 =$	(a) 4.871	(b) 51.010	(c) 2.878	(d) .288
(21) $3,897 - 2,509 =$	(a) 2,508	(b) 1,388	(c) 2,376	(d) 3,388
(22) $2,785 + 1,165 =$	(a) 2,950	(b) 5,338	(c) 3,950	(d) 4,850

Estimate the following answers and then determine them exactly, rounded to 3 decimal places.

	Estimated Answer	Correct Digits	Answer
5.29×3.74	_____ (23)	01978460	_____ (24)
3.42×29.8	_____ (25)	01019160	_____ (26)
$7.92 \div 3.816$	_____ (27)	20754716	_____ (28)
$13.812 \div 2.016$	_____ (29)	68511904	_____ (30)
$7.4471 \times .09831$	_____ (31)	7321244	_____ (32)
$52.384 \div 27.756$	_____ (33)	18873036	_____ (34)
7.8952×527.5	_____ (35)	4164718	_____ (36)
$431.54 \div 1.8079$	_____ (37)	23869683	_____ (38)
$563.34 \times .00491$	_____ (39)	2765999	_____ (40)
$5.3341 \div 10.088$	_____ (41)	52875693	_____ (42)
435.52×1.9086	_____ (43)	83123347	_____ (44)
$694.14 \div 589.41$	_____ (45)	11776861	_____ (46)
78.142×2.0018	_____ (47)	15642465	_____ (48)
$43.181 \div 1019$	_____ (49)	42375858	_____ (50)

CHAPTER 4

Special Functions and Operations With an Electronic Calculator

LEARNING GOALS

After completing this chapter, you should be able to:

- Perform accumulative multiplication and division
- Work with fractions on a calculator
- Solve percentage problems
- Use a constant function
- Raise numbers to a power
- Do mixed problems using storage

You also will be able to pass Pretest IV, a 15-minute timed test of your ability to use the special functions and perform special operations with a business electronic calculator. You will be able to complete correctly at least 15 of the 25 problems on the test and the number correct will be at least 90 percent of all the problems you attempt.

TOO BAD ABOUT WIGHAM. HE NEVER DID LEARN HOW TO USE THE SPECIAL FUNCTIONS ON HIS CALCULATOR.

Having completed Chapters 1 and 2 you have developed touch control on a 10-key calculator and should be able to use its functions of addition, subtraction, multiplication, and division with speed and accuracy. You have also proved you can work with numbers and add, subtract, multiply, and divide without a calculator. And you have developed skill at estimating answers.

This chapter introduces you to additional capabilities found on business calculators. These special calculator functions are easy to use and readily available to most people because they are found on hand-held calculators and on the pull down screens of popular computer software programs such as Microsoft Word. Because they increase speed and accuracy they can increase your productivity. In fact if you are doing repetitious processes they may save you more than an hour in just one day's work.

As you go through the chapter, remember a concentrated effort is required to understand and utilize fully the capabilities of a business calculator. Although you must be able to understand and solve the problems, you should give at least equal concern to building skill in calculator operation.

While the many available makes and models of business calculators are quite similar in their operation, you will find numerous differences among them: location of function keys, type of *zero* key or keys, key and tape symbols, display mechanisms, and certain special features. For this reason, when a function or machine operation you need is not apparent to you, you should review the operating manual for your particular machine or have your instructor acquaint you with that function or machine operation.

Accumulative Multiplication and Division

Most popular business desk calculators have memory or storage registers for accumulating products and quotients from a series of problems and for storing numbers used repeatedly in successive calculations. Many machines have a *sigma* (Σ) or *accumulation* (A) key that when engaged will accumulate answers in the machine's memory. On other machines this operation is performed with the *equal plus* (= +) or *equal minus* (= –) key. To print out or display an accumulative total, on most machines, the operator must depress the total key. On other electronic calculators, however, the operator multiplies normally and then enters the individually printed or displayed answers into memory for accumulation. Some machines even have multiple storage or memory registers.

General Instructions for Accumulative Multiplication and Division

(1) Clear machine and memory.

(2) Do individual multiplication or division problem.

(3) Add to memory.

(4) Repeat steps (2) and (3) as often as necessary.

(5) Depress *recall from memory* or *total* key to find the accumulated total.

With an Accumulation Key	Without an Accumulation Key
(1) Engage accumulation key.	(1) Clear machine.
(2) Clear machine and memory.	(2) Multiply or divide directly into storage.
(3) Do individual multiplication or division.	(3) Repeat step 2 as often as necessary.
(4) Repeat step 3 as often as necessary.	(4) Depress recall from memory or total key to find the accumulated total.
(5) Depress recall from memory or total key to find the accumulated total.	

Please check with your instructor for the most efficient use of your calculator.

Do the following sample accumulation problems without recording intermediate products.

$(5 \times 2) + (4 \times 6) + (2 \times 7) + (8 \times 3) = 72$

$(47 \times 32) + (56 \times 78) + (89 \times 24) + (47 \times 63) = 10{,}969$

$(5.83 \times 30.3) + (73.5 \times .159) + (6.21 \times 8.69) + (.357 \times .475) = 242.470$

$(4 \div 2) + (6 \div 3) + (8 \div 4) + (10 \div 5) = 8$

$(5.43 \div 8) + (21.4 \div 9) + (37.8 \div 8) + (22.7 \div 16) = 9.200$

If you understand the examples, work the problems in Exercise 1. If not, consult your operating manual again or ask your instructor to explain.

1. Solve the following accumulative multiplication problems.

   (1) $(8 \times 3) + (5 \times 6) + (9 \times 9) + (7 \times 8) = $ _____

   (2) $(77 \times 51) + (30 \times 38) + (20 \times 86) + (42 \times 83) = $ _____

   (3) $(21 \times 81) + (85 \times 93) + (13 \times 27) + (88 \times 55) = $ _____

   (4) $(3 \times 27) + (6 \times 89) + (11 \times 303) + (32 \times 92) = $ _____

   (5) $(651 \times 440) + (10 \times 21) + (817 \times 191) + (716 \times 29) = $ _____

   (6) $(6{,}052 \times 8) + (306 \times 95) + (4 \times 83) + (5 \times 7) = $ _____

   (7) $(4 \times 36) + (6{,}442 \times 1{,}808) + (2{,}376 \times 177) + (82 \times 676) = $ _____

   (8) $(.07 \times 47) + (1.7 \times 98) + (289 \times .766) + (5{,}413 \times .0432) = $ _____

   (9) $(12.88 \times 73.43) + (19.523 \times 755) + (.009 \times .17) = $ _____

   (10) $(6.07 \times .901) + (700 \times 800) + (1.1 \times 13.001) + (.089 \times 732) = $ _____

   Answers: (1) 191; (2) 10,273; (3) 14,797; (4) 6,892; (5) 463,461; (6) 77,853; (7) 12,123,264; (8) 625.106; (9) 15,685.645; (10) 560,084.918

2. Solve the following accumulative division problems.

   (1) $(9 \div 3) + (8 \div 4) + (6 \div 2) + (10 \div 5) = $ _____

   (2) $(8 \div 3) + (5 \div 8) + (9 \div 6) + (1 \div 9) = $ _____

   (3) $(78 \div 5) + (42 \div 4) + (27 \div 8) + (51 \div 3) = $ _____

   (4) $(13 \div 6) + (61 \div 5) + (88 \div 7) + (30 \div 4) = $ _____

   (5) $(55 \div 78) + (17 \div 65) + (14 \div 83) + (48 \div 34) = $ _____

   (6) $(89 \div 4.1) + (59 \div 2.6) + (94 \div 3.9) + (60 \div 7.1) = $ _____

   (7) $(7.48 \div 19) + (7.88 \div 49) + (6.55 \div 84) + (4.49 \div 69) = $ _____

(8) $(605 \div 288) + (34 \div 4.1) + (107 \div 95) + (98 \div 14.5) =$ _____

(9) $(5 \div 1.28) + (.09 \div 7.1) + (9.71 \div 9) + (43.3 \div 53) =$ _____

(10) $(12.88 \div 39.7) + (73.4 \div 36) + (11 \div 8.4) + (40.4 \div 2.8) =$ _____

Answers: (1) 10; (2) 4.903; (3) 46.475; (4) 34.438; (5) 2.547; (6) 76.953; (7) .698; (8) 18.278; (9) 5.815; (10) 18.101

Mixed positive and negative accumulation problems also can be worked easily. Simply depress the *minus* (–) or *equal minus* (= –) key instead of the *plus* (+) or *equal plus* (= +) key. Remember to enter the sign *after* the numbers you are subtracting.

3. Solve these mixed positive and negative accumulation problems.

(1) $(5 \times 3) - (2 \times 3) - (4 \times 6) + (8 \times 7) =$ _____

(2) $(12 \div 6) - (6 \div 2) + (15 \div 3) - (8 \div 4) =$ _____

(3) $(94 \times 7) + (89 \times 9) - (3 \times 42) - (22 \times 6) =$ _____

(4) $(4.3 \div 6) + (5.1 \div 7) - (.77 \div 8) - (72 \div .7) =$ _____

(5) $(2.08 \times 2.6) - (66 \times 9.5) - (7.6 \times 8) + (.79 \times 3.6) =$ _____

Answers: (1) 41; (2) 2; (3) 1,201; (4) –101.508; (5) –679.548

4. It is even easy to mix positive accumulation and negative accumulation while accumulating products and quotients, as you will find by solving the following problems.

(1) $(65 \div 5) + (5 \times 8) - (9 \div 3) + (9 \times 8) =$ _____

(2) $(47 \times 3) - (15 \div 5) + (31 \times 6) - (99 \div 11) =$ _____

(3) $(17.2 \div 8) - (28.81 \times 1.7) + (8.97 \times .33) - (4.3 \div 6) =$ _____

(4) $(9.07 \times 3) + (.435 \div .59) - (43 \div 44) + (.37 \times 8.1) =$ _____

(5) $(45 \div .8) + (84 \times .51) - (.47 \times 5.9) - (.37 \div .13) =$ _____

Answers: (1) 122; (2) 315; (3) –44.584; (4) 29.967; (5) 93.471

FRACTIONS

A fraction is a way of expressing division, ratios, parts, percentages, quartiles, and decimals. For example, the fraction 7/8 is a way of saying, divide the numerator 7 by the denominator 8.

There are three types of fractions:

■ **Proper fractions**—the value is always less than one because the numerator is less than the denominator. Examples: 1/2, 5/8, 13/15.

■ **Improper fractions**—the value is always more than one because the numerator is greater than the denominator. Examples: 3/2, 8/5, 13/7.

■ **Mixed numbers**—a whole number combined with a fraction. Examples: 1 1/2, 3 5/6, 11 1/8.

Since calculators do not solve problems with fractions directly, we usually convert the fraction to its decimal equivalent during machine calculations by dividing the numerator (top number) of the fraction by the denominator (bottom number), as shown in the following examples.

Fraction				Decimal Equivalent
1/2	=	$1 \div 2$	=	.5
5/8	=	$5 \div 8$	=	.625
5/6	=	$5 \div 6$	=	.8333 ...
11/9	=	$11 \div 9$	=	1.2222 ...
8 2/3	=	$8 + (2 \div 3)$	=	8.6666 ...

1. Convert the following fractions and mixed numbers to decimals. Round to three decimals.

   (1) 1/4 = _____   (2) 8/3 = _____

   (3) 1/9 = _____   (4) 7/12 = _____

   (5) 1/8 = _____   (6) 59/33 = _____

   (7) 5/9 = _____   (8) 1 9/17 = _____

   (9) 8 4/7 = _____   (10) 16 2/15 = _____

   (11) 9 4/19 = _____   (12) 17 3/22 = _____

   Answers: (1) .250; (2) 2.667; (3) .111; (4) .583; (5) .125; (6) 1.788; (7) .556; (8) 1.529; (9) 8.571; (10) 16.133; (11) 9.211; (12) 17.136

It is easy to add and subtract fractions on an electronic calculator. You need only first convert the fraction to its decimal equivalent by dividing the numerator of the fraction by the denominator. Then accumulate the decimal equivalents. For example:

1/6	=	.1667
3/8	=	.3750
3/5	=	.6000
		1.1417

Rounded 1.142

2. Solve each of the following problems as you would in accumulative division problems in the accumulation exercise on

page 146. Use the machine efficiently, **do not** convert each fraction to a decimal and then re-enter the decimals to get your answer. (Set the decimal at 4 places.)

(1)	1/3	(2)	2/3	(3)	5/6	(4)	1/6
	1/4		1/2		7/8		3/8
	1/5		3/4		1/8		3/4
	1/8		1/6		3/5		5/6
	1/2		5/8		2/3		7/8

(5)	1/9	(6)	1/3	(7)	5/9	(8)	1/6
	3/8		3/4		3/4		2/3
	7/8		1/3		1/3		1/4
	5/6		5/6		4/5		3/4
	3/4		2/3		2/3		1/2

Answers: (1) 1.408; (2) 2.708; (3) 3.100; (4) 3; (5) 2.944; (6) 2.917; (7) 3.106; (8) 2.333

3. When adding mixed numbers, it is best to add the whole numbers first, retaining the sum and then accumulate the fractions, as shown in the following example:

46 1/9
34 5/8
13 2/3
———

```
46.0000    +
34.0000    +
13.0000    +
 1.0000  ÷
 9.0000  = +
 0.1111    *

 5.0000  ÷
 8.0000  = +
 0.6250    *

 2.0000  ÷
 3.0000  = +
 0.6667    *

94.4028    *
```

(1)	26 1/4	(2)	8 1/9	(3)	40 3/7	(4)	5 1/6
	5 1/2		22 7/9		12 5/9		96 5/9
	50 1/3		70 5/7		5 4/5		5 3/4
	39 1/6		5 1/5		11 2/7		9 2/3
	4 8/9		54 4/9		26 4/7		36 3/8

(5) 6 2/7	(6) 25 1/3	(7) 5 5/9	(8) 4 1/6
18 4/5	5 3/4	42 3/4	19 2/3
7 2/3	9 1/3	23 1/3	16 1/4
10 1/3	7 5/6	7 4/5	9 3/4
27 5/8	57 2/3	11 2/3	48 1/2

Answers: (1) 126.139; (2) 161.248; (3) 96.641; (4) 153.514; (5) 70.711; (6) 105.917; (7) 91.106; (8) 98.333

4. When subtracting mixed numbers, it is usually easier to subtract the whole numbers first, retain the difference, and then using negative accumulation, accumulate the fractions as shown in the following examples:

635 3/7
−87 5/9

```
     635.0000   +
      87.0000   −

       3.0000   ÷
       7.0000   = +
       0.4286   *

       5.0000   ÷
       9.0000   = −
       0.5556   *

     547.8730   *
```

(1) 892 3/4	(2) 19 2/7	(3) 4,448 4/9	(4) 929 2/3
−99 4/5	−9 5/7	−449 1/4	−628 3/5

(5) 3,497 5/8	(6) 9,620 4/7	(7) 8,097 1/9	(8) 8,883 4/5
−489 5/6	−841 5/6	−908 3/7	−869 2/9

Answers: (1) 792.950; (2) 9.571; (3) 3,999.194; (4) 301.067; (5) 3,007.792; (6) 8,778.738; (7) 7,188.683; (8) 8,014.578

MULTIPLYING FRACTIONS

You probably already have a feel for how to multiply fractions. For example, if you divide a candy bar with another person and each of you in turn shares your half equally with a friend, what part of the candy bar does each of you have? Each of you has 1/2 × 1/2 or 1/4 of the candy bar. This example shows that if you have less than a whole number and multiply it by less than a whole number you end up with an even smaller part of the whole number.

Stocks may be owned in fractions of a share. Few people actually get stock certificates of shares traded on stock exchanges; the shares are held in an account electronically.

Since division is the opposite of multiplication, you should not be surprised that when we divide by a fraction we often get a larger number. In the candy bar example above, we started with one candy bar. When we divided it by 1/2 we had two pieces. When we divided it again, we really divided it by 1/4 and had four pieces. Remember, to divide a number by a fraction, invert the divisor and multiply.

Multiplying fractions is quite easy on most electronic calculators, even those without a special memory function. Try the following procedure on your machine to multiply 5/8 by 3/4.

Key	
5	
÷	
8	
×	
3	
÷	
4	
=	.4688
Rounded	.469

```
          5.  ÷
          8.  ×
          3.  ÷
          4.  =
     0.4688  *
```

5. Multiply the following fractions. Round answers to three decimal digits.

(1) $2/3 \times 7/9 =$ _____   (2) $1/8 \times 1/6 =$ _____

(3) $7/9 \times 4/17 =$ _____   (4) $1/44 \times 7/15 =$ _____

(5) $2/3 \times 5/9 =$ _____   (6) $7/18 \times 5/13 =$ _____

(7) $2/19 \times 4/7 =$ _____   (8) $2/89 \times 7/34 =$ _____

(9) $5/31 \times 5/8 =$ _____   (10) $9/34 \times 9/52 =$ _____

Answers: (1) .519; (2) .021; (3) .183; (4) .011; (5) .370; (6) .150; (7) .060; (8) .005; (9) .101; (10) .046

DIVIDING FRACTIONS

Again, since division is the opposite of multiplication, you should not be surprised that when we divide by a fraction we often get a larger number. For example, if you divide one large cake into sixty-fourths, how many pieces of cake do you have? You have 64 pieces. Remember, to divide a number by a fraction, invert the divisor and multiply:

Even though you see $2/3 \div 5/6$

Input as $2/3 \times 6/5 = .8$

6. Divide the following fractions by mentally inverting the divisor and then multiplying the fractions.

(1) $2/3 \div 1/2 =$ _____   (2) $2/9 \div 3/4 =$ _____

(3) $1/2 \div 2/3 =$ _____   (4) $7/11 \div 3/8 =$ _____

(5) $5/8 \div 2/3 =$ _____   (6) $1/6 \div 5/9 =$ _____

(7) $5/6 \div 2/7 =$ _____   (8) $3/8 \div 2/11 =$ _____

(9) $13/14 \div 2/31 =$ _____   (10) $5/24 \div 2/33 =$ _____

Answers: (1) 1.333; (2) .296; (3) .750; (4) 1.697; (5) .938; (6) .300; (7) 2.917; (8) 2.063; (9) 14.393; (10) 3.438

MIXED PRACTICE

Remember, fractions such as 1/3 do not convert to decimals exactly. That is, 1/3 is approximately but not exactly equal to .333. Thus,

$$\$669.39 \times 1/3 = \$223.13 \qquad \$598.15 \times 3/7 = \$256.35$$

$$\$669.39 \times .333 = \$222.91 \qquad \$598.15 \times .429 = \$256.61$$

To avoid this inexactness, we first multiply by the numerator and then divide by the denominator. Thus:

$$\$598.15 \times 3/7 = \frac{\$598.15 \times 3}{7} = \$256.35$$

7. Solve the following problems.

(1) $\$678.31 \times 5/9 =$ _____   (2) $\$451.92 \times 4/9 =$ _____

(3) $\$362.81 \times 2/3 =$ _____   (4) $\$637.55 \times 5/17 =$ _____

(5) $\$251.78 \times 1/3 =$ _____   (6) $\$942.73 \div 9/52 =$ _____

(7) $\$894.63 \div 3/7 =$ _____   (8) $\$833.21 \div 7/34 =$ _____

(9) $\$711.11 \div 7/9 =$ _____   (10) $\$578.58 \div 19/31 =$ _____

Answers: (1) $376.84; (2) $200.85; (3) $241.87; (4) $187.51; (5) $83.93; (6) $5,446.88; (7) $2,087.47; (8) $4,047.02; (9) $914.28; (10) $944.00

Percentages

Business people need a way to compare data within departments, between departments, between competing companies, and within the entire economy. We use **percentage principles** to express these comparisons. Percentages have a wide range of application and are universally understood, making them a valuable business tool. This section reviews percentages and provides the background necessary to solve many business application problems using percents.

The *percent* key is useful for certain special functions, but it is mostly for people who do not understand percentage principles. The functions of a percent key also differ from machine to machine. We will not use the percent key in this section.

Percent means "per hundred" or hundredths. Percents are fractions whose denominators are always 100. Thus, 3 percent represents three parts of 100 or three hundredths (3/100) of a unit. The percent sign (%) should be thought of as representing the decimal fraction .01 or the proper fraction 1/100. It is easy to equate percentages with dollars and cents:

25% means 1/4 of 1	1% means 1/l00 of 1
25¢ means 1/4 of $1	1¢ means 1/l00 of $1

To express cents in terms of dollars, move the decimal point two places to the left. Thus, 132 pennies equal $1.32. Likewise, when percents are changed to decimals, the decimal point is moved two places to the left. Thus, 132% equals 1.32. The same is true with fractions. Thirty pennies is 30/100 or 3/10 of a dollar; 30% is 30/100 or 3/10 of a unit.

CONVERTING PERCENTS TO DECIMALS AND FRACTIONS

In order to have a common basis for comparing fractions and decimals we often change both to percents. But before percents can be used in machine calculations they must be converted to either decimals or common fractions. The following examples illustrate the conversion of a percent to its fractional or decimal form.

Percent	Fraction	Decimal
50	50/100 or 1/2	.50
10	10/100 or 1/10	.10
300	300/100 or 3/1	3.00
225	225/100 or 2 1/4	2.25
1/2	5/1,000 or 1/200	.005
.08	8/10,000 or 1/1,250	.0008

As the examples show, any number can be expressed in three ways: as a percent, a fraction, and a decimal.

1. Write the following percents as decimals. Remember, the % sign is equivalent to two decimal places (hundredths). To change a percent to a decimal, drop the % sign and move the decimal point two places to the left.

   15% = _____ (1)   2 1/2%* = _____ (2)   106.7% = _____ (3)

   Answers: (1) .15; (2) .02 1/2 or .025; (3) 1.067

2. Write the following decimals as percents. Remember, to change a decimal to a percent, move the decimal point two places to the right and use the % sign.

   .06 = _____ (1)   .875 = _____ (2)   1.83 1/3 = _____ (3)

   Answers: (1) 6%; (2) 87 1/2% or 87.5%; (3) 183 1/3%

3. Write the following percents as fractions. Remember, to change a percent to a fraction, drop the % sign, divide the percent quantity by 100, and reduce to lowest terms.

   75% = _____ (1)   250% = _____ (2)   12.5% = _____ (3)

   Answers: (1) 75/100 = 3/4; (2) 250/100 = 2 1/2; (3) 12.5/100 or 125/1,000 = 1/8

4. Complete the following table of conversions.

Percent		Fraction		Decimal
25	=	_____ (1)	=	_____ (2)
_____ (3)	=	_____ (4)	=	.70
5	=	_____ (5)	=	_____ (6)
_____ (7)	=	1/2	=	_____ (8)

   Answers: (1) 25/l00 = 1/4; (2) .25; (3) 70%; (4) 70/100 = 7/10; (5) 1/20; (6) .05; (7) 50%; (8) .50

---

*2 1/2% = 2.5% =.025

THE PERCENTAGE FORMULA

Percentage problems have only three basic parts:

- **The base**—always the beginning or initial value (100% or the whole amount of anything).
- **The rate**—generally expressed as a percent (%); can be thought of as the number of hundredths of the base number.
- **The part**—the product of rate and base.

Following are the formulas for finding: the part when the base and rate are known, the rate when the part and base are known, and the base when the part and rate are known.

Part = Base × Rate   P = BR

Rate = Part ÷ Base   R = P/B

Base = Part ÷ Rate   B = P/R

An easy way to remember these different variations of the percentage formula is to remember just one triangle formula. When "reading" the formula remember that RB means multiply and P/R means to divide.

To find the formula for part (P), eliminate P from the triangle, leaving RB.

To find the formula for rate (R), eliminate R from the triangle, leaving P/B.

To find the formula for base (B), eliminate B from the triangle, leaving P/R.

Hint

The secret of solving any problem successfully is being able to distinguish the known factors from the unknown factors. Because there are only three basic elements—part, rate, and base—percentage problems can easily be solved by estimating the result.

1. Identify the three parts of the following problem. Use this as an example: 25% of 24 = 6; .25 × 24 = 6 or 1/4 × 24 = 6; the rate is 25%, the base is 24, and the part is 6.

   In the problem 33 1/3% of 150 = 50, the rate is _____(1), the base is _____(2) and the part is _____(3). The base always represents the initial value, the whole amount, or _____% (4).

   Answers: (1) 33 1/3%; (2) 150; (3) 50; (4) 100

FINDING THE PART (PERCENTAGE)

$$B \times R = P \quad \text{or} \quad \triangle \frac{P}{RB}$$

The following examples use the triangle formula.

Example 1:   Find 15% of 72.

R = 15%. B = 72. Therefore, P = .15 × 72 = 10.8

Example 2:   Mr. Jones earns $42,800 a year and his tax is 25% of this amount. How much tax does he pay?

R = 25%. B = $42,800. Therefore, P = .25 or 1/4 × $42,800 = $10,700

2. Use your calculator to find the part, given the rate and base.

20% of 468 = _____ (1)   35% of 352 = _____(2)

179% of 268 = _____ (3)   .6% of 119 = _____(4)

Answers: (1) 93.6; (2) 123.2; (3) 479.72; (4) .714

FINDING THE RATE (PERCENT)

$$R = P/B \quad \text{or} \quad \triangle \frac{P}{\cancel{R}B}$$

> ### Hint
>
> Usually the base is designated by "of", the part by "is", and the rate by "%". Another way to remember the percentage formula (P = R × B) is:
>
> $$\text{"(is) = (\%) (of)"} \quad \text{or} \quad \triangle \frac{\text{is}}{\text{\% of}}$$

The following examples use the triangle formula.

Example 1:   25¢ is what percent of 75¢?

P = 25. B = 75. Therefore, R = 25/75 = 1/3 = 33 1/3%.

Example 2:   Out of 48 cars that started in an auto race, 36 cars completed. What percent finished?

P = 36. B = 48. Therefore, R = 36/48 = 3/4 = 75%.

3. Use the calculator to find the rate, given the part and base.

41 is what % of 46? _____ (1)   52 is what % of 11? _____ (2)

What % of 65 is 3.2? _____ (3)   What % of .29 is 1.5? _____ (4)

Answers: (1) 89.1%; (2) 472.7%; (3) 4.9%; (4) 517.2%

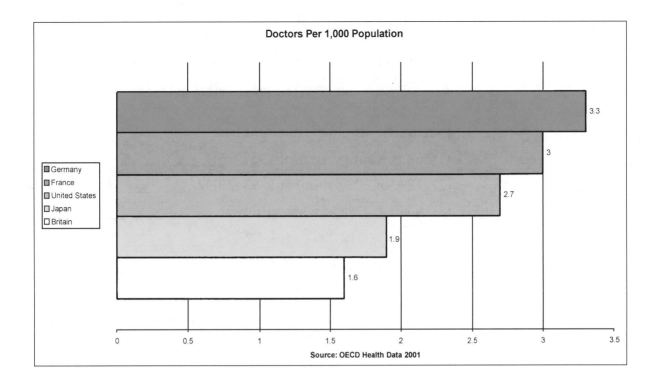

Doctors Per 1,000 Population

- Germany — 3.3
- France — 3
- United States — 2.7
- Japan — 1.9
- Britain — 1.6

Source: OECD Health Data 2001

(5) From the chart above, what is the percent of doctors per 1000 population in Japan compared to doctors in Germany?

(6) What is the percent of doctors per 1000 population in France compared to Britain?

Answers: (5) 57.6%; (6) 187.5%

FINDING THE BASE (100%)

$$B = P/R \quad \text{or} \quad \frac{P}{RB}$$

The following examples use the triangle formula.

Example 1: 150 is 75% of what number?

P = 150. R = .75. Therefore, B = 150/.75 = 15,000/75 = 200.

Example 2: Erin bought a sack of candy at the store and was charged $.12 tax. If the tax rate was 8%, what was the price tag on the candy?

P = $.12. R = .08 Therefore B = .12/.08 = 12/8 = $1.50

4. Use the calculator to find the base (100%), given the part and rate.

$83 is 14% of what number _____ (1)

15% of _____ (2) = $2.97

$7.80 is 1/2% of what amount? _____ (3)

If $43.00 is 18%, what is 100%? _____ (4)

Answers: (1) $592.86; (2) $19.80; (3) $1,560.00; (4) $238.89

Practice finding part, rate and base.

(1) 62 is what percent of 195? _____

(2) 12% of what number is $342.09? _____

(3) $69 is 142% of what number? _____

(4) What is 312.2% of $59.32? _____

(5) What percent of 277 is 82? _____

(6) 5.5% of 94 is what number? _____

Answers: (1) 31.8%; (2) $2,850.75; (3) $48.59; (4) $185.20; (5) 29.6%; (6) 5.170

Percent of Increase or Decrease

$$R = \frac{P}{B} \quad \text{or} \quad \frac{P}{RB}$$

To find the percent of increase or decrease you must first find the part, the amount of increase or decrease. Then use the same formula you used in finding the rate, remembering the base is always the original amount.

The following examples use the triangle formula.

Example 1: What is the percent decrease from $14.57 to $11.35?

$14.57 − $11.35 = a $3.22 decrease, P = $3.22. B = $14.57. Therefore, R = $3.22/$14.57 = a 22.1% decrease.

Example 2: Only 24 cars finished last year's auto race. If 36 cars finished this year, what was the percent of increase?

36 − 24 = a 12 car increase. P = 12. B = 24. Therefore, R = 12/24 = 1/2 = 50% increase.

5. Use the calculator to find the percent increase or decrease.

What is the percent of increase from 31 to 46? _____(1)

What is the percent of decrease from 52 to 25? _____(2)

The average price of a two-bedroom flat is very different in different cities of the World. In 2004 prices ranged from $840,000 in New York City to $180,000 in Brussels. In real dollars (inflation adjusted) in 1980 the average price was $396,000 in New

York City and $114,000 in Brussels. What percent did the average price of a two bedroom flat increase in New York City from 1980 to 2004?_____(3)

In Toronto the average price, in real dollars, of a two bedroom flat was $254,000 in 1984. If the average price was $231,000 in 2004 what was the percent decrease in the cost of a two bedroom flat from 1984 to 2004?_____(4)

Answers: (1) 48.4% (the increase, 15 divided by the original amount, 31); (2) (51.9%) (the decrease or difference, 27, divided by the original amount, 52); (3) 112.1%; (4) 9.1%

Increasing or Decreasing the Base

$$P = RB \quad \text{or} \quad \frac{P}{RB}$$

When a problem changes the value of the base, it is always a multiplication problem, after you adjust the rate by adding 100% or subtracting from 100%.

Example 1: 120 increased by 25% is how much?

The base is 100%. It is increased by 25%. The problem could be solved: $120 \times .25 = 30$ and $120 + 30 = 150$. But since all of 120 is 100%, it is easier to mentally add 100% + 25% = 125%, and then $1.25 \times 120 = 150$.

Example 2: 36 decreased by 25% is how much?

The base is 100%. It is decreased by 25%. The problem could be solved: $36 \times .25 = 9$ and $36 - 9 = 27$. But since all of 36 is 100%, it is easier to mentally subtract 100% - 25% = 75%, and then $36 \times .75 = 27$. You may do the subtraction on the calculator as shown on the following tape.

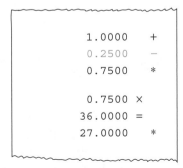

```
   1.0000    +
   0.2500    −
   0.7500    *

   0.7500  ×
  36.0000  =
  27.0000    *
```

6. Use the calculator to find the part after adjusting the rate.

$58.72 increased by 16.2% is how much _____ (1)

$85.32 decreased by 23% is how much? _____ (2)

$437.81 less 5.8% equals what amount? _____ (3)

What is 37.8% more than $589.98? _____ (4)

Answers: (1) $68.23 (Think all of $58.72 plus 16.2% more, or $58.72 × 1.162); (2) $65.70 (Think all of $85.32 less 23%, or $85.32 × .77); (3) $412.42; (4) $812.99

Additional Practice Finding Part, Rate, and Base

In the following practice problems, notice how one "main" formula can be used to find part, rate, and base.

Find 25% of 168. Think $\triangle$ P / RB $\triangle$ Therefore, .25 × 168 = _____(1)

91 is what % of 43? Think $\triangle$ P / RB $\triangle$ Therefore, 91 ÷ 43 = _____(2)

55 increased by 24% is how much? Think $\triangle$ P / RB $\triangle$ Since all of 55 is 100%, 100% plus 24% = 124%, 124% of 55 is the same as 55 × 1.24 = _____(3)

34 decreased by 18% is how much? Think $\triangle$ P / RB $\triangle$ Therefore, all of 34 × (100% − 18%) = 34 × .82 = _____ (4)

81.61 is 16.1% of what number? Think $\triangle$ P / RB $\triangle$ Therefore, 81.61 ÷ .161 = _____(5)

Answers: (1) 42; (2) 211.6%; (3) 68.2; (4) 27.88; (5) 506.894

Hint

The best way to solve these problems is to use the estimating techniques you have learned. Read the problem and ask yourself, should the answer be larger or smaller. That will let you know if you multiply or divide. Even if you goof and arrive at an answer that is not logical, just try the opposite process. Remember to always ask yourself if your answer is reasonable.

REVIEW PROBLEMS

Find 13.2% of $243.28. _____(1)

$87 is what % of $314? _____(2)

$3.14 increased by 15.1% is how much? _____(3)

$79.23 decreased by 11.1% is how much? _____(4)

$92.63 is 17.2% of what number? _____(5)

$401.80 less 8.2% equals what amount? _____(6)

109.7% of $.68 is how much? _____(7)

What is 32.1% of $514.27? _____(8)

$681.42 increased by 5.1% is how much? _____(9)

What is $8,927.15 decreased by 18.3%? _____(10)

Answers: (1) $32.11; (2) 27.7%; (3) $3.61; (4) $70.44; (5) $538.55; (6) $368.85; (7) $.75; (8) $165.08; (9) $716.17; (10) $7,293.48

What is 31.7% of $914.27? _____(11)

$53.97 increased by 32.9% is how much? _____(12)

246.3% of $79.83 is how much? _____(13)

$3,527.32 is what % of $593.81? _____(14)

What is $392.41 less 27.1%? _____(15)

$311.11 is what % of $7,528.37? _____(16)

What is $937.52 decreased by 5.1%? _____(17)

Find 89.3% of $2,721.31. _____(18)

What is 323% of $216.38? _____(19)

$631.83 increased by 31.5% is how much? _____(20)

Answers: (11) $289.82; (12) $71.73; (13) $196.62; (14) 594%; (15) $286.07; (16) 4.1%; (17) $889.71; (18) $2,430.13; (19) $698.91; (20) $830.86

WORD PROBLEMS

Four Steps For Solving Word Problems

Step 1 Read the question carefully and identify what is given and what must be found.

Step 2 Estimate a reasonable answer. This will often let you know what needs to be done to solve the problem—add, subtract, multiply, or divide.

Step 3 Solve the problem.

Step 4 Reread the question. Does the answer make sense? If the answer is reasonable check your work. If not, start over again or ask your instructor for help.

Work the following problems.

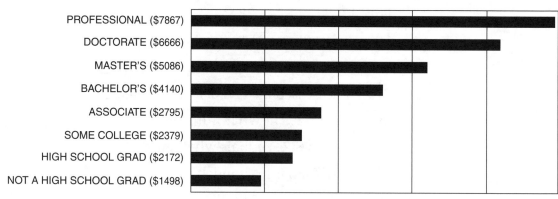

AVERAGE MONTHLY EARNINGS BY EDUCATIONAL LEVEL ACHIEVED
U.S. CENSUS BUREAU DATA, 2000

Using the chart above, what is the percent of increase in average monthly earnings between a high school graduate and a person with a masters degree?

_____(1)

What is the percent of decrease in the average monthly earnings between a person with an associate degree and those who do not have a high school education?

_____(2)

If a day in the hospital cost $36.50 in 1975, how much would a day in the hospital cost today if the price increased 1184 percent?

_____(3)

The consumer price index rose 240.8% in an eleven year period. If the price of a $17.01 blouse increased the same amount, what would the blouse cost at the end of the period?

_____(4)

The first portable PC, Osborne I in 1981, weighed 24 lbs. Many of today's notebook computers weigh about 5 lbs. Find the percent of decrease.

_____(5)

If the price of a new home increased 172% over a ten year period, what would it cost at the end of the period if the price was $84,600 at the beginning of the period?

_____(6)

Americans are delaying marriage. The average age is now 25.0 for women and 26.7 for men. Forty years ago the average age was 20.3 for women and 22.8 for men. Did women or men have the greatest percentage change in the last forty years?

_____(7)

The price of a man's suit was $194 eleven years ago. What would the price be today if the price had increased 127%?

_____(8)

In 1945, when gas was rationed because of World War II, Americans took a record 23.4 billion trips on mass transportation. Trips dropped to 6.5 billion in 1972 and rose to 9.4 billion in 2000. What was the percent of decrease in trips from 1945 to 1972?

_____(9)

Referring to the previous problem, what was the percent of increase in trips from 1972 to 2000?

_____(10)

Answers: (1) 134.2%; (2) 46.4%; (3) $468.66; (4) $57.97; (5) 79.2%; (6) $230,112; (7) Women by 6.1%; (8) $440.38; (9) 72.2%; (10) 44.6%

Constants

A **constant** is a numerical value that remains unchanged during a given problem. It is often used to increase the speed and accuracy of business problems. The function and capability of constants varies widely with different machines. Most business machines have a constant function for use with multiplication and division but are unlikely to have constants directly usable in addition and subtraction. Check with your instructor or your operating manual to find the capability and use of the constant function and storage functions on your machine. It will describe the use of constants and storage and give example problems. Follow the examples carefully.

If your machine has any type of constant, you should be able to do all of the following sample problems without reentering the constant. If your machine has a storage register, be sure to use it for accumulative multiplication and division.

MULTIPLICATION WITH A CONSTANT

On most machines, the constant multiplier is entered first, as in the following example. If your machine does not have an automatic constant, depress the constant key (usually K) first. Index $35.29 only once.

			Key	
			35.29	35.2900 ×
			×	2.0000 =
			2	70.5800 *
$35.29 × 2	=	$70.58	=	4.0000 =
			4	141.1600 *
$35.29 × 4	=	$141.16	=	
			18	18.0000 =
$35.29 × 18	=	$635.22	=	635.2200 *
			427	427.0000 =
$35.29 × 427	=	$15,068.83	=	15,068.8300 *
			2,876	2,876.0000 =
$35.29 × 2,876	=	$101,494.04	=	101,494.0400 *

Accumulative Multiplication With a Constant

While the constant multiplier is entered last on some machines, on most machines it is entered first, as in the previous example. If your machine lacks an automatic constant, depress the *constant* key (usually K); if your machine has automatic accumulative capacity, depress the *accumulator* key before working the following problem, or use the = + or M+ key.

			Key	
			27	27.0000 ×
			×	2.0000 = +
			2	54.0000 *
27 × 2	=	54	= or = +	
			5	5.0000 = +
27 × 5	=	135	= or = +	135.0000 *
			32	
27 × 32	=	864	= or = +	32.0000 = +
			75	864.0000 *
27 × 75	=	2,025	= or = +	
			25.78	75.0000 = +
27 × 25.78 =		696.060	= or = +	2,025.0000 *
Total		= 3,774.060	Recall	
			Accumulation	25.7800 = +
				696.0600 *
				3,774.0600 *

If your machine has automatic accumulator capabilities and you did not get 3,774.060, recheck your work or refer back to the section on accumulative multiplication and division. If your machine has neither automatic accumulator capability nor storage capacity, you can find the total of the products by finding each product separately and then adding them all up.

2,378 × 5 = _____	(1)	3,276 @ $2.12 = _____	(8)
2,378 × 16 = _____	(2)	3,276 @ $.87 = _____	(9)
2,378 × 81 = _____	(3)	3,276 @ $.04 = _____	(10)
2,378 × 132 = _____	(4)	3,276 @ $3.45 = _____	(11)
2,378 × 37 = _____	(5)	3,276 @ $2.75 = _____	(12)
2,378 × 48 = _____	(6)	3,276 @ $.83 = _____	(13)
Total = _____	(7)	Total = _____	(14)

Answers: (1) 11,890; (2) 38,048; (3) 192,618; (4) 313,896; (5) 87,986; (6) 114,144; (7) 758,582; (8) $6,945.12; (9) $2,850.12; (10) $131.04; (11) $11,302.20; (12) $9,009.00; (13) $2,719.08; (14) $32,956.56

DIVISION WITH CONSTANTS

The constant divisor is usually entered last, as in the following example. If your machine does not have an automatic constant, depress the *constant* key (usually K). Index 714 only once.

		Key
		1,428
		÷
		714
$1,428 \div 714 =$	2	=
		4,284
$4,284 \div 714 =$	6	=
		16,422
$16,422 \div 714 =$	23	=
		3,478
$3,478 \div 714 =$	4.871	=
		31,340
$31,340 \div 714 =$	43.894	=

```
   1,428.0000 ÷
     714.0000 =
          2.0000    *

   4,284.0000 =
          6.0000    *

  16,422.0000 =
         23.0000    *

   3,478.0000 =
          4.8711    *

  31,340.0000 =
         43.8936    *
```

Accumulative Division With a Constant

The constant divisor is usually entered last, as in the previous example. If your machine does not have an automatic constant, depress the *constant* key (usually K); if your machine has automatic accumulative capacity, depress the *accumulator* key before working the examples or use the = + or +I key.

		Key
		54
		÷
		27
$54 \div 27$	=	2.000	= or = +
		11
$11 \div 27$	=	.407	= or = +
		897
$897 \div 27$	=	33.222	= or = +
		92.61
$92.61 \div 27$	=	3.430	= or = +
		Recall
Total	=	39.060	Accumulation

```
     54.0000 ÷
     27.0000 = +
      2.0000    *

     11.0000 = +
      0.4074    *

    897.0000 = +
     33.2222    *

     92.6100 = +
      3.4300    *

     39.0596    *
```

If your machine has automatic accumulative capabilities and you did not get 39.060, recheck your work or refer back to the section on accumulative multiplication and division. If your machine has neither automatic accumulative capability nor storage capacity, you can find the sum of the quotients by calculating each quotient separately and then adding them all up.

901 ÷ 3.2057 = _____ (1)   374 ÷ 7.0321 = _____ (8)

37 ÷ 3.2057 = _____ (2)   584 ÷ 7.0321 = _____ (9)

85 ÷ 3.2057 = _____ (3)   581 ÷ 7.0321 = _____ (10)

623 ÷ 3.2057 = _____ (4)   72 ÷ 7.0321 = _____ (11)

871 ÷ 3.2057 = _____ (5)   692 ÷ 7.0321 = _____ (12)

69 ÷ 3.2057 = _____ (6)   84 ÷ 7.0321 = _____ (13)

Total = _____ (7)   Total = _____ (14)

Answers: (1) 281.062; (2) 11.542; (3) 26.515; (4) 194.341; (5) 271.704; (6) 21.524; (7) 806.688; (8) 53.185; (9) 83.048; (10) 82.621; (11) 10.239; (12) 98.406; (13) 11.945; (14) 339.443

ADDITION AND SUBTRACTION WITH MEMORY OR STORAGE

The examples that follows are quite easy and can be worked almost as efficiently without using a constant in memory or storage. However, if constants are large and used numerous times as they sometimes are in business and government using memory or storage definitely increases speed and accuracy. This exercise is designed to help introduce the storage or memory functions of your calculator more than to help you do addition and subtraction more efficiently.

Addition With a Constant Using Storage or Memory

The constant is usually entered into storage or memory and recalled by using the subtotal key each time it is used. Enter 4,986 into storage or memory and do the following examples.

			Key
			4,986 M+
			5
			+
			Memory Recall
			+
5 + 4,986	=	4,991	Total
			1,678
			+
			Memory Recall
			+
1,678 + 4,986	=	6,664	Total
			5,324
			+
			Memory Recall
			+
5,324 + 4,986	=	10,310	Total

```
4,986. M +
    5.   +
4,986. M ◊

4,986.   +
4,991.   *

1,678.   +
4,986. M ◊

4,986.   +
6,664.   *

5,324.   +
4,986. M ◊

4,986.   +
10,310.  *
```

Subtraction With a Constant Using Storage or Memory

As with addition, the constant for subtraction is usually entered into storage or memory and recalled each time it is used. Enter 4,986 into memory and work the following problems.

			Key
			4,986 M+
			5,000
			+
			Memory Recall
			−
5,000 − 4,986	=	14	Total
			8,541
			+
			Memory Recall
			−
8,541 − 4,986	=	3,555	Total
			6,085
			+
			Memory Recall
			−
6,085 − 4,986	=	1,099	Total

```
4,986. M +
5,000.   +
4,986. M ◊

4,986.   −
   14.   *

8,541.   +
4,986. M ◊

4,986.   −
3,555.   *

6,085.   +
4,986. M ◊

4,986.   −
1,099.   *
```

If you understand the examples and know which processes your machine is capable of working with a constant, you should continue. If not, consult your operating manual again or ask your instructor for assistance.

3,781 + 5,271 = _____	(1)	3,892 – 2,495 = _____	(11)
87 + 5,271 = _____	(2)	7,831 – 2,495 = _____	(12)
432 + 5,271 = _____	(3)	8,931 – 2,495 = _____	(13)
8,721 + 5,271 = _____	(4)	8,257 – 2,495 = _____	(14)
945 + 5,271 = _____	(5)	9,481 – 2,495 = _____	(15)
$438.16 + $1,425.25 = _____	(6)	$78.39 – $26.75 = _____	(16)
$21.32 + $1,425.25 = _____	(7)	$93.13 – $26.75 = _____	(17)
$5.78 + $1,425.25 = _____	(8)	$37.65 – $26.75 = _____	(18)
$16.66 + $1,425.25 = _____	(9)	$132.11 – $26.75 = _____	(19)
$77.87 + $1,425.25 = _____	(10)	$161.10 – $26.75 = _____	(20)

Answers: (1) 9,052; (2) 5,358; (3) 5,703; (4) 13,992; (5) 6,216; (6) $1,863.41; (7) $1,446.57; (8) $1,431.03; (9) $1,441.91; (10) $1,503.12; (11) 1,397; (12) 5,336; (13) 6,436; (14) 5,762; (15) 6,986; (16) $51.64; (17) $66.38; (18) $10.90; (19) $105.36; (20) $134.35

REVIEW PROBLEMS (ENTER CONSTANTS ONLY ONCE)

1. Do the following problems on accumulative multiplication with a constant in the most efficient manner possible on your machine.

   21 × 3 = _____ (1)   88 @ $15.12 = _____(7)

   21 × 99 = _____ (2)   88 @ $50.26 = _____(8)

   21 × 436 = _____ (3)   88 @ $94.04 = _____(9)

   21 × 755 = _____ (4)   88 @ $69.77 = _____(10)

   21 × 8,237 = _____ (5)   88 @ $519.26 = _____(11)

   Total = _____ (6)   Total = _____(12)

   Answers: (1) 63; (2) 2,079; (3) 9,156; (4) 15,855; (5) 172,977; (6) 200,130; (7) $1,330.56; (8) $4,422.88; (9) $8,275.52; (10) $6,139.76; (11) $45,694.88; (12) $65,863.60

2. Do the following problems on accumulative division with a constant as efficiently as possible on your machine.

   90 ÷ 45 = _____ (1) $24.49 ÷ 9.83 = _____(7)

   357 ÷ 45 = _____ (2) $95.94 ÷ 9.83 = _____(8)

   11.88 ÷ 45 = _____ (3) $87.19 ÷ 9.83 = _____(9)

   913.4 ÷ 45 = _____ (4) $957.25 ÷ 9.83 = _____(10)

   7,820 ÷ 45 = _____ (5) $878.98 ÷ 9.83 = _____(11)

   Total = _____ (6)   Total = _____(12)

   Answers: (1) 2; (2) 7.933; (3) .264; (4) 20.298; (5) 173.778; (6) 204.273; (7) $2.49; (8) $9.76; (9) $8.87; (10) $97.38; (11) $89.42; (12) $207.92

3. Do the following addition problems in the most efficient manner possible on your machine.

   27 + 3,994 = _____ (1) $69.24 + $119.85 = _____(6)

   68 + 3,994 = _____ (2) $8.89 + $119.85 = _____(7)

   522 + 3,994 = _____ (3) $87.06 + $119.85 = _____(8)

   1,104 + 3,994 = _____ (4) $55.38 + $119.85 = _____(9)

   8,706 + 3,994 = _____ (5) $39.67 + $119.85 = _____(10)

   Answers: (1) 4,021; (2) 4,062; (3) 4,516; (4) 5,098; (5) 12,700; (6) $189.09; (7) $128.74; (8) $206.91; (9) $175.23; (10) $159.52

4. Compute the following problems as efficiently as possible.

86 − 5,775 = _____ (1)	$888.82 − $433.92 = _____ (6)	
6,859 − 5,775 = _____ (2)	$912.84 − $433.92 = _____ (7)	
1,247 − 5,775 = _____ (3)	$803.82 − $433.92 = _____ (8)	
6,101 − 5,775 = _____ (4)	$603.01 − $433.92 = _____ (9)	
8,403 − 5,775 = _____ (5)	$488.32 − $433.92 = _____ (10)	

Answers: (1) −5,689; (2) 1,084; (3) −4,528; (4) 326; (5) 2,628; (6) $454.90; (7) $478.92; (8) $369.90; (9) $169.09; (10) $54.40

Raising a Number to a Power

To raise a number to a power means to multiply the number by itself a certain number of times. Thus 5^4 equals 5 times itself 4 times, or $5 \times 5 \times 5 \times 5$. The process is useful for problems involving volume, statistics, and compound interest, and is simple to perform on most electronic calculators. A common way to raise a number to a power is shown in the next example.

With a Pencil

$$2^5 = 2 \times 2 \times 2 \times 2 \times 2 = 32$$

Key

2
×
=
=
=
=

```
           2. ×
           2. =
           4.      *

           4. =
           8.      *

           8. =
          16.      *

          16. =
          32.      *
```

Hint

When raising a number to a power, your machine obtains intermediate answers. To match the answers in this book, set the decimal at four places and then round your final answer to three places.

1. Using the constant key, raise each of the following numbers to the indicated power.

$5^2 =$ _____ (1) $5^4 =$ _____ (2)

$37^3 =$ _____ (3) $58^2 =$ _____ (4)

$74^3 =$ _____ (5) $1.03^8 =$ _____ (6)

$1.0712^5 =$ _____ (7) $1.003^4 =$ _____ (8)

$49.34^3 =$ _____ (9) $5.3^6 =$ _____ (10)

$2.351^{11} =$ _____ (11) $3.46^{10} =$ _____ (12)

Answers: (1) 25; (2) 625; (3) 50,653; (4) 3,364; (5) 405,224; (6) 1.267; (7) 1.410; (8) 1.012; (9) 120,115.053; (10) 22,164.361; (11) 12,127.655; (12) 245,901.217

The formula for finding the volume of a box is Volume = Height × Width × Length (V = HWL). Since a cube has sides of equal length, the formula for the volume of a cube is Volume = Length of one side cubed ($V = L^3$).

2. Find the volume of the following cubes, given the length of one side.

12 inches _____ (1)   3 feet _____ (2)

7 yards _____ (3)   1 1/8 yards _____ (4)

1 1/2 feet _____ (5)   13 meters _____ (6)

Answers: (1) 1,728 cu in; (2) 27 cu ft; (3) 343 cu yd; (4) 1.424 cu yd; (5) 3.375 cu ft; (6) 2,197 cu m

Mixed Problems Using Storage, or Memory

Do these problems using storage or memory.

$$\frac{17}{(2 \times 34)} =$$

Key
2
×
34
add to storage
17
÷
total from storage
=

```
        2.0000  ×
       34.0000  = +
       68.0000    *

       17.0000  ÷
       68.0000    *

       68.0000  =
        0.2500    *
```

$$\frac{5{,}838}{(17 \times 27 \times 5)} =$$

Key
17
×
27
×
5
add to storage
5,838
÷
total from storage
=

```
        17.0000  ×
        27.0000  ×
         5.0000  =  +
     2,295.0000     *

     5,838.0000  ÷
     2,295.0000     *

     2,295.0000  =
         2.5438     *
```

Hint

When solving mixed problems like those listed above always work the bottom of the equation first and store the results. Then enter the top number and divide by the quantity you stored.

$$\frac{8}{(83 + 14 + 17)} =$$

Key
83
+
14
+
17
+
add to storage if needed
8
÷
total from storage
=

```
        83.0000     +
        14.0000     +
        17.0000     +
         8.0000  ÷
       114.0000     *

       114.0000  =
         0.0702     *
```

1. Solve the following problems without reentering a number.

$$\frac{96}{(7 \times 44)} = \underline{\hspace{6cm}} \quad (1)$$

$$\frac{491}{(22 + 67 - 78)} = \underline{\hspace{6cm}} \quad (2)$$

$$\frac{93}{(4 + 17 + 13)} = \underline{\hspace{6cm}} \quad (3)$$

$$\frac{19}{(39 \times 52)} = \underline{\hspace{6cm}} \quad (4)$$

$$\frac{167}{(67 \times 78)} = \underline{\hspace{5cm}} \quad (5)$$

$$\frac{78}{(17 \times 18 \times 43)} = \underline{\hspace{5cm}} \quad (6)$$

$$\frac{42}{(40 \times 16) + (13 \times 10)} = \underline{\hspace{5cm}} \quad (7)$$

$$\frac{18}{(42 \times 15) - (8 \times 31)} = \underline{\hspace{5cm}} \quad (8)$$

$$\frac{97}{(2 \times 6) + (9 \times 12) + (3 \div 14)} = \underline{\hspace{5cm}} \quad (9)$$

$$\frac{57}{(16 \times 18) + (17 \times 8)} = \underline{\hspace{5cm}} \quad (10)$$

Answers: (1) .312; (2) 44.636; (3) 2.735; (4) .009; (5) .032; (6) .006; (7) .055; (8) .047; (9) .807; (10) .134

2. A customer was billed $1,204.67 for carpeting three rooms that measured 9' × 14', 22' × 15', and 21' × 18'. What was the average price per yard?

$$\frac{\$1,204.67}{[(9 \times 14) + (22 \times 15) + (21 \times 18)]} \times 9 \text{ square feet per yard}$$

Answer: $13 per square yard of carpet. (Work the bottom first, store, enter $1,204.67, divide by what you stored and multiply by 9.)

Hint

It should be worthwhile at this point to review the operating manual for your machine to learn the specific capabilities of your machine that you are unfamilar with before proceeding to Chapter 5.

Stop

You are now ready to take Pretest IV, a 15-minute test of your skill in performing certain special functions on a calculator.

If your machine has accumulative capacity and a constant key, you should be able to complete correctly at least 15 of the 25 problems on the test and get better than 90 percent of all the problems you attempt. Unless instructed otherwise, turn in your *calculator tape* and Pretest for correction and review before taking Test IV.

If your machine does not have accumulative capacity or a constant key, simply be certain you understand the problems on Pretest IV before proceeding to **Test IV.** The test may take you longer than 15 minutes.

Hint

Remember the rules for rounding. Since this test has intermediate answers, set your decimal at four places.

Pretest IV

SPECIAL FUNCTIONS AND OPERATIONS WITH AN ELECTRONIC CALCULATOR

15 minutes

Turn in your calculator tape with this test. This test must be worked in sequence using the special features on your machine. If a problem is skipped or if special features are not used correctly that problem will count as an error! You need 90 percent accuracy and at least 15 problems correct to pass.

Compute the following accumulative problems.

(1) $(37 \times 77) + (39 \times 43) + (19 \times 76) + (73 \times 77) =$ _____

(2) $(13.9 \div 8.89) + (1.051 \div .247) + (35.8 \div 7.9) + (3.27 \div .987) =$ _____

Combine the following fractions.

(3)	4/7	(4)	25 2/7	(5)	54 1/7	(6)	277 5/7
	4/5		2 4/9		−8 1/6		−80 7/9
	1/6		3 2/3				
	3/8		25 1/6				
	5/9		13 7/8				

Multiply the following problems.

(7) $7/8 \times 5/31 =$ _____   (8) $9/34 \times 7/52 =$ _____

Divide the following fractions.

(9) $5/6 \div 3/7 =$ _____   (10) $5/24 \div 3/8 =$ _____

Solve the following accumulative problems using constants.

(11)	147 @ $.88	(12)	$27.13 ÷ 1.37
	75 @ .88		$184.75 ÷ 1.37
	192 @ .88		$98.75 ÷ 1.37
	37 @ .88		$874.32 ÷ 1.37
	128 @ .88		$14.78 ÷ 1.37

Raise the following numbers to the indicated power.

(13) $1.7034^5 = $ _____

(14) $1.004^7 = $ _____

Solve the following problems.

(15) $\dfrac{93}{75 + 17 + 81} = $ _____

(16) $\dfrac{\$79.83}{(9 \times 4) + (13 \times 8) - (8 \times 7)} = $ _____

(17) What is 125% of $374? _____

(18) $75 is 5 1/2% of what amount? _____

(19) $132 is what percent of $348? _____

(20) $401.25 less 15% equals what amount? _____

Addition and Subtraction Using Memory or Storage.

(21) $6.27 + $191.38 _____

$7.37 + $191.38 _____

$1.54 + $191.38 _____

$.58 + $191.38 _____

$8.79 + $191.38 _____

(22) $87.14 − $13.71 _____

$57.13 − $13.71 _____

$71.27 − $13.71 _____

$75.00 − $13.71 _____

$55.13 − $13.71 _____

Perform the indicated operations.

(23) $(2.83 \div .9) - (27.4 \times 3.1) + (8.97 \times 94.7) - (38.4 \div 871) = $ _____

(24) $1/7 + 3/4 + 3/8 - 7/8 + 1/3 - 2/5 = $ _____

(25) $\dfrac{\$120.45}{(75 \times 27) + (7 \div 31)} = $ _____

Additional Practice for Developing Touch Control, Speed, and Accuracy With a Calculator

The following problems should help improve your touch control. Work as fast as possible while maintaining accuracy. Use correct finger placement. Operate the keys without looking. (After completing these exercises you might want to retake Test IB; you may be surprised at the improvement.)

PROGRESSIVE ADDITION

(1)		(2)		(3)		(4)		(5)	
	45		54		65		454		456
	66		44		54		546		544
	54		56		44		444		556
	46		65		54		465		554
	56		44		44		565		665
	44		45		54		464		555
	46		54		65		656		454
	45		45		46		566		554
	64		64		45		455		654
	54		56		56		646		554

(6)		(7)		(8)		(9)		(10)	
	54		52		52		321		266
	55		45		25		654		432
	52		25		52		245		333
	41		14		61		354		111
	53		43		36		131		256
	36		41		14		414		435
	14		54		53		254		626
	25		52		35		363		644
	63		63		36		143		563
	41		14		51		241		456

(11)	(12)	(13)	(14)	(15)
213	313	512	5,423	3,223
313	323	351	2,345	3,442
414	516	462	6,123	5,353
151	342	132	2,534	6,364
161	231	321	2,135	1,515
212	145	256	5,124	2,525
322	346	625	3,514	3,132
543	343	613	5,621	4,252
123	526	321	5,236	4,454
343	624	543	5,342	5,646

Answer: (1) 520; (2) 527; (3) 527; (4) 5,261; (5) 5,546; (6) 434; (7) 403; (8) 415; (9) 3,120; (10) 4,122; (11) 2,795; (12) 3,709; (13) 4,136; (14) 43,397; (15) 39,906

PROGRESSIVE ADDITION

(1)	(2)	(3)	(4)	(5)
45	24	66	747	699
55	35	55	848	588
66	61	44	949	677
64	35	74	789	876
45	24	74	987	549
44	36	84	876	854
46	41	94	797	549
45	15	57	849	947
44	16	76	946	876
55	42	69	875	945

(6)	(7)	(8)	(9)	(10)
10	35	43	422	800
85	52	96	479	213
82	97	89	588	500
20	81	27	629	486
51	20	24	760	527
30	43	32	657	380
83	79	64	891	406
92	26	78	208	895
76	60	91	696	472
90	37	10	704	202

(11)	(12)	(13)	(14)	(15)
201	541	347	8,040	5,091
689	811	639	5,060	8,342
513	219	768	1,080	6,070
485	578	587	7,071	1,008
821	436	922	1,401	5,102
406	420	204	1,008	6,809
816	680	624	8,020	3,037
706	207	955	5,840	2,104
596	621	703	9,008	5,101
708	433	426	4,001	9,300

Answers: (1) 509; (2) 329; (3) 693; (4) 8,663; (5) 7,560; (6) 619; (7) 530; (8) 554; (9) 6,034; (10) 4,881; (11) 5,941; (12) 4,946; (13) 6,175; (14) 50,529; (15) 51,964

ADDING DOLLARS AND CENTS

Hint

To increase your speed when adding a column of dollars and cents, do not index the decimal. However, if your calculator is equipped with an "adding machine" decimal setting, you may want to use it to automatically set the decimal at 2 places so you do not have to index it.

(1)	$3.06	(2)	$7.82	(3)	$7.99	(4)	$5.67	(5)	$3.34
	9.10		5.00		9.88		8.44		5.30
	4.74		4.63		6.56		3.13		6.31
	7.47		6.20		2.14		6.34		4.33
	3.43		8.00		3.76		9.49		5.30
	2.19		2.43		5.01		5.67		2.91
	5.58		1.62		5.75		3.56		9.43
	4.02		3.21		6.50		9.08		7.07
	3.33		2.64		3.50		5.19		1.12
	5.31		3.85		5.99		3.12		7.21

(6)	$6.42	(7)	$9.36	(8)	$7.58	(9)	$7.14	(10)	$1.16
	7.12		5.78		4.62		6.20		2.25
	9.72		8.63		7.97		2.88		3.34
	1.63		4.87		1.22		9.74		4.11
	7.53		3.24		9.52		7.82		5.63
	2.71		3.36		6.09		5.04		6.03
	9.46		9.51		8.43		6.74		7.97
	2.03		2.68		3.91		9.12		8.54
	4.00		2.36		5.94		8.94		9.01
	3.12		6.66		6.41		6.05		1.00

(11)	$11.26	(12)	$25.43	(13)	$29.25	(14)	$265.54	(15)	$885.30
	58.12		12.11		79.99		371.98		655.62
	40.32		68.06		81.13		701.77		140.02
	87.21		10.97		49.33		780.36		344.03
	93.98		43.93		40.55		222.10		321.92
	56.76		93.62		17.92		637.43		972.85
	70.49		34.47		84.79		213.19		604.37
	32.52		19.82		88.96		519.84		275.48
	10.01		58.19		92.36		967.53		343.81
	23.45		60.13		14.97		776.50		528.91

Answers: (1) $48.23; (2) $45.40; (3) $57.08; (4) $59.69; (5) $52.32; (6) $53.74; (7) $56.45; (8) $61.69; (9) $69.67; (10) $49.04; (11) $484.12; (12) $426.73; (13) $579.25; (14) $5,456.24; (15) $5,072.31

MIXED PRACTICE

(1) $581.43	(2) $758.18	(3) $918.84	(4) $785.14	(5) $389.55
654.59	207.91	137.98	813.33	851.24
18.27	248.21	757.86	815.95	826.70
432.81	543.54	504.61	616.36	502.34
178.62	84.50	208.66	705.83	934.81

(6) 3,214	(7) 8,832	(8) 7,284	(9) 3,481	(10) 1,374
−984	−941	−596	−792	−587

(11) 426	(12) 5,270	(13) 287	(14) 8,152	(15) 2,414
2,716	6,881	3,111	7,184	5,263
5,184	6,778	4,552	1,381	1,591
1,109	2,288	2,669	2,661	3,020
8,004	2,743	511	671	6,070
3,358	4,650	2,344	6,080	9,982
644	1,744	8,010	5,098	4,742
9,191	9,616	4,295	4,782	3,000
5,087	9,782	3,827	1,325	4,050
4,807	5,004	5,944	5,784	4,263

(16) $806 + 390 - 471 - 827 + 432 =$ _____

(17) $177 - 431 + 524 - 821 + 873 =$ _____

(18) $76.728 + 209 - 12,431 + 4.91 =$ _____

(19) $8,241 + 61.58 - 3.255 + .1678 =$ _____

(20) $67.54 - 7.351 + .4728 - 762.8 =$ _____

Answers: (1) $1,865.72; (2) $1,842.34; (3) $2,527.95; (4) $3,736.61; (5) $3,504.64; (6) 2,230; (7) 7,891; (8) 6,688; (9) 2,689; (10) 787; (11) 40,526; (12) 54,756; (13) 35,550; (14) 43,118; (15) 44,395; (16) 330; (17) 322; (18) −12,140.362; (19) 8,299.493; (20) −702.138

CHAPTER 5

Introducing the Metric System

LEARNING GOALS

After completing this chapter, you should know:

- Why the metric system is important
- The standard metric units for length, weight, volume, and temperature
- The standard metric prefixes
- Relate metric measurements to familiar items

You also will show your ability to "think metric" by completing a 25-question test with at least 90 percent accuracy.

The speech bubble reads: "IF IT'S FARENHEIT HE'S O.K. IF IT'S CELSIUS HE IS TOTALLY FRIED."

This chapter will introduce you to the metric system of measurement and help you "think metric." It will not ask you to memorize conversion factors for finding metric equivalents nor will it teach you all of the specialized vocabulary of SI (Systeme International) metric.

The Metric System

Since 1993 metric specifications have been required for U.S. government construction projects: General Services Administration, the Pentagon, Department of Veterans Affairs and others. Contractors who deal with the government need to know metric. The United States, however, is moving slowly to metric. President Gerald Ford signed the Metric Conversion Act of 1975 on December 8, 1975. Since then, many industries such as Ford Motor Co. and General Motors have made major movements to metric. Some highway signs show distance in both miles and kilometers. Pharmacists use metric measurements. Weather forecasters sometimes report a warm sunny day as 20° Celsius (SELL-sea-us). Wine and soda pop sell by the liter; so does gasoline. Starting February 14, 1994 a Federal Trade Commission regulation began requiring all consumer packaging labels to list metric measurements in addition to feet, pounds or gallons.

Why Metric?

We in America cherish freedom, and the push for metric is not by government decree. The United States is moving toward metric because of economic necessity. With 5% of the world's population, we do about 20% of the world's commerce; but, that means the rest of the world, which is metric, has 95% of the population and does 80% of the world's commerce. A common language of measurement is needed by scientists, engineers, business people, educators, and government officials to communicate more freely and with less misunderstanding. We truly are a nation isolated in a world that is metric.

United States' dependence on world trade necessitates accommodation with the metric system. For example, the U.S. Office of Emergency Preparedness designated 72 materials and commodities as vital, of which 69 must be imported in whole or in part. Although the names of many of these raw materials, such as columbite, manganese, and bauxite, are not everyday household words, the products manufactured from them are: braces for teeth, autos, and auto fuel, washing machines and dryers, TV sets, drilling rigs, earth-moving equipment, aircraft, telephones, and on and on. Other items that we are almost entirely dependent on other countries for include: bananas, cocoa, coffee, spices, tea, raw silk, nickel, tin, natural rubber and diamonds.

History

The metric system should not be all that foreign to us. America first considered going metric in 1816 when President James Madison reminded Congress of a need for uniform weights and measures. In 1866, Congress recognized the metric system as valid for "contracts, dealings, or other court proceedings." Since 1892, it has actually served as the basis for all United States standards of measurement: our customary units of length and mass are defined as fractions of metric units. For example, an inch is officially 25.4 millimeters.

The English system of measurement that we have been using evolved over thousands of years and had its origin in the civilizations of Babylonia, Egypt, Rome, the Anglo-Saxons, and the Norman French. Rome contributed inches and the base 12. Our 12-inch foot comes from the Roman "pes," meaning foot. The word "yard" can be traced back to the Saxon word "gird," meaning the circumference of a person's waist. Early Saxon kings wore a sash or girdle around the waist that could be removed and used as a convenient measuring device. Tradition also holds that King Henry I of England decreed that a yard should be the distance from the tip of his nose to the end of his thumb. The length of a furlong (or "furrow long") was established by an early Tudor ruler as 220 yards. This led Queen Elizabeth I in the 16th century to replace the traditional Roman mile of 4,000 feet with one of 5,280 feet, making a mile exactly 8 furlongs and providing a convenient relationship between two measures previously awkwardly related.

England by the 18th century had achieved, through royal edicts, a greater degree of standardization than the continental countries of Europe. English units had developed to meet the needs of commerce. England's colonization and dominance of world commerce during the 17th, 18th, and 19th centuries spread the English system of weights and measures to many parts of the world, including America.

By contrast, a French commission in 1790 created the metric system of measurement, at once simple and scientific. It did not evolve, it was planned. The unit of length was made a fraction of the earth's circumference. (For scientists, it is now defined as 1,650,763.73 wavelengths in a vacuum of the orange-red line of the light spectrum of Krypton-86.) Measures of capacity (volume) and mass (weight) were derived from the unit of length, thus relating the basic units of the metric system to each other as well as to nature.

Although the metric system was first accepted by the French without enthusiasm, other nations have steadily adopted it. France made its use compulsory in 1840. Its standardized character and decimal features made it well suited to science and engineering. In 1875, the Metric Convention set up well-defined metric standards for length and mass and established permanent machinery to recommend and adopt further refinements. This "Treaty of the Meter" was signed by 17 countries, including the United States. By 1900, 35 nations had officially accepted the metric system. In 1965, Great Britain started conversion to metric. It had success in industry and education, but encountered problems in the consumer field. New Zealand and Australia started their shift to metric in 1970 and by 1973 were ahead of England in consumer acceptance. Canada, too, is metric. Today, with the exception of the United States and a few small countries, the world uses the metric system. The result is that our outmoded system of measurement creates problems not only in foreign trade, but in education, engineering, and other areas.

Benefits

There are numerous gains from going metric, especially in the export of goods manufactured to metric standards. Since metric countries give preference to the metric-designed products, foreign consumers who prefer a certain American product might not buy it unless standard parts for repair and maintenance are available in their country. There are substantial savings, both here and abroad, in using metric standards for American-made goods:

- Fewer jobs will be exported. American companies that manufacture for foreign markets have found it advantageous to build where they can employ workers who know the metric system.
- The compatibility and interchangeability of military equipment between the United States and its allies will expedite repairs, make possible mutual military support in areas where such support has been unavailable, and simplify procurement across national boundaries.
- We could see a great reduction in the number of sizes of products, such as fasteners (bolts, nuts, etc.)., spark plugs, electric motors, and bearings.
- Scarce resources can be better utilized by reducing inventories.
- Money can be saved by producing larger quantities in each size.
- International standards are a must if nations are to cooperate in space travel (for instance, hatches and docking equipment must be uniform).
- Perhaps most important, a standard system of measurement will improve communication and enhance international relations.

Metric and the Current System Compared

To know metric is to love it. Once learned, the metric system is actually much simpler and more logical than the current conglomeration of inches, feet, yards, ounces, pounds, quarts, and so on. Surveys show that a large majority of people who understand metric are in favor of the change, while many of those who do not understand metric are opposed.

Under our current system, we must divide feet by 12 (or yards by 36) to get inches, and pounds by 16 (or quarts by 32) to get ounces. By contrast, much of the metric system is based on a single unit. For example, the standard unit of length is the meter (a little over a yard). And there is a simple relationship between the linear meter and the metric units of weight and volume. The standard unit of weight, the gram, is the weight of a volume of water measuring one centimeter (one hundredth of a meter) on a side (one cubic centimeter). The standard unit of volume, the liter (a little more than a quart), is the volume of a cube 10 centimeters on a side or 1,000 cubic centimeters.

Metric and the Decimal System

The metric system is a decimal system, meaning it's based on the number 10. Thus, one meter divided by 100 and 1,000 gives centimeters and millimeters, respectively, and multiplied by 1,000 it gives kilometers.

The decimal system may appear different, but it is not unfamiliar. At its founding, the United States pioneered the adoption of a decimal system for its money—in which currency denominations are related by tens. (Ten pennies equals one dime and one hundred pennies equals one dollar.) All other nations of the world have since followed our lead, with Great Britain the last to adopt a decimal monetary system. Now we find it advantageous to follow the rest of the world in adopting the decimal metric system of measurement.

As we change to the metric system, several current units of measure will remain unchanged. Time will continue to be measured in hours, minutes, and seconds; electricity in watts; and light from a light bulb in lumens.

Learning the Metric System

The metric system is easy to learn. It also reduces the need for troublesome skills for dealing with feet, inches, pounds, and ounces, such as finding the lowest common denominator, reducing improper fractions, adding mixed numbers, and reducing fractions to their lowest terms. Since, currently, almost one classroom hour of every five spent on elementary math focuses on learning these skills, think of the savings in student effort, time, and money. And this doesn't count remedial and review work in junior high, high school, and college.

This section will teach the most common units of the metric system by using the term in a practical context. With practice, you will be able to think metric even better than you have been able to think in the archaic system of inches, pounds, quarts and so on. You will also be able to conceptualize distances, volumes, weights, and temperature.

The speedometer in Figure 5-1 shows the use of both systems.

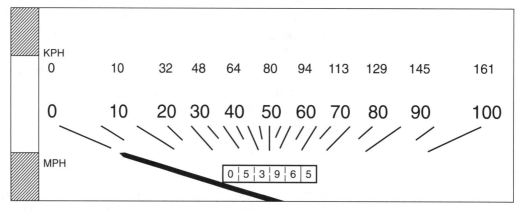

Figure 5-1.

The small numbers at the top are kilometers per hour, the larger numbers are miles per hour. As you can see, 50 miles per hour is about the same as 80 kilometers per hour. Both show how fast we are going; however, since we think in terms of miles (speed limits are posted in miles per hour and distances in miles), miles-per-hour means more to us. Speeds posted in kilometers per hour and distances in kilometers would be just as easy to use.

The metric system will clearly make conversions easier. We can see this if we equate miles to other measures of distance. One mile is 320 rods, 1,760 yards, 5,280 feet, or 63,360 inches—all cumbersome and somewhat difficult to relate one to the other. A kilometer equals 1,000 meters or 100,000 centimeters—easy to convert and relate to each other. Calculations involving weight are also simpler with metric units. Take the following example.

How many pounds of apples are there in three boxes, one containing 48 lbs., 14 oz., one containing 31 lbs., 15 oz., and one containing 37 lbs., 7 oz.?

(1) Add the pounds: 48 lbs. + 31 lbs. + 37 lbs. = 116 lbs.

(2) Add the ounces: 14 oz. + 15 oz. + 7 oz. = 36 oz.

(3) Convert ounces to pounds and ounces: 36 ÷ 16 = 2 lbs., 4 oz.

(4) Add: 116 lbs. + 2 lbs. + 4 oz. = 118 lbs., 4 oz.

In the metric system, the problem would be:

How many kilograms of apples are there in three boxes, one containing 14.67 kg, one containing 22.14 kg, and one containing 16.96 kg?

Simply add: 14.67 kg + 22.14 kg + 16.96 kg = 53.77 kg

1. Judging by the previous two examples, which method is easier, the metric system or our current system?

   Answer: The metric system is easier. It took only one step while adding pounds and ounces took four.

2. Liquid measures are another example. Which of the following problems is easier, (a) or (b)?

(a)	1 gallon		11 oz.	(b)	4.100 liters
	3 quarts		14 oz.		+ 3.252 liters
		1 pint	15 oz.		+ .916 liters
	2 gallons	1 pint	8 oz.		8.268 liters

Answer: b. Is it any wonder pharmacists are using metric instead of gallons, quarts, pints, gills, fluidounces, fluidrams, and minims? (60 min = 1 fl dr, 8 fl dr = 1 fl oz, 4 fl oz = 1 gi, 4 gi = 1 pt, 2 pt = 1 qt, 4 qt = 1 gal)

Why is the metric system so much simpler? It uses the decimal system, that is, it's based on multiples of ten. Our currency is a decimal system (a dime is one-tenth of a dollar, a penny one-hundredth of a dollar) and you already know how simple it is.

Metric Units

All physical entities have properties that can be measured: matter or mass, extent in space (length), duration in time, energy, temperature, color, and electrical charge. These properties have many units to measure them: tons, pounds, grain, grams, chains, paces, furlongs, feet, meters, moons, days, hours, BTUs, calories, Fahrenheit, Celsius, and so forth. A measuring system need meet only two conditions, consistency and convenience. The metric system meets these conditions better than the system we have been using.

Metric is based on Decimal system

The metric system is simple to learn. To use the metric system in your everyday life you will need only a few new units. You will also need to get familiar with a few new temperatures. There are even some metric units with which you are already familiar: those for time and electricity are the same as you use now.

BASIC UNITS

METER: a little longer than a yard (about 1.1 yards)

LITER: a little larger than a quart (about 1.06 quarts)

GRAM: a little more than the weight of a paper clip

(comparative sizes are shown)

1 METER

1 YARD

25 DEGREES FAHRENHEIT

COMMON PREFIXES
(to be used with basic units)

milli: one-thousandth (0.001)
centi: one-hundredth (0.01)
kilo: one-thousand times (1000)

For example:
1000 millimeters = 1 meter
100 centimeters = 1 meter
1000 meters = 1 kilometer

1 LITER   1 QUART

MILK   MILK

25 DEGREES CELSIUS

OTHER COMMONLY USED UNITS

millimeter:	0.001 meter	diameter of paper clip wire
centimeter:	0.01 meter	a little more than the width of a paper clip (about 0.4 inch)
kilometer:	1000 meters	somewhat further than ½ mile (about 0.6 mile)
kilogram:	1000 grams	a little more than 2 pounds (about 2.2 pounds)
milliliter:	0.001 liter	five of them make a teaspoon

1 KILOGRAM   1 POUND

OTHER USEFUL UNITS
hectare: about 2 ½ acres
tonne: about one ton

TEMPERATURE
degrees Celsius are used

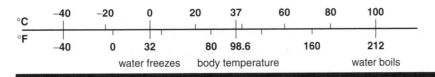

°C	−40	−20	0	20	37	60	80	100
°F	−40	0	32	80	98.6		160	212

water freezes   body temperature   water boils

In 1960, representatives of most of the important international scientific organizations adopted a simplified form of the metric system for use throughout the world. This system, which was reaffirmed in 1964, 1968, and 1971, is called **Systeme International d'Units**, which translates as **International System of Units** and which is abbreviated **SI**. Since many of these units are used only in highly technical fields, you need not learn them all; however, a list of all the SI metric units can be found in most libraries.

The chart on page 189 (from the U.S. Bureau of Standards) shows that you need to know only four basic metric units. This is all we will concentrate on. The four basic metric units are:

Physical Property	Unit of Measure	Symbol
length	meter	m
mass or weight	gram	g
volume	liter	l
temperature	degrees Celsius	°C

3. In the following list, match the descriptions with one of the following units: *meter, gram, liter, 0° Celsius*. Use the symbol for the unit rather than its full name

(a)_____ a little larger than a quart

(b)_____ a little longer than a yard

(c)_____ about the weight of a paper clip

(d)_____ temperature at which water freezes

Answers: (a) l; (b) m; (c) g; (d) 0°C

We use different units for different distances, the distance between Seattle, Washington, and Boise, Idaho, is 505 miles; the length of a desk might be 4 ft. 7 in.; the length of a pencil is 4 $\frac{1}{8}$ in. We could measure all distances in miles, but then your little finger would measure .000047 miles. It is for convenience that we use different units to express different measurements. In the system we now use, however, the units require cumbersome conversions. For example:

12 inches = 1 foot
3 feet = 1 yard
1,760 yards = 1 mile

16 drams = 1 ounce
16 ounces = 1 pound
2,000 pounds = 1 short ton

4. Conversions are not only difficult to make, but they are easy to forget. Many people must consult a guide for all but the ones they use every day. For example:

(a) How many items are there in a gross? _____

(b) How many fluid ounces are in a pint? _____

(c) How many feet make a mile? _____

(d) How many quarts fill a bushel?_____

Answers: (1) 144, or 12 dozen; (b) 16 fl oz; (c) 5,280 ft; (d) 32 quarts. (If you answered all four correctly, you are well above average.)

In the metric system, we use the same basic units but change the prefix. To make it easier, each prefix is a multiple of 10. Eight common prefixes are:

Prefix	Meaning	Prefix	Meaning
micro- (MI-kro)	one millionth of (0.000001)	deca- (DEK-a)	ten times (10)
milli- (MILL-e)	one thousandth of (0.001)	hecto- (HEK-te)	a hundred times (100)
centi- (SENT-e)	one hundredth of (0.01)	kilo- (KIL-e)	a thousand times(1,000)
deci- (DES-e)	one tenth of (0.1)	mega- (MEG-a)	a million times (1,000,000)

The three most common prefixes are kilo, centi, and milli. Be certain to memorize these symbols.

5. Change each of the following measures to their basic unit; for example, 1 kilometer = 1,000 meters.

(a) 1 milliliter = _____   (b) 1 centimeter = _____

(c) 1 kilogram = _____   (d) 1 millimeter = _____

Answers: (a) .001 liter; (b) .01 meter; (c) 1,000 grams; (d) .001 meter

6. Name the following prefixes:

(a) .001 = _____   (b) 1,000 times = _____

(c) .01 = _____

Answers: (a) milli-; (b) kilo-; (c) centi-. (That is all you need to memorize to effectively use metric.)

7. Use prefixes to rewrite the following (for example, .001 of a meter equals a millimeter):

(a) 1,000 meters equals a _____.

(b) .01 meter equals a _____.

(c) 1,000 grams equals a _____.

(d) .001 liter equals a _____.

Answers: (a) kilometer; (b) centimeter; (c) kilogram; (d) milliliter

Metric Symbols

Metric prefix symbols are really very simple. Note in the table that follows that each symbol is the first letter of the prefix—except micro-, for which the Greek letter m (μ) is the symbol. Capital M is the symbol for mega-, to distinguish it from milli- and micro-.

Prefix	Symbol	Meaning
mega-	M	a million times
kilo-	k	a thousand times
hecto-	h	a hundred times
deca-	D	ten times
deci-	d	one tenth of
centi-	c	one hundredth of
milli-	m	one thousandth of
micro-	μ	one millionth of

Symbols for the basic metric units also are very easy. As shown in the following table they are simply the first letter of the unit.

Unit	Symbol
meter	m
gram	g
liter	l

8. Complete the following list.

   (a) 25 kilometers = 25 km   (b) 31 milliliters = 31 ml

   (c) 16 hectograms = _____   (d) 14 centimeters = _____

   (e) 7 kilograms = _____

   Answers: (c) 16 hg; (d) 14 cm; (e) 7 kg

9. Use abbreviations to complete the following list.

   (a) 5 decigrams = 5 dg   (b) 7 micrometers = _____

   (c) 3 millimeters = _____   (d) 14 megagrams = _____

   (e) 9 centiliters = _____   (f) 13 kilograms = _____

   (g) 11 kilometers = _____   (h) 4 centiliters = _____

   Answers: (b) 7 μm; (c) 3 mm; (d) 14 Mg; (e) 9 cl; (f) 13 kg; (g) 11 km; (h) 4 cl

Measuring Distance and Speed

Once the metric system is fully adopted, all speed limits will be designated in kilometers per hour (km/h); measurements of bolts, service tools, and ammunition will be in millimeters; measurements of carpet and tile, in square meters or square centimeters; and the width and length of a building, in meters.

For the lay person, small distances are normally expressed in centimeters; in scientific or engineering work, however, the millimeter and the meter in decimal form are the most frequent units of measure. Small distances are easy to relate to, for example, parts of the body. A very popular size for men's jeans is 32×32 or $80 \text{ cm} \times 80 \text{ cm}$.

Figure 5-2.

Use the ruler in Figure 5-2 for the following measurement problems.

10. Measure the width of your pencil or pen. It is _____ m, _____ cm, or _____ mm.

    Answers: .007m; .7 cm; 7 mm

11. What is the distance from the first joint of your index finger to the second joint? _____ cm

    Answer: about 3 cm (Some people say this was the origin of the inch.)

12. What is the width of your hand in centimeters? _____ cm. In millimeters? _____ mm

    Answers: about 8 centimeters; about 80 millimeters

13. If a man's height is 6 feet, he is just over 180 centimeters tall; about how tall are you in centimeters? (1 inch equals 2.54 cm) _____

    Answers: 5' = 153 cm; 5'2" = 157 cm; 5'4" = 163 cm; 5'6" = 168 cm; 5'8" = 173 cm; 5'10" = 178 cm; 6' = 183 cm; 6'2" = 188 cm; 6'4" = 193 cm

14. What is the width of the tip of your little finger or the width of a fingernail? _____

    Answer: about 10 mm

Distance is often translated into time, as when we ask how long it takes to get somewhere. For instance, the 463 km from Spokane, Washington to Seattle, Washington, can be thought of as a little less than 5 hours. That is, driving 463 km at the legal speed limit of about 100 km/h would take 463 km ÷ 100 km/h = 4.63 hours.

Study the following table of speeds of everyday activities.

Activity	Speed (km/h)	Activity	Speed (km/h)
Walking	5	Jogging	10
Bicycling	20	Highway Driving	100
City Driving	50	High-speed Train	150
Airliner	1,000		

Table 5-1

Highway Distance Between U.S. Cities (in kilometers)

	Atlanta GA	Boston MA	Chicago IL	Dallas TX	Los Angeles CA	Miami FL	New York NY	Seattle WA	Washington DC
Atlanta GA	-------	1728	1175	1320	3565	1073	1387	4330	1025
Boston MA	1728	------	1600	2931	4896	2482	348	4867	703
Chicago IL	1175	1600	------	1508	3367	2211	1352	3307	1146
Dallas TX	1320	2931	1508	------	2261	2106	2583	3426	2227
Denver CO	2271	3214	1630	1262	1862	3338	3003	2184	2752
Los Angeles CA	3565	4896	3367	2261	------	4398	4501	1883	4263
Miami FL	1073	2482	2211	2106	4398	------	2150	5477	1777
New York NY	1387	348	1352	2583	4501	2150	-------	4649	369
Seattle WA	4330	4867	3307	3426	1883	5477	4649	-------	4405
Spokane WA	3867	4564	2844	3034	2005	5077	4176	463	3941
Washington DC	1025	703	1146	2227	4263	1777	369	4405	------

15. Match the activities in column one with an appropriate speed from column two.

 (a) Hiking in Yellowstone Park _____ 25 km/h

 (b) Flying in a Piper Cub _____ 135 km/h

 (c) Driving in a school zone _____ 5 km/h

 (d) Driving over the maximum speed limit _____ 200 km/h

Answers: (a) 5 km/h; (b) 200 km/h; (c) 25 km/h; (d) 135 km/h

16. Estimate the time it would take to do the following:

 (a) Hike 20 km _____

 (b) Jog 5 km _____

 (c) Drive from Boston to Seattle, averaging 80 km/h (see Table 5-1) _____

 (d) Drive from Chicago to Boston, averaging 80 km/h (see Table 5-1) _____

Answers: (a) 4 hours; (b) 30 minutes; (c) about 60 hours; (d) 20 hours

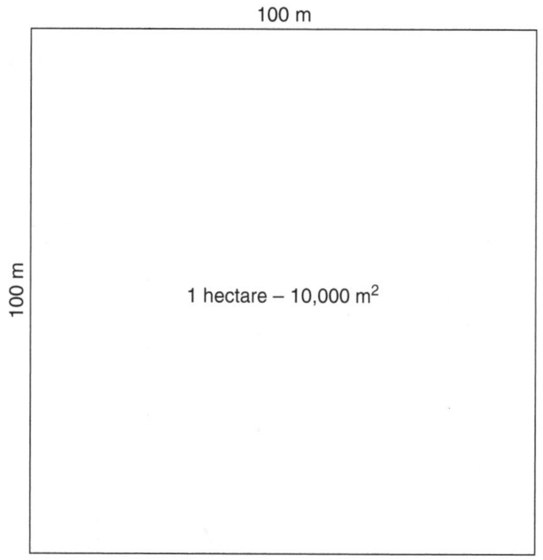

Figure 5-3.

Land Area

The basic metric unit of land area is an **are** (pronounced AIR), which is 10 m on a side, or 100 m². Metric real estate, however, is usually sold in **hectares** (100 ares), which is 100 m on a side, or 10,000 m² (see Figure 5-3). One hectare is 2.5 acres. A large suburban lot (about 1/2 acre) is about 0.2 hectare.

17. If a city block in Columbia, South Carolina, is 100 meters long, its area is _____ hectare.

Answer: one

18. If a city block in New York City is 50 m by 50 m, its area is _____ hectares.

Answer: 0.25

19. If a farm is 1,000 m by 2,590 m, it is _____ hectares.

Answer: 259 (about one section of land, or 640 acres)

Mass and Weight

Weight is the result of the pull of gravity. You weigh less on a mountaintop than at sea level because things weigh less when they are farther from the center of the earth. You would weigh even less in space or on the moon, where gravitational pull is even lower. Your **mass** (or matter), however, is the same whether at sea level, on a mountaintop, or on the moon. This is because, no matter where you are when you are weighed, there is still the same amount of you.

The distinction between weight and mass is important in science, but for ordinary business purposes, we estimate the mass of an object by weighing it. The four metric units of mass, then, can be thought of as units of weight; the **milligram** (mg), the **gram** (g), the **kilogram** (kg), and the **metric ton**.

Small Weights

When we convert to metric, small quantities of something like candy will be weighed in grams instead of ounces. For example, 9 ounces of gum drops will be sold as 250 grams.

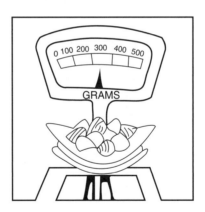

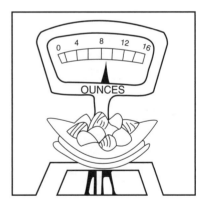

Larger Weights

The purchase of large items, such as meat, will be figured in kilograms rather than pounds. In the example shown, instead of buying a 4.5-pound roast, we will be getting one weighing 2 kilograms.

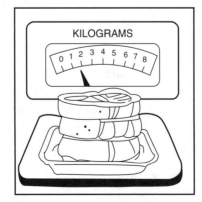

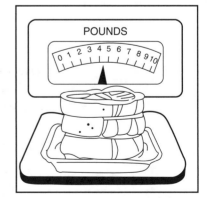

The two most common metric units of weight are the **gram** and the **kilogram**. The weight of packaged goods like breakfast cereals and prepared foods will be marked in grams. In fact, many such packages now show their weight in grams as well as pounds and ounces. This means we can compare price per unit without the added bother of converting pounds to ounces or the like. Weightier purchases such as meat or watermelon will be measured in kilograms.

The two extremes of weight are the milligram (seldom used except in medicine or chemistry) and the metric ton (more or less equivalent to the ton we now use). A **milligram** is about the weight of one grain of salt. To visualize a **metric ton**, think of one cubic meter of water: the water in a container one meter high, one meter wide, and one meter long weighs 1,000,000 grams, 1,000 kilograms, or 1 metric ton.

20. What unit would you use to measure the weight of the following items?

    (a) a pork roast _____   (b) a truck load of coal _____

    (c) aspirin _____   (d) a chair _____

Answers: (a) kilogram; (b) metric ton; (c) milligram; (d) kilogram

The following tabulation should help you relate to the gram.

(a) A nickel weighs 5 grams.      = 5 g

(b) A small can of soup weighs about 300 grams      = 300 g

21. About how much do 10 nickels weigh? _____

Answer: 50 grams

An easy way to remember kilograms is to learn your weight in kilograms.

22. How much do you weigh if one pound equals .453529 kg (about one-half kilogram)?

Answer:	Pounds	100	110	120	130	140	150	160	170	180
		190	200	210	220					
	Kilograms	45	50	54	59	64	68	73	77	82
		86	91	95	100					

A large man weighs about 100 kg; a small woman, about 50 kg.

Tables 5-2 and 5-3 might be of interest to any of you who are weight watchers.

Table 5-2

NORMAL WEIGHT FOR MEN[1] in kilograms, by Height and Build			
	BUILD		
Height (cm)	**Small**	**Medium**	**Large**
157.48	58.1 – 60.8	59.4 – 64.0	62.6 – 68.0
160.02	59.0 – 61.7	60.3 – 64.9	63.5 – 69.4
162.56	59.9 – 62.6	61.2 – 65.8	64.4 – 70.8
165.10	60.8 – 63.5	62.1 – 67.1	65.3 – 72.6
167.64	61.7 – 64.4	63.1 – 68.5	66.2 – 74.4
170.18	62.6 – 65.8	64.4 – 69.9	67.6 – 76.2
172.72	63.5 – 67.1	65.8 – 71.2	68.9 – 78.0
175.26	64.4 – 68.5	67.1 – 72.6	70.3 – 79.8
177.80	65.3 – 69.9	68.5 – 73.9	71.7 – 81.6
180.34	66.2 – 71.2	69.9 – 75.3	73.0 – 83.5
182.88	67.6 – 72.6	71.2 – 77.1	74.4 – 85.3
185.42	68.9 – 74.4	72.6 – 78.9	76.2 – 87.1
187.96	70.3 – 76.2	74.4 – 80.7	78.0 – 89.4
190.50	71.7 – 78.0	75.8 – 82.6	79.8 – 91.6
193.04	73.5 – 79.8	77.6 – 84.8	82.1 – 93.9

[1]Men wearing 2.27 kg of clothing, in shoes with 2.54 cm heels.
Sources: Metropolitan Life Insurance Company; National Academy of Sciences

Table 5-3

NORMAL WEIGHT FOR WOMEN[1]			
in kilograms, by Height and Build			
	BUILD		
Height (cm)	Small	Medium	Large
147.32	46.3 – 50.3	49.4 – 54.9	53.5 – 59.4
149.86	46.7 – 51.3	50.3 – 55.8	54.4 – 60.8
152.40	47.2 – 52.2	51.3 – 57.2	55.3 – 62.1
154.94	48.1 – 53.5	52.2 – 58.5	56.7 – 63.5
157.48	50.0 – 54.9	53.5 – 59.9	58.1 – 64.9
160.02	50.3 – 56.2	54.9 – 61.2	59.4 – 66.7
162.56	51.7 – 57.6	56.2 – 62.6	60.8 – 68.5
165.10	53.1 – 59.0	57.6 – 64.0	62.1 – 70.3
167.64	54.4 – 60.3	59.0 – 65.3	63.5 – 72.1
170.18	55.8 – 61.7	60.3 – 66.7	64.9 – 73.9
172.72	56.2 – 63.1	61.7 – 68.0	66.2 – 75.8
175.26	58.5 – 64.4	63.1 – 69.4	67.6 – 77.1
177.80	59.9 – 65.8	64.4 – 70.8	68.9 – 78.5
180.34	61.2 – 67.1	65.8 – 72.1	70.3 – 79.8
182.88	62.6 – 68.5	67.1 – 73.5	71.7 – 81.2

[1]Women wearing 1.36 kg of clothing, in shoes with 2.54 cm heels.
Sources: Metropolitan Life Insurance Company; National Academy of Sciences

23. About how much should a woman weigh if she is 160 cm tall (5 ft 3 in) and of medium build?

_____ kg

Answer: about 55

24. About how much should a man weigh if he is 182.88 cm tall (6 ft) and of medium build?

_____ kg

Answer: about 75

25. Match the following items with their approximate weight.

_____	(1)	10 nickels	100 g
_____	(2)	a size D flashlight battery	4 mg
_____	(3)	4 grains of salt	600 g
_____	(4)	one cubic meter (m³) of water	10 kg
_____	(5)	a large can of soup	1 metric ton
_____	(6)	a watermelon	50 g
_____	(7)	a college coed	90 kg
_____	(8)	a liter of milk	0.1 g
_____	(9)	a straight pin	60 kg
_____	(10)	a basketball player 200 cm tall	1 kg

Volume

Unlike the system we now use, which has two separate sets of measures for volume—one dry and one liquid, the metric system has only three basic units for both dry and liquid measures: the **liter** (l), the **milliliter** (ml), and the **cubic meter** (m^3). A liter is a little more than a quart (actually 1.05669 quarts) and is related to the meter by being defined as 1 cubic decimeter (dm^3) in volume. Most liquid medicines are already sold by the **milliliter** (one-thousandth of a liter). Soon you will buy such things as vegetable coloring and peppermint oil by the milliliter. A **cubic meter** (the volume of a cube measuring 1 m on a side) is for large volumes such as the capacity of a railroad car or truck trailer.

26. Match the following with their approximate volume.

    _____ (a) a bottle of cough medicine   310 m^3

    _____ (b) the amount of air in a room   .7 liter

    _____ (c) a large can of beef stew   100 ml

    Answers: (a) 100 ml; (b) 310 m^3; (c) .7 liter

27. Since a liter equals approximately 1 quart, about how many liters of milk would a gallon milk carton hold?

    _____

    Answer: about 4 liters (3.7854 liters to be exact)

28. Match the following items with their appropriate measure.

    _____ (1) a cup of vinegar   7 liters

    _____ (2) a can of soda pop   75 ml

    _____ (3) a large kettle   1 liter

    _____ (4) the volume of a   .25 liters
                                 walk-in freezer

    _____ (5) a bottle of wine   300 m^3

    _____ (6) a bottle of medicine   354 ml

    Answers: (1) .25 liters; (2) 354 ml; (3) 7 liters; (4) 300 m^3; (5) 1 liter; (6) 75 ml

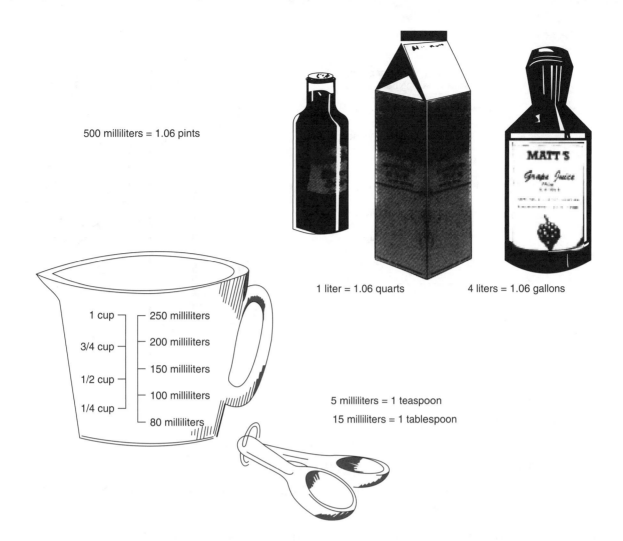

500 milliliters = 1.06 pints

1 liter = 1.06 quarts

4 liters = 1.06 gallons

1 cup — 250 milliliters
3/4 cup — 200 milliliters
1/2 cup — 150 milliliters
1/4 cup — 100 milliliters
— 80 milliliters

5 milliliters = 1 teaspoon
15 milliliters = 1 tablespoon

Temperature

Everyone understands temperature. It measures something we all experience and hear a great deal about. The two temperature scales we see most often are Fahrenheit and Celsius.

The temperature scale we now use is the **Fahrenheit scale.** It was devised by Gabriel Fahrenheit, the same German scientist who developed the mercury thermometer. While 0° Fahrenheit was the coldest he could make a mixture of salt and ice, since his time we have measured much colder temperatures. Consequently, such convenient points as 0, 10, and 100 have no special significance on the Fahrenheit scale. Water boils at 212°F and freezes at 32°F.

The **Celsius scale** was devised by Anders Celsius, a Swede who wanted a scale where the freezing point of water would be 0° and the boiling point would be 100°. Because of this 0–100 range, this scale has been called centigrade scale; now, however, the official name of this scale is Celsius.

With experience, you can learn to recognize temperatures in degrees Celsius. The following table will help orient you to temperatures encountered normally.

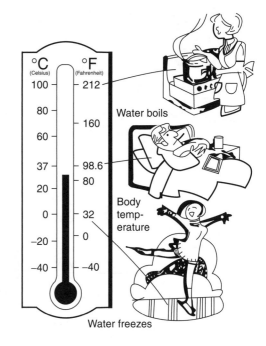

200°C	Oven setting for baking potatoes or roasting beef
100°C	Boiling point of water
40°C	Sweltering summer heat
37°C	Normal body temperature
30°C	A warm summer day
20°C	A mild spring or fall day
10°C	A warm winter day
0°C	Freezing point of water

29. Complete each of the statements in column one with the appropriate temperature from column two.

(1) The record high temperature in California was ——————— °C recorded at Greenland Ranch on July 10, 1913.   –53°C

(2) The record high temperature in New York was ——————— °C recorded at Troy on July 22, 1926.   57°C

(3) The record low temperature in Wyoming was ——————— °C recorded at Moran on February 9, 1933.   –62°C

(4) The record low temperature in Alaska was ——————— °C recorded at Prospect Creek Camp on January 23, 1971.   17°C

(5) The normal temperature in Spokane, Washington, during June is ——————— °C   42°C

Answers: (1) 57; (2) 42; (3) –53; (4) –62; (5) 17

Converting to Metric Units

Once you begin to think metric, you will have little need to convert from metric to inches, pounds, and so on. However, since it is so much easier to work with metric measurements, you often may want to convert inches and so forth to metric. This is easy to do with the conversion factors shown in Figure 5-4 and Appendix 3.

U.S. DEPARTMENT OF COMMERCE
National Bureau of Standards
Washington, D.C. 20234

METRIC CONVERSION CARD
Approximate Conversions
to Metric Measures

Symbol	When You Know	Multiply by	To Find	Symbol
	LENGTH			
in	inches	2.5	centimeters	cm
ft	feet	30	centimeters	cm
yd	yards	0.9	meters	m
mi	miles	1.6	kilometers	km
	AREA			
in^2	square inches	6.5	square centimeters	cm^2
ft^2	square feet	0.09	square meters	m^2
yd^2	square yards	0.8	square meters	m^2
mi^2	square miles	2.6	square kilometers	km^2
	acres	0.4	hectares	ha
	MASS (weight)			
oz	ounces	28	grams	g
lb	pounds	0.45	kilograms	kg
	short tons	0.9	tonnes	t
	(2000 lb)			
	VOLUME			
tap	teaspoons	5	milliliters	ml
Tbsp	tablespoons	15	milliliters	ml
fl oz	fluid ounces	30	milliliters	ml
c	cups	0.24	liters	l
pt	pints	0.47	liters	l
qt	quarts	0.95	liters	l
gal	gallons	3.8	liters	l
ft^2	cubic feet	0.03	cubic meters	m^2
yd^2	cubic yards	0.76	cubic meters	m^2
	TEMPERATURE (exact)			
°F	Fahrenheit temperature	5/9 (after subtracting 32)	Celsius temperature	°C

°F
32   98.6   212
-40   0   40   80   120   160   200
-40 -20   0   20   40   60   80   100
°C   37

Approximate Conversions
from Metric Measures

Symbol	When You Know	Multiply by	To Find	Symbol
	LENGTH			
mm	millimeters	0.04	inches	in
cm	centimeters	0.4	inches	in
m	meters	3.3	feet	ft
m	meters	1.1	yards	yd
km	kilometers	0.6	miles	ml
	AREA			
cm^2	square centimeters	0.16	square inches	in^2
m^2	square meters	1.2	square yards	yd^2
km^2	square kilometers	0.4	square miles	ml^2
ha	hectares (10,000 m^3)	2.5	acres	
	MASS (weight)			
g	grams	0.035	ounces	oz
kg	kilograms	2.2	pounds	lb
t	tonnes (1000 kg)	1.1	short tons	
	VOLUME			
ml	milliliters	0.03	fluid ounces	fl oz
l	liters	2.1	pints	pt
l	liters	1.06	quarts	qt
l	liters	0.26	gallons	gal
m^3	cubic meters	35	cubic feet	ft^3
m^3	cubic meters	1.3	cubic yards	yd^3
	TEMPERATURE (exact)			
°C	Celsius temperature	9/5 (then add 32)	Fahrenheit temperature	°F

For

U.S. Government Printing Office
Washington, D.C., 20402

*1 in = 2.54 cm (exactly). For other exact conversions and more detailed tables, see NBS Misc. Publ. 286, Units of Weights and Measures, Price $2.25, SD Catalog No.
C13.10 : 286.

✩U.S. GOVERNMENT PRINTING OFFICE   0–520–706

Figure 5-4.

30. How many liters of gasoline are equivalent to 10 American gallons?

_____ liters

Answer: 38 (10 × 3.8)

31. John Blanchard purchased 6 pounds of potatoes at the local market. How many kilograms is that?

_____ kg

Answer: 2.7 (6 × .45)

32. Shell Oil Co. plans to build a new plant in Australia. If they need a storage tank with a capacity equivalent to 50,000 American gallons, what size tank should they order from their Japanese supplier, 100,000 liter, 200,000 liter, or 250,000 liter?

_____

Answer: 200,000 liter, since 50,000 gals equals about 190,000 liters

33. Libby's sells their canned vegetables internationally. What equivalent metric weight should they list on the label of a can with a net weight of 15 ounces?

_____

Answer: 420 grams (1 oz = 28 g; therefore, 28 × 15 = 420)

34. One European sports car has a top speed of 200 kilometers per hour. What is the equivalent speed in miles per hour?

_____

Answer: 120 mph (1 km = 0.6 mi; therefore, 0.6 × 200 = 120)

35. If an ideal temperature for skiing is 21°F, what is it in Celsius?

_____

Answer: –6° Celsius [(21°F – 32°) × 5/9]

36. Complete the following table.

My Metric Measurements

Height _____ in × 2.5 cm/in. = _____ cm

Chest (bust) _____ in × 2.5 cm/in. = _____ cm

Waist _____ in × 2.5 cm/in. = _____ cm

Hips _____ in × 2.5 cm/in. = _____ cm

Weight _____ lbs × .45 kg/lb = _____ kg

Shoe size _____ × 5.125 = _____

Distance to work
or school _____ miles × 1.6 mi/km = _____ km

Temperature (98.6°F – 32) × 5/9 = 37°C

Stop

You are now ready to take Pretest V on the metric system. This test will tell you if you know the International System of Measurement. Unless instructed otherwise, turn in your Pretest for correction and review before taking Test V.

Pretest V

METRIC SYSTEM

Untimed Test

To pass this test, you must have 90 percent accuracy.

Write the basic metric measurements for the following.

(1) Length _____ (2) Weight _____

(3) Volume _____ (4) Temperature _____

Write the prefixes for each of the following multiples.

(5) One millionth of (0.000001) _____

(6) One hundredth of (0.01) _____

(7) One tenth of (0.1) _____

(8) A hundred times (100) _____

Fill in the blanks with metric units.

(9) A quart is a little smaller than a _____.

(10) A woman who is 5'6" tall is 168 _____.

(11) People walk at about 5 _____.

(12) Metric real estate is measured in _____.

(13) A 5 _____ roast weighs about 11 lbs.

Match the following items or definitions with the appropriate measurements or terms.

_____ (14) The system of measurement created by a French Commission in 1790 that was to be at once simple and scientific, and which has served as the basis for all United States standards since 1892.

_____ (15) A man 6 feet tall is just over this tall.

_____ (16) It would take about this long to drive from Chicago, Illinois to Denver, Colorado, which is 1,630 km if you drove near the speed limit.

_____ (17) A large suburban lot is about this large.

_____ (18) A man who is 175 cm tall and of medium build should weigh about this much.

_____ (19) This is the temperature of a warm, sunny summer day.

_____ (20) The record high temperature in California.

(a) 150 g	(b) 180 cm	(c) 4 hours	(d) 6,194 m
(e) 2.5 cm	(f) 68 kg	(g) 57°C	(h) 17 hours
(i) 5°C	(k) 30°C	(l) metric system	(m) .2 hectares

Circle the T if the statements are true, F if false.

T   F   (21)   The United States is highly dependent on foreign trade.

T   F   (22)   The symbols for most metric prefixes are arbitrary.

T   F   (23)   A 6-inch ruler is about 15 centimeters long.

T   F   (24)   A car traveling 60 mph is going faster than a car traveling 80 km/hr.

T   F   (25)   A reasonable temperature at which to bake a pie would be 220°C.

Part II
Calculator Applications

In the first five chapters of this book you had a chance to review basic arithmetic, to build proficiency on a 10-Key keyboard, and to acquaint yourself with the capabilities of most business desk calculators. Part II of *Basic Business Math and Electronic Calculators* gives you the opportunity to apply these skills to realistic problems. These application problems will refine your ability to operate calculators, enhance your ability to communicate with numbers and expand your knowledge of business activity.

After completing Part II you will be able to:

■ Perform essential business math applications such as word problems, percentage, simple interest and compound interest.
■ Use and understand the computations needed for buying and selling goods.
■ Use and understand the numbers involved in consumer economics.
■ Be able to perform such business operations as prorating expenses, computing depreciation and financial analysis.
■ Use ratio and proportions, time value concept, index numbers, graphs and charts, and statistics to better understand business analysis.

Hint

Do not skip around. Work at least a few problems from each section to be certain you understand the concept. Working every problem is even better.

You will also learn more in less time if you use this text as a workbook. Write notes to yourself in the book. Make a commitment, before you check your answers, write the answers in the spaces provided in your book.

Essential Applications

LEARNING GOALS

After completing Chapter 6, you will have improved your ability to operate business calculators and expanded your knowledge of business activity in the following areas:

- Word problems
- Percentages
- Simple Interest
- Compound Interest
- Inventory
- Payroll

You also will be able to pass a pretest of typical business problems, with at least 70 percent accuracy in less than 50 minutes.

Word Problems

Competence in math is a vocational advantage. Math avoidance limits people at all work levels. Research is quite conclusive that, for both men and women, anxiety about mathematics is often the result of their negative experiences with mathematics, not the cause. We want everyone who suffers such anxiety to give themselves one more chance. Math anxiety and math avoidance are not uncommon. Many men and women have been denied the pleasure and power that competence with numbers can provide. Everyone has the potential for success with numbers.

Origins of Math Anxiety

People who elect to study business are sometimes uncomfortable with mathematics in general, and word problems specifically. Most business students would rather deal with people than with things or with data. And what begins as a preference often becomes a mental prison. The longer such a phobia is maintained the more difficult it is to overcome. Being a young beginner is difficult enough; to be a beginner as an adult takes a special kind of courage. It is not uncommon for a discomfort with mathematics (particularly with story problems) during elementary or secondary school years to develop into full-fledged anxiety and avoidance by the time of graduation from high school or going to work. Yet to succeed in the business world, we must be able to get facts from the figures we encounter. We must be able to interpret quantitative data such as balance statements, budgets, and records of sales, and make sound decisions based on them. Such quantitative data are almost always in the form of word problems.

Guesstimation

People who are good with numbers trust their intuition in solving problems. They guess. They visualize. They test for reasonableness. They may even work backward from a reasonable guess. Most real-life problems that deal with numbers can be solved in several ways. When, for instance, I give college students a problem cold, one that requires several steps to solve, I frequently see at least five different ways of solving the problem from the top achievers.

Intuition is not irrational or emotional. People who are good at problem solving trust their intuition. They perceive intuition as flashes of insight into the rational. Victims of math anxiety also need to understand this. They need to understand that they "guesstimate" too little, that there is more than one way to solve a problem, and that the best way to check most any business math problem is to ask yourself, "Does the answer make sense?"

Learning to Solve Word Problems

To develop your ability to solve word problems, recognize that math is not a spectator sport. Like skiing, swimming, or playing the piano, if you want to be able to solve word problems, the best way is TO DO IT. Experience with success will make you more tolerant of occasional failure, which most everyone experiences.

Math ideas that might have been difficult to learn at age seven or eight are much easier to comprehend as an adult. As adults, our facility with language has improved. We understand more mathematical concepts just from everyday living. We are also able to ask more and better questions. How, then, can a person overcome a block to the solving of math problems? To answer this question, let's try a problem.

A car travels 15,000 miles. The five tires including a full-size spare are rotated equally so they will wear evenly. How many miles will each tire have gone by the end of the trip?

(a)   (b)

Figure 6-1.

Most people know that if a car has five tires, counting the spare, four are in use at any one time. A person who is not math anxious but knows no algebra will poke around at the problem for a while and then come up with an answer of "four-fifths of 15,000 miles," or 12,000 miles. They're pretty sure they're right, although they may not know why. Perhaps they thought of the four tires on the car and one in the trunk. Perhaps they even made another important step, the "reasonableness test"; that is, 12,000 miles makes sense—it is less than 15,000 miles but not much less. Most important, they tried.

Another student might draw a picture (Figure 6-1a) and think, each tire is in the trunk one-fifth of the time (Figure 6-1b) 15,000 miles less one-fifth (3,000 miles) equals 12,000 miles.

Math-anxious students respond very differently. Unless they have a formula memorized for the specific problems, they give up. They don't try. Even if they guess four-fifths, they won't trust their intuition.

To solve word problems let's revisit the four steps found in Chapter Four:

Step 1 Read the question. Where applicable, draw a sketch and label the parts both known and unknown. Be careful to identify what is given and what must be found. Use equations if you like them.

Step 2 "Guesstimate". Use your intuition. In other words, estimate or ask yourself what would be a reasonable answer. This will often let you know what needs to be done to solve the problem—add, subtract, multiply, or divide.

Step 3 Solve the problem. Sometimes it is helpful to work backwards from your "guesstimate." If your answer "feels" wrong when you multiply or divide, try the opposite process.

Step 4 Reread the question. Use a "Reasonableness Test," check the results against the original problem and ask yourself, "Does the answer make sense?"

For example, a problem many people have trouble with is finding the selling price when only the amount of sales tax and the sales tax rate is known. It is easy if we simplify the problem using the steps listed above.

If you are asked to find the selling price of a sport coat when an 8.5 percent sales tax is $15.64.

Step 1 After reading the question carefully, draw a picture and label the parts both known and unknown.

Price of sport coat	Tax ($15.64)
100%	8.5%

Step 2 "Guesstimate" a reasonable answer. Since the tax $15.64 is less than 10 percent of the price of the coat you know the coat must cost more than $156.40.

Step 3 Dividing $15.64 by .085 gives you $184.

Step 4 The price of the sport coat could be $184 and since $184 is a little more than $156.40 it passes the "Reasonableness Test."

Here is another example of a question given on a national test that just two of the steps in our process might help with: José ate 1/2 of a pizza. Ella ate 1/2 of another pizza. José said that he ate more pizza than Ella, but Ella said they both ate the same amount. Use words and pictures to show that José could be right. Nationally, only 16 percent of the students had the correct response.

Step 1   After reading the question carefully draw a picture and label the parts

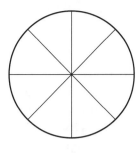

José's Pizza

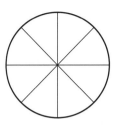

Ella's Pizza

Step 4   Yes, it makes sense that José could have eaten half of a larger pizza than Ella.

Using the guidelines above solve the following word problems:

Mark Adams owes $2,382.35 plus $76.93 interest on his credit union loan. If he wants to pay the loan in full, how much must he pay?

_____ (1)

If 450 ski lift tickets are sold on an average day, how many tickets could you expect to be sold in 5 days?

_____ (2)

If profits of $489,514 are divided equally among 311 employees, how much will each employee receive?

_____ (3)

The annual payroll deductions of Kim Nygent are $2,456.88. If equal deductions are made each month, what is her monthly deduction?

_____ (4)

At least 12 million American women have taken up arms in recent years. The National Rifle Association says that as many as 70 percent of its basic pistol course students are female, up from 3 percent in the late '80s. If the average basic pistol course has 23 students how many would you expect to be women?

_____ (5)

China Garden Restaurant had 73 customers on Sunday, 53 on Monday, 39 on Tuesday, and a total of 213 Wednesday to Saturday. If the average customer spends $7.59 what were the total sales for the week?

_____ (6)

Design Associates projected gross sales at $850,000. During the year they earned $432,922 in sales from their major clients and $589,219 in sales from the remainder of their clients. How much did the agency underestimate its sales?

_____ (7)

John Simko bought 4 new tires from Discount Tire for a total for $431.63. Discount also charged John $1.54 per tire for a state required environmental fee, $2.00 per tire for a waste disposal fee, $12.99 per tire for a passenger lifetime spin balance service, and $3.25 per tire for valve stems. What was John's final bill?

_____ (8)

Norma Katz bought a new sweater at Nordstroms for $78.25. If the sales tax is 7.8% how much change would Norma get back from five $20 bills.

_____ (9)

Takashi Shioyama is traveling to a computer convention by car. His company will reimburse him $.28 per mile. If Takashi travels 542 miles how much will his company reimburse him for mileage?

_____ (10)

A TREK mountain bike priced at $432 was reduced or marked down to $349. What percent was the price decreased?

_____ (11)

There are 36 men on the school football team. This number represents 6 percent of the school's total enrollment. What is the school's total enrollment?

_____ (12)

Arne has read 138 pages of a library book. He has 20 percent left to read. How many pages are there in the book? (*Hint*: What percent has he already read?)

_____ (13)

Several years ago the Internal Revenue Service (IRS) was encouraging people to file their income tax returns electronically because it is more accurate and efficient than paper and pencil. The first year they pushed for electronic filling there were 28.9 million tax returns filed electronically, three years later there were 42.3 million returns filed electronically. What was the percent of increase in returns field electronically from year one to year three?

_____ (14)

Last year exports to China from T & W Manufacturing were $37 million. To the nearest tenth of a million what would exports be this year if they dropped 28 percent due to the new regulations?

_____ (15)

Vietnam is the second largest exporter of rice in the world exceeded only by Thailand. If Vietnam exported 4,555 thousand metric tons of rice last year, to the nearest thousand tons how much rice will Vietnam export in 12 years if exports increase 16.8 percent.

_____ (16)

If Canada produced 26,900 thousand metric tons of wheat and the U.S. produced 62,569 thousand metric tons of wheat, Canada's wheat production was what percent of that in the United States?

_____ (17)

If U.S. Corn production totaling 241 metric tons was 40 percent of the world's production of corn, how many metric tons of corn were produced in the world?

_____ (18)

Junko's total sales were 15 percent less last week than this week. If her total sales were $72,894 this week what were her total sales last week?

_____ (19)

Sixty-six percent of the Business Statistics students earned a grade above a 2.5. If there were 47 students in the class how many earned a grade above a 2.5?

_____ (20)

Answers: (1) $2,459.28; (2) 2,250 tickets; (3) $1,574; (4) $204.74; (5) 16 women; (6) $2,869.02; (7) $172,141; (8) $510.75; (9) $15.65; (10) $151.76; (11) 19.2%; (12) 600; (13) 173; (14) 46.4%; (15) $26.6 million; (16) 5320 thousand metric tons; (17) 43.0%; (18) 602.5 metric tons; (19) $61,959.90; (20) 31 students

Percentages in Business

Percentages are a common means of expressing relationships in business: rates of interest, discounts, taxes, and fluctuations in prices. Percent means one hundredth, or compared to 100. In other words, 15% is the same as 15 parts out of 100 and is equivalent to the decimal .15.

This section will use the percentage formula: P = RB for several business forms.

To better understand the concept of percent, we will not use the percent key in this section. We change 15% to .15, the decimal equivalent of 15/100.

Commissions

1. Adams Wholesale pays their sales people on a commission basis. On Table 6-1, calculate the commission paid each salesperson for the week of April 14. Use the memory feature of your machine to accumulate the total commissions earned.

Hint

To find percentage (part), use the formula P = RB. To find the commission, multiply sales by the commission rate.

Table 6-1

ADAMS WHOLESALE CORPORATION
Salespersons Commissions for Week Ending: April 14

Salesperson	Sales	Rate of Commission	Commission
Allen	$ 718.57	8.4%	_____ (1)
Bradley	927.84	29.7%	_____ (2)
Cotter	1,049.27	5.9%	_____ (3)
Deno	451.97	7.6%	_____ (4)
Halpin	1,151.91	29.5%	_____ (5)
Knowles	3,012.14	6.1%	_____ (6)
Pooley	3,188.47	10.0%	_____ (7)
Victor	661.44	3.5%	_____ (8)
Williams	728.81	19.2%	_____ (9)
		Total Commissions	_____ (10)

Answers: (1) $60.36; (2) $275.57; (3) $61.91; (4) $34.35; (5) $339.81; (6) $183.74; (7) $318.85; (8) $23.15; (9) 139.93; (10) $1,437.67

Earnings per Share

2. Joe Bradley's stock portfolio is detailed in Table 6-2. Calculate his earnings as a percent of purchase price per share. This return per dollar invested is one way of determining the value of stock investment.

Table 6-2

Stock	Earnings per Share	Price per Share	Earnings as Percent of Price
ABT	$ 1.73	$ 39.86	_____ (1)
BWA	3.60	54.07	_____ (2)
DSL	4.12	41.20	_____ (3)
NWFI	2.57	28.24	_____ (4)
OCAS	2.00	18.00	_____ (5)
QBAK	0.29	5.25	_____ (6)
RACN	1.26	17.65	_____ (7)
TUP	1.02	17.36	_____ (8)
VIP	1.93	23.20	_____ (9)
WAT	0.81	22.08	_____ (10)

Answers: (1) 4.3%; (2) 6.7%; (3) 10.0%; (4) 9.1%; (5) 11.1%; (6) 5.5%; (7) 7.1%; (8) 5.9%; (9) 8.3%; (10) 3.7%

Pricing

3. Peoples Department Store had a special furniture sale with discounts shown in Table 6-3. If discounts were based on the regular price, what was the sale price of each item?

Table 6-3

Description	Discount	Regular Price	Sale price	
Buffet	31%	$ 273.61	_____	(1)
Dinette	37%	217.68	_____	(2)
Bedroom suite	44%	321.13	_____	(3)
Occasional chair	28%	97.15	_____	(4)
Desk	53%	243.13	_____	(5)
Recliner	33%	189.99	_____	(6)
Lamp	16%	47.94	_____	(7)
Sofa	26%	199.70	_____	(8)
Chair	66%	36.93	_____	(9)
Stereo	25%	292.51	_____	(10)

Answers: (1) $188.79; (2) $137.14; (3) $179.83; (4) $69.95; (5) $114.27; (6) $127.29; (7) $40.27; (8) $147.78; (9) $12.56; (10) $219.38

4. Some employees are paid a commission based on the amount of their sales. If the employees listed in Table 6-4 are paid a commission of 12%, what are their earnings?

Hint

Use .12 as a constant multiplier and the accumulative function of your machine to accumulate the total commission.

Table 6-4

Employee	Sales	12% Commission	
Fred Jones	$ 735.40	_____	(1)
Carl Ames	662.10	_____	(2)
Bob Allen	940.06	_____	(3)
Cora Brown	880.44	_____	(4)
Ella Martin	320.00	_____	(5)
Dick Green	605.25	_____	(6)
	TOTAL	_____	(7)

Answers: (1) $88.25; (2) $79.45; (3) $112.81; (4) $105.65; (5) $38.40; (6) $72.63; (7) $497.19

Percent of Net Sales

5. A portion of Sunset Supply Company's comparative income statement is shown in Table 6-5. Calculate the percent of net sales for each account. Net sales in each year is the base (100%) to which the other amounts in that year are compared. This changes absolute numbers (dollars) to relative numbers (percents), and enables management to make comparisons between years, with other companies, with industry averages, and so on. You will learn more about this if you study accounting, but for now, it is an excellent example of how you can use a constant divisor. Simply divide each item in column one by 533 and each item in column two by 303.

Hint

Use the percentage formula $R = P/B$. Let each account figure equal P and net sales for each period equal B. To avoid having to reenter the net sales figure (B), use division with a constant. For example, in the first column, net sales this year of $533 is a constant divisor: $554 \div 533 = 1.039$ or 103.9%, $21 \div 533 = .039$ or 3.9%, $533 \div 533 = 1$ or 100%, etc.

Table 6-5

SUNSET SUPPLY COMPANY
Comparative Income Statement
for period Ending: December 31, 20XX

Account	Amount (000s omitted)		Percent of Net Sales	
	This Year	Last Year	This Year	Last Year
Gross sales	$554	$329	_____ (1)	_____ (11)
Less returns	21	26	_____ (2)	_____ (12)
Net sales	$533	$303	_____ (3)	_____ (13)
Cost of goods sold	$311	$181	_____ (4)	_____ (14)
Gross profit	$222	$122	_____ (5)	_____ (15)
Expenses				
Commissions	$ 78	$ 38	_____ (6)	_____ (16)
Overhead	12	11	_____ (7)	_____ (17)
Freight	11	7	_____ (8)	_____ (18)
Total Expenses	$101	$ 56	_____ (9)	_____ (19)
Net income	$121	$ 66	_____ (10)	_____ (20)

Answers: (1) 103.9%; (2) 3.9%; (3) 100.0%; (4) 58.4%; (5) 41.7%; (6) 14.6%; (7) 2.3%; (8) 2.1%; (9) 19.0%; (10) 22.7%; (11) 108.6%; (12) 8.6%; (13) 100.0%; (14) 59.7%; (15) 40.3%; (16) 12.5%; (17) 3.6%; (18) 2.3%; (19) 18.5%; (20) 21.8%

6. A portion of sales for Edwards Mens Wear, Inc., is shown in Table 6-6. Calculate the amount and percent of increase or decrease for each item. Label all credit balances.

> ## Hint
>
> Use the percentage formula R = P/B. The earliest year (last year) should always be used as the base. If you store the figure for last year when finding the difference you will not need to re-enter it when finding the percent increase or decrease. A decrease can be shown by parentheses.

Table 6-6

EDWARDS MENS WEAR, INC.
Comparative Sales

Item	Sales Last Year	Sales This Year	Amount of Increase (Decrease)	Percent of Increase (Decrease)
Pants, dress	$ 284,214	$ 315,219	_____ (1)	_____ (2)
Pants, casual	121,278	221,097	_____ (3)	_____ (4)
Shirts, dress	97,997	94,205	_____ (5)	_____ (6)
Shirts, casual	172,488	182,037	_____ (7)	_____ (8)
Shoes	79,406	87,481	_____ (9)	_____ (10)
Shorts	872	1,932	_____ (11)	_____ (12)
Sport Coats	115,899	144,137	_____ (13)	_____ (14)
Suits	468,691	396,637	_____ (15)	_____ (16)
Sweaters	1,348	884	_____ (17)	_____ (18)
Ties	3,478	1,062	_____ (19)	_____ (20)

Answers: (1) $31,005; (2) 10.9%; (3) $99,819; (4) 82.3%; (5) ($3,792); (6) (3.9%); (7) $9,549; (8) 5.5%; (9) $8,075; (10) 10.2%; (11) $1,060; (12) 121.6%; (13) $28,238; (14) 24.4%; (15) ($72,054); (16) (15.4%); (17) ($464); (18) (34.4%); (19) ($2,416); (20) (69.5%)

7. Carrying charges are sometimes computed as a percent of sales price and added to the amount owed by a credit-purchase customer. For example, a purchase of three items at $6 each to be charged a 10% additional carrying charge would be computed as shown in Table 6-7. Compute the amounts owed on the remaining purchases.

Table 6-7

No. of Items	Price Each	Amount	Rate	Carrying Charge	Total Owed
3	$6.00	$18.00	10%	$1.80	$19.80
2	1.20	_____ (1)	15%	_____ (2)	_____ (3)
1	4.50	_____ (4)	12%	_____ (5)	_____ (6)
4	.95	_____ (7)	12%	_____ (8)	_____ (9)
12	2.00	_____ (10)	10%	_____ (11)	_____ (12)
5	1.50	_____ (13)	10%	_____ (14)	_____ (15)
2	4.00	_____ (16)	5%	_____ (17)	_____ (18)
6	.75	_____ (19)	15%	_____ (20)	_____ (21)

Answers: (1) $2.40; (2) $.36; (3) $2.76; (4) $4.50; (5) $.54; (6) $5.04; (7) $3.80; (8) $.46; (9) $4.26; (10) $24.00; (11) $2.40; (12) $26.40; (13) $7.50; (14) $.75; (15) $8.25; (16) $8.00; (17) $.40; (18) $8.40; (19) $4.50; (20) $.68; (21) $5.18

Simple Interest

Businesses as well as individuals often borrow money for purchases that could not be readily made with cash only. Such credit is typically used for financing of new industrial plant and equipment, the purchase of goods for resale by wholesalers and retailers, and the purchase of major appliances and automobiles by individuals.

Interest is the added amount paid for the use of borrowed money. **Simple interest** is calculated by multiplying **principal** (amount borrowed) by **rate** of interest and by length of **time** to repay the loan. Expressed as a formula, we have:

$$I = PRT \quad \text{or} \quad \frac{I}{PRT}$$

where I = interest, P = principal or face value, R = rate of interest on an annual basis, and T = time in years.

Similar to the percentage formula, one triangle formula makes it easy to remember the different variations of the simple interest formula:

To Find	Eliminate	Leaving
Interest (I)	I	PRT
Principal (P)	P	I/RT
Rate (R)	R	I/PT
Time (T)	T	I/PR

There are two methods commonly used to calculate time on credit instruments. The **exact method**, customary in government, uses the exact number of days in a month and the exact number of days in a year (365). The **Banker's Method,** more common in business, uses the exact number of days in a month, but 360 days per year. The following examples use the Banker's Method.

Example 1. Calculate simple interest on $975.00 at $15\frac{1}{4}\%$ for 53 days.

$$I = PRT \text{ or } \frac{I}{PRT} = \$975.00 \times .1525 \times \frac{53}{360} = \frac{975 \times .1525 \times 53}{360} = \$21.89$$

Example 2. What investment is necessary to earn $512.00 interest in 180 days at $19\frac{1}{2}\%$

$$P = \frac{I}{RT} = \frac{I}{PRT} = \frac{\$512.00}{\frac{180}{360} \times .195} = \frac{\$512.00}{\frac{180 \times .195}{360}} = \frac{512}{.0975} = \$5,251.28$$

Example 3. What interest rate is necessary to earn $440.00 on a $55,000 investment for 37 days?

$$R = \frac{I}{PT} = \frac{I}{PRT} = \frac{440}{55,000 \times \frac{37}{360}} = \frac{440}{\frac{55,000 \times 37}{360}} = \frac{440}{5,652.7778} = 7.8\%$$

Example 4. How long would it take to earn $8,125.00 on a $10,000 investment at $16\frac{1}{4}\%$ simple interest?

$$T = \frac{I}{PR} = \frac{I}{PRT} = \frac{8,125}{10,000 \times .1625} = 5 \text{ years}^*$$

1. Using the Banker's Method, fill in the blanks on the following simple interest loans. Give time in years and days, to the nearest day.

Hint

Remember the rules for rounding all final answers, given in the front of the book (.001, .1% and $.01)

---

* Since days are a fractional part of a year, 5 years need not be converted to days.

Principal	Rate	Time	Interest
$1,687	15 1/2%	54 days	_____ (1)
$2,245	16 1/4%	56 days	_____ (2)
_____ (3)	11 1/4%	3 years*	$1,687.50
$5,643	_____ (4)	2 years	$1,410.75
$1,399	18 3/4%	_____ (5)**	$33.32
$3,524	7 1/4%	_____ (6)	$177.42
_____ (7)	8%	180 days	$460.20
$7,333	_____ (8)	87 days	$150.63
$2,578	15 1/2%	133 days	_____ (9)
$5,819	_____ (10)	289 days	$443.78

* When time is in years, do not convert it to a fraction.
** Time answers will always be a decimal part of a year. Therefore, to change a decimal part of a year into days, multiply by 360.

Answers: (1) $39.22; (2) $56.75; (3) $5,000; (4) 12 1/2%; (5) 46 days; (6) 250 days; (7) $11,505.00; (8) 8.5%; (9) $147.63; (10) 9.5%

2. Using the Banker's Method, fill in the blanks on the following table of simple interest loans. Give time in years and days, to the nearest day.

Hint

Notice that when interest is given in the above problems, the last step always is to divide interest by the product of all the other factors.

Principal	Rate	Time	Interest
$5,253.00	16 1/4%	77 days	_____ (1)
_____ (2)	10 1/2%	96 days	$56.00
$4,139.00	16 3/4%	_____ (3)	$83.81
$9,888.00	14 3/8%	185 days	_____ (4)
$2,103.68	_____ (5)	280 days	$147.26
$474.58	13 1/2%	110 days	_____ (6)
$9,117.81	_____ (7)	310 days	$863.66
$2,572.20	9 1/8%	_____ (8)	$208.63
$870.64	16 1/2%	_____ (9)	$53.87
_____ (10)	8 3/4%	215 days	$5.23

Answers: (1) $182.58; (2) $2,000.00; (3) 44 days; (4) $730.44; (5) 9%; (6) $19.58; (7) 11%; (8) 320 days; (9) 135 days; (10) $100.00

3. In Table 6-8, complete ABC Bank's schedule of notes, which mature on July 31, 20xx. **The total of principal and interest should equal maturity value.** Use the Banker's Method in all calculations.

> **Hint**
>
> If you store the principal in memory, you need only add interest to memory to find maturity value.

Table 6-8

					Maturity
Customer	Principal	Rate	Time	Interest	Value
Willie C. Chan	$ 870	12 1/2%	60 days	_____ (1)	_____ (2)
Pearl N. Chaney	1 060	13 1/2%	120 days	_____ (3)	_____ (4)
Ralph S. Dorn	4 075	14 1/4%	90 days	_____ (5)	_____ (6)
W.M. Fields	2 360	15 3/4%	180 days	_____ (7)	_____ (8)
Max T. Fry	7 828	9 1/2%	180 days	_____ (9)	_____ (10),
John R. Harris	1 165	16 3/4%	45 days	_____ (11)	_____ (12)
J. J. Knoll	9 936	11 1/4%	180 days	_____ (13)	_____ (14)
Bill R. Long	185	18 %	30 days	_____ (15)	_____ (16)
J. A. Morales	3 235	10 1/2%	90 days	_____ (17)	_____ (18)
J. H. Rusk	665	13 1/4%	60 days	_____ (19)	_____ (20)
TOTAL	$_____ (21)			_____ (22)	_____ (23)

ABC BANK
Schedule of Notes that Mature on July 31, 20xx

Answers: (1) $18.13; (2) $888.13; (3) $47.70; (4) $1,107.70; (5) $145.17; (6) $4,220.17; (7) $185.85; (8) $2,545.85; (9) $371.83; (10) $8,199.83; (11) $24.39; (12) $1,189.39; (13) $558.90; (14) $10, 494.90; (15) $2.78; (16) $187.78; (17) $84.92; (18) $3,319.92; (19) $14.69; (20) $679.69; (21) $31,379.00; (22) $1,454.36; (23) $32,833.36

4. A personal finance student surveyed a group of people who had borrowed money from a variety of lending institutions (Table 6-9). For each loan, calculate the amount of interest paid and the annual rate of interest. Use the Banker's Method in all calculations.

This interest rate is very similar to the Annual Percentage Rate (APR), the annual rate of interest based on total finance charges including interest, carrying charges, insurance, and special fees. Disclosure of the APR is now required by the Federal

Truth in Lending Act so that consumers are more aware of the true cost of credit. Because this law requires the accrual method of computation which is somewhat complicated, most lending institutions use tables to assist in computing the APR.

Table 6-9

SMALL LOAN INTEREST RATES				
Amount Borrowed	Amount Paid Back	Time of Loan	Amount of Interest	Interest Rate
$ 73.00	$ 79.57	180 days	_____ (1)	_____ (2)
47.00	61.90	180 days	_____ (3)	_____ (4)
143.00	158.87	120 days	_____ (5)	_____ (6)
173.00	187.59	60 days	_____ (7)	_____ (8)
210.00	224.85	76 days	_____ (9)	_____ (10)
119.00	138.18	183 days	_____ (11)	_____ (12)

Answers: (1) $6.57; (2) 18%; (3) $14.90; (4) 63.4%; (5) $15.87; (6) 33.3%; (7) $14.59; (8) 50.6%; (9) $14.85; (10) 33.5%; (11) $19.18; (12) 31.7%

Word Problems

What is the maturity value on a 90-day note for $4,827.75 at 15 3/4%? _____ (1)

To the nearest thousand dollars, how much money would you need to invest at 11 1/2% simple interest to earn $500 in 30 days? _____ (2)

What rate of simple interest is necessary to earn $80 on $4,000 in 60 days? _____ (3)

How many days would it take for $15,000 to grow to $16,000 at 13 1/2% interest? _____ (4)

What is the ordinary interest on a $7,426.87 loan for 67 days at $19_{3/4}$% _____ (5)

Answers: (1) $5,017.84; (2) $52,000; (3) 12%; (4) 178 days; (5) $272.99

Compound Interest

Compound interest differs from simple interest in that the amount of interest obtained on an investment is added to the original amount each period, and calculations for succeeding interest periods are based on the new value (principal plus interest). Although the concept of simple interest underlies most financial transactions, its use in the business world is less common than compound interest.

For example, suppose you invested $10,000 for two years at 12%. How much interest would your investment earn? Using simple interest, the answer would be $2,400—$1,200 at the end of the first year plus $1,200 at the end of the second year. What would happen if at the end of the first year, the $1,200 of interest were invested for the second year along with the initial $10,000? At the end of the second year, the $10,000 and the $1,200 together would earn $1,344—$144 more than the initial $10,000 earned the first year. Each time interest is paid, it is added to the balance. In effect, the interest is earning interest.

This method of reinvesting earned interest is much more common and has wider application than interest on principal alone. Compound interest is usually stated as an annual rate, although it may be compounded (calculated) daily, monthly, quarterly, or semi-annually.

The symbols used in the formula for compound interest are somewhat different from those used in the simple-interest formula. The symbol T in the simple-interest formula changes to n in the compound-interest formula. The symbol n represents the **number of** interest or **conversion periods**. For example, if an investor lent money for 5 years with interest compounded quarterly, the number of conversion periods would be 20 (5 years times 4 periods per year). The symbol R changes to i, the **periodic interest rate**, which is found by dividing the nominal (annual) interest rate by the number of conversion periods per year. For example, if a sum of money is invested at a nominal rate of 8% converted semi-annually, the period rate (i) would be 4% (8% divided by 2 conversion periods per year).

Compound-interest calculations may be based on one conversion per year (annual), two conversion periods per year (semi-annual), four conversion periods (quarterly), twelve conversion periods (monthly), and so forth. Remember, both the number of conversion periods (n) and the periodic interest rate (i) must be known before compound-interest calculations can be made.

The formula for compound interest is:

$$S = P(1 + i)^n$$

where   S = the maturity value or future value at compound interest
P = the principal or original amount
1 = 100% of the principal
i = the periodic interest rate
n = the number of conversion periods

Example 1. What would a $1,000 savings certificate be worth after 12 years if it pays 6% interest compounded annually?

Instead of a formula you may want to use an intuitive approach. First, find the growth factor, one plus the interest rate per period (1.06). Enter this growth factor as a constant multiplier.

Enter the amount ($1,000). When you depress the equal key, the new principal plus interest is displayed, so depress the equal key once for each conversion period (12).

The usual way of solving this problem is to use 1.06 as a constant. To do this, engage the constant function if your machine does not have an automatic constant. Adding 1 to the periodic interest rate allows you to calculate the balance without reentering the principal each time.

Key	Display
1.06	1.06
×	1.06
1,000	1,000.00
=	1,060.00
=	1,123.60
=	1,191.02
=	1,262.48
=	1,338.23
=	1,418.52
=	1,503.63
=	1,593.85
=	1,689.48
=	1,790.85
=	1,898.30
=	2,012.20

If this approach is not clear, review the sections on "Use of Constants" and "Raising a Number to a Power" in Chapter 4.

Example 2. Assume that $950 is deposited in a savings account on January 1. What will be the balance of the account at the end of 3 years if interest is compounded semi-annually at a rate of 4 1/2%?

Enter one plus the interest rate per period (1.0225) as a constant multiplier. Enter the amount ($950) and depress the equal key once for each conversion period. (There are six semi-annual periods in 3 years).

or

Period	Balance
1	$ 971.38
2	993.23
3	1,015.58
4	1,038.43
5	1,061.79
6	1,085.68

1. Compute the amount of principal plus interest (maturity value) in the following problems. To match the answers given, set your calculator to round to four decimal digits for all intermediate answers. Round your final answer to two places.

Principal	Time	Annual Rate	Frequency of Conversions	No. of Periods	Rate per Periods as a Decimal	Amount
$ 200.00	2 yr.	6%	quarterly	_____	_____	_____ (1)
1,120.00	3 yr.	7%	annual	_____	_____	_____ (2)
350.00	5 yr.	4 1/2%	semi-annual	_____	_____	_____ (3)
2,500.00	3 yr.	5%	semi-annual	_____	_____	_____ (4)
7,050.00	2 yr.	8%	quarterly	_____	_____	_____ (5)
4,333.33	3 yr.	4%	annual	_____	_____	_____ (6)
3,200.50	4 yr.	9%	quarterly	_____	_____	_____ (7)
2,100.65	2 yr.	12%	monthly	_____	_____	_____ (8)
4,555.67	3 yr.	16%	quarterly	_____	_____	_____ (9)
852.55	5 yr.	5 1/2%	annual	_____	_____	_____ (10)

Answers: (1) 8, .015, $225.30; (2) 3, .07, $1,372.05; (3) 10, .0225, $437.22; (4) 6, .025, $2,899.23; (5) 8, .02, $8,260.20; (6) 3, .04, $4,874.41; (7) 16, .0225, $4,569.10; (8) 24, .01, $2, 667.27; (9) 12, .04, $7,293.77; (10) 5, .055, $1,114.25

Hint

An easy way to estimate the effect of compound interest is the "Rule of 70." To find how long it takes to double the money value of a deposit, divide 70 by the rate of interest. For example, at 5% interest compounded annually it would take 14 years for the money value of a deposit to double (70 ÷ 5 = 14). You can also quickly calculate the impact of inflation by finding the number of years for prices to double. For example, at a 7% annual rate of inflation, prices will double in about 10 years (70 ÷ 7 = 10), whereas at a 2% rate of inflation, it would take 35 years (70 ÷ 2 = 35).

2. The schedule for the J.P. Jones Investment Company (Table 6-10) shows a long-term investment of $1,000 over three different time periods at various rates of interest. Complete the schedule. Notice what a difference an increase in time and rate of interest makes.

Hint

To save time, after calculating the amount of 4% for 5 years, calculate the amounts at 4% for 10 years and at 4% for 20 years. Then do the same for 8%, 12%, 16%, and 20%.

Table 6-10

J.P. JONES INVESTMENT COMPANY
Investment Growth at Various Interest Rates

Principal	Time	Annual Rate	Frequency of Conversion	Amount
$1,000.00	5 yr	4%	annual	_____ (1)
1,000.00	5 yr	8%	annual	_____ (2)
1,000.00	5 yr	12%	annual	_____ (3)
1,000.00	5 yr	16%	annual	_____ (4)
1,000.00	5 yr	20%	annual	_____ (5)
$1,000.00	10 yr	4%	annual	_____ (6)
1,000.00	10 yr	8%	annual	_____ (7)
1,000.00	10 yr	12%	annual	_____ (8)
1,000.00	10 yr	16%	annual	_____ (9)
1,000.00	10 yr	20%	annual	_____ (10)
$1,000.00	20 yr	4%	annual	_____ (11)
1,000.00	20 yr	8%	annual	_____ (12)
1,000.00	20 yr	12%	annual	_____ (13)
1,000.00	20 yr	16%	annual	_____ (14)
1,000.00	20 yr	20%	annual	_____ (15)

Answers: (1)$1,216.65; (2) $1,469.33; (3) $1,762.34; (4) $2,100.34; (5) $2,488.32; (6) $1,480.24; (7) $2,158.92 (8) $3,105.85; (9) $4,411.44; (10) $6,191.74; (11) $2,191.12; (12) $4,660.96; (13) $9,646.29; (14) $19,460.76; (15) $38,337.60

Word Problems

If your investment of $10,247.86 grew at 16$\frac{1}{2}$% compounded annually for 18 years, what would the dollar value of the investment be at the end of 18 years?

_____ (1)

If the inflation rate were 3.5% each year for 12 years, how much money would you have to make per month at the end of 12 years to stay even with inflation if you now earn $1,978.25 per month?

_____ (2)

The population of Lexington, Kentucky, is 251,794 today. What will the population be in 21 years if Lexington's annual growth rate is 7.4%?

_____ (3)

ACS had sales of $52,341.87 this year. What will sales be in 9 years if they grow at 17.2% per year?

_____ (4)

What is the maturity value of $4,287.62 compounded quarterly at 16% for 7 years?

_____ (5)

The civilian labor force in the United States grew at a rate of 2.5 percent from 1973 to 1986, faster than at any time in the peace time history of any country. If the civilian labor force was 82 million in 1973, to the nearest million, what was it in 1986?

_____ (6)

Empty nesters and young professionals are reversing the downtown decline, shunning the suburbs for central business districts, where mass transit and other amenities beckon. Chicago had an average growth rate of 4.2 percent for the last ten years giving it a downtown population of 42,039. If the downtown population of Chicago continued to grow at this rate for another ten years what would the population be?

_____ (7)

If you purchased a home today at $205,000, to the nearest thousand what would it sell for in 15 years if it appreciated 6.3% per year?

_____ (8)

Diana has an antique Ford automobile that has been increasing in market value at 13% per year for the last 10 years. If its value is $8,000 today, to the nearest thousand dollars, what will it be worth in another 10 years if its value continues to increase at 13% per year?

_____ (9)

Assume that the national debt of the United States is $6.4 trillion. To the nearest tenth of a trillion what would the national debt be in 15 years if it grew at an average annual rate of 3.3 percent?

_____ (10)

Answers: (1) $160,140.01; (2) $2,989.27; (3) 1,127,549; (4) $218,372.40; (5) $12,857.30; (6) 113 million; (7) 63,435; (8) $513,000; (9) $27,000; (10) $10.4 trillion

Inventory

For firms that buy merchandise for resale, tracking the value and specific type of merchandise they have on hand is very important. Obviously inventory is important because a business's ability to serve customers often depends on what they have to sell. Tracking inventory helps management obtain a picture of what is selling. It helps buyers know what to order. It is a way of knowing more about such costs as insurance, spoilage, damaged merchandise, and theft. It is also required information for each tax period.

At the beginning of an accounting time period a firm has an inventory of merchandise on hand to sell. This amount is termed **beginning inventory**, the value of inventory that the firm begins with in a period. During the period the firm will buy more merchandise to add to the inventory. The total value bought is termed **purchases.** Beginning inventory plus purchases equals **goods available for sale**, all of the merchandise that can be sold during this period; although not necessarily all available at any one time in the period.

The value of the goods on hand at the end of the period is termed **ending inventory.** By subtracting the ending inventory from the goods available for sale, the value of the goods that were sold during the period can be found. The price of the goods that were sold during the period is termed **cost of goods sold.**

One way of finding out how many of each item are on hand is to actually count the items. This is often referred to as taking a **physical inventory.** Another way of determining how many of each item are on hand is to maintain a **perpetual inventory.** Perpetual inventory means that inventory records are constantly being adjusted for receipts (incoming items) and issues (outgoing shipments or sales). The receipts are added to the inventory; the issues are subtracted. This was once a very time consuming task but today most inventory records are kept with the aid of computers and some form of **database** software. Database software programs are like electronic filing cabinets and are used for many other types of records as well as inventory control. In food and other retail stores a laser scanner is often used in conjunction with cash registers that are connected to a computer. As each sale is made, the computer reduces the inventory of that item accordingly.

The computer may also be programmed to reorder merchandise whenever the number on hand reaches a preset minimum level.

Merchandise is often purchased at different time periods and at different prices. Therefore, inventory could be valued using several different methods. This text uses the **average-cost method** as shown below:

$$\text{Average cost per unit} = \frac{\text{Total cost of units available for sale}}{\text{Total number of units available for sale}}$$

The average cost per unit is multiplied by the number of units on hand to arrive at the total value of the items.

Example 1 BEST Company

	Number of Units Purchased	Cost per Unit	Total Cost
Beginning inventory	31	$ 6.50	$ 201.50
First purchase	12	5.37	64.44
Second purchase	20	7.25	145.00
Third purchase	15	8.34	125.10
Fourth purchase	24	6.69	160.56
Goods available for sale	**102**		**696.60**
Units sold	81		
Units in ending inventory	21		

Using the average cost method what is the value of BEST's ending inventory?

$$\frac{\text{Total cost}}{\text{Total units available for sale}} = \text{Average cost per unit}$$

$$\frac{\$696.60}{102} = \$6.83 \quad \text{(Rounded to Nearest cent)}$$

Units in ending inventory × Average cost per unit = Value of ending inventory

21   × $6.83   = $143.43

What was BEST's cost of goods sold?

Cost of Goods Available for Sale − Cost of Ending Inventory = Cost of Goods Sold

$696.60   −$143.43   = $553.17

If BEST wants to maintain an inventory of 40 units how many units should be reordered?

Units desired − Units in ending inventory = Reorder

| 40 | −21 | = 19 |

Inventory is usually one of the most expensive assets a company has. Too much inventory results in the use of needed space, extra insurance cost, etc. Too little inventory may mean shortage and loss of business. Because tracking inventory is so important companies should compare their inventory with competitors, industry standards, and so on.

1. Maria Vasquez is the proud owner of a bookstore that sells only classic novels. Maria received word from the TV station manager that the **Last Retreat** would be shown on television on March 23. Maria knew from past experience that after a classic film has been aired on television, scores of people flock to her bookstore to buy copies of the book on which the film was based. Maria found that she still has thirty copies of **Last Retreat.** To the nearest cent, what would be the average cost per book?

Purchases

July 27	15 copies @ $3.16 =	_____ (1)
October 12	24 copies @ $2.89 =	_____ (2)
December 23	13 copies @ $3.45 =	_____ (3)

Total copies _____ (4)   Total Cost _____ (5)

Average cost per book _____ (6)

(Round to the nearest cent)

2. Partial Income Statement of Oklahoma Oil

Cost of goods sold:

Beginning inventory   2,328 barrels @ $35 =   _____ (7)
(carried over from last year)

Purchases during the current year:

January 13	6,000 barrels @ $29 =	_____ (8)
May 30	4,000 barrels @ $32 =	_____ (9)
August 14	7,000 barrels @ $35 =	_____ (10)
November 22	5,000 barrels @ $26 =	_____ (11)

Total available for sale   _____ (12)   _____ (13)

Oklahoma Oil sold 19,712 barrels during the above period. What is the inventory value at the end of the period using the average cost method?

Units in ending inventory × Average Cost per Unit = Value of ending inventory

_____ (14) × _____ (15) = _____ (16)

What was Oklahoma Oil's cost of goods sold?

Cost of Goods Available for Sale − Cost of Ending Inventory = Cost of Goods sold

_____ (17) − _____ (18) = _____ (19)

3. Find the cost of goods sold using the following information.

Beginning Inventory	3,342 units @ $1.50 =	$ _____	(20)

Purchases:

June 15	2,000 units @ $1.55 =	$ _____	(21)
July 10	4,000 units @ $2.00 =	$ _____	(22)
August 1	2,500 units @ $2.00 =	$ _____	(23)
Total Cost of Goods Available for Sale:		$ _____	(24)
Less Ending Inventory:			
3,547 units @ _____ (25)		$ _____	(26)
Cost of Goods Sold		$ _____	(27)

4. Michelle opened a shoe store during the month of May. Using the following information regarding the purchases for Michelle's Shoe Store, find the value of her ending inventory using the average cost method, and the cost of goods sold.

Purchases:

April 30	1,000 pairs @ $12
May 10	1,500 pairs @ $13
July 20	1,000 pairs @ $18
Ending Inventory:	967 pairs

Value of Ending Inventory	a) _____	(28)
Cost of Goods Sold	b) _____	(29)

5. Use the following partial income statement for Jeffrey's Hardware Store to determine (a) the value of his ending inventory of outside base white paint using the average cost method and (b) the cost of goods sold.

Beginning Inventory: 432 gallons @ $12.87

Ending Inventory: 278 gallons

Purchases:

March 1   143 gallons @ $11.98

June 1   219 gallons @ $13.32

November 1   289 gallons @ $12.73

Value of Ending
    Inventory   a) _____ (30)
Cost of Goods
    Sold   b)_____ (31)

Answers: (1) $47.40; (2) $69.36; (3) $44.85; (4) 52; (5) $161.61; (6) $3.11; (7) $81,480; (8) $174,000; (9) $128,000 (10) $245,000; (11) $130,000; (12) 24,328; (13) $758,480; (14) 4,616; (15) $31.18; (16) $143,926.88; (17) $758,480; (18) $143,926.88; (19) $614,553.12; (20) $5,013; (21) $3,100; (22) $8,000; (23) $5,000; (24) $21,113; (25) $1.78; (26) $6,313.66; (27) $14,799.34; (28) $13,673.38; (29) $35,826.62; (30) $3,561.18; (31) $10,307.85

Payroll

Payroll accuracy is extremely important. Perhaps nothing is more important for good employee relations. Consequently, even though wages and salaries are relatively easy to calculate, great care must be exercised to make sure all calculations are accurate.

1. Complete the payroll schedule for Snook Wrecking Company (Table 6-12). If you use the following step-by-step instructions, no figures will need to be reentered on the sample pay lines in your totals.

   1. Calculate regular pay (for 40 hours or less) by multiplying into the memory or storage register the rate per hour by the hours worked ($10.00 × 40 = $400.00).

   2. Calculate overtime pay by multiplying into memory the rate times the overtime hours times one and one-half ($10.00 × 8 × 1.5 = $120.00)

   3. Recall overtime pay and regular pay from the memory register ($520.00)

   4. Multiply total pay by 7.65% to find the deduction for FICA (Federal Insurance Contributions Act or Social Security) and subtract this amount ($520 × .0765 = $39.78) from the storage register. For the payrolls in this section, FICA taxes are computed at 7.65% of total pay.

   5. Look up in Appendix 2 the appropriate federal income tax based on a single person's total pay and the given number of exemptions and subtract this amount ($55.00) from memory.

   6. Subtract miscellaneous ($25.00) from memory.

   7. Total the memory to find net pay ($400.22).

Table 6-12

SNOOK WRECKING COMPANY

Hourly Employee Payroll for Week Ending April 14, 20xx

Employee	Exemptions	Rate	Hrs	OT Hrs	Pay	OT Pay	Total Pay	FICA*	Tax**	Misc	Net Pay
Anders, J.	1	10.00	40	8	400	120	520	39.78	55	25.00	400.22 (1)
Bellow, M.	6	9.85	40	2						23.16	(2)
Black, W.	1	10.76	40	5						26.42	(3)
Chang, T.	1	9.40	38	0						13.71	(4)
Dillon, M.	4	9.20	40	1						18.00	(5)
Gomez, R.	2	12.00	40	5						14.40	(6)
Hall, R.	0	8.85	40	2						16.95	(7)
Higgin, P.	4	8.15	36	0						18.37	(8)
West, G.	3	11.66	40	12						18.25	(9)
Zenith, R.	2	10.25	39	0						41.25	(10)
Total					(11)	(12)	(13)	(14)	(15)	(16)	(17)

*FICA Taxes are computed at 7.65% of total pay

**Assume all persons are single

Answers: (1) $400.22; (2) $365.99; (3) $391.58; (4) $286.16; (5) $324.59; (6) $457.99; (7) $291.49; (8) $251.58; (9) $546.29; (10) $300.92; (11) $3,943.15; (12) $570.48; (13) $4,513.63; (14) $345.31; (15) $336; (16) $215.51; (17) $3,616.81

Hint

To use your machine as efficiently as possible, pretend the keyboard is hot and touch it only when absolutely necessary. Make use of constants, memories, and extra storage registers if your machine is so equipped.

2. Complete the payroll schedule for Breumsbach Brush Implements (Table 6-13). You will need to look at the married persons Federal tax chart for this payroll.

Table 6-13

BREUMSBACH BRUSH IMPLEMENTS

Hourly Employee Payroll for Week Ending September 8, 20xx

Employee	Exemptions	Rate	Hrs	OT Hrs	Pay	OT Pay	Total Pay	FICA*	Tax**	Misc	Net Pay
Anders, J.	0	9.15	40	0						18.46	(1)
Bellow, M.	2	9.12	40	6						22.95	(2)
Black, W.	4	10.86	40	9						26.25	(3)
Chang, T.	3	12.00	35	0						19.56	(4)
Dillon, M.	6	11.10	40	4						37.46	(5)
Gomez, R.	2	11.85	35	0						19.92	(6)
Hall, R.	1	10.35	40	6						17.42	(7)
Higgin, P.	2	8.88	40	2						15.49	(8)
West, G.	3	9.42	40	0						16.85	(9)
Zenith, R.	1	10.30	38	0						28.65	(10)
Total					(11)	(12)	(13)	(14)	(15)	(16)	(17)

*FICA Taxes are computed at 7.65% of total pay

**Assume all persons are married

Answers: (1) $298.54; (2) $372.74; (3) $491.31; (4) $359.31; (5) $434.08; (6) $349.10; (7) $420.93; (8) $326.14; (9) $327.12; (10) $314.81; (11) $3,981.35; (12) $415.08; (13) $4,396.43; (14) $336.34; (15) $143; (16) $223.01; (17) $3,694.08

Stop

You are now ready to take Pretest VI to check your skill in using an electronic calculator to solve business problems. You should be able to correctly complete at least 70 of the 100 problems on the test in less than 50 minutes. Be certain you understand each problem on the Self-Test before attempting your graded examination. Unless instructed otherwise, turn in your Pretest for correction and review before taking Test VI.

When you pass Test VI, you will have proven your ability to efficiently use electronic calculators to solve word problems and work problems using percentage, simple interest and compound interest. You will have the ability to apply these skills to inventory and payroll questions.

NOTE: The questions with double numbers count twice as much (two points each).

Notes

Pretest VI

ESSENTIAL APPLICATIONS

50 minutes

This test need NOT be worked in sequence. Work the problems you know best first. You need 70 problems correct to pass.

Word problems.

To solve word problems _READ_ (1) the question carefully and use your intuition. Work backward from a _GUESSTIMATE_ (2). Draw a _PICTURE_ (3) and label the parts known and unknown. If you like equations, use them; but always ask yourself whether the answer makes sense—use a _Reasonableness_ (4) test.

Complete the following form.

SUNSET SUPPLY COMPANY
Comparative Income Statement for Period Ending: **December 31, 20xx**

	Amount (000s omitted)		Percent of Net Sales	
Account	This Year	Last Year	This Year	Last Year
Gross sales	$671	$554	_____ (5)	_____ (15)
Less returns	18	21	_____ (6)	_____ (16)
Net sales	$653	$533	_____ (7)	_____ (17)
Cost of goods sold	$382	$310	_____ (8)	_____ (18)
Gross profit	$271	$223	_____ (9)	_____ (19)
Expenses				
Commissions	$84	$78	_____ (10)	_____ (20)
Overhead	14	12	_____ (11)	_____ (21)
Freight	15	13	_____ (12)	_____ (22)
Total Expenses	$113	$103	_____ (13)	_____ (23)
Net Income	$158	$120	_____ (14)	_____ (24)

Percents.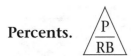

Calculate the amount and percentage of increase or decrease for the following items. Indicate decreases with a minus sign.

Item	Last Year	This Year	Amount of Increase/Decrease	Percent of Increase/Decrease
Skirts	$ 97,832	$ 111,081	_____ (25)	_____ (26)
Blouses	121,382	132,421	_____ (27)	_____ (28)
Shorts	48,523	32,518	_____ (29)	_____ (30)
Sweaters	9,856	14,327	_____ (31)	_____ (32)
Shoes	81,526	71,238	_____ (33)	_____ (34)

Word problems using percents.

What is 52.8% of $824.36? _____ (35)

How much is 53.9% increased by 26.6%? _____ (36)

How much is 437.3% of $88.73? _____ (37)

What is $391.32 less 19.8%? _____ (38)

What % of $328.70 is $458.85? _____ (39)

What is $827.48 decreased by 6.8%? _____ (40)

If your net pay is 76.8% of your gross pay, what is your net pay? Your gross pay is $1,286.71. _____ (41/42)

Opal Gray paid $121.23 on a debt. If the payment was 31.8% of the total debt, what was her total debt? _____ (43/44)

If sales tax of 6.2% of an item is $18.45, what is the price of the item? _____ (45/46)

Last year, Keystone Products had a payroll of $532,182.28. This year, its payroll increased to $593,873.59. What is the percent increase in payroll? _____ (47/48)

Simple Interest.

Using the Banker's Method, fill in the blanks on the following simple interest loans. Give time in years and days, to the nearest day.

Principal	Rate	Time	Interest	
$1,732.58	5 1/4%	80 days	_____	(49)
_____ (50)	3 3/5%	307 days	$105.47	
$5,436.72	7 1/2%	_____ (51)	$57.84	
$2,678.38	_____ (52)	350 days	$283.98	

Word problems using simple interest.

To the nearest dollar, how much money would you need to
invest at 10 4/5% simple interest to earn $5,200 in 90 days? _____ (53/54)

What rate of simple interest will earn $60.00 on $3,000 in 120 days? _____ (55/56)

How many days would it take for $1,000 to grow to $1,100 at 12.278%? _____ (57/58)

What is the maturity value of a $5,486.98 loan at 17 1/2% for 78 days _____ (59/60)

Compound Interest. (HINT: First find rate per period and number of periods.)

Principal	Time	Annual Rate	Frequency of Conversion	Amount	
$ 383.47	1 yr.	8%	quarterly	_____	(61)
$4,686.39	8 yrs.	14 3/4%	annually	_____	(62)
$ 487.42	3 yrs.	16%	semi-annual	_____	(63)
$ 142.53	9 mos.	24%	monthly	_____	(64)
$ 429.98	3 yrs.	9%	quarterly	_____	(65)

Word problems using compound interest.

If the inflation rate were 11% each year for five years, how much money would you have to make per month to stay even with inflation at the end of the five years? You now earn $1,238 per month.

_____ (66/67)

If the population of a certain country is 2.4 million today, to the nearest tenth of a million, what will the population be in 15 years if the country has an annual growth rate of 3.8%?

_____ (68/69)

If IBC had sales of $49 thousand this year, to the nearest thousand, what will their sales be in 11 years if they grow at 22% per year?

_____ (70/71)

If the value of a home increases at a rate of 4.1% per year, to the nearest thousand, what would the value be of a $87,250.00 home after 17 years?

_____ (72/73)

Inventory.
With the information given below and using the average cost method of valuing inventory find the cost of goods sold.

Beginning Inventory	642 units @ $1.53 = $_____	(74)
Purchases		
June 15	345 units @ $1.55 = $_____	(75)
July 10	362 units @ $2.03 = $_____	(76)
July 23	289 units @ $1.97 = $_____	(77)
August 1	235 units @ $2.04 = $_____	(78)
August 27	186 units @ $2.13 = $_____	(79)
Total cost of goods available for sale:	$_____	(80)
Less Ending Inventory: 547 units @ _____ (81)	$_____	(82)
Cost of goods sold	$_____	(83)

Hourly Employee Payroll for Week Ending March 5, 20xx

Employee	Exemptions	Rate	Hrs	OT Hrs	Pay	OT Pay	Total Pay	FICA*	Tax**	Misc	Net Pay
Anders, J.	1	11.25	40	6						22.27	(1)
Bellow, M.	2	12.30	40	7						24.57	(2)
Black, W.	1	11.20	40	5						27.25	(3)
Chang, T.	3	11.25	40	0					27.00	28.32	(4)
Dillon, M.	5	9.25	40	4					8.00	20.32	(5)
Gomez, R.	4	10.10	39	0					11.00	17.51	(6)
Hall, R.	3	11.26	40	3					35.00	51.10	(7)
Higgin, P.	2	9.15	40	4					31.00	24.32	(8)
West, G.	1	11.25	40	8					64.00	27.81	(9)
Zenith, R.	1	10.25	40	12					66.00	19.32	(10)
Total					(11)	(12)	(13)	(14)	(15)	(16)	(17)

*FICA Taxes are computed at 7.65% of total pay

**Assume all persons are single

Buying and Selling Goods

LEARNING GOALS

After completing Chapter 7, you will have improved your ability to operate electronic calculators and expanded your knowledge of business activity in the following areas:

- Cash Discounts
- Trade Discounts
- Invoices and Business Forms
- Transportation Costs
- Merchandising

You also will be able to pass a pretest of typical business problems, with at least 70 percent accuracy in less than 50 minutes.

Cash Discounts

Some companies deduct a part of the amount owed if payment is made before a specific time. This deduction is called a **discount** and is usually stated in the terms of the sale. For example, the terms may be "2/10, n/30." The n/30 means the customer has a 30-day charge period beginning at the date of the invoice. The 2/10 means that if payment is made on or before the tenth day after the invoice date, 2% of the amount owed may be deducted. Terms vary according to the agreements made.

For a sale of $200, terms 2/10, n/30, invoice on Jan. 6, the net amount of $200 would be overdue after 30 days (Feb. 5). If payment is made on or before Jan. 16, a discount of $4 (2% of $200) may be taken, and payment of $196 will satisfy the debt.

Hint

With terms like 2/10, n/30, if payment is not made within the discount period, only 20 days are left to pay before the account is delinquent since the total credit period is 30 days. To help find the days in each month consult Appendix 4.

1. Fill in the dates in Table 7-1. You may want to use the representative calendar in Appendix 4 for help with dates.

Table 7-1

Terms	Invoice Date	Last Date for Cash Discount	Last Date for Final Payment
2/10, n/30	Mar. 4	Mar. 14, 20XX	Apr. 3, 20XX
3/10, n/30	July 1	_____ (1)	_____ (2)
3/15, n/30	Aug. 5	_____ (3)	_____ (4)
3/20, n/60	May 17	_____ (5)	_____ (6)
3/10, n/60	Apr. 4	_____ (7)	_____ (8)
8/10, n/30	Nov. 19	_____ (9)	_____ (10)

Answers: (1) July 11; (2) July 31; (3) Aug. 20; (4) Sept. 4; (5) June 6; (6) July 16; (7) Apr. 14; (8) June 3; (9) Nov. 29; (10) Dec. 19

2. Compute the net amounts due if the invoices listed in Table 7-2 are paid on June 27. Remember, if a discount date is passed, the full amount must be paid.

Table 7-2

Invoice Date	Terms	Amount	Discount	Remittance
June 19	2/10, n/30	$500	_____ (1)	_____ (2)
June 26	1/10, n/30	600	_____ (3)	_____ (4)
June 15	2/10, n/30	800	_____ (5)	_____ (6)
June 27	2/10, n/30	400	_____ (7)	_____ (8)
June 20	2/10, n/30	220	_____ (9)	_____ (10)
June 10	1/10, n/30	600	_____ (11)	_____ (12)
June 10	2/20, n/60	300	_____ (13)	_____ (14)

Answers: (1) $10.00; (2) $490.00; (3) $6.00; (4) $594.00; (5) None; (6) $800.00; (7) $8.00; (8) $392.00; (9) $4.40; (10) $215.60; (11) None; (12) $600.00; (13) $6.00; (14) $294.00

3. Complete the invoice of Table 7-3.

Table 7-3

Mr. Joseph Martin
W. 1234 Evergreen Ave.
Seattle, Washington

Jan. 4, 20XX

Terms: 2/10, n/30

No. of Items	Item	Price Each	Total Price
1 dozen	cups	$ .73	$ _____ (1)
14	spoons	.15	_____ (2)
3	plates	1.45	_____ (3)
		TOTAL	_____ (4)

On Jan. 12 the amount to pay is $ _____ (5)

Answers: (1) $8.76; (2) $2.10; (3) $4.35; (4) $15.21; (5) $14.91

Trade Discounts

Trade discounts are another application of percentages. A dealer pays a reduced price for the goods he will sell; that is, he buys **wholesale**. The manufacturer or the supplier maintains a list of suggested retail prices and gives discounts to adjust these prices downward to wholesale for the dealer price. When manufacturers' prices change, only the discounts need to change; the suggested retail prices can remain the same.

Trade discounts are often stated as multiple percent rates. For example, discounts of "40%, 10%, 5%" might mean: 40% if the dealer is buying and reselling; 10% more if the dealer handles warranty adjustments; 5% more if the dealer attains a certain volume. Thus, some dealers may get only the 40% discount; others may get additional discounts.

These multiple trade discounts are often called **chain** or **series discounts** because they must be computed in succession. They cannot simply be summed to get the total discount. Thus, for the two discounts "40%, 10%," the 10% applies to what is **left** to pay **after** the first discount. For example:

$$
\begin{array}{ll}
\$100 & \text{invoice amount} \\
\underline{-40} & (40\% \text{ of } \$100) \\
60 & \text{left to pay} \\
\underline{-6} & (10\% \text{ of } \$60) \\
\$54 & \text{left to pay}
\end{array}
$$

In this example, the overall discount was 46% ([$40 + $6] ÷ $100). Adding the rates 40% and 10% does not give the overall discount. The trade discounts should be taken as a series or chain.

A shorter method for computing the after-discount amount is to multiply the amount before each discount by the percentage left to pay. Thus, on an invoice amount of $100 with trade discounts of 40%, 10%, after the first discount there will be only 60% left to pay:

$$\$100 \times .60 = \$60$$

And, after the second discount, only 90% of the previous amount will be left to pay.

$$\$60 \times .90 = \$54$$

The shortcut is to combine the steps.

$$\$100 \times .60 \times .90 = \$54$$

Another way to think of a 40% discount is: if you get 40% off, what percentage would you pay? 60%. Therefore, if you had chain discounts of 40%, 10%, and 5%, you would pay 60% of 90% of 95% or $.60 \times .90 \times .95$ or .513.

There is another shortcut if there are several invoices with the same set of trade discounts. For example, the series 40%, 10%, 5% means the constant percent left to pay is 51.3%. This constant factor can be obtained by multiplying the percentages left to pay ($.60 \times .90 \times .95 = .513$). The complement .487 is the overall discount.

1. What percentage is left to pay after the following discounts? (Remember to combine steps, using the complement of each discount.)

   10%, 10%, 10% = _____ % (1)

   40%, 10% = _____ % (2)

20%, 10%, 5% = _____% (3)

47%, 42%, 13% = _____% (4)

30%, 15%, 8% = _____% (5)

42%, 20%, 9% = _____% (6)

22%, 18%, 7% = _____% (7)

Answers: (1) 72.9% (.90 × .90 × .90); (2) 54%; (3) 68.4%; (4) 26.7%; (5) 54.7%;
(6) 42.2%; (7) 59.5%

2. Compute the amount due after trade discounts for the following invoice amounts.

			Left to Pay
$130.40	less	12%, 9%, 5%	$ _____ (1)
845.44	less	40%, 10%	$ _____ (2)
643.71	less	20%, 10%, 5%	$ _____ (3)
543.86	less	30%, 5%	$ _____ (4)
224.37	less	15%, 10%	$ _____ (5)
143.99	less	40%, 5%	$ _____ (6)
220.05	less	15%, 5%, 5%	$ _____ (7)
662.75	less	10%, 10%	$ _____ (8)
301.40	less	15%, 15%, 15%	$ _____ (9)
561.72	less	30%, 12 1/2%, 2 1/2%	$ _____ (10)

Answers: (1) $130.40 × .88 × .91 × .95 = $99.20; (2) $456.54; (3) $440.30;
(4) $361.67; (5) $171.64; (6) $82.07; (7) $168.81; (8) $536.83; (9) $185.10;
(10) $335.45

3. Compute the invoice totals in Tables 7-4 and 7-5 and then compute the amount to be paid after trade discount.

Table 7-4

Date: August 10, 20XX		Terms: 2/10, n/30 Discount: 30%, 15%	
	Price Per Carton	Total Amount	
386 cartons paper cups	$41.36	$ _____ (1)
62 cartons paper plates	71.83	_____ (2)
508 cartons paper napkins	18.37	_____ (3)
		TOTAL _____ (4)

The amount to pay after trade discount is $_____(5)

Table 7-5

	Cost Each	Total Amount
Date: August 3, 20XX   Terms: 3/10, n/30   Discount: 20%, 20%

	Cost Each	Total Amount
1 reamer	$6.27	$_____ (6)
3 files	1.39	_____ (7)
2 oilers	2.45	_____ (8)
		TOTAL _____ (9)

The amount to pay after trade discount is $ _____ (10)

In addition to the trade discounts that are always deducted when a company is "in the trade," a cash discount may apply. For instance, on August 15, the amounts needed to pay these two invoices would be:

Invoice 1: $ _____ (11)

Invoice 2: $ _____ (12)

Answers: (1) $15,964.96; (2) $4,453.46; (3) $9,331.96; (4) $29,750.38; (5) $17,701.48; (6) $6.27; (7) $4.17; (8) $4.90; (9) $15.34; (10) $9.82; (11) $17,347.45; (12) $9.82

Invoices and Business Forms

Electronic calculators, especially those with more than one storage device, greatly simplify the job of extending invoices and completing business forms. In this section, you will complete some business forms. Remember, the objective in completing the forms is to learn to use the machine with maximum efficiency, not just to arrive at correct answers.

Sales tax is computed as a percentage of purchase amount. This tax is usually levied by a state or city and paid by the purchaser as part of the total price. For a sales tax rate of 8%, a sale of $9.35 would cost a total of $10.10:

$$
\begin{array}{ll}
\$\ 9.35 & \text{purchase} \\
\underline{\quad .75} & \text{tax } (.08 \times \$9.35) \\
\$10.10 & \text{total}
\end{array}
$$

1. Complete the following invoices

No. of Items	Price Each	Amount	
2	$ .98	$ _____	(1)
1	.40	$ _____	(2)
3	.25	$ _____	(3)
	Subtotal	$ _____	(4)
	4% sales tax	$ _____	(5)
	TOTAL	$ _____	(6)

No. of Items	Price Each	Amount	
4	$21.36	$ _____	(7)
1	19.98	$ _____	(8)
5	9.37	$ _____	(9)
	Subtotal	$ _____	(10)
	4% sales tax	$ _____	(11)
	TOTAL	$ _____	(12)

No. of Items	Price Each	Amount	
3	$3.49	$ _____	(13)
1	1.98	$ _____	(14)
	Subtotal	$ _____	(15)
	3% sales tax	$ _____	(16)
	TOTAL	$ _____	(17)

No. of Items	Price Each	Amount	
42	$ .29	$ _____	(18)
8	.89	$ _____	(19)
	Subtotal	$ _____	(20)
	5% sales tax	$ _____	(21)
	TOTAL	$ _____	(22)

No. of Items	Price Each	Amount	
1	$32.95	$ _____	(23)
7	1.38	$ _____	(24)
	Subtotal	$ _____	(25)
	5% sales tax	$ _____	(26)
	TOTAL	$ _____	(27)

No. of Items	Price Each	Amount	
2	$11.98	$ _____	(28)
3	4.00	$ _____	(29)
	Subtotal	$ _____	(30)
	3% sales tax	$ _____	(31)
	TOTAL	$ _____	(32)

Hint

If you are misplacing the decimal point, refer to Estimating Decimal Placement, in Chapter 3.

Answers: (1) $1.96; (2) $.40; (3) $.75; (4) $3.11; (5) $.12; (6) $3.23; (7) $85.44; (8) $19.98; (9) $46.85; (10) $152.27; (11) $6.09; (12) $158.36; (13) $10.47; (14) $1.98; (15) $12.45; (16) $.37; (17) $12.82; (18) $12.18; (19) $7.12; (20) $19.30; (21) $.97; (22) $20.27; (23) $32.95; (24) $9.66; (25) $42.61; (26) $2.13; (27) $44.74; (28) $23.96; (29) $12.00; (30) $35.96; (31) $1.08; (32) $37.04

2. Complete the invoice for UN Industries, Inc. (7-1), using accumulative multiplication to calculate the total.

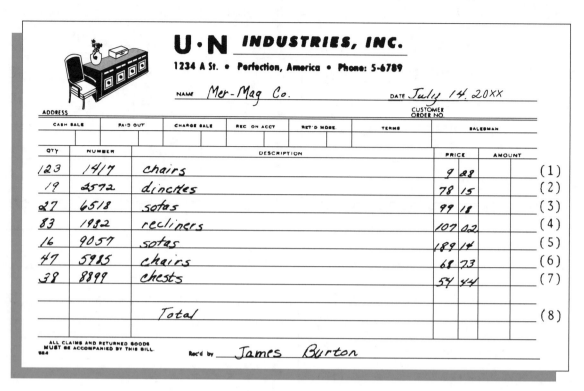

U·N INDUSTRIES, INC.

1234 A St. • Perfection, America • Phone: 5-6789

NAME _Mer-Mag Co._   DATE _July 14, 20XX_

ADDRESS   CUSTOMER ORDER NO.

CASH SALE	PAID OUT	CHARGE SALE	REC ON ACCT	RET'D MDSE.	TERMS	SALESMAN

QTY	NUMBER	DESCRIPTION	PRICE	AMOUNT	
123	1417	chairs	9 28		(1)
19	2572	dinettes	78 15		(2)
27	6518	sofas	99 18		(3)
83	1932	recliners	107 02		(4)
16	9057	sofas	189 14		(5)
47	5985	chairs	68 73		(6)
38	8899	chests	54 44		(7)
		Total			(8)

ALL CLAIMS AND RETURNED GOODS MUST BE ACCOMPANIED BY THIS BILL.
984   Rec'd by _James Burton_

Figure 7-1.

Answers: (1) $1,141.44; (2) $1,484.85; (3) $2,677.86; (4) $8,882.66; (5) $3,026.24; (6) $3,230.31; (7) $2,068.72; (8) $22,512.08

3. Figure 7-2 shows sales slips for Jimmy's Sporting Goods and Harder Enterprises, Inc. Complete each sales slip. Use accumulative multiplication to find the subtotal; then add tax and total.

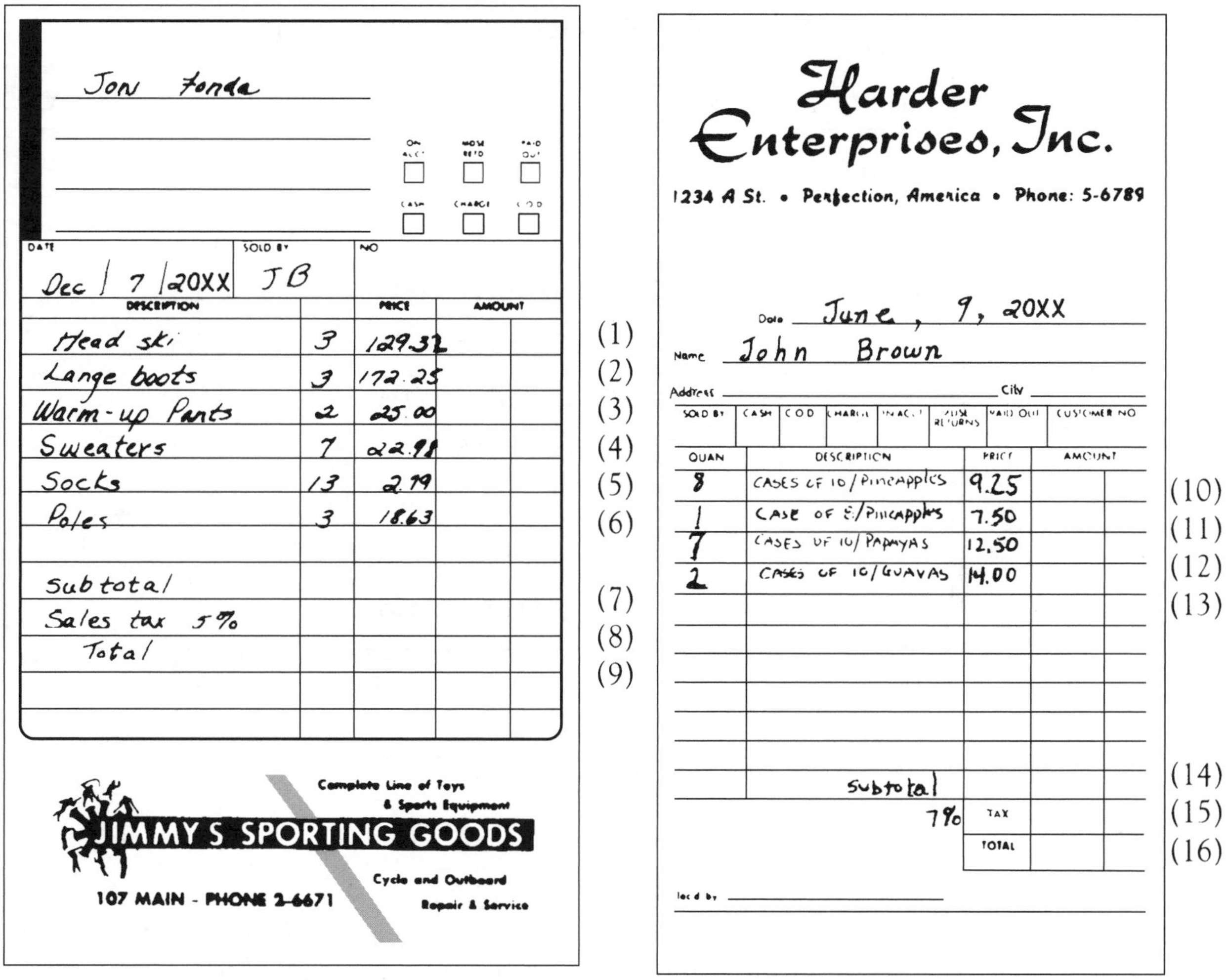

(a)

(b)

Figure 7-2.

Answers: (1) $387.96; (2) $516.75; (3) $50.00; (4) $160.86; (5) $36.27; (6) $55.89; (7) $1,207.73; (8) $60.39; (9) $1,268.12; (10) $74.00; (11) $7.50; (12) $87.50; (13) $28.00; (14) $197.00; (15) $13.79; (16) $210.79

4. Complete the invoice of Perfection Tire Company in Table 7-6. Use accumulative multiplication to calculate the total.

Table 7-6

PERFECTION TIRE COMPANY		
Invoice		
Sold to: Ken's 76		*Date: June 11, 20XX*
Quantity	*Description*	*Unit Price*
5	#453 P155/80R13 B/W	$41.71
4	#321 P185/75R13 W/W	55.31
8	#723 P195/75R14 W/W	57.81
4	#576 P225/75R14 W/W	65.16
2	#711 P235/75R15 W/W	73.32
	Subtotal	_____ (1)
	Plus 6.2% sales tax	_____ (2)
	TOTAL PAYMENT	_____ (3)

Answers: (1) $1,299.55; (2) $80.57; (3) $1,380.12

Transportation Costs

Transportation charges can have a major influence on final price. For example, oil has a much higher price at a refinery in California than at the well in Prudhoe Bay, Alaska. A Honda automobile has a higher price at a showroom in Spokane, Washington, than at the manufacturer's site in Japan. Costs of transportation from seller to buyer may be paid by the seller or the buyer, depending on the terms of sale. If a sale is made **FOB Origin**, the buyer pays transportation costs; if the sale is made **FOB Destination**, the seller must pay freight charges. (FOB stands for "free on board.") In practice, when the terms of sale are FOB Origin, the seller usually prepays for shipment and then adds the shipping costs to the invoice.

Remember: Freight charges are always excluded when figuring discounts. That is, a cash discount, if offered, is based on the net amount following the trade discount but before the freight charge is added.

Washington Produce ships 2,000 boxes of apples to Nelson's Distributors at a price of $18.00 a box, with trade discounts of 15%, 5%, a cash discount of 2/10, n/30, and shipping charges of $314.79. Assuming FOB Origin and payment made within 10 days:

Solution

2,000 boxes @ $18 ea. =	$36,000.00
Less trade discounts 15%, 5% =	29,070.00
Less cash discounts 2/10, n/30 =	28,488.60
Plus freight charges =	314.79
TOTAL REMITTANCE	$28,803.39

Assuming FOB Destination and payment made after 10 days:

Solution

2,000 boxes @ $18 ea. =	$36,000.00
Less trade discounts 15%, 5% =	29,070.00
No cash discount	
No freight charges	
TOTAL REMITTANCE	$29,070.00

1. If the following invoices are paid June 8, decide which cash discounts and freight charges apply and fill in the amount due the seller.

Date of Invoice	Amount	Transportation FOB Costs	Trade Discounts	Cash Discounts	Amount Due the Seller
May 28	$ 832.16	Origin $ 32.81	2%, 5%, 3%	1/15, n/45	_____ (1)
April 10	1,334.51	Origin 152.37	10%, 22%, 35%	2/15, n/60	_____ (2)
May 30	581.37	Origin 67.90	15%, 25%	3/10, n/30	_____ (3)
June 1	837.43	Destination 50.00	5%, 7%, 16%	1/10, n/60	_____ (4)
May 25	21,456.87	Destination 487.23	2%, 18%, 24%	3/15, n/45	_____ (5)

Answers: (1) $776.79; (2) $761.31; (3) $427.40; (4) $615.28; (5) $12,711.35

2. What would the remittance be on the invoice in Table 7-7 from Center Fish Market if it were paid February 25?

Table 7-7

Center Fish Market 634 Lake Street Pikesville, Michigan		

Invoice No.	**7983**
Invoice Date	Feb. 10, 20XX

Sold To:	Harder Enterprises, Inc. 1234 A Street Flour, Michigan	**Ship To:**	same

Selling Broker Gerber Bros., Inc.	**Transportation Company** Santa Fe	**Shipping Date** 2/10/20XX

Customer Purchase Order Y2879	**Terms of Sale** 1 1/2/15, n/30

Cases	Size	Description	Number	Price	Amount	
1700	48/2	Sea Star Tuna	7845	28.25	_____	(1)
	After trade discount of 5%, 15%, 17%				_____	(2)

☐ **FOB Destination**

☒ **FOB Origin**
28253 lbs @ $3.80 cwt*

Freight _____ (3)	
if paid by Feb. 25, 20XX	**Total** _____ (4)

*per hundred weight (282.53 × $3.80)

Answers: (1) $48,025.00; (2) $32,187.56; (3) $1,073.61; (4) $32,778.36

3. What would be the remittance on the invoice in Table 7-8 from Allied Industries if the transportation costs were $173.15 and the invoice were paid on June 1?

Table 7-8

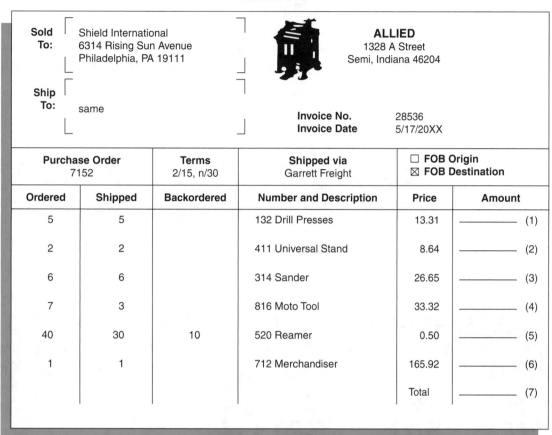

Sold To:	Shield International 6314 Rising Sun Avenue Philadelphia, PA 19111			**ALLIED** 1328 A Street Semi, Indiana 46204		
Ship To:	same			Invoice No. 28536 Invoice Date 5/17/20XX		

Purchase Order 7152		Terms 2/15, n/30	Shipped via Garrett Freight		☐ FOB Origin ☒ FOB Destination	
Ordered	**Shipped**	**Backordered**	**Number and Description**	**Price**	**Amount**	
5	5		132 Drill Presses	13.31	———	(1)
2	2		411 Universal Stand	8.64	———	(2)
6	6		314 Sander	26.65	———	(3)
7	3		816 Moto Tool	33.32	———	(4)
40	30	10	520 Reamer	0.50	———	(5)
1	1		712 Merchandiser	165.92	———	(6)
				Total	———	(7)

Freight   ——— (8)

Net if paid by 6/1/20xx ——— (9)

Answers: (1) $66.55; (2) $17.28; (3) $159.90; (4) $99.96; (5) $15.00; (6) $165.92; (7) $524.61; (8) 0; (9) $514.12

Merchandising

Pricing merchandise is a crucial decision in marketing or selling goods. Prices are based on relative scarcity. Relative scarcity is determined by supply and demand, cost of production, competition, economic conditions, and so forth. Because of the many variables in pricing, each situation is unique.

The sale price of a product must cover the costs of the product, including administrative and selling expenses, plus provide a reasonable profit. Profit is the incentive for businesses to serve consumers. Without a fair profit, businesses cannot stay alive for long. Making a profit is the reason most businesses exist in a free-enterprise society.

There are two types of profit in business—gross profit and net profit. **Gross profit**, also known as **markon**, or **margin**, is the difference between selling price and cost price. **Net profit** or **loss** is the amount that remains after operating expenses are deducted from gross profit.

The difference between the cost of a good and its selling price is called **markon**. (See Figure 7-3.) If an item does not sell well at the original price, the price may be decreased. Conversely, if the price is too low, it may be increased. Reductions and increases from the original selling price are referred to as **markdowns** and **markups**.

There are two bases for pricing merchandise: cost and selling price. We will consider these in the sections that follow.

Markon Based on Cost

Many wholesale businesses use markon based on costs. Retail businesses that face frequent price changes, such as those selling fruit and vegetables, also like the cost method because it provides a more stable base. The cost method is a logical base for pricing because cost data are readily available and tend to remain more stable than selling prices.

Selling Price

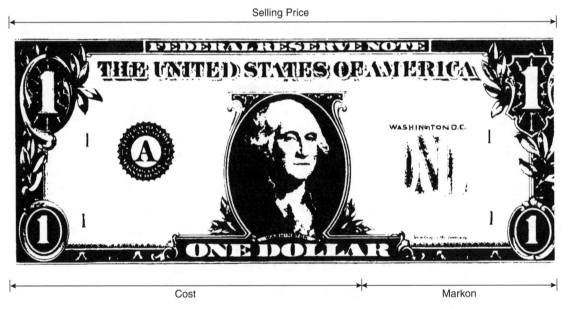

Cost — Markon

Figure 7-3.

There is a simple formula for relating selling price to cost and markon that you probably already know, which will be useful in all the problems in this section:

$$C + M = S$$

where C = cost, M = markon, and S = selling price. For example, if cost is $7.00 and markon is $3.50, then selling price is $7.00 + $3.50 = $10.50.

Cost is what the store pays for an item. Selling price is the price they want to sell the item for. Markon is the difference, the amount needed to cover such overhead expenses as rent, labor, utilities, etc., and maybe even have something left for profit.

Markon is often expressed as a percent instead of a dollar amount. Thus, if cost is $7.00 and markon is $3.50, we find the markon percent by dividing the base (cost) into the part (markon). Since $3.50 is half of $7.00, markon is 50%. Using the symbols, we have:

C	+	M	=	S
$ 7.00	+	$ 3.50	=	$10.50, or
100%	+	50%	=	150%

1. The best way to solve merchandising problems is with a picture. First, write the formula:

C + M = S

Then place a blank line with a dollar sign under each letter of the formula.

C + M = S

$ _____ + $ _____ = $ _____

Then fill in the blanks from the question you are asked. For example, fill in the blanks from the first problem below to compute selling price(s).

C	+	M	=	S
$ 3.50	+	$ 1.74	=	$?

So you know to combine cost (C), and markon (M), to find selling price (S).

C	M	S	
$3.50	$1.74	_____	(1)
$3.24	$1.08	_____	(2)
$12.30	$4.10	_____	(3)
$15.75	$3.15	_____	(4)
$27.99	$9.33	_____	(5)

Answers: (1) $5.24; (2) $4.32; (3) $16.40; (4) $18.90; (5) $37.32

To compute markon (M) just fill in the blanks from the first problem below.

C	+	M	=	S
$ 3.00	+	$?	=	$ 5.00

You then know to subtract cost (C) from selling price (S) to find markon (M).

C	M		S
$3.00	_____	(1)	$5.00
$12.32	_____	(2)	$16.27
$29.73	_____	(3)	$85.71
$13.72	_____	(4)	$18.27
$25.31	_____	(5)	$75.87

Answers: (1) $2.00; (2) $3.95; (3) $55.98; (4) $4.55; (5) $50.56

3. To compute cost (C) fill in the blanks from the first problem below.

C	+	M	=	S
$?	+	$ 2.00	=	$ 5.00

You then know to subtract markon (M) from selling price (S) to find cost (C).

C		M	S
_____	(1)	$2.00	$5.00
_____	(2)	$12.27	$18.37
_____	(3)	$11.36	$29.43
_____	(4)	$12.71	$24.31
_____	(5)	$27.32	$76.89

Answers: (1) $3.00; (2) $6.10; (3) $18.07; (4) $11.60; (5) $49.57

4. To compute percent of markon based on cost (C%) place two blanks below each letter in the formula. Label the first row with dollar signs and the second row with percent signs. On the percent line the base (cost percent) will be 100% and the markon based on cost (C%) is what you are trying to find. Fill in the blanks from the first problem below.

C	+	M	=	S
$ 1.30	+	$ .65	=	$____
100%	+	? %	=	____ %

You then know to divide markon (M) by cost (C) to find markon based on cost (C%).

C		M	C%	
$1.30	÷	$.65	_____	(1)
$12.27		$1.72	_____	(2)
$23.75		$3.39	_____	(3)
$27.85		$13.59	_____	(4)
$89.11		$22.05	_____	(5)

Answers: (1) 50%; (2) 14%; (3) 14.3%; (4) 48.8%; (5) 24.7%

5. To compute markon (M) based on cost, draw the picture and fill in the appropriate blanks.

C	+	M	=	S
$10.00	+	$?	=	$____
100%	+	20%	=	120%

You know that if markon based on cost is 20% (C%) then markon is 20% of the cost (C), or you multiply cost (C) times markon based on cost (C%).

C	C%	M	
$10.00	20%	_____	(1)
$13.26	16%	_____	(2)
$8.73	12%	_____	(3)
$19.72	28%	_____	(4)
$37.14	103%	_____	(5)

Answers: (1) $2.00; (2) $2.12; (3) $1.05; (4) $5.52; (5) $38.25

6. To compute cost (C) when the percent of markon based on cost (C%) and markon (M) are given, draw the picture and fill in the appropriate blanks.

C	+	M	=	S
$?	+	$ 4.00	=	$____
100%	+	25%	=	____ %

With the picture you know that markon (M) is 25% of the base cost (C). Divide markon (M) by percent of markon based on cost (25%) to find cost (C).

C%	M	C
25%	$4.00	_____ (1)
37%	$2.23	_____ (2)
41%	$14.32	_____ (3)
76%	$16.84	_____ (4)
62%	$89.31	_____ (5)

Answers: (1) $16.00; (2) $6.03; (3) $34.93; (4) $22.16; (5) $144.05

7. To compute selling price (S) based on cost draw the picture and fill in the appropriate blanks.

base ↘

C	+	M	=	S
$ 4.40	+	$ 1.10	=	$? 5.50
100%	+	25%	=	125%

↑ rate

First combine the base (cost percent) and the markon percent to find the selling percent, then find selling price by multiplying the selling percent times the cost (C).

C%	C	S
25%	$4.40	_____ (1)
100%	$5.00	_____ (2)
37%	$5.37	_____ (3)
41%	$58.75	_____ (4)
87%	$71.32	_____ (5)

Answers: (1) $5.50; (2) $10.00; (3) $7.36; (4) $82.84; (5) $133.37

8. To compute cost (C) based on cost, draw the picture and fill in the appropriate blanks.

C	+	M	=	S
$____	+	$____	=	$59.72
100%	+	38%	=	138%

First combine the base (cost percent) and the markon percent to find the selling percent, then find cost price by dividing selling price (S) by the selling price percent.

C%	S	C	
38%	$59.72	_____	(1)
13%	$27.83	_____	(2)
10%	$11.00	_____	(3)
51%	$67.31	_____	(4)
104%	$71.98	_____	(5)

Answers: (1) $43.28; (2) $24.63; (3) $10.00; (4) $44.58; (5) $35.28

9. Fill in the blanks using the C + M = S picture.

C	M	S	C%				
$5.00	_____(1)	_____(2)	20%				
_____(3)	$1.00	$4.00	_____(4)				
$7.15	$3.14	_____(5)	_____(6)				
$13.28	_____(7)	$16.73	_____(8)				
_____(9)	$8.14	_____(10)	16%				

Answers: (1) $1.00; (2) $6.00; (3) $3.00; (4) 33.3%; (5) $10.29; (6) 43.9%; (7) $3.45; (8) 26.0%; (9) $50.88; (10) $59.02

Markon Based on Selling Price

Many retail firms base markon on selling price, or retail price. This **retail method** is preferred to the cost method by many retailers because numerous bookkeeping procedures are based on retail price. For example, commissions are often figured as a percentage of retail sales; sales tax is usually a percentage of selling price; and inventory-taking needs no cost coding per item. In addition, the retail industry publishes certain statistics using the retail method, such as sales per square foot, budget amounts per retail sales, and store rents as percent of sales.

We use the formula C + M = S to base markups on retail price, except the base is selling price instead of cost. For example, if retail price (S) is $10.50 and markon (M) is $3.50, the markon percentage is the ratio of markon to selling price. Since $3.50 is one-third of

$10.50, the markon is 33 1/3% based on retail price. Based on cost, this same markon was 50%. Let us compare the cost method and the retail method using this same example.

Based on Selling Price					**Based on Cost**				
C	+	M	=	S	C	+	M	=	S
$7.00	+	$3.50	=	$10.50	$7.00	+	$3.50	=	$10.50
66 2/3%	+	33 1/3%	=	100%	100%	+	50%	=	150%

Or we could more easily write the problem:

	C	+	M	=	S
	$7.00	+	$3.50	=	$10.50
Based on Selling	66 2/3%	+	33 1/3%	=	100%
Based on Cost	100%	+	50%	=	150%

Hint

The only difference between the cost method and the retail method is the position of the base. If you learn the formula C + M = S (Cost + Markon = Selling Price) and remember to ask whether the base is cost or retail, you will find these problems quite simple.

10. To compute percent of markon based on selling price (S%) draw the picture and fill in the appropriate blanks. Since the base is selling price, remember to place 100% under selling price.

C	+	M	=	S
$____	+	$5.27	=	$13.28
____%	+	____%	=	100%

From the picture, you should be able to visualize that markon (M) divided by selling price (S) would equal percent of markon based on selling price (S%).

S	M	S%
$13.28	$5.27	_____ (1)
$3.57	$1.19	_____ (2)
$4.00	$2.00	_____ (3)
$89.99	$17.63	_____ (4)
$98.71	$63.17	_____ (5)

Answers: (1) 39.7%; (2) 33.3%; (3) 50%; (4) 19.6%; (5) 64%

11. To compute markon (M) based on selling price (S%) draw the picture and fill in the appropriate blanks.

C	+	M	=	S
$____	+	$_?_	=	$28.31
____%	+	27%	=	100%

From the picture you see that percent of markon based on selling price (S%) times selling price (S) equals markon (M).

S	S%	M
$28.31	27%	_____(1)
$8.24	13%	_____(2)
$5.00	50%	_____(3)
$31.72	39%	_____(4)
$57.19	89%	_____(5)

Answers: (1) $7.64; (2) $1.07; (3) $2.50; (4) $12.37; (5) $50.90

12. To compute selling price (S), when the percent of markon based on selling price (S%) and markon (M) are given, sketch the problem and fill in the blanks.

C	+	M	=	S
$____	+	$8.00	=	$?
____%	+	20%	=	100%

From this sketch you see that to find selling price (S) you would divide markon (M) by percent of markon based on selling price (S%).

S%	M	S
20%	$8.00	_____(1)
15%	$8.32	_____(2)
27%	$17.63	_____(3)
19%	$18.72	_____(4)
89%	$76.73	_____(5)

Answers: (1) $40.00; (2) $55.47; (3) $65.30; (4) $98.53; (5) $86.21

13. To compute cost (C) based on selling price, sketch the problem and fill in the blanks.

C	+	M	=	S
$?	+	$___	=	$10.00
90%	+	10%	=	100%

This time you will need to first find percent of cost based on selling by subtracting percent of markon based on selling (S%) from the base (100%, then from the sketch you see that to find cost (C) just multiply percent of cost based on selling, times selling price (S).

S%	S	C	
10%	$10.00	_____	(1)
23%	$8.73	_____	(2)
17%	$25.00	_____	(3)
33%	$45.00	_____	(4)
43%	$47.83	_____	(5)

Answers: (1) $9.00; (2) $6.72; (3) $20.75; (4) $30.15; (5) $27.26

14. To compute selling price (S) based on selling price, sketch the problem and fill in the blanks.

C	+	M	=	S
$89.95	+	$___	=	$___
65%	+	35%	=	100%

First subtract percent of markon based on selling from the base (100%), then divide this number into cost (C) to find selling price (S).

S%	C	S	
35%	$89.95	_____	(1)
25%	$75.00	_____	(2)
50%	$5.00	_____	(3)
72%	$33.33	_____	(4)
84%	$35.72	_____	(5)

Answers: (1) $138.38; (2) $100.00; (3) $10.00; (4) $119.04; (5) $223.25

15. The management of Roundup Wholesale Market wants to compare the markups based on cost and retail. From the schedule in Table 7-9 calculate percent markup on cost and percent markup on retail.

Table 7-9

ROUNDUP WHOLESALE MARKET Markup Schedule					
Item	Cost	Retail Price	Markup	% Markup on Cost	% Markup on Retail
Asparagus	$80.58	$90.19	_____ (1)	_____ (2)	_____ (3)
Beans, green	43.17	57.04	_____ (4)	_____ (5)	_____ (6)
Corn	38.78	47.98	_____ (7)	_____ (8)	_____ (9)
Peas	47.45	58.30	_____ (10)	_____ (11)	_____ (12)
Spinach	32.78	41.60	_____ (13)	_____ (14)	_____ (15)

Answers: (1) $9.61; (2) 11.9%; think markup divided by cost. (3) 10.7%; think markup divided by retail. (4) $13.87; (5) 32.1%; (6) 24.3%; (7) $9.20; (8) 23.7%; (9) 19.2%; (10) $10.85; (11) 22.9%; (12) 18.6%; (13) $8.82; (14) 26.9%; (15) 21.2%

Retailers sometimes know the retail price at which they can sell a given product and the percent markup needed to make a transaction profitable. This knowledge tells them how much they can pay for a certain item and still market it profitably.

16. Calculate the maximum cost a retailer could pay for the following items.

Hint

Remember the sketch

C	+	M	=	S
$?	+	$____	=	$17.37
80%	+	20%	=	100%

Retail Value	% Markup on Retail	Maximum Cost
$ 17.37	20%	_____ (1)
59.20	13%	_____ (2)
83.01	49%	_____ (3)
9.50	52%	_____ (4)
98.52	26%	_____ (5)
108.89	14%	_____ (6)
55.38	12%	_____ (7)
183.96	19%	_____ (8)
35.82	39%	_____ (9)
136.63	46%	_____ (10)

Answers: (1) $13.90; (2) $51.50; (3) $42.34; (4) $4.56; (5) $72.90; (6) $93.65; (7) $48.73; (8) $149.01; (9) $21.85; (10) $73.78

17. The Peoria Manufacturing Company produces widgets for Caterpillar Tractors. They mark up each widget $39^{1/4}\%$ over manufacturing cost. Find the selling price for each widget (Table 7-10).

Table 7-10

PEORIA MANUFACTURING COMPANY
Price Schedule: January 1, 20XX

Product Number	Cost to Manufacture	% Markup on Cost	Selling Price	
AM 3663	$ 9.40	$39^{1/4}\%$	_____	(1)
AM 4678	7.41	$39^{1/4}\%$	_____	(2)
BA 5886	62.88	$39^{1/4}\%$	_____	(3)
BA 1104	51.74	$39^{1/4}\%$	_____	(4)
JL 8693	17.94	$39^{1/4}\%$	_____	(5)
JM 9322	16.06	$39^{1/4}\%$	_____	(6)
KQ 3663	143.68	$39^{1/4}\%$	_____	(7)
NA 2678	25.80	$39^{1/4}\%$	_____	(8)
OP 3034	106.17	$39^{1/4}\%$	_____	(9)
RS 5538	77.93	$39^{1/4}\%$	_____	(10)

Answers: (1) $13.09; (2) $10.32; (3) $87.56; (4) $72.05; (5) $24.98; (6) $22.36; (7) $200.07; (8) $35.93; (9) $147.84; (10) $108.52

18. Kinley's Parts House calculates the markup on parts at 47% of retail price. Calculate the retail price for each part shown on the partial invoice in Table 7-11. Don't forget to use the constant key.

Hint

Remember the sketch

C	+	M	=	S
$9.32	+	$___	=	$?
53%	+	47%	=	100%

Table 7-11

KINNLEY'S PARTS HOUSE

Sold to: Jo's Auto   Invoice: 22184

Part Number	Cost per Unit	Retail Price
L669-4A	$ 9.32	_____ (1)
L806-2B	88.57	_____ (2)
N554-1A	8.05	_____ (3)
N950-8C	.60	_____ (4)
M907-2A	9.50	_____ (5)
O210-3B	45.54	_____ (6)
Q911-8C	31.73	_____ (7)
R981-89	103.58	_____ (8)
S581-37	5.32	_____ (9)
T476-48	19.81	_____ (10)

Answers: (1) $17.58; (2) $167.11; (3) $15.19; (4) $1.13; (5) $17.92; (6) $85.92; (7) $59.87; (8) $195.43; (9) $10.04; (10) $37.38

Markdowns

Sale prices or markdowns help a business dispose of merchandise that is overstocked, seasonal, no longer stylish, damaged, or perishable like fruit, flowers, and pastry. Markdowns are very easy to compute. Just remember the percentage problems from Chapter 4. The "part" is the amount of markdown. The "rate" is the percent or fraction of markdown. The "base" is the original selling price. And the sales price is found by multiplying the original selling price by the compliment of the markdown. For example:

If a dress with a retail price of $64.95 is marked down 35% what is the sale price?

We could find the markdown by taking 35% (percent of markdown) times $64.95 (original sales price) which would equal $22.73 (the markdown). Then by subtracting $22.73 from $64.95 we would arrive at a sales price of $42.22.

The most efficient use of the calculator, however, is to use the compliment method. Simply think, if you do not pay 35% then you do pay 65%. So:

$$.65 \times \$64.95 = \$42.22$$

Calculate the sale price on the following items using the compliment method.

Original Selling Price	Markdown Rate	Sale Price	
$235.89	27%	_____	(1)
$97.25	39%	_____	(2)
$22.87	45%	_____	(3)
$450.90	35%	_____	(4)
$12.35	50%	_____	(5)

An oak desk that was damaged in shipment was marked down 25% from the original sale price of $1,269.95. Determine the new sale price.

_____ (6)

At the end of summer all swim wear was marked 65% off. What would be the price of a swimming suit that had an original price of $48.89?

_____ (7)

If day old pastries were marked down 35%, what would a day old cherry pie cost that was priced at $7.79?

_____ (8)

Jane's Fashion shop was overstocked and advertised a reduction of inventory sale with everything 20% off. What would the sale price of a blouse be with an original selling price of $42.81?

_____ (9)

A somewhat out of fashion men's suit which had an original price of $378.89 was marked down 23%, then 31% and then 50% before it sold. What was the sale price of the suit?

_____ (10)

Answers: (1) $172.20; (2) $59.32; (3) $12.58; (4) $293.09; (5) $6.18; (6) $952.46; (7) $17.11; (8) $5.06; (9) $34.25; (10) $100.65; think $378.89 \times (1 - .23) \times (1 - .31) \times (1 - .5)$

Word Problems

A furniture store buys a lounge chair for $214.84 and marks it up 60% on retail. Calculate the selling price.

_____ (1)

A head of lettuce sells for $.83. It has a markon of 40% based on cost. Find the cost to the supermarket.

_____ (2)

A buyer for Stan's Men's Wear needs to find a line of coats that retail for $95 each and have a percent markon of 37.5% of retail. What is the most the buyer could pay for each coat?

_____ (3)

The markon on a small piece of gold jewelry is $25.97. If the percent markon based on selling price is 65%, what is the retail price?

_____ (4)

What is the cost price?

_____ (5)

If the cost price on an item is $15.30 and the selling price is $22.95, what is the percent markon based on retail?

_____ (6)

What is the percent markon based on cost?

_____ (7)

O'Malley's Book Store stocks an atlas that costs $27.95 and sells it at a markon of 32% selling price. Find the selling price.

_____ (8)

Find the markon.

_____ (9)

A golf club which had an original price of $43.95 was marked down 35%. What was the new sale price?

_____ (10)

Jenny Williams, a contractor, needs to submit a bid at least 34% markon over cost. If she calculates the cost of the home to be $189,650, what must she ask for a selling price?

_____ (11)

A dress manufacturer sells to a wholesaler at a markon of 29% cost. If a dress sells for $19, what is the cost to manufacture the dress?

_____ (12)

If an item sells for $25.25 that cost $15.38, what is the percent markon based on selling price?

_____ (13)

Based on cost?

_____ (14)

Gonzales's Furniture pays $238.24 for a chair and sells it for $495.95. What is the percent markon based on selling price?

_____ (15)

Sara's Health Food Store buys dried apricots for $.71 per pound. If it needs 23% profit on selling price, what should the selling price per pound be?

_____ (16)

A department store has a 35% off sale on a special purchase of men's shirts. If regular retail price was $22.95, what is the sale price?

_____ (17)

What is the amount of markon on an item selling for $313.16 if the markup is 38% of retail?

_____ (18)

What is the percent markon on an item that cost $39.45 and sells for $52.98 based on cost?

_____ (19)

Based on selling price?

_____ (20)

Answers: (1) $537.10; (2) $.59; (3) $59.38; (4) $39.95; (5) $13.98; (6) $33^{1/3}$%; (7) 50%; (8) $41.10; (9) $13.15; (10) $28.57; (11) $254,131; (12) $14.73; (13) 39.1%; (14) 64.2%; (15) 52.0%; (16) $.92; (17) $14.92; (18) $119.00; (19) 34.3%; (20) 25.5%

Stop

You are now ready to take Pretest VII to check your skill using a calculator to solve business problems involving Buying and Selling Goods. You should be able to complete this test in less than 50 minutes with better than 70 percent accuracy. Unless instructed to do otherwise, turn in your Pretest for correction and review before taking Test VII. Be certain you understand each problem in Pretest VII before attempting your graded examination.

When you pass Test VII you will have proven your ability to use calculators effectively to solve merchandising problems.

Pretest VII

CALCULATOR APPLICATIONS—BUYING AND SELLING GOODS

50 minutes

This test need not be worked in sequence. Do the problems you know best first. You need 70 percent correct to pass.

Compute the total of these invoices.

Items	Price	Amount	
3	$ .75	_____	(1)
8	2.77	_____	(2)
21	14.43	_____	(3)
72	.29	_____	(4)
	Subtotal	_____	(5)
	6.2% sales tax	_____	(6)
	TOTAL	_____	(7)

Compute these invoices including trade and cash discounts.

Date: March 3, 20XX	Terms: 2.5/15, n/45 Discount: 10%, 5%, 5%	[ ] FOB Origin [X] FOB Destination

Quantity	Item #	Item	Cost Each	Amount	
3	#3225	microwave	$445.93	$ _____	(8)
7	#1172	stove	500.00	_____	(9)
6	#5783	refrigerator	562.12	_____	(10)
12	#8424	freezer	516.80	_____	(11)
			Total	_____	(12)
		After trade discounts		_____	(13)
		Freight Charges ($131.72)			
		Net (if paid March 17)		_____	(14/15)

Date: January 17, 20XX		Terms: 2/10, n/30 Discount: 15%, 3%, 1%		[X] FOB Origin [ ] FOB Destination	

Quantity	Item #	Item	Cost Each	Amount	
16 cases	#21	beans	$ 6.81	$ _____	(16)
7 cases	#28	peas	5.99	_____	(17)
8 cases	#9	asparagus	13.65	_____	(18)
10 cases	#31	corn	9.88	_____	(19)
3 cases	#33	corn	6.78	_____	(20)
			Total	_____	(21)
		After trade discounts		_____	(22)
		Freight Charges $42.45			
		Net (if paid Jan. 23)		_____	(23/24)
		Net (if paid Jan. 29)		_____	(25)

Merchandising.

Item	Cost	Retail	Markup	% Markup on Cost	% Markup on Retail
C32	$34.78	$42.68	_____ (26)	_____ (27)	_____ (28)
D71	$67.29	_____ (29)	$9.62	_____ (30)	_____ (31)
E32	_____ (32)	$3.08	$1.09	_____ (33)	_____ (34)
F29	$47.12	_____ (35)	_____ (36)	39%	_____ (37)
H41	_____ (38)	$29.95	_____ (39)	_____ (40)	48%

Word Problems.

Gem Book store sells an atlas the cost them $22.95 at a markup of 18% of selling price. What is the selling price?

_____ (41/42)

If the selling price of a suit is $188.72 and the markup based on retail is 35%, what is the cost of the suit?

_____ (43/44)

If Stanford Payless sells a digital camera for $399.55 and markup based on cost is 39%, what is the cost?

_____ (45/46)

What should be the selling price of a pair of shoes if the cost is $29.25 and markup based on retail is 28%?

_____ (47/48)

What should be the selling price of a custom trailer if the cost is $1,995.74 and the markup based on cost is 42%?

_____ (49/50)

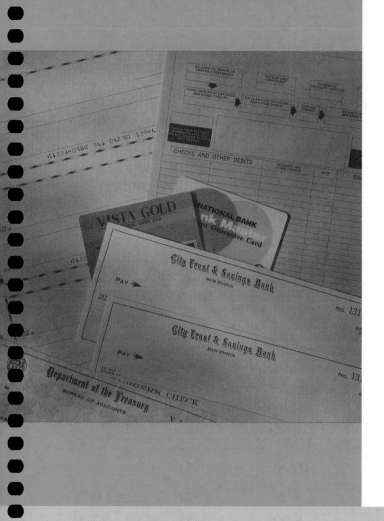

CHAPTER

Consumer Economics

LEARNING GOALS

After completing Chapter 8, you will have improved your ability to operate electronic calculators and expanded your knowledge in the following areas:

- Consumer Credit
- Balancing a Checking Account
- Personal Taxes
- Insurance
- Investments

You will also be able to pass a pretest of typical business problems, with at least 70 percent accuracy in less than 50 minutes.

Consumer Credit

When buying on time, shopping for credit is often as beneficial as shopping for the article itself. Even with the Truth-in-Lending law, a purchaser of goods should always determine the difference between the cost on a cash basis and the cost on an installment credit plan.

The **installment price** is found by multiplying the amount of each payment times the number of payments and adding the down payment. The **carrying charge** (cost of credit) is found by subtracting the cash price from the installment price.

1. In the last three years Jim Smith has bought a number of items on credit (Table 8-1). Calculate the total installment price and cost of credit on each item.

Table 8-1

Item	Cash Price	Down Payment	No. of Monthly Payments	Amount of Payment	Installment Price	Cost of Credit
Desk	$214.43	$50.00	20 ×	$10.00	250.00 (1)	35.57 (2)
File	54.78	10.00	12 ×	4.00	58.00 (3)	3.22 (4)
Rifle	153.38	25.00	24 ×	6.00	169.00 (5)	15.62 (6)
Shotgun	211.13	30.00	25 ×	12.53	343.25 (7)	132.12 (8)
Television	842.40	10% 84.24	36 ×	25.00	984.24 (9)	141.84 (10)
Dishwasher	293.90	15% 44.09	21 ×	13.21	321.50 (11)	27.60 (12)
DVD recorder	378.31	25% 94.58	30 ×	11.83	449.40 (13)	71.09 (14)

TOTAL COST OF CREDIT 427.06 (15)

20 × 10 = 200

Answers: (1) $250.00; (2) $35.57; (3) $58.00; (4) $3.22; (5) $169.00; (6) $15.62; (7) $343.25; (8) $132.12; (9) $984.24; (10) $141.84; (11) $321.50; (12) $27.60; (13) $449.49; (14) $71.12; (15) $427.09

2. A consumer protection group collected data on credit costs charged consumers on installment purchases (Table 8-2). For each loan, calculate the credit price and the credit cost.

Table 8-2

COST OF CREDIT
A Consumer Protection Study: September 1

Loan Value	No. of Payments	Payment Schedule	Amount of Payment	Credit Price	Credit Cost
$200.00	12	monthly	$ 20.00	$= 240.00(1)^{-200.00}$	$= 40.00$ (2)
147.13	32	weekly	5.00	160.0 (3)	12.87 (4)
746.99	4	semi-annual	219.74	878.96 (5)	131.97 (6)
310.48	10	monthly	34.06	340.60 (7)	30.12 (8)
86.70	26	weekly	3.93	102.18 (9)	15.48 (10)

Answers: (1) $240.00; (2) $40.00; (3) $160.00; (4) $12.87; (5) $878.96; (6) $131.97; (7) $340.60; (8) $30.12; (9) $102.18; (10) $15.48

Balancing a Checking Account

To enable you to know how much money you have in your checking account day by day, banks have a procedure for balancing checkbooks, which makes use of your bank statement and your checkbook. Your **bank statement** is the bank's record of all the activity in your checking account; it is issued regularly each month (or quarter). Your **checkbook** is the record you keep of the activity in your checking account. It is the most important part of balancing, for it makes balancing possible.

Maintaining Your Checkbook

Maintaining your checkbook record need not be complicated, but it does require consistency:

1. Record each check when you write it and each deposit when it's made.
2. Subtract each check or add each deposit immediately.
3. Keep a running balance in your checkbook.

Since a checking account is a contractual relationship with a bank, you have a legal duty to promptly examine statements, canceled checks, and other items and to report errors, suspected forgeries, or alterations on any check or item. You also have the responsibility not to write checks for more than you have in the account. For your own protection, you should also promptly report lost or stolen checks.

Balancing your checkbook every time you receive your bank statement is something you do for your own benefit. Bringing both the bank statement and your records into balance promptly upon receipt of the statement allows you to:

■ review the checks you've written during the past month (or quarter)
■ verify the amounts of deposits, checks, and charges
■ correct errors in your account record
■ correct errors in the bank's record of your account

The Problem of Bouncing Checks

Bounced checks are embarrassing and costly. Banks charge a fee for each overdraft or returned check. Supermarkets and other businesses that allow you to cash checks also may charge a fee for checks returned to them. With today's computers, checks are being processed faster than ever. (Most banks process thousands of checks a day.) A check you cash today has a good chance of being posted to your account tonight. Planning on "float time"—time to cover your check with a deposit—is risking an overdraft. Knowing your account balance is the best way to avoid bouncing your checks.

Checks and Other Debits

The following charges appear on your bank statement as **subtractions** from your checking account during the statement period.

Checks—A written order directing the bank to pay a specified amount of money to a specified party.

Personalized Check Charge—for blank checks; the amount depends on the check design you order.

Service Charge—for maintaining your checking account; the amount depends on the type of account you have and will be explained when you open your account.

Bounced Check Charge—Whenever your account hasn't enough funds to pay for checks you've written, you have "insufficient funds." Depending on how you've handled the account, the bank may: (a) create an overdraft and pay the check (the person or firm you made the check out to is unaware your account is overdrawn); or (b) return the check unpaid to the person or firm you made it out to. To cover the extra time, handling, and paperwork for overdrafts or returns, there is usually a charge per check. The bank notifies you of the amount of the charge and the amount of the overdraft if you are overdrawn.

If you have a line of credit, or Instant Cash Service, overdraft checks can be covered by automatic deposits to your checking account that are billed to your loan account. (Special arrangements must be made with your bank to provide this service.)

Automatic Transfer of Funds

You may authorize your bank to transfer money automatically from your checking account, on a regular basis and on a date you select, for the following:

- Savings account—regular savings, investors passbook, or Christmas Club
- Loan payment on real estate loans, personal loans, auto or other loans
- Insurance premiums
- Safe deposit box rental fee
- Other fixed monthly payments for services, dues, tuition, leasing, and so on, if automatic payment option is offered by the service provider

There is usually no charge for automatic transfer of funds and you may cancel such service at any time.

Credits

The following deposits appear on your bank statements as **additions** to your checking account during the statement period.

In-Person Deposits—Use the personalized deposit slips in the back of your checkbook, they are already encoded with your account number for faster and more accurate processing.

By-Mail Deposits—Use the personalized deposit slips in the back of your checkbook. Banks often provide envelopes and receipt cards for such mail deposits.

Overdraft Protection—Such deposits require separate application and approval.

Certain miscellaneous credits may appear on your bank statement in the following ways:

R (Reversing Entry)—"R" next to a deposit means the deposit is offset by a debit for an identical amount listed in the "Checks and Other Debits" area of the statement.

M (Miscellaneous Entry)—"M" next to a deposit entry means the bank itself has initiated a miscellaneous addition of adjustment to your account. Generally, you will be aware of such an item. If you have questions, visit your bank's customer service representative.

Automatic Deposits—You may authorize the bank to make regular, automatic deposits from the following sources:

- Paycheck, if your employer offers Payroll Service
- Interest earned on your savings accounts or certificates of deposit with the bank

- Another checking account, such as your individual or joint account, a parent's account, or a commercial account
- Other income, such as from trusts, property management programs, or installment or rent collection services

Automatic deposits require your authorization and may be canceled at any time. There is usually no charge.

How to Balance Your Checkbook

1. Find the new balance on your bank statement and copy it onto the T account on the back of the statement.

2. Compare the deposits listed in the "Deposits" area of your bank statement with deposits recorded in your checkbook. If a deposit recorded in your checkbook is not listed on your statement (not yet credited by the bank), write it on the back of your statement or T account. Add all the deposits not yet credited by the bank to the new balance to get a sub-total.

3. If there is a deposit on the bank account that you did not record in your checkbook, first verify that it's your deposit. If it is not, notify the bank. If it is, record it in your checkbook and add the amount to the last balance in your checkbook. All additions to your account during this statement period are now recorded on both your record and the bank's.

4. Mark off (✓) canceled checks in your checkbook. This tells you what checks the bank has already paid and subtracted from your account. If you find that a canceled check is not recorded in your checkbook, record it now and subtract the amount from your checkbook balance.

5. On the back of the bank statement or T account, list the checks not marked off in your checkbook. These are "checks outstanding," which the bank had not received and paid by the statement date. Total the "checks outstanding" and subtract the total from the sub-total to get the Adjusted Bank Statement Balance. (Since you have already subtracted these checks from your checkbook, you must also subtract them from the bank statement so that your record and the bank's show the same subtractions.)

6. Find the "Service Charge" listed at the top of the "Checks and Other Debits" area of your bank statement. Subtract the Service Charge from your checkbook balance if you have not already subtracted it. If other charges are listed that you have not subtracted from your checkbook balance, do so now. What remains is your "Adjusted Checkbook Balance."

7. Compare your "Adjusted Bank Statement Balance" with your "Adjusted Checkbook Balance"—they should be equal. If you

have followed Steps 1 through 6, your record should show the same additions, subtractions, and balance as the bank's. You have balanced your checkbook. This balance is how much money you have in your checking account today. If you can't balance your checkbook, see the next section, "Tracking Down Errors," or visit the customer service representative at your bank.

Tracking Down Errors

If you've gone through the balancing procedure and your checkbook still won't balance, the following checklist may help you locate the error.

Automatic Transactions—Make sure you've added to or subtracted from your record all automatic deposits and deductions and all miscellaneous credits and charges that appear on your statement. Don't forget Instant Cash deposits.

Arithmetic—Check the addition and subtraction in your checkbook and in the balancing procedure. (If the difference between your balance and the bank's can be evenly divided by 2, the error could be caused by adding instead of subtracting a check in your checkbook.)

Transposing—If the difference between your balance and the bank's can be evenly divided by 9, there's a good chance the error was caused by transposing numbers, for example, recording a $23 check as $32, or $5.17 as $7.15.

Recording Errors—Compare the check numbers and check amounts recorded in your checkbook with the numbers and amounts on the canceled checks you received. On each check, the amount recorded by the computer is encoded on the bottom right corner under your signature. This should also be the same as the check amount you wrote and recorded.

Last Month's "Checks Outstanding"—Any checks outstanding from last month's balancing that are still unpaid by the bank (and don't show up on your statement) must be included in this month's list of checks outstanding.

Balance Carry-Forward—In your checkbook, be sure that you correctly carried forward the balance from the bottom of one page to the top of the next.

Unrecorded Canceled Checks—Have you recorded and subtracted from your checkbook balance all the canceled checks listed on your statement and enclosed with it?

Missing Check—(missing from your checkbook record or from the numerical listing on your statement). Did you forget to record a check? A saved sales receipt might help jog your memory. Have you destroyed a check? You can visit the customer service representative at your bank and learn about your canceled checks before they're normally returned to you.

"Less Cash" Deposit—When you deposit a check and simultaneously withdraw part of the deposit in cash (using one deposit slip) you have a "less cash" deposit. Be sure you recorded the correct amount to be added to your account. Check the teller's stamped entry on the Deposit Record page of your checkbook or your deposit receipt (stamped duplicate deposit slip).

Same Deposits—Do you and the bank show the same number of deposits and for the same amounts? You should have a receipt or a stamped entry in your checkbook to verify the amount of each deposit.

Matching Statement Balance—Be sure the Previous Balance on this month's statement is the same as the New Balance on last month's statement.

If your checkbook still won't balance, you need further help. Gather all your records—checkbook, deposit receipts, statement and canceled checks—and visit the statement window at your bank.

Here's an important point to remember: Today's Balance, as given to you by your bank, may not necessarily be the true balance of your account. It won't include checks you've written or deposits made that have not yet reached the bank. You need to make allowance for these checks to prevent overdrawing your account.

Bringing Your Records Up to Date

Where do you begin if you haven't balanced your checkbook for several months? If you have a record of deposits and checks written you must balance your checkbook one statement at a time. Start with the oldest statement and canceled checks and:

1. In your checkbook, draw a line under the last check listed on that statement (the check with the highest number enclosed with that statement).

2. Balance that statement as far as the checkbook balance on the line you just drew.

3. Go to the next oldest statement and canceled checks and repeat steps 1–2 until your checkbook balance is up to date.

If you don't have a complete record of deposits and checks written, visit the customer service representative at your bank for help in reaching an accurate balance. Bring your checkbook and your last two bank statements with the enclosed canceled checks.

Once your checkbook balance is up to date, keep your future records current so you will know how much money you have in your checking account from day to day. Regular balancing will get easier.

Bank Reconciliation—T-Account Form

Because bank statement forms vary widely, we will use a T-account form to apply the principles of bank statement reconciliation in the following example.

Sam Bear received his bank statement on January 23. The bank balance was (a) $723.19. Sam's checkbook showed a balance of (b) $2,405.16. Sam made one deposit that did not appear on the bank statement in the amount of (c) $1,276.49. The bank statement showed an automatic transfer for a life insurance payment for (d) $87.75 and an automatic transfer for a house payment of (e) $368. Bank service charges were (f) $2. There were three outstanding checks: (g) No. 532 for $17.21; No. 533 for $7.93; No. 535 for $27.13. Reconcile the bank statement balance with the checkbook balance.

BANK

BANK SAYS I HAVE :

Jan 23rd.

ME

BANK RECONCILIATION WHAT I HAVE RECORDED :

BANK SAYS I HAVE			ME / WHAT I HAVE RECORDED		
Bank Balance	(a)	$ 723.19	Checkbook Balance	(b)	$2,405.16
Additions to bank statement:			Additions to checkbooks:		
Deposits in transit	(c)	1,276.49			
SUBTOTAL		$1,999.68	SUBTOTAL		$2,405.16
Deductions from bank statement:			Deductions from checkbook:		
Outstanding checks (g)			Automatic transfers		
No. 532 $17.21				(d) $ 87.75	Ins. Payment.
No. 533 7.93				(e) 368.00	House Payment
No. 535 27.13			Service charge (f)	2.00	Service Charges
Total		– 52.27	Total		– 457.75
ADJUSTED BANK BALANCE		$1,947.41	ADJUSTED CHECKBOOK BALANCE		$1,947.41

1. On Juanita Bolivar's bank statement for the previous month, the balance is $631.82. Her check stubs show a balance of $1,727.81. Two deposits she made do not appear on the bank statement: $372.10 and $2,489.31. Juanita ordered personalized checks and the bank charge for them is $10.00. There is a bank service charge of $2.50. The bank credited Juanita's account automatically for $1,637.28, which is her biweekly paycheck. An automatic transfer was made by the bank for a car payment in the amount of $220.37. Juanita sold a junker automobile for $475.00; the check was returned marked insufficient funds (therefore, Juanita had $475 less in her account). Outstanding checks are: No. 871 for $15.27, No. 874 for $87.93, No. 875 for $732.81. Reconcile the bank statement balance with Juanita's checkbook balance.

BANK RECONCILIATION

Bank Balance	_____	Checkbook Balance		_____
Additions:		Additions:		
SUBTOTAL	_____		SUBTOTAL	_____
Subtractions:		Subtractions:		
TOTAL	_____		TOTAL	_____
ADJUSTED BANK BALANCE	======	ADJUSTED CHECKBOOK BALANCE		======

ANSWER

BANK RECONCILIATION

Bank Balance	$631.82		Checkbook Balance	$1,727.81

Additions: | | | Additions: | |
Deposits in transit	372.10		Automatic payroll deposit	$1,637.28
	2,489.31			
SUBTOTAL	$3,493.23		SUBTOTAL	$3,365.09

Subtractions: | | | Subtractions: | |
Outstanding checks			Personalized checks	$ 10.00
No. 871 $ 15.27			Service charge	2.50
No. 871 87.93			Car payment	220.37
No. 875 732.81			Returned check	475.00
Total	836.01		Total	707.87
ADJUSTED			ADJUSTED	
BANK BALANCE	$2,657.22		CHECKBOOK BALANCE	$2,657.22

2. The H.S. Sharp Co.s' latest bank statement indicated a $1,517.67 balance. The checkbook shows a $2,714.27 balance. After the canceled checks are organized, it is found that checks No. 2517 for $157.18 and No. 2519 for $389.25 are still outstanding. A deposit for $2,541.30 is not shown on the statement. Service charges were $3.00 for the account, $9.00 for printing checks, and $4.00 for an $814.27 note that was collected by the bank. Reconcile, using the following T-account form.

BANK RECONCILIATION

Bank Balance	_____	Checkbook Balance	_____
Additions:		Additions:	
SUBTOTAL	_____	SUBTOTAL	_____
Subtractions:		Subtractions:	
TOTAL	_____	TOTAL	_____
ADJUSTED		ADJUSTED	
BANK BALANCE	_____	CHECKBOOK BALANCE	_____

BANK RECONCILIATION

Bank Balance	$1,517.67		Checkbook Balance	$2.714.27
Additions:			Additions:	
Deposits in transit	$2,541.30		Note collected	814.27
SUBTOTAL	$4,058.97		SUBTOTAL	$3,528.54
Subtractions:			Subtractions:	
Outstanding checks:			Service charge $3.00	
No. 2517 $157.18			Printing check 9.00	
No. 2519 389.25			Collection charge 4.00	
	Total 546.43			Total 16.00
ADJUSTED			ADJUSTED	
BANK BALANCE	$3,512.54		CHECKBOOK BALANCE	$3,512.54

3. Justin Davis has a checkbook balance of $12,180.37 as of April 30. The bank statement that he received on May 2 indicates a balance of $15,824.37. He has outstanding checks No. 681 for $98.00 and No. 684 for $6,000.00; service charge of $11.00, overdraft charges of $24.00, and a late deposit of $155.86 not yet recorded by the bank. Justin also found two errors in his checkbook: a $35 check listed as $53, and an unrecorded check for $2,281.14. Reconcile the statement using the T-account form.

BANK RECONCILIATION

Bank Balance	_____		Checkbook Balance	_____
Additions:			Additions:	
SUBTOTAL	_____		SUBTOTAL	_____
Subtractions:			Subtractions:	
TOTAL	_____		TOTAL	_____
ADJUSTED			ADJUSTED	
BANK BALANCE	_____		CHECKBOOK BALANCE	_____

BANK RECONCILIATION

Bank Balance	*$15,824.37*	*Checkbook Balance*	*$12,180.37*
Additions:		*Additions:*	
Deposits in transit	*155.86*	*Transposition error*	*18.00*
SUBTOTAL	*$15,980.23*	*SUBTOTAL*	*$12,198.37*
Subtractions:		*Subtractions*	
Outstanding checks:		*Unrecorded check* $2,281.14	
No. 681 *$ 98.00*		*Service charge* 11.00	
No. 684 *6,000.00*		*Overdraft charges* 24.00	
Total *6,098.00*		*Total* 2,316.14	
ADJUSTED		*ADJUSTED*	
BANK BALANCE	*$9,882.23*	*CHECKBOOK BALANCE*	*$9,882.23*

Personal Taxes

In Chapter 6 you computed social security taxes and income taxes. In this unit we will focus on sales tax and property taxes.

Sales tax is the most important source of revenue for state governments.

Sales Taxes

A tax on the selling price of an item or service that you purchase is called a **sales tax**. Sales taxes are **consumption taxes** imposed on the retail value of most items we buy. However, food purchased for consumption off-premises is exempt from sales taxes in many states.

The sales tax rate is expressed as a percent and varies from state to state as shown in Table 8-3:

Property taxes pay for the many important services of state and local governments including education, welfare, hospitals and health services, highways, libraries, fire and police services, and a variety of other public services.

Table 8-3

COMPARISON OF STATE AND LOCAL RETAIL SALES TAXES

	Food Items [1] Taxable (T) Exempt (E)	State Rate	Maximum Local Rate [2]	Maximum State/Local Rate [2]
Alabama	T	4.00	5.00	9.00
Alaska	T	—	6.00 [4]	6.00
Arizona	E	5.60	3.00	8.60
Arkansas	T	5.125	3.00	8.125
California	E	5.75	2.50	8.25
Colorado	E	2.90	4.50	7.40
Connecticut	E	6.00	—	6.00
District of Columbia	E	5.75	—	5.75
Florida	E	6.00	2.50	8.50
Georgia	E	4.00	3.00	7.00
Hawaii	T*	4.00	—	4.00
Idaho	T*	5.00	2.00	7.00
Illinois	T**	6.25	2.50	8.75
Indiana	E	5.00	—	5.00
Iowa	E	5.00	2.00	7.00
Kansas	T*	4.90	3.00	7.90
Kentucky	E	6.00	—	6.00
Louisiana	T [3]	4.00	5.50	9.50
Maine	E	5.00	—	5.00
Maryland	E	5.00	—	5.00
Massachusetts	E	5.00	—	5.00
Michigan	E	6.00	—	6.00
Minnesota	E	6.50	1.00	7.50
Mississippi	T	7.00	—	7.00
Missouri	T	4.225	4.00	8.225
Nebraska	E	5.00	1.50	6.50

Continued

Nevada	E	6.50	0.75	7.25
New Jersey	E	6.00	—	6.00
New Mexico	T	5.00	2.1875	7.1875
New York	E	4.00	4.50	8.50
North Carolina	E [5]	4.00	2.00	6.00
North Dakota	E	5.00	2.00	7.00
Ohio	E	5.00	2.00	7.00
Oklahoma	T	4.50	5.25	9.75
Pennsylvania	E	6.00	1.00	7.00
Rhode Island	E	7.00	—	7.00
South Carolina	T**	5.00	1.00	6.00
South Dakota	T*	4.00	2.00	6.00
Tennessee	T	6.00	2.75	8.75
Texas	E	6.25	2.00	8.25
Utah	T	4.75	2.00	6.75
Vermont	E	5.00	—	5.00
Virginia	T**	3.50	1.00	4.50
WASHINGTON	E	6.50	2.30	8.80
West Virginia	T	6.00	—	6.00
Wisconsin	E	5.00	0.60	5.60
Wyoming	T*	4.00	2.00	6.00

[1] Food purchased for consumption off-premises.
[2] Highest local rate known to be actually levied by at least one jurisdiction. Includes local taxes for general purposes and those earmarked for specific purposes (e.g. transit). Taxes applying only to specified sales (e.g. lodging or meals) are excluded.
[3] Exemption has been temporarily suspended for the state tax; food remains subject to local taxes.
[4] Alaskan cities and boroughs may levy local sales taxes from 1% to 6%.
[5] Food exempt from state tax, but subject to local taxes.
*Income tax credit allowed to offset sales tax on food.
**Food taxed at lower rate.
Source: "State Tax Guide," Commerce Clearing House, Inc.; Federation of Tax Administrators. Table was compiled by the Washington Dept. of Revenue. Updated 10/18/2001, from state websites and input from state revenue/tax agency responses

Note that State and Federal taxes frequently change; this table is for mathematical instruction examples.

The triangle you used in Chapter 4 works well for solving sales tax problems, with some minor modifications.

NOTE: When using Table 8-3 assume all sales taxes are at the maximum state and local level.

The total purchase price is found by adding the sales tax to the purchase price of an item.

Example 1. Kenney's Shoe Store sells a certain shoe for $28.95 in Cleveland, Ohio. What is the sales tax? What is the total purchase price?

Solution: Sales tax = Sales tax rate × Selling price
$$= 7\% \times \$28.95 \quad \text{Note the sales tax rate is 7\% from}$$
$$\text{Table 8-3}$$
$$= .07 \times \$28.95$$
$$= \$2.0265$$
$$= \$2.03 \text{ (rounded)}$$

Total purchase price = Selling price + Sales tax
$$= \$28.95 + \$2.03$$
$$= \$30.98 \quad \text{Note } \$30.98 \text{ is } 107\% \text{ of } \$28.95$$

When the total purchase price is given, the selling price can be found by dividing the total purchase price by 100 percent + the tax rate.

Example 2. At the end of the day The Fashion Bug had $3,869.09 in the cash register. The $3,869.09 is the total purchase price of all items sold during the day. If the sales tax rate is 8 percent, what is the selling price of the items sold?

Solution: Total purchase price = (Selling price percent + Sales tax percent) × Selling price.
$$\$3,869.09 = (100\% + 8\%) \times \text{Selling price}$$
$$\$3,869.09 = 108\% \times \text{Selling price}$$
$$\$3,869.09 = 1.08 \times \text{Selling price}$$

Since division is the opposite process of multiplication
$$\$3,869.09/1.08 = \$3,582.49 \text{ (Selling Price)}$$

NOTE: We want to find what the tax is based on. The total purchase price ($3,869.09) is the "part" and the selling price percent plus the sales tax rate is the rate (108%). We can find base by dividing the part by the rate.

If the amount of sales tax and the tax rate is known, the selling price can be determined by dividing the sales tax by the sales tax rate.

Example 3. If the sales tax is $4.50 and the sales tax rate is 9 percent what was the selling price?

Solution: Selling price = Sales tax/Sales tax rate
Selling price = $4.50/9%
Selling price = $4.50/.09
Selling price = $50.00

Solve the following word problems.

What is the total purchase price of a pair of Docker slacks if the selling price is $34.50 and they are purchased in Omaha, Nebraska?

_____ (1)

If you purchased a Prince "PRO" oversize tennis racket priced at $49.95 in Virginia how much change should you receive from $60.00?

_____ (2)

The total purchase price for a Led Zepplin, Volume 1 gift set purchased in Ohio is $37.45. What was the selling price of Volume l?

_____ (3)

What would the total purchase price of a Yamaha SY-55 Music Synthesizer priced at $1,219.00 be in Provo, Utah?

_____ (4)

Find the price of a Robin Hood Professional Bow Hunting Set bought in Spokane, Washington state if $8.12 is paid in sales tax.

_____ (5)

Find the price of a pair of Hush Puppies shoes bought in Castleton, Vermont if $2.14 is paid in sales tax.

_____ (6)

A pair of Dan Post "ELK" Cowboy Boots at the Boot Ranch in Waco, Texas is priced at $155.00. What would the total price be including sales tax?

_____ (7)

If $25.60 sales tax was collected in Hershey, Pennsylvania for the purchase of a Seiko Ladies' Diamond Quartz Watch, what was the sale price of the watch?

_____ (8)

The sales clerk told Sarah the total purchase price of a London Fog "Ashley" All Weather Coat was $159.86 in Knoxville, Tennessee. What was the sale price of the coat?

_____ (9)

If Zoe wanted to by a Zwilling 9 pc. Knife and Block Set that sells for $145 how much would the sales tax be in Charleston, West Virginia?

_____ (10)

Answers: (1) $36.74; (2) $7.80; (3) $35.00; (4) $1,301.28; (5) $92.27; (6) $42.80; (7) $167.79; (8) $365.71; (9) $147.00; (10) $8.70

Property Taxes

Property tax is the major source funding for local governments providing about 75 percent of all local tax revenues in the United States. Property tax is levied primarily on real estate—land and buildings. Each locality sets an annual tax rate. Chicago, for example, sets a nominal tax rate of 9.66 percent of "assessed value" (i.e., of the value as determined by the city and/or county). If a house in Chicago was assessed at $100,000 the tax would be $9,660. In most places assessed valuations tend to be a fraction of the true market value. In Chicago, assessments are about 16 percent of market value, so the true tax rate is really about 1.55 percent of market value.

Property tax has been very controversial since the 1970's. During the housing boom of the 1970's, housing valuations and taxes skyrocketed. Taxpayers revolted. In Massachusetts voters passed "Proposition 2 1/2 ," limiting tax payments to 2 1/2 percent of market value. California passed "Proposition 13" and Oregon passed "Measure 5." Today almost half the states have limitations on property taxes preventing property taxes from rising as rapidly as they did in the 1970's. During recessions these tax limits have led several local governments into severe fiscal crises as they ran out of tax funds and were forced to cut services. Since education is the major expenditure of most local government, education has usually felt these cuts.

The tax assessor's office is responsible for determining the amount of tax to be levied on each piece of property. First the assessor must determine the **market value** of each piece of property. Market value, defined as the worth of the property (land and buildings) if the property were to be sold today, is found using such data as real estate sales and construction costs.

The rate of assessment usually ranges from 15 percent to 60 percent of market value. This is the formula:

$$\text{Assessed Value} = \text{Assessment Rate} \times \text{Market Value}$$

Example 1. What is the assessed value of a home where the assessment rate is 45% and the market value is $98,000?

Solution:
$$\begin{aligned}
\text{Assessed Value} &= \text{Assessment Rate} \times \text{Market Value} \\
&= 45\% \times \$98,000 \\
&= .45 \times \$98,000 \\
&= \$44,100
\end{aligned}$$

Within the limits of local regulations the first step in determining the property tax rate is deciding the total amount of revenue needed to pay for local government services. The total amount of money needed from property taxes to pay for these services is then divided by the total assessed value of all the property in the local government's boundaries to find the property tax rate. Tax rates are expressed in different ways in different parts of the country. However, they can always be found with this formula:

$$\text{Tax Rate} = \text{Budget Needed}/\text{Total Assessed Value}$$

Example 2. What should the tax rate be if a local government needs to collect $2,456,900 from property that has a total assessed value of $189,800,000?

Solution: Tax rate = Budget Needed/Total Assessed Value
= $2,456,900/$189,800,000
= $.0129

This tax rate could be expressed as a *percent (dollars per $100) or mills (dollars per $1,000)*. As a percent the tax rate in Example 2 would be 1.29%. Since percent means hundredths, as dollars per $100 the tax rate would be almost the same thing $1.29 per hundred. With dollars per $1,000 we just move the decimal one more place to the right giving us a tax rate of $12.90 per thousand. Expressed in mills which is one-tenth of a cent or one-thousandth of a dollar the tax rate would be 12.9 mills.

The dollar amount of property tax that a property owner pays is determined by assessed value of the property and the tax rate.

Property Tax = Tax Rate × Assessed Value

Example 3. What are the property taxes on a home with an assessed value of $67,800 where the tax rate is 24.5 mills?

Solution: Property Tax = Tax Rate × Assessed Value
= 24.5 mills × $67,800   Note: since mills means one-thousandth we shift the decimal three places to the left.

= .0245 × $67,800
= $1,661.10

Practice Problems
Find the assessed valuations for each of the following pieces of property.

Market Value	Rate of Assessment	Assessed Valuation	
$34,000	48%	_____	(1)
$56,000	37%	_____	(2)
$137,000	31%	_____	(3)
$82,000	24%	_____	(4)
$219,000	45%	_____	(5)

Find the tax rate to the nearest ten-thousandth (four decimal places) for the following.

Total Tax Amount Needed	Total Assessed Value	Tax Rate
$956,800	$20,457,000	_____ (6)
$2,894,100	$59,783,000	_____ (7)
$456,300	$1,429,000	_____ (8)
$1,927,300	$492,519,000	_____ (9)
$4,318,200	$71,935,000	_____ (10)

Complete the following list comparing tax rates.

Percent	Per $100	Per $1,000	Mills
2.18%	_____ (11)	_____ (12)	_____ (13)
_____ (14)	$7.21	_____ (15)	_____ (16)
_____ (17)	_____ (18)	$21.90	_____ (19)
_____ (20)	_____ (21)	_____ (22)	32.8

Answers: (1) $16,320; (2) $20,720; (3) $42,470; (4) $19,680; (5) $98,550; (6) .0468; (7) .0484; (8) .3193; (9) .0039; (10) .0600; (11) $2.18; (12) $21.80; (13) 21.8; (14) 7.21%; (15) $72.10; (16) 72.1; (17) 2.19%; (18) $2.19; (19) 21.9; (20) 3.28%; (21) $3.28; (22) $32.80

Find the following taxes.

Assessed Valuation	Tax Rate	Tax
$12,900	$12.20 per $100	_____ (23)
$45,200	34.7 mills	_____ (24)
$182,700	$51.90 per $1,000	_____ (25)
$87,300	3.72%	_____ (26)

Solve the following word problems.

A piece of land in Valley County is appraised at $34,300. What are the property taxes for this piece of land if the tax rate is 31.7 mills?

_____ (27)

The market value of a home in Peoria, Illinois, is $129,000. The tax rate is $9.56 per $1,000. If the assessed valuation is 46% of market value, find the property tax.

_____ (28)

If the total value of assessed property in Jackson Hole, Wyoming is $216,589,000 and they need to raise $5,396,000 in property taxes, what should the tax rate be in mills?

_____ (29)

If the tax rate in Newark, New Jersey, is $3.24 per $100 of assessed valuation, what is the tax on property assessed at $82,400?

_____ (30)

Answers: (23) $1,573.80; (24) $1,568.44; (25) $9,482.13; (26) $3,247.56; (27) $1,087.31; (28) $567.29; (29) 24.9 mills; (30) $2,669.76

Insurance

Our lives are fraught with many areas of uncertainty. We can exercise and eat right to protect our health. We can drive defensively to decrease the chance of an auto accident. We can monitor our property to decrease the risk of loss or damage due to fire, theft and vandalism. However, we live in an uncertain world and we cannot eliminate chance from our lives. One of the ways we can deal with this uncertainty is with insurance. Insurance provides financial protection in situations that cause economic loss such as loss of life, loss of health, loss of employment and loss of or damage to property.

This unit will deal with life insurance and automobile insurance.

Life Insurance

A few terms basic to all types of insurance are: **Beneficiary**, the individual or firm who is designated to receive the benefits or the value paid by the insurance policy in the event of a loss. **Claim**, a form filed to request payment for losses covered in an insurance policy. **Insurance**, protection against loss. **Policy**, a written contract between the insurance company and the insured that explains the benefits of the protection purchased. **Policyholder**, the purchaser of the insurance. **Premium**, the payment to the insurance company for the purchase of an insurance policy. **Term**, the time period for which the insurance policy is in effect.

Types of Life Insurance

Term insurance is the least expensive type of life insurance, but it only provides temporary protection. This type of insurance pays the face amount to your beneficiary only if you die within the period of the insurance coverage (1, 5, 10 years and so on).

Whole Life, Ordinary Life, or Straight Life insurance provides permanent protection rather than the temporary protection of term insurance. Protection is assured for life, so long as the premiums are paid. The premiums for this type of policy are higher and it usually has a built-in savings feature.

Endowment insurance is one of the most expensive, because it is a combination of term insurance and cash value accumulation. You receive term insurance protection during the time you pay premiums, or it pays a certain amount of money to the insured at the end of a specified period of time if the insured is still living. You do not need to die to collect.

Limited Pay insurance provides protection for the insured's entire life, but is paid up with a limited number of premium payments.

Annuity insurance provides financial protection to the beneficiary for a specified amount upon the death of the insured, or if the insured lives past a specified age it pays a regular periodic payment to the insured for the remainder of his/her life (or for a predetermined time period).

Universal Life insurance is a contract that combines the features of term insurance and a tax deferred savings program. The cost of the life insurance is deducted on a regular basis from the total amount of the premiums collected. The remaining accumulated funds draw interest on an ongoing basis. The cash value eventually reverts to the insured.

Example 1. Barney Miller is a 30-year-old male and wishes to purchase $50,000 of life insurance. Determine the annual premium payments he would be required to pay for (a) 5-year renewable term, (b) Whole life, (c) 20-year limited pay life, and (d) 20-year endowment life.

Solution: We first determine the number of $1,000 units of face value of life insurance Barney wants to purchase:

Number of Units = Face Value/$1,000
                = $50,000/$1,000
                = 50

Then we multiply the number of units by the appropriate premium rate per unit from Table 8.4 as shown on the next page:

Table 8-4

TYPICAL ANNUAL PREMIUMS PER $1,000 OF LIFE INSURANCE

Age	5-Year Renewable Term Male	5-Year Renewable Term Female	Whole Life Male	Whole Life Female	20-Year Limited Pay Male	20-Year Limited Pay Female	20-Year Endowment Male	20-Year Endowment Female
18	$ 2.64	$ 1.83	$ 6.98	$ 5.76	$17.98	$15.73	$33.45	$29.46
19	2.67	1.86	7.04	5.94	18.37	16.31	33.52	29.55
20	2.70	1.91	8.05	6.29	19.18	18.02	33.69	27.93
21	2.76	1.95	8.27	6.47	19.55	18.23	33.80	28.01
22	2.83	1.97	8.52	6.71	19.89	18.56	33.86	28.22
23	2.88	1.99	8.81	6.95	20.24	19.01	33.89	28.30
24	2.95	2.01	9.11	7.20	20.60	19.22	33.99	28.45
25	3.01	2.05	9.45	7.46	20.97	19.37	34.11	28.58
30	3.20	2.26	11.67	9.13	22.60	20.81	34.45	29.41
35	3.83	2.99	14.91	11.42	25.26	22.14	35.22	29.64
40	5.79	4.48	19.45	14.57	28.29	24.81	36.42	30.54
45	8.86	6.36	25.59	18.63	31.38	26.87	38.44	31.75
50	14.10	9.26	34.04	24.21	36.53	30.91	41.04	33.35
55	23.54	13.87	46.51	32.37	42.17	35.22	44.38	36.27
60	29.80	15.85	55.76	37.63	50.74	41.72	——	——

a. 5-year term premium = number of units × rate
$$= 50 \times \$3.20$$
$$= \$160.00$$

b. Whole life premium = number of units × rate
$$= 50 \times \$11.67$$
$$= \$583.50$$

c. 20-year limited pay = number of units × rate
$$= 50 \times 22.60$$
$$= \$1,130.00$$

d. 20-year endowment = number of units × rate
$$= 50 \times \$34.45$$
$$= \$1,722.50$$

Using Table 8-4 solve the following word problems.

Tamara Hall, a female age 35, wants to buy a $45,000 5-year renewable term life insurance policy. What is the annual premium?

_____ (1)

What would the annual premium be for Jim Hundrup, a 25-year-old male, to purchase a $150,000 20-year endowment life insurance policy?

_____ (2)

How much more would the annual premium be to purchase $80,000 a 20-year limited pay policy than a whole life policy on Kay Pacheco, a 22-year-old female?

_____ (3)

What would the annual premium be for a $200,000 20-year endowment policy on Dave Reikosfski, a 45-year-old male?

_____ (4)

Sue Frankovich, a 30-year-old female, just took out a mortgage of $159,000 to purchase a new home. The finance company wanted to sell her mortgage insurance for $587.00 per year. How much would Sue save the first year if she purchased the same amount of 5-year renewable term life insurance?

_____ (5)

Answers: (1) $134.55; (2) $5,116.50; (3) $948.00; (4) $7,688.00; (5) $227.66

Automobile Insurance

Auto insurance is designed to provide protection from loss or damage to property and persons due to an automobile accident.

Some basic types of auto insurance are explained as follows:

Automotive Liability insurance covers the policy holder against claims for **bodily injury** or **property damage** as a result of an accident. The combined coverage is often listed as 50/100/25. In most cases, the amount of bodily injury insurance is indicated in the first fraction. For example, 50/100 means the insurance company pays up $50,000 for injury to one person and up to a total of $100,000 for injury to two or more persons in the same accident. The 25 refers to a property damage limit of $25,000. Property damage insurance covers damage done to property other than that of the insured. This type of coverage will pay for damages done to the other auto, buildings, or landscaping when it is determined that the insured is at fault. The drivers age and driving record are the primary determinants of the cost of liability coverage.

Comprehensive insurance provides coverage for loss caused by vandalism, theft, fire, windstorm, etc. The insurance premium rate for this type of coverage is heavily dependent on the area that the auto will be used, the age of the vehicle and its cost.

Collision insurance is designed to fix or replace the vehicle in case of a collision with another object. The cost of this type of coverage is based on (1) the age and type of auto, (2) the age and sex of the driver, (3) the record of the driver, (4) the number of miles driven each year, and (5) the size of the deductible. The **deductible** clause indicates that for example the insured must pay for the first $100, $200, or $500 of damage. Damages beyond the specified deductible are paid up to the limit of the insurance coverage. Like comprehensive insurance, the premium rate for collision coverage is heavily dependent on the area that the auto will be used, the age of the vehicle and its cost.

In addition to the basic coverages of liability, comprehensive and collision, numerous other types of coverage are available on an optional basis. **Medical** coverage can be obtained to pay for medical expenses resulting from injuries suffered by the insured and/or passengers while riding in the insured's car. **Uninsured motorist** insurance pays for injuries and damages caused by a motorist with no insurance. **Loss-of-earnings** insurance reimburses the insured for a percent of earnings lost because of an automobile accident. **Rental car** insurance reimburses the insured for the cost of a rental car to provide transportation until the insured vehicle is again available for use. There are even policies for disability and death that are sometimes written into automobile insurance.

Insurance companies sometimes divide the nation into territories based on past claims in all areas. Four territories are used in the following table:

Table 8-5

LIABILITY INSURANCE (SEMIANNUAL PREMIUM)

Territory	50/100/25	100/200/50	150/300/75	200/400/100
1	$116	$129	$136	$151
2	134	149	157	174
3	104	116	122	135
4	148	164	173	192

Example 1. What would a 100/200/50 liability insurance semiannual premium be in territory 3?

Solution: The premium of $116 is found in row 3 column 2 of Table 8-5.

Comprehensive and collision insurance rates are determined not only by territories, but also by vehicle age group and symbol. Age group 1 is a vehicle up to 1 year of age, and age group 6 is a vehicle 6 years of age or older. The symbol is determined by the cost of the vehicle. For example, a Mazda 323 might have a symbol 6, and a Aerostar Van might be symbol 8.

Example 2. What is the semiannual comprehensive and $200 deductible collision premium for a 3-year-old Ford with a symbol of 7 driven in territory 4.

Solution: The comprehensive would be $37 and the collision $147, so both would be $184

Table 8-6

COMPREHENSIVE AND COLLISION INSURANCE
(SEMIANNUAL PREMIUM)

Territory	Age Group	Comprehensive			Collision ($200 Deductible)		
		Symbol 6	Symbol 7	Symbol 8	Symbol 6	Symbol 7	Symbol 8
1	1	$28	$31	$43	$120	$135	$150
	2, 3	24	29	39	105	115	140
	4, 5	20	24	36	84	96	115
	6	16	18	26	54	60	82
2	1	$32	$36	$50	$139	$156	$174
	2, 3	28	34	45	122	133	162
	4, 5	23	28	42	97	111	133
	6	19	21	30	63	69	95
3	1	$25	$28	$39	$108	$121	$135
	2, 3	22	26	35	94	103	126
	4, 5	18	22	32	75	86	103
	6	14	16	23	48	54	74
4	1	$36	$40	$55	$153	$172	$150
	2, 3	31	37	50	134	147	179
	4, 5	26	31	46	107	122	147
	6	20	23	33	69	77	105

Actuaries, the people who collect and analyze insurance statistics have found accidents involving males under age 25 are higher than for females under 25 and much higher than adults over age 25. Because of this most insurance companies charge more for young male drivers than females or people over 25 years of age. Young drivers with driver's education experience fewer accidents than those without driver's education. And for the same reason some insurance companies also offer good student discounts. Table 8-7 shows the factors for age, sex and driver's education.

Table 8-7

YOUTHFUL OPERATOR FACTOR

Sex	Age	With Driver's Education	Without Driver's Education
Male	20 or less	1.95	2.45
Female	20 or less	1.35	1.85
Male	21 to 25	1.65	1.95
Female	21 to 25	1.15	1.45

Example 3.　What would the annual cost be for a 50/100/25 liability, comprehensive, and $200 deductible collision insurance policy? The car is a 6-year-old Dodge with a symbol of 7 driven in area 4 by a 23-year-old male without driver's education?

Solution:

Liability	$148
Comprehensive	23
Collision	77
Total	$248.0

$$\times 1.95 \quad \text{(youthful operator factor)}$$
$$\$483.60 \quad \text{semiannual premium}$$

Multiplied by two would give an annual cost of $967.20.

Find the following automobile insurance premiums:

Using the tables on the previous pages, what would a 150/300/75 liability insurance semiannual premium be in territory 1?

_____ (1)

What is the semiannual comprehensive and $200 deductible collision premium for a 2-year-old Mercury with a symbol of 8 driven in territory 4?

_____ (2)

According to the tables how much more would a 19-year-old male pay semiannually for comprehensive and $200 deductible collision insurance for a car in territory 2, age group 3, symbol 7, than a 19-year-old female? (Assume both have driver's education.)

_____ (3)

Frank Hernandez is 32 years old and lives in territory 2. He drives a new Buick with a symbol of 7. If he wants 100/200/50 liability, comprehensive, and $200 deductible collision insurance policy, what would his semiannual premium be?

_____ (4)

Janet Reno has taken driver's education, is 22 years old and lives in territory 4. If she drives an 8-year-old Chevrolet, symbol 6 and wants a 50/100/25 liability, comprehensive, and $200 deductible collision insurance policy what would her annual premium be?

_____ (5)

Answers: (1) $136.00; (2) $229.00; (3) $100.20; (4) $341.00; (5) $545.10 (272.55 × 2)

Investments

The **Wall Street Journal** and many other newspapers in America publish an entire section every day devoted to news and statistics on the financial markets. Many newspaper readers turn first to these because they want to find the value of securities they own or plan to buy. Others are looking for data to use in research for business or educational needs.

Investment risks vary not only with the kind of investment but also with the length of time involved. For short term investments there is less risks in bonds or money in the bank. For long run investments of 20 to 40 years inflation threatens the value of fixed-dollar assets like bonds or money in the bank and there may less risk in stocks or real estate. An extreme example of this is that a dollar invested in 1800 would be worth about $1,000 in 2000, a dollar invested in stocks in the same time period would be worth more than $500,000. All this is in real terms, with inflation taken into account. Meanwhile a dollar invested in gold during the same time period would be worth less than $.80. This comparison gives new meaning to the phrase "good as gold" when talking about the long run. There have been several short run periods, however, when bonds or gold have held their value and stock prices have plummeted. To make it harder to predict the patterns seem to be different in all eras.

The real rate of return after adjusting for inflation was only slightly positive in the 1930s. The real rate of return for bonds in the 1940s, 1950s, 1960s, and 1970s was negative, that is during these inflationary decades money invested in bonds would not buy as much when the bonds were sold as when they were purchased even though larger sums of money was were received at the end. Both stocks and bonds had real positive rates of returns in the 1980s and 1990s.

This section will help you become more familiar with two major types of investments in America, Stocks and Bonds.

Stocks

About 80 million Americans own stock. This stock ownership is in many forms. Some people have bought stock in individual companies, others have pooled their investment in the form of mutual funds, and still others own stock as part of the employer's retirement plan.

Stocks are at the heart of the U.S. economic system. They represent shares in the ownership of corporations. Companies issue stock to raise money for their activities. Investors buy stock in hopes that their price will rise as the company's business prospers and that maybe some of the profits will be paid to the investors as dividends.

The New York Stock Exchange traces its origins back more than 200 years to 1792. Centuries of growth and innovation later, the NYSE remains the world's foremost securities marketplace. The NYSE is an agency auction market. Trading at the NYSE takes place by open bids and offers by Exchange members, acting as agents for institutions or individuals investors. Buy and sell orders meet directly on the trading floor and prices are determined by the interplay of supply and demand. Each listed stock is assigned to a single post where the specialist manages the auction process. All orders for a NYSE-listed stock are brought electronically or by a floor broker to this single location. The result is a heavy flow of diverse orders that allows securities to be bought and sold without wide price fluctuations.

NASDAQ (The National Association of Securities Dealers Automated Quotation System) began trading in February of 1971. Today it is the world's largest electronic stock market listing nearly 4,100 of the world's leading companies. NASDAQ is not limited to one central trading location; instead it uses a sophisticated computer and telecommunications network, which transmits real-time quote, and trade data to more than 1.3 million users in 83 countries. A core of more than 500 market-making firms are key to NASDAQ's market structure. These market makers, also known as dealers, commit their own capital to NASDAQ listed securities then turn around and re-distribute the stock as needed. They post their bid and ask prices in the NASDAQ network where they can be viewed and accessed by all participants. By being willing to buy and sell stock using their own funds, market makers add liquidity to NASDAQ's market, ensuring that there are always buyers and sellers.

Reputable Companies whose stocks, for one reason or another, aren't quoted on the NYSE or the NASDAQ may be traded on the American Stock Exchange, Amex, in New York or on one or more of the regional exchanges in other cities.

Again, stock ownership is equity in a business. Stocks represent ownership. This ownership usually carries with it voting rights and the risk of profits or losses.

Bonds

In contrast to stocks, bonds don't convey an ownership in the business entity that issues them. Bonds represent **debt.** A bond is a loan. It pays interest to the investor and the loan must be repaid after a stipulated period called maturity date. Bonds are issued by a variety of borrowers, including corporations, governments and agencies of governments, such as school districts.

The interest rate on a bond is partly a reflection of the investor's risk of losing his money. Corporations occasionally go bankrupt, for example. Governments are considered the least risky of borrowers, so government bonds such as those of the U.S. Treasury generally pay lower interest rates. The rates also vary according to the maturity, or duration, of the loans. The lowest interest rates are on the shortest loans such as common borrowing for about three months in the form of U.S. Treasury Bills, or for about one month in the form of commercial paper issued by corporations.

Mutual Funds

Investments that pool the money of many different shareholders and invest in a diversified portfolio of securities are called mutual funds. Depending on the funds objectives, securities that make up a mutual fund will differ in mixes of stocks, bonds and money market instruments.

Money market funds have the goal of keeping your investment safe, while providing income potential. To pursue those goals, these funds are made up of a portfolio with short maturities and high credit ratings such as T-bills, commercial paper, negotiable CDs banker's acceptances, and even Eurodollars. There are still no guarantees. Money market funds are not insured by the Federal Deposit Insurance Corporation (FDIC) or any other U.S. government agency. However, they are considered pretty safe investments.

Bonds funds usually have the goal of providing income. They invest in short, medium, and/or long-term debt obligations such as government, corporate, and municipal bonds. Bond funds offer higher income potential than money market funds, but involve more risks. Because a bond fund's net asset value goes up and down depending on what happens in the bond market you may lose money when you sell your bond fund shares.

Stock funds have the goal of growth over time. To reach their stated goals stock fund portfolio managers invest in a variety stocks or equities of different companies both domestic and foreign. The value of these funds tend to be more volatile than money market funds or bond funds because they go up and down with the stock market. But as illustrated in the beginning of this section, if you are able to maintain a long-term focus, stock funds have the highest potential for growth.

Reading a Stock Table

Stock tables like the one below are found in most daily newspapers, although the most extensive listing appears in **The Wall Street Journal**. The columns in the table have been numbered to help you locate the information.
Explanation:

1	2	3	4	5	6	7	8	9	10	11
14.1	53.50	32.35	BlockHR	HRB	.72	1.4	22	11846	51.01	−0.29
−8.5	30.25	16.40	Blkbstr	BBI	.08	.3	—	2308	23.06	−0.17
−4.9	53.59	27.60	Boeing	BA	.68	1.8	14	30047	36.89	−0.24
−18.1	38.81	25.87	BoiseCasc	BCC	.60	2.2	—	2993	27.86	0.11
26.3	5.25	2.01	Bombay	BBA	—	—	36	1167	2.88	0.20

1. Year to date percent change in the price of the stock.

2. The highest price at which the stock traded during the year.

3. The lowest price at which the stock traded during the year.

4. The name of the stock, which is often abbreviated.

5. The symbol for the stock.

6. The dividend paid per share.

7. The stock yield, found by dividing the annual dividend per share by the closing price per share. The percent may be very low because people often buy stock with the expectation of the price increasing as much or more than returns in the form of dividends.

8. The price-earnings ratio will vary in a range depending on the quality, future expectations, economic conditions and so on. It is the closing price per share divided by the annual earning per share.

9. The number of shares traded in hundreds.

10. The price per share of the last trade of the day.

11. The change in the last trade of the day from the previous day's closing price.

Calculating the cost of buying and selling stock.

You buy or sell stock from a stockbroker not directly from the stock exchange. The broker charges a commission for either a purchase or a sale. The rates for this commission will vary between brokers and will depend on such factors as the size and price of the transaction. The amount of the commission will also depend on whether the shares of stock are traded according to round lots (multiples of 100) or odd lots (fewer than 100). If the order is an odd lot (less than 100 shares) the commission is usually an additional 1% on the odd lot portion.

Example 1. What would it cost to purchase 126 shares of PepsiCo 43.86 if the commission on round lots is 1.5% with odd lots an additional 1% of the cost of the stock?

Solution:

Buying Stock

Step 1. Multiply the number of shares times the price per share. (126 times $43.86 = $5,526.36)

Step 2. Multiply the result from step one by the commission rate to find the commission charge. ($5,526.36 × .015 = $82.90 + the odd lot 26 × $43.86 × .01 = $11.40. Total $82.90 + $11.40 = $94.30.)

Step 3. Add steps one and two to find the total cost. ($5,526.36 + $94.30 = $5,620.66)

Example 2. Eighteen months later the 126 shares of PepsiCo in the question above was sold at 51.89 with a sales commission of 1.5%, with odd lots an additional 1%. (a) How much profit would be made?

(b) What is the return on the investment?

Solution:

Selling Stock

Step 1. Multiply the number of shares times the price per share. $(126 \times 51.89 = 6{,}538.14)$

Step 2. Multiply the result from step one by the selling commission rate to find the commission charge. $(6{,}538.14 \times .015 = 98.07 +$ the odd lot $26 \times 51.89 \times .01 = 13.49$. Total $98.07 + 13.49 = 111.56)$

Step 3. Subtract step two from step one to find the amount received from the sale. $(6{,}538.14 - 111.56 = 6{,}426.58)$

(a) The profit would be the net proceeds from the sale $(6{,}426.58)$ less the total cost (5620.66) or $805.92)$

(b) Return on investment is the profit $(805.92)/$[total cost $(5620.66) \times$ the time in years (18 months/12 months in a year or 1.5)] = 9.6% [Don't forget to do the equation in brackets first]

Solve the following stock problems:

What is the Total cost of 300 shares of Potlach stock purchased at 25.37 with a 2.25% commission?

_____ (1)

What is the total cost of 221 shares of SnapOnTools purchased at 31.23 with a 1.75% commission? (Remember the 1% for the odd lot.)

_____ (2)

How much profit or loss would there be from the sale of the 300 shares of Potlach stock in problem (1) if the shares were sold at 21.45? Use a selling commission rate of 1.75%.

_____ (3)

What would be the return on investment from 400 shares of Manpower bought at 13.50, held for 27 months, and sold at 42.73? Use a buying and selling commission of 2%.

_____ (4)

What would be the return on investment from 500 shares of six flags bought at 4.12, held for 11 months, and sold at 15.88? Use a buying and selling commission of 1.5%.

_____ (5)

Answers: (1) 7,782.25; (2) 7,029.17; (3) 1,459.86 loss; (4) 90.7%; (5) 299.0%

Stop

You're now ready to take Pretest VIII to check your skill using a calculator to solve business problems involving Consumer Economics. You should be able to complete this test in less than 50 minutes with better than 70 percent accuracy. Unless instructed to do otherwise, turn in your Pretest for correction and review before taking Test VIII. Be certain you understand each problem on Pretest VIII before attempting your graded examination.

When you pass Test VIII you will have proven your ability to use calculators effectively to solve consumer economics problems.

Pretest VIII

CALCULATOR APPLICATIONS—CONSUMER ECONOMICS

50 minutes

This test need NOT be worked in sequence. Do the problems you know best first. You need 70 percent correct to pass.

Consumer credit.

Compute the credit price and credit cost.

Value	No. of Payments	Payments Schedule	Size of Payment	Credit Price	Credit Cost
$ 94.87	6	monthly	$19.56	_____ (1)	_____ (2)
205.59	12	monthly	29.00	_____ (3)	_____ (4)
583.14	24	monthly	25.14	_____ (5)	_____ (6)
110.14	22	weekly	10.57	_____ (7)	_____ (8)

If you purchased a Bushnell 345 × 60 Telescope priced at $125.50 in Omaha, Nebraska with a sales tax of 6.5%. what would be the total purchase price?

_____ (9/10)

If a 6% sales tax of $7.38 was collected for the purchase of a Phone-Mate Cordless Phone what was the sales price of the phone?

_____ (11/12)

How much would the sales tax for AMA Espresso Coffee Machine be if the total purchase price was $137.50 and the sales tax rate 6.25%?

_____ (13/14)

Personal taxes.

If the total value of assessed property in Podunk is $834,892,000 and $9,471,000 is needed in property taxes, what should the property tax rate be in mills?

_____ (15/16)

The market value of a home in Springfield is $126,000. The tax rate is 31.7 mills. If the assessed valuation is 44% of market value, find the property tax.

_____ (17/18)

If the property tax rate in Pleasant Grove is $4.87 per $100 of assessed valuation, what is the property tax on property assessed at $56,923 in that city?

_____ (19/20)

Bank problem.

Below is a list of eight items to be used in the T-account at the bottom of this page. Enter the following data in the appropriate places and compute the adjusted balances.

Wrote check for $23, entered it as $32.

Outstanding checks:	#368	$56.80	Overdraft charges	$16.00
	#372	$18.00	Unrecorded check	$10.00
	#373	$16.00	Late deposit not listed by bank	$516.34
			Service charge	$3.50

BANK RECONCILIATION

Bank Balance	$244.20	Checkbook Balance	$690.24
Additions:		Additions:	
TOTAL _____ (21)		TOTAL _____ (25)	
SUBTOTAL _____ (22)		SUBTOTAL _____ (26)	
Subtractions:		Subtractions:	
TOTAL _____ (23)		TOTAL _____ (27)	
ADJUSTED BANK BALANCE _____ (24)		ADJUSTED CHECKBOOK BALANCE _____ (28)	

Insurance.

TYPICAL ANNUAL PREMIUMS PER $1,000 OF LIFE INSURANCE

Age	5-Year Renewable Term		Whole Life		20-Year Limited Pay		20-Year Endowment	
	Male	Female	Male	Female	Male	Female	Male	Female
18	$ 2.64	$ 1.83	$ 6.98	$ 5.76	$17.98	$15.73	$33.45	$29.46
19	2.67	1.86	7.04	5.94	18.37	16.31	33.52	29.55
20	2.70	1.91	8.05	6.29	19.18	18.02	33.69	27.93
21	2.76	1.95	8.27	6.47	19.55	18.23	33.80	28.01
22	2.83	1.97	8.52	6.71	19.89	18.56	33.86	28.22
23	2.88	1.99	8.81	6.95	20.24	19.01	33.89	28.30
24	2.95	2.01	9.11	7.20	20.60	19.22	33.99	28.45
25	3.01	2.05	9.45	7.46	20.97	19.37	34.11	28.58
30	3.20	2.26	11.67	9.13	22.60	20.81	34.45	29.41
35	3.83	2.99	14.91	11.42	25.26	22.14	35.22	29.64
40	5.79	4.48	19.45	14.57	28.29	24.81	36.42	30.54
45	8.86	6.36	25.59	18.63	31.38	26.87	38.44	31.75
50	14.10	9.26	34.04	24.21	36.53	30.91	41.04	33.35
55	23.54	13.87	46.51	32.37	42.17	35.22	44.38	36.27
60	29.80	15.85	55.76	37.63	50.74	41.72	——	——

Tracy Nechanicky, a female age 25, wants to buy a $50,000 5-year renewable term life insurance policy. What is the annual premium?

_____ (29/30)

What would the annual premium be for a $300,000 20-year endowment policy on Paul Geibel a 35-year-old male?

_____ (31/32)

What would the annual premium be for $150,000 whole life policy on Joshua Swekeer, a 22-year-old male?

_____ (33/34)

LIABILITY INSURANCE (SEMIANNUAL PREMIUM)

Territory	50/100/25	100/200/50	150/300/75	200/400/100
1	$116	$129	$136	$151
2	134	149	157	174
3	104	116	122	135
4	148	164	173	192

COMPREHENSIVE AND COLLISION INSURANCE (SEMIANNUAL PREMIUM)

Territory	Age Group	Comprehensive Symbol 6	Symbol 7	Symbol 8	Collision ($200 Deductible) Symbol 6	Symbol 7	Symbol 8
1	1	$28	$31	$43	$120	$135	$150
	2, 3	24	29	39	105	115	140
	4, 5	20	24	36	84	96	115
	6	16	18	26	54	60	82
2	1	$32	$36	$50	$139	$156	$174
	2, 3	28	34	45	122	133	162
	4, 5	23	28	42	97	111	133
	6	19	21	30	63	69	95
3	1	$25	$28	$39	$108	$121	$135
	2, 3	22	26	35	94	103	126
	4, 5	18	22	32	75	86	103
	6	14	16	23	48	54	74
4	1	$36	$40	$55	$153	$172	$150
	2, 3	31	37	50	134	147	179
	4, 5	26	31	46	107	122	147
	6	20	23	33	69	77	105

YOUTHFUL DRIVER FACTOR

Sex	Age	With Driver's Education	Without Driver's Education
Male	20 or less	1.95	2.45
Female	20 or less	1.35	1.85
Male	21 to 25	1.65	1.95
Female	21 to 25	1.15	1.45

Use the tables on the previous page for the following problems.

What would a 100/200/50 liability insurance semiannual premium be in territory 2?

_____ (35/36)

If you were a 19-year-old male who lives in territory 1 without driver education and just purchased a new Ford with a symbol of 8 and want 150/300/75 liability, comprehensive, and $200 deductible collision automobile insurance policy, what would your annual premium be?

_____ (37/38)

What is the semiannual comprehensive and $200 deductible collision premium for a 5-year-old Plymouth with a symbol of 6 driven in territory 3?

_____ (39/40)

Investments.

What would 600 shares of Ford Motor Company cost, selling at 15.65? Use a buying commission of 1.75%.

_____ (41/42)

How much would you receive if you sold 300 shares of Ingersoll-Rand Company Limited at 67.92? Use a selling commission of 1.5%.

_____ (43/44)

How much profit or loss would there be from the sale of 400 shares of The Home Depot, Inc. bought at 21.11 and sold at 35.04 if the buying and selling commissions were 1.25%?

_____ (45/46)

How much profit or loss would there be from the sale of 800 shares of The Boeing Company bought at 65.18 and sold at 49.67? Use a buying and selling commission of 1.5%.

_____ (47/48)

What would be the return on investment from 1,200 shares of Apollo Group, Inc. bought at 28.67, held for 36 months, and sold for 94.17? Use a buying and selling commission of 1%.

_____ (49/50)

Business Operations

LEARNING GOALS

After completing Chapter 9, you will have improved your ability to operate electronic calculators and expanded your knowledge of business activity in the following areas:

- Prorating Expenses
- Depreciation
- Financial Analysis

You will also be able to pass a pretest of typical business problems, with at least 70 percent accuracy in less than 50 minutes.

Prorated Expenses

It is easy to charge the direct costs of labor, materials, and certain kinds of advertising to a single department within a business. But what about the indirect costs or **overhead** expenses, such as executive salaries, office supplies, rent, heat, general advertising, and community relations? The two distribution techniques used in this section show how business firms **prorate** indirect or overhead costs.

1. Idaho Department Store prorates its overhead expenses on the basis of the square footage occupied by each department. Complete Table 9-1 for the month of June, when overhead expenses were $52,826. Round answers to the nearest whole dollar.

Hint

Calculate overhead cost per square foot by dividing overhead expenses by the total square footage of all departments. Then enter cost per square foot as a constant multiplier. Multiply square footage for each department by this constant to find the prorated cost per department. If your machine is so equipped, use the accumulative techniques to check your work by accumulating Total Overhead (13), which must equal $52,826.

Allocation per square foot of floor space at Idaho Department Store is ($52,826 ÷ 24,750) = _2.1344_ (1)

Since this is an intermediate answer, don't round, carry to at least 4 decimal places.

Table 9-1

IDAHO DEPARTMENT STORE
Overhead Costs for Month Ending June 30, 20XX

Department	Square Footage	Overhead Expense	
Appliances	2,950	6296. 23	(2)
Automotive	2,100	4482	(3)
Pharmacy	1,150	2455	(4)
Books & Records	790	1686	(5)
Garden Shop	4,330	9242	6)
Hardware	3,050	6570	(7)
Men's Wear	1,980	4226	(8)
Shoes	980	2092	(9)
Sporting Goods	1,810	3863	(10)
Toys	1,970	4205	(11)
Women's Wear	3,640	7769	(12)
TOTAL	24,750	52,826	(13)

Answers: (1) 2.1344; (2) $6,296; (3) $4,482; (4) $2,455; (5) $1,686; (6) $9,242; (7) $6,510; (8) $4,226; (9) $2,092; (10) $3,863; (11) $4,205; (12) $7,769; (13) $52,826

2. The Summit Sales Corporation prorates its advertising costs on the basis of sales generated in its various offices. Complete Table 9-2 for the month of October, when advertising expenses were $895,098. Round answers to the nearest dollar.

Hint

Use the same procedure as in prorating on the basis of square footage. Think of the chances of making an error and the amount of time it would take to work each of these problems with a pencil only or even without a constant.

The allocation of $1,000 of sales for Summit Sales Corporation is $895,098 ÷ 71,522 = _12.5750_ (1). (Remember to use at least 4 decimal places for this factor.)

Table 9-2

SUMMIT SALES CORPORATION
Advertising Expenses for Month Ending October 31, 20XX

Office	Total Sales (000's omitted)	Advertising Expense	
Atlanta	$7,303	91,397	(2)
Boston	4,743	59,359	(3)
Denver	6,698	83,825	(4)
Los Angeles	18,062	232,804	(5)
Phoenix	5,541	69,346	(6)
Portland	6,898	86,328	(7)
Seattle	3,263	40,836	(8)
St. Louis	7,066	88,431	(9)
St. Paul	3,242	40,574	(10)
Toledo	8,706	108,956	(11)
TOTAL	$71,522	895,098	(12)

Answers: (1) $12.5150; (2) $91,397; (3) $59,359; (4) $83,825; (5) $226,046; (6) $69,346; (7) $86,328; (8) $40,836; (9) $88,431; (10) $40,574; (11) $108,956; (12) $895,098

Depreciation

Depreciation is the loss in value of assets such as building and equipment due to wear or obsolescence. An understanding of depreciation is important to all business people, especially accountants, income tax services, and individuals who maintain their own business records.

The depreciation of items which are used for more than one year are classified by the Internal Revenue Service into one of eight categories based on the IRS's Asset Depreciation Range (ADR) as follows:

The 3-year category consists of over-the-road tractors, special tools, items used for research and experimentation, etc.

The 5-year category consists of such items as automobiles, pick-ups, trucks, computers, typewriters, copiers, cattle, and most construction equipment.

The 7-year category consists of office furniture and fixtures, desks, chairs, single-use agricultural and horticultural buildings, most farm equipment, etc.

The 10-year category consists of water transportation items, some manufacturing machinery, mobile homes, etc.

The 15-year category consists of depreciable land improvements such as roads, fences, landscaping, etc.

The 20-year category consists of such things as farm buildings, railroad structures, electric utility plants, water utilities, etc.

The 27.5-year category consists of rental residential property such as houses, duplexes, apartments, condos, and co-ops.

The 31.5-year category includes all nonresidential real property, for example, office buildings, shopping centers, hotels, and motels.

The 1986 tax reform eliminated investment tax credit.

The above time frames and the accelerated method (ACRS) or prescribed method as it is sometimes called is used most often. Ordinarily, you will want to use the depreciation method which writes off the expense or claims the tax deduction the most rapidly. However, you can use the straight-line method or certain longer periods if you choose. However, it is rare that choosing any of these longer write-off periods would be to one's advantage.

Depreciation Methods for 3-Year and 5-Year Property

The following table shows the percentage that would be deducted each year under the accelerated and straight-line methods for 3-year and 5-year items.

Regular Depreciation Table

3-YEAR PROPERTY			5-YEAR PROPERTY		
Year	Acclerated Method	Straight-Line Method	Year	Acclerated Method	Straight-Line Method
1	33%	16.7%	1	20.0%	10.0%
2	45%	33.3%	2	32.0%	20.0%
3	15%	33.3%	3	19.2%	20.0%
4	7%	16.7%	4	11.5%	20.0%
			5	11.5%	20.0%
			6	5.8%	10.0%

The above table applies to items placed into service anytime during the year. The table yields the same depreciation deductions for a 3-year or 5-year item purchased early in the year as for one purchased late in the year. It is assumed that you continue to use the item for business purposes throughout the period indicated in the table. The 7, 10, 15, and 20-year classes have a similar but longer schedule.

Depreciation Methods for 27.5-Year and 31.5-Year Categories

These categories consist of houses, apartments, and other buildings. Because the tables are similar we will use only one table in this unit. Items in the 31.5-year category can be depreciated according to the method given by the following table. You use the column in the table corresponding to the month in the first year that the item starts being used for business purposes. The entries in each column give the percentage of the cost which is deducted in each year of use.

31.5-Year Nonresidential (Commercial) Real Property Tables

If the recovery year is:	The applicable percentage is: (Use the column for month property placed in service)											
	Jan	Feb	Mar	Apr	May	Jun	Jul	Aug	Sep	Oct	Nov	Dec
1	.030	.028	.025	.022	.020	.017	.015	.012	.009	.007	.004	.001
2	.032	.032	.032	.032	.032	.032	.032	.032	.032	.032	.032	.032
3	.032	.032	.032	.032	.032	.032	.032	.032	.032	.032	.032	.032
4	.032	.032	.032	.032	.032	.032	.032	.032	.032	.032	.032	.032
5	.032	.032	.032	.032	.032	.032	.032	.032	.032	.032	.032	.032
6	.032	.032	.032	.032	.032	.032	.032	.032	.032	.032	.032	.032
7	.032	.032	.032	.032	.032	.032	.032	.032	.032	.032	.032	.032
8	.032	.032	.032	.032	.032	.032	.032	.032	.032	.032	.032	.032
9	.032	.032	.032	.032	.032	.032	.032	.032	.032	.032	.032	.032
10	.032	.032	.032	.032	.032	.032	.032	.032	.032	.032	.032	.032
11	.032	.032	.032	.032	.032	.032	.032	.032	.032	.032	.032	.032
12	.032	.032	.032	.032	.032	.032	.032	.032	.032	.032	.032	.032
13	.032	.032	.032	.032	.032	.032	.032	.032	.032	.032	.032	.032
14	.032	.032	.032	.032	.032	.032	.032	.032	.032	.032	.032	.032
15	.032	.032	.032	.032	.032	.032	.032	.032	.032	.032	.032	.032
16	.032	.032	.032	.032	.032	.032	.032	.032	.032	.032	.032	.032
17	.032	.032	.032	.032	.032	.032	.032	.032	.032	.032	.032	.032
18	.032	.032	.032	.032	.032	.032	.032	.032	.032	.032	.032	.032
19	.032	.032	.032	.032	.032	.032	.032	.032	.032	.032	.032	.032
20	.032	.032	.032	.032	.032	.032	.032	.032	.032	.032	.032	.032
21	.032	.032	.032	.032	.032	.032	.032	.032	.032	.032	.032	.032
22	.032	.032	.032	.032	.032	.032	.032	.032	.032	.032	.032	.032
23	.032	.032	.032	.032	.032	.032	.032	.032	.032	.032	.032	.032
24	.032	.032	.032	.032	.032	.032	.032	.032	.032	.032	.032	.032
25	.032	.032	.032	.032	.032	.032	.032	.032	.032	.032	.032	.032
26	.032	.032	.032	.032	.032	.032	.032	.032	.032	.032	.032	.032
27	.032	.032	.032	.032	.032	.032	.032	.032	.032	.032	.032	.032
28	.032	.032	.032	.032	.032	.032	.032	.032	.032	.032	.032	.032
29	.032	.032	.032	.032	.032	.032	.032	.032	.032	.032	.032	.032
30	.032	.032	.032	.032	.032	.032	.032	.032	.032	.032	.032	.032
31	.032	.032	.032	.032	.032	.032	.032	.032	.032	.032	.032	.032
32	.010	.012	.015	.018	.020	.023	.025	.028	.031	.032	.032	.032
33	0	0	0	0	0	0	0	0	0	.001	.004	.007
	100%	100%	100%	100%	100%	100%	100%	100%	100%	100%	100%	100%

Brown's Machine Shop recently purchased some special tools, a new pickup truck, and a new shop building. They want depreciation schedules on these items including comparison depreciation schedules made for the special tools and the pickup truck using straight-line, and accelerated methods. Complete the following depreciation schedules. Some of the answers have been furnished as examples.

Depreciation Schedules for Special Metal Lathe

Year	Purchase Price $9,820 ACCELERATED METHOD Depreciation	3-Year Category STRAIGHT-LINE METHOD Depreciation
1	$3,240.60	$1,639.94
2	4,419.00	3,270.06
3	_____ (1)	_____ (4)
4	_____ (2)	_____ (5)
Total (100% of cost)	_____ (3)	_____ (6)

Answers: (1) 1,473.00; (2) $687.40; (3) $9,820.00; (4) $3,270.06; (5) $1,639.94; (6) $9,820.00

Depreciation Schedules for Pickup Truck

Year	Purchase Price $12,894 ACCELERATED METHOD Depreciation	5-Year Category STRAIGHT-LINE METHOD Depreciation
1	_____ (7)	_____ (14)
2	_____ (8)	_____ (15)
3	_____ (9)	_____ (16)
4	_____ (10)	_____ (17)
5	_____ (11)	_____ (18)
6	_____ (12)	_____ (19)
Total (100% of cost)	_____ (13)	_____ (20)

Answers: (7) $2,578.80; (8) $4,126.08; (9) $2,475.65; (10) $1,482.81; (11) $1,482.81; (12) $747.85; (13) $12,894; (14) $1,289.40; (15) $2,578.80; (16) $2,578.80; (17) $2,578.80; (18) $2,578.80; (19) $1,289.40; (20) $12,894

Depreciation Schedule for Shop Building

Placed into service in June
Purchase Price $211,500   31.5-Year Category
PRESCRIBED METHOD

Year	Depreciation		Year	Depreciation	
1	_____	(22)	17	_____	(38)
2	_____	(23)	18	_____	(39)
3	_____	(24)	19	_____	(40)
4	_____	(25)	20	_____	(41)
5	_____	(26)	21	_____	(42)
6	_____	(27)	22	_____	(43)
7	_____	(28)	23	_____	(44)
8	_____	(29)	24	_____	(45)
9	_____	(30)	25	_____	(46)
10	_____	(31)	26	_____	(47)
11	_____	(32)	27	_____	(48)
12	_____	(33)	28	_____	(49)
13	_____	(34)	29	_____	(50)
14	_____	(35)	30	_____	(51)
15	_____	(36)	31	_____	(52)
16	_____	(37)	32	_____	(53)
Total	(100% of Cost)			$211,500	

Answers: (22) $3,595.50; (23) $6,768.00; (24) $6,768.00; (25) $6,768.00; (26) $6,768.00; (27) $6,768.00; (28) $6,768.00; (29) $6,768.00; (30) $6,768.00; (31) $6,768.00; (32) $6,768.00; (33) $6,768.00; (34) $6,768.00; (35) $6,768.00; (36) $6,768.00; (37) $6,768.00; (38) $6,768.00; (39) $6,768.00; (40) $6,768.00; (41) $6,768.00; (42) $6,768.00; (43) $6,768.00; (44) $6,768.001; (45) $6,768.00; (46) $6,768.00; (47) $6,768.00; (48) $6,768.00; (49) $6,768.00; (50) $6,768.00; (51) $6,768.00; (52) $6,768.00; (53) $4,864.50

Financial Analysis

Business organizations, from individuals such as accountants and farmers, to retail outlets that sell groceries or hardware, to large companies that have offices and factories in many parts of the world, must keep careful records of expenses and income. These records and financial statements are needed by managers and owners to evaluate business performance. How profitable is the operation?

This financial information is also required by people more indirectly related to business operations. Before a business, regardless of its size, will be able to obtain a bank loan, the banker will want some indication of profitability and assurance that enough funds will be available to repay the loan. Financial statements will also be required if a business wants to buy supplies or floor inventory on credit. If a firm wants to raise money for expansion, potential investors will have questions about the performance of the business. Certainly financial statements are required when a business is sold.

Analysis of the two most important financial statements, balance sheets and income statements, along with some important financial ratios are covered in this section. These statements and ratios tend to be standardized throughout the business world so if you can understand the financial statements and ratios of one company you will be able to interpret the statements and ratios of other companies.

Balance Sheets

The **Balance Sheet**, which is sometimes a "snapshot" of the business, reveals the financial condition of a business at a specific moment in time only. It is a statement of what is owned (assets), what is owed (liabilities), and net worth (owner's equity, stockholder's equity, or capital) which is the difference between assets and liabilities on a given date.

Assets are usually divided into two categories; current assets and fixed assets.

Current Assets are cash and other assets that can be converted into cash or will be realized within one year or one operating cycle, whichever is longer. Current assets include:

- **Cash** in checking and savings accounts on the date the balance sheet is made.
- **Accounts Receivable** from customers of the firm.
- **Notes Receivable** from customers to the firm. Normally a note receivable is for a period of less than one year.
- **Inventory**, the cost of the merchandise the firm has for sale.

Fixed Assets are those tangible assets used in the operation of the business that have a useful life longer than one accounting period. Fixed assets include:

- **Land**, the value of the land owned by the firm.
- **Buildings**, the value of the buildings owned by the firm.
- **Equipment**, the value of the store fixtures, furniture, equipment, and similar items used by the firm.

Liabilities, like assets, are divided into two categories, current and long term.

Current liabilities are obligations that must be paid or liquidated within one year or one operating cycle, whichever is longer. Current liabilities include:

- **Accounts Payable** to other firms.
- **Notes Payable** to other firms.

Long-Term Liabilities are items that will be paid over a period of more than one year:

- **Mortgages Payable**, include the total balance on all mortgages on which the firm is paying.
- **Long-Term Notes Payable**, are the total of all other debts of the firm.

A balance sheet might look as follows:

TRAVIS MANUFACTURING
Balance Sheet
December 31, 20XX

Current Assets		
Cash	$78,217	
Accounts Receivable	51,083	
Inventory	29,872	
Total Current Assets		$159,172
Fixed Assets		
Land	$117,832	
Building	93,801	
Equipment	301,726	
Total Fixed Assets		$513,359
Total Assets		$672,531

LIABILITIES

Current Liabilities:		
Accounts Payable	$21,137	
Taxes Payable	31,816	
Total Current Liabilities		$52,953
Long-Term Liabilities:		
Mortgage Payable	$28,615	
Notes Payable (over 1 year)	5,317	
Total Long-Term Liabilities		$33,932
Total Liabilities		$86,885

OWNER'S EQUITY

Capital	$585,646
Total Liabilities and Owner's Equity	$672,531

Using the balance sheet for Travis Manufacturing as an example, solve the following problems:

Claxton Mayo runs a small proprietorship business. His balance sheet shows the following items and amounts: cash, $6,138; accounts receivable, $15,221; merchandise inventory, $24,783; furniture, $7,587; equipment, $4,783; and total liabilities of $33,538. Determine Mr. Mayo's owner's equity in this business

_____ (1)

Jane Gallagher operates a sporting goods store. Her balance sheet shows the following: inventory, $21,894; accounts receivable, $7,314; accounts payable, $9,214; cash, $4,917; equipment, $3,819; notes payable, $6,218; and wages payable, $827. Determine (a) total assets, (b) total liabilities, and (c) owner's equity.

_____ (2)

_____ (3)

_____ (4)

Joseph Graziano has his own insurance business. On the current balance sheet, his owner's equity is $31,258. The balance sheet shows he has the following liabilities: accounts payable $1,983; notes payable, $5,416; salaries payable, $1,487; interest payable, $225. What is the amount of total assets on the current balance sheet?

_____ (5)

Answers: (1) $24,974; (2) $37,944; (3) $16,259; (4) $21,685; (5) $40,369

Income Statements

An Income Statement is a record of income and expenses. People in business need to know if they are making a profit or experiencing a loss. The form shows the revenue, expenses and net income for a certain period of time, such as one month, one quarter or one year.

Gross Sales represent the total amount of income received from customers for the goods or services sold by the firm.

Returns and Allowances are defined as the total value of all goods returned by customers.

Net Sales represent the value of goods bought and kept by customers. (Net Sales = Gross Sales − Returns and Allowances.)

Cost of Goods Sold is the initial inventory plus goods purchased plus shipping and handling charges less the inventory at the end of the time period.

Gross Margin is the difference between the amount received from customers for goods and what the firm paid for the goods. Gross margin is sometimes called gross profit on sales. (Gross Margin = Net Sales − Cost of Goods Sold.)

Expenses represent the amount paid by firms in an attempt to sell its goods. Rent, salaries and wages, advertising, utilities, and taxes are examples of these expenses which are sometimes called overhead.

Net Income is the difference between gross margin and expenses.

DO-LITTLE'S PRODUCTS
Income Statement
For the Year Ending December 31, 20XX

Gross Sales		$134,615	
Returns and Allowances		2,587	
Net Sales			$132,028
Inventory, January 1		61,874	
Cost of Goods Purchased	95,214		
Freight	2,117		
Total Cost of Goods Purchased		97,331	
Total Goods Available for Sales		159,205	
Inventory, December 31		68,854	
Cost of Goods Sold			90,351
Gross Margin			41,677
Expenses			
Salaries & Wages		15,721	
Rent		6,521	
Advertising		1,452	
Utilities		942	
Taxes on Inventory, Payroll		3,415	
Miscellaneous Expenses		1,895	
Total Expenses			29,946
NET INCOME			$11,731

Using the income statement for Do-Little's Products as an example, solve the following problems:

What is the cost of goods sold if the beginning inventory was $7,898, the total cost of goods purchased was $71,213, and the ending inventory was $5,619?

_____ (1)

What is the gross margin if sales were $193,812, beginning inventory $7,856, purchases $162,314, sales returns and allowances $2,187, and ending inventory $8,514?

_____ (2)

What is the net income if net sales were $59,872, cost of goods sold $32,714, and total expenses $5,618?

_____ (3)

Answers: (1) $73,492; (2) $29,969; (3) $21,540

Horizontal and Vertical Analysis

Now you know what balance sheets and income statements are. But, what if you need to know how well a business did compared to other firms, both large and small, in a similar industry. How do you compare the results of one year with another. Business financial statements can be analyzed to find answers to a variety of practical and important questions. Let's look at the two most common methods of analysis, vertical and horizontal analysis.

Horizontal Analysis is the comparison of an item on one statement to the same item in a preceding or succeeding statement. Changes in assets, liabilities, and stockholder's (owner's) equity indicate whether a business is growing or receding. When two different time periods are involved the earlier statement is used as a base.

HORIZONTAL ANALYSIS

Assets	This Year	Last Year	Change Amount	%	Calculations
Cash	15,300	14,200	1,100	7.7	$\dfrac{15,300 - 14,200}{14,200} = 7.7\%$
Supplies	903	860	43	5.0	$\dfrac{903 - 860}{860} = 5.0\%$
Equipment	8,200	7,500	700	9.3	$\dfrac{8,200 - 7,500}{7,500} = 9.3\%$

Vertical Analysis is the comparison of a single item in a financial statement to another item in the same statement. On a balance sheet the percent of each asset is based on the total assets. The percent of each liability item and stockholder's (owner's) equity item is based on the total liabilities and stockholder's equity. Total assets and the sum of total liabilities and owner's equity are each therefore considered to be 100%. All other items on the balance sheet are thus reported as a percent of total assets or sum of total liabilities and owner's equity.

VERTICAL ANALYSIS

Assets	Amount	Percent of Total	Calculations
Cash	15,300	68.6	$\dfrac{15,300}{22,300} = 68.6\%$
Supplies	800	3.6	$\dfrac{800}{22,300} = 3.6\%$
Equipment	6,200	27.8	$\dfrac{6,200}{22,300} = 27.8\%$
TOTAL	22,300	100.0	100%

On an income statement it is customary to compare all amounts with the net sales (revenue) figure. Net sales are therefore considered to be 100%. This changes absolute numbers, dollars, to relative numbers, percents, and enables management to make comparisons between years, with other companies with industry averages, and so on.

COMPARATIVE BALANCE SHEET

Brandon Supply House Inc.

	This Year	Last Year	Increase (Decrease) Amount	%	Percents This Year	Percents Last Year
Assets						
Cash	78,432	62,971	15,461	24.6	8.2	7.8
Account Receivable	211,241	183,742	27,499	15.0	22.2	22.6
Merchandise Inventory	287,238	202,681	84,557	41.7	30.2	25.0
Plant & Equipment	374,816	361,824	12,992	3.6	39.4	44.6
Total Assets	951,727	811,218	140,509	17.3	100.0	100.0
Liabilities & Equity						
Current Liabilities	127,832	139,816	(11,984)	(8.6)	13.4	17.2
Long-Term Liabilities	372,841	351,618	21,223	6.0	39.2	43.4
Stockholder's Equity	451,054	319,784	131,270	41.0	47.4	39.4
Total Liabilities & Owner's Equity	951,727	811,218	140,509	17.3	100.0	100.0

COMPARATIVE INCOME STATEMENT

Brandon Supply House Inc.

	This Year	Last Year	Increase (Decrease) Amount	%	Percents This Year	Percents Last Year
Gross Sales	607,832	488,751	119,081	24.4	100.4	100.4
Returns	2,257	1,821	436	23.9	0.4	0.4
Net Sales	605,575	486,930	118,645	24.4	100.0	100.0
Cost of Goods Sold	379,542	267,215	112,327	42.0	62.7	54.9
Gross Margin	226,033	219,715	6,318	2.9	37.3	45.1
Wages	63,015	79,819	(16,804)	(21.1)	10.4	16.4
Rent	4,021	4,017	4	0.1	0.7	0.8
Advertising	11,598	11,681	(83)	(0.7)	1.9	2.4
Utilities	12,284	12,064	220	1.8	2.0	2.5
Taxes on Inventory & Payroll	22,872	19,018	3,854	20.3	3.8	3.9
Miscellaneous Expenses	1,492	1,783	(291)	(16.3)	0.2	0.4
Total Expenses	115,282	128,382	(13,100)	(10.2)	19.0	26.4
Net Income	110,751	91,333	19,418	21.3	18.3	18.8

Fill in the missing items in the following comparative balance sheet.

COMPARATIVE BALANCE SHEETS

Sharon Co.

	This Year	Last Year	Increase (Decrease) Amount	%	Percents This Year	Last Year
Assets						
Current Assets						
Cash	49,385	52,106	__(17)	__(36)	__(55)	__(72)
Notes Receivable	8,716	7,219	__(18)	__(37)	__(56)	__(73)
Accounts Receivable	152,613	125,182	__(19)	__(38)	__(57)	__(74)
Inventory	148,214	151,932	__(20)	__(39)	__(58)	__(75)
Total Current Assets	__(1)	__(9)	__(21)	__(40)	__(59)	__(76)
Plant & Equipment						
Land	10,000	10,000	__(22)	__(41)	__(60)	__(77)
Buildings	89,800	86,700	__(23)	__(42)	__(61)	__(78)
Fixtures	18,200	16,900	__(24)	__(43)	__(62)	__(79)
Total Plant & Equip.	__(2)	__(10)	__(25)	__(44)	__(63)	__(80)
Total Assets	__(3)	__(11)	__(26)	__(45)	100%	100%
LIABILITIES						
Current Liabilities						
Accounts Payable	4,512	7,814	__(27)	__(46)	__(64)	__(81)
Notes Payable	135,863	146,918	__(28)	__(47)	__(65)	__(82)
Total Current Liabilities	__(4)	__(12)	__(29)	__(48)	__(66)	__(83)
Long-Term Liabilities						
Mortgages Payable	15,816	14,683	__(30)	__(49)	__(67)	__(84)
Long-Term Notes	25,763	21,871	__(31)	__(50)	__(68)	__(85)
Total Long-Term Liab.	__(5)	__(13)	__(32)	__(51)	__(69)	__(86)
Total Liabilities	__(6)	__(14)	__(33)	__(52)	__(70)	__(87)
CAPITAL	__(7)	__(15)	__(34)	__(53)	__(71)	__(88)
TOTAL LIABILITIES AND CAPITAL	__(8)	__(16)	__(35)	__(54)	100%	100%

Answers: (1) 358,928; (2) 118,000; (3) 476,928; (4) 140,375; (5) 41,579; (6) 181,954; (7) 294,974; (8) 476,928; (9) 336,439; (10) 113,600; (11) 450,039; (12) 154,732; (13) 36,554; (14) 191,286; (15) 258,753; (16) 450,039; (17) (2,721); (18) 1,497; (19) 27,431; (20) (3,718); (21) 22,489; (22) 0; (23) 3,100; (24) 1,300; (25) 4,400; (26) 26,889; (27) (3,302); (28) (11,055); (29) (14,357); (30) 1,133; (31) 3,892; (32) 5,025; (33) (9,332); (34) 36,221; (35) 26,889;

(36) (5.2); (37) 20.7; (38) 21.9; (39) (2.5); (40) 6.7; (41) 0; (42) 3.6; (43) 7.7; (44) 3.9; (45) 6.0; (46) (42.3); (47) (7.5); (48) (9.3); (49) 7.7; (50) 17.8; (51) 13.7; (52) (4.9); (53) 14.0; (54) 6.0; (55) 10.4; (56) 1.8; (57) 32.0; (58) 31.1; (59) 75.3; (60) 2.1; (61) 18.8; (62) 3.8; (63) 24.7; (64) 1.0; (65) 28.5; (66) 29.4; (67) 3.3; (68) 5.4; (69) 8.7; (70) 38.2; (71) 61.9; (72) 11.6; (73) 1.6; (74) 27.8; (75) 33.8; (76) 74.8; (77) 2.2; (78) 19.3; (79) 3.8; (80) 25.2; (81) 1.7; (82) 32.6; (83) 34.4; (84) 3.3; (85) 4.9; (86) 8.1; (87) 42.5; (88) 57.5

Fill in the missing items in the following comparative income statement.

United Specialty Inc.

	This Year	Last Year	Increase (Decrease) Amount	%	Percents This Year	Last Year
Gross Sales	846,319	928,174	__(7)	__(20)	__(33)	__(45)
Returns	6,415	3,287	__(8)	__(21)	__(34)	__(46)
Net Sales	__(1)	__(4)	__(9)	__(22)	100%	100%
Cost of Goods Sold	525,817	601,967	__(10)	__(23)	__(35)	__(47)
Gross Margin	314,087	322,920	__(11)	__(24)	__(36)	__(48)
Wages	74,563	75,914	__(12)	__(25)	__(37)	__(49)
Rent	39,416	38,951	__(13)	__(26)	__(38)	__(50)
Advertising	61,832	55,183	__(14)	__(27)	__(39)	__(51)
Utilities	18,621	16,851	__(15)	__(28)	__(40)	__(52)
Taxes on Inv. & Payroll	9,207	8,785	__(16)	__(29)	__(41)	__(53)
Miscellaneous	29,872	27,532	__(17)	__(30)	__(42)	__(54)
Total Expenses	__(2)	__(5)	__(18)	__(31)	__(43)	__(55)
Net Income	__(3)	__(6)	__(19)	__(32)	__(44)	__(56)

Answers: (1) 839,904; (2) 233,511; (3) 80,576; (4) 924,887; (5) 223,216; (6) 99,704; (7) (81,855); (8) 3,128; (9) (84,983); (10) (76,150); (11) (8,833); (12) (1,351); (13) 465; (14) 6,649; (15) 1,770; (16) 422; (17) 2,340; (18) 10,295; (19) (19,128); (20) (8.8); (21) 95.2; (22) (9.2); (23) (12.7); (24) (2.7); (25) (1.8); (26) 1.2; (27) 12.0; (28) 10.5; (29) 4.8; (30) 8.5; (31) 4.6; (32) (19.2); (33) 100.8; (34) 0.8; (35) 62.6; (36) 37.4; (37) 8.9; (38) 4.7; (39) 7.4; (40) 2.2; (41) 1.1; (42) 3.6; (43) 27.8; (44) 9.6; (45) 100.4; (46) 0.4; (47) 65.1; (48) 34.9; (49) 8.2; (50) 4.2; (51) 6.0; (52) 1.8; (53) 0.9; (54) 3.0; (55) 24.1; (56) 10.8

Financial Ratios

Ratio Analysis is a common tool used in analyzing financial reports. A ratio is a relative comparison of one number to another. Companies compare their ratios with other companies in their industry and with their own ratios from previous years. Ratios are also used by creditors and investors.

Current Ratio is a ratio between current assets and current liabilities and is sometimes referred to as the working capital ratio. It is one of the most common measures of an organization's financial position, and is given by the following formula:

$$\text{Current Ratio} = \frac{\text{Current Assets}}{\text{Current Liabilities}}$$

A commonly used rule is that a firm may have financial problems if the current ratio is less than 2. Since current assets are to be converted into cash during the current period and current liabilities are to be met by use of current assets, a current ratio of less than 2 may indicate an organization's lack of financial strength on a day-to-day basis. There are exceptions to this rule because much depends on the type of industry a firm works within, for example, a utility company usually does not have a need for a current ratio as high as 2. Like other financial ratios, current ratios should be observed over time and compared with similar ratios from other time periods for the individual firm and other firms within the same industry.

The **Acid-Test Ratio** which is sometimes called a **Quick Ratio** is a measure of a company's ability to quickly convert current assets into cash to meet its current debt. This acid-test ratio is found by the following formula:

$$\text{Acid-Test Ratio} = \frac{\text{Quick Assets}}{\text{Current Liabilities}}$$

Quick assets are defined as cash plus those current assets such as accounts receivable and marketable securities that can easily be converted into cash. They do not include inventory because often inventory cannot be converted quickly to cash. An acid-test ratio of 1 or more is usually considered acceptable because it indicates that an organization can pay its current liabilities in a short period. There are exceptions, however, and like other ratios, trends over time should be studied.

The **Debt Asset Ratio** or simply the **Debt Ratio** is concerned with a firm's stability beyond the current period. This long run ratio is found by:

$$\text{Debt-Asset Ratio} = \frac{\text{Total Liabilities}}{\text{Total Assets}}$$

By convention, this ratio is always expressed as a percent.

Low debt-asset ratios are preferred over higher ones. Firms going out of business usually are not able to sell their assets for the entire amounts showing on their books. Therefore, creditors usually want to see total assets significantly higher than total liabilities.

Return on Equity can be thought of as the rate of return on investment. This ratio is found by:

$$\text{Return on Equity Ratio} = \frac{\text{Net Income}}{\text{Owner's Equity}}$$

By convention, this ratio is also expressed as a percent.

No specific rule is available to determine whether a rate of return is satisfactory. As with other ratios, the rate of return needs to be compared with similar businesses. Trends over time also must be considered. In general, of course, the higher the rate of return the better. The question of opportunity costs or if a higher rate of return could be received somewhere else is always asked.

Data for Jen's Florist is given below:

Total current assets	$284,135
Total current liabilities	123,010
Cash	75,881
Accounts receivable	98,742
Total liabilities	205,153
Total assets	483,721
Stockholder's equity	278,568
Net income	52,831

Using the data above find the following ratios:

$$\text{Current Ratio} = \frac{\text{Current Assets}}{\text{Current Liabilities}} \qquad \underline{\hspace{2cm}} (1)$$

$$\text{Acid-Test Ratio} = \frac{\text{Quick Assetss}}{\text{Current Liabilities}} \qquad \underline{\hspace{2cm}} (2)$$

$$\text{Debt-Asset Ratio} = \frac{\text{Total Liabilities}}{\text{Total Assets}} \qquad \underline{\hspace{2cm}} (3)$$

$$\text{Return on Equity Ratio} = \frac{\text{Net Income}}{\text{Owner's Equity}} \qquad \underline{\hspace{2cm}} (4)$$

Frank's Backhoe Service has current assets of $349,215; current liabilities $202,514; cash $3,215; notes and accounts receivable total $78,452; inventory is $4,216.

Find the current ratio: _____ (5)

Find the quick ratio: _____ (6)

Jose Supply has current assets of $783,152; current liabilities are $287,413, quick assets are $315,847, total assets are $984,321, and total liabilities are $495,624 and net income is $96,853.

Find the current ratio: _____ (7)

Find the quick ratio: _____ (8)

Find the debt-asset ratio: _____ (9)

Find the return on equity (remember owner's equity equals total assets minus total liabilities): _____ (10)

Answers: (1) 2.31; (2) 1.42; (3) 42.4%; (4) 19.0%; (5) 1.72; (6) .40 (Frank has a problem); (7) 2.72; (8) 1.10; (9) 50.4%; (10) 19.8%

Stop

You are now ready to take Pretest IX to check your skill in using a calculator to solve problems involving Business Operations. You should be able to complete this test in less than 50 minutes with better than 70 percent accuracy. Unless instructed to do otherwise, turn in your Pretest for correction and review before taking Test IX. Be certain you understand each problem on Pretest IX before attempting your graded examination.

When you pass Test IX you will have proven your ability to use calculators effectively to solve Business Operations problems.

Pretest IX

CALCULATOR APPLICATIONS—BUSINESS OPERATIONS

50 minutes

This test need not be worked in sequence. Do the problems you know best first. You need 70 percent correct to pass.

Prorating.

Complete the following table of advertising expenses (total of $68,418.00). Round to the nearest dollar.

Allocation per thousand dollars of sales   _____ (1)

Office	Total Sales (000's omitted)	
Albuquerque, NM	$ 2,288	_____ (2)
Atlanta, GA	1,354	_____ (3)
Baltimore, MD	1,712	_____ (4)
Boise, ID	2,157	_____ (5)
Chicago, IL	3,896	_____ (6)
Dallas, TX	2,285	_____ (7)
Denver, CO	1,559	_____ (8)
Grand Forks, ND	1,981	_____ (9)
Los Angeles, CA	5,243	_____ (10)
Oakland, CA	1,275	_____ (11)
Orlando, FL	4,812	_____ (12)
Portland, OR	1,264	_____ (13)
Scranton, PA	1,748	_____ (14)
St. Louis, MO	1,989	_____ (15)
TOTAL	$33,563	$68,418

Depreciation.

Using the tables from the test or handout, complete the following depreciation schedules.

DEPRECIATION SCHEDULES FOR SPECIAL TOOLS

Year	Purchase Price $14,900 ACCELERATED METHOD Depreciation	3-Year Category STRAIGHT-LINE METHOD Depreciation
1	_____ (16)	_____ (21)
2	_____ (17)	_____ (22)
3	_____ (18)	_____ (23)
4	_____ (19)	_____ (24)
TOTAL (100% of cost)	_____ (20)	_____ (25)

DEPRECIATION SCHEDULES FOR DELIVERY VAN

Year	Purchase Price $22,800 ACCELERATED METHOD Depreciation	5-Year Category STRAIGHT-LINE METHOD Depreciation
1	_____ (26)	_____ (33)
2	_____ (27)	_____ (34)
3	_____ (28)	_____ (35)
4	_____ (29)	_____ (36)
5	_____ (30)	_____ (37)
6	_____ (31)	_____ (38)
TOTAL (100% of cost)	_____ (32)	_____ (39)

Placed into service in February
Purchase Price $221,500   31.5-Year Category
PRESCRIBED METHOD

Year	Depreciation	Year	Depreciation
1	_____ (40)	17	same as above
2	_____ (41)	18	same as above
3	_____ (42)	19	same as above
4	_____ (43)	20	same as above
5	_____ (44)	21	same as above
6	_____ (45)	22	same as above
7	same as above	23	same as above
8	same as above	24	same as above
9	same as above	25	same as above
10	same as above	26	same as above
11	same as above	27	same as above
12	same as above	28	same as above
13	same as above	29	same as above
14	same as above	30	same as above
15	same as above	31	same as above
16	same as above	32	_____(46)
Total			
(100% of cost)			_____(47)

COMPARATIVE BALANCE SHEET

Brandon Supply House Inc.

	This Year	Last Year	Increase/Decrease Amount	%
Assets				
Cash	88,423	52,971	_____ (48)	_____ (49)
Account Receivale	110,241	183,742	_____ (50)	_____ (51)
Merchandise Inventory	287,796	214,681	_____ (52)	_____ (53)
Plant & Equipment	474,817	361,859	_____ (54)	_____ (55)
Total Assets	961,277	813,253	_____ (56)	_____ (57)
Liabilities & Equity				
Current Liabilities	87,382	102,484	_____ (58)	_____ (59)
Long-Term Liabilities	372,333	267,985	_____ (60)	_____ (61)
Stockholder's Equity	501,562	442,784	_____ (62)	_____ (63)
Total Liabilities & Owner's Equity	961,277	813,253	_____ (64)	_____ (65)

COMPARATIVE INCOME STATEMENT

Brandon Supply House Inc.

	This Year	Last Year	Percent of Net Sales This Year	Last Year
Gross Sales	407,575	388,477	_____ (66)	_____ (67)
Returns	2,364	1,821	_____ (68)	_____ (69)
Net Sales	405,211	386,656	_____ (70)	_____ (71)
Cost of Goods Sold	201,320	192,697	_____ (72)	_____ (73)
Gross Margin	203,891	193,959	_____ (74)	_____ (75)
Wages	55,212	65,819	_____ (76)	_____ (77)
Rent	4,021	4,982	_____ (78)	_____ (79)
Advertising	10,628	9,412	_____ (80)	_____ (81)
Utilities	11,284	11,063	_____ (82)	_____ (83)
Taxes on Inventory & Payroll	21,872	17,018	_____ (84)	_____ (85)
Miscellaneous Expenses	1,516	1,612	_____ (86)	_____ (87)
Total Expenses	104,533	109,906	_____ (88)	_____ (89)
Net Income	99,358	84,053	_____ (90)	_____ (91)

The Dillon Company had: current assets of $416,341, current liabilities of $211,957, quick assets of $203,052, total liabilities of $299,766, total assets of $534,293, owner's equity of $234,527, and net income of $58,499.

$$\text{Current Ratio} = \frac{\text{Current Assets}}{\text{Current Liabilities}}$$ _____ (92)

$$\text{Acid-Test Ratio} = \frac{\text{Quick Assets}}{\text{Current Liabilities}}$$ _____ (93)

$$\text{Return on Equity Ratio} = \frac{\text{Net Income}}{\text{Owner's Equity}}$$ _____ (94)

$$\text{Debt-Asset Ratio} = \frac{\text{Total Liabilities}}{\text{Total Assets}}$$ _____ (95)

What is the gross margin if sales were $702,419, beginning inventory $7,246, purchases $87,899, returns and allowances $1,015, and ending inventory $8,538?

_____(96)

What is the net income if net sales were $240,225, cost of goods sold $98,357, and total expenses $9,816?

_____(97)

Lori Jenson's business had a balance sheet with: inventory $44,364, accounts receivable $10,730, accounts payable $22,581, cash $6,089, equipment $21,432, notes payable $7,600, and wages payable $14,146. Determine (a) total assets, (b) total liabilities, and (c) owner's equity.

_____(98)

_____(99)

_____(100)

10

Business Analysis

LEARNING GOALS

After completing Chapter 10, you will have improved your ability to operate electronic calculators and expanded your knowledge in the following areas:

- Ration and Proportions
- Time Value Concepts
- Index Numbers
- Statistics

You will also be able to pass a pretest of typical business problems, with at least 70 percent accuracy in less than 50 minutes.

Ratio and Proportions

Often fractions and percents, which are widely used in business, will be called ratios or proportions. Since a fraction represents a portion of a whole, business problems can often be solved by constructing the appropriate fraction, ratio, or proportion and then multiplying.

Example 1. If an automobile salesman sold 5 cars on Friday and 8 on Saturday, the ratio of cars sold on Friday to cars sold on Saturday would be 5 to 8. If the ratio was the same for the entire dealership and it sold 90 cars on Friday, how many cars did the dealership sell on Saturday?

Solution:

think $\dfrac{5}{8} = \dfrac{90}{?}$

We know the salesman's ratio was 5 to 8 (a ratio of the number of units sold on Friday to the number of units sold on Saturday). We also know the number of units sold by the dealership Friday (90) has the same ratio as the salesman. That is:

$$\frac{5 \text{ (Friday)}}{8 \text{ (Saturday)}} = \frac{90 \text{ (Friday)}}{? \text{ (Saturday)}}$$

The most common way to solve this problem is by cross multiplication:

$$\frac{5}{8} \diagdown\!\!\!\!\!\diagup \frac{90}{?}$$

or 8 times 90 equals 5 times some other number. To find the other number simply divide 5 into the product, 720 (the answer of 8 times 90).

$$720 \div 5 = 144$$

Hint

Ratio proportion problems can always be checked by changing them to a decimal or percent, since each ratio or proportion must be equal. For example: 5/8 = 90/144. 5 ÷ 8 = .625 and 90 ÷ 144 = .625

Example 2. Last week sales were $7,000. This week they were $3,000. Expressed as a fraction, what was the ratio of sales this week to last week?

Solution: 3 to 7 or 3/7.

Example 3. If 30 pounds of material cost $86, what is the cost of 9 pounds?

Solution: $\dfrac{30 \text{ lbs.}}{\$86} = \dfrac{9 \text{ lbs.}}{\$?}$ $\qquad \dfrac{30}{86} \bowtie \dfrac{9}{?}$

$86 \times 9 = 774$ and $774 \div 30 = \$25.80$

Example 4. A new owner will occupy a house at the end of February. The seller has already paid annual real estate taxes of $1,345 on the house. How much should be repaid to the seller?

Solution: $\dfrac{10 \text{ (the number of months left in the year)}}{12 \text{ (the number of months in a year)}} = \dfrac{?}{1345}$

or $\dfrac{10}{12} \bowtie \dfrac{?}{1345}$

$10 \times 1,345 = 13,450$ and $13,450 \div 12 = \$1,120.83$

The concept of ratio and proportions was utilized in Chapter 9 in the section on Prorating Expenses and Financial Analysis.

Solve the following problems as efficiently as possible:

1. If James is paid $493 per week and he only works 3 days, what portion of weekly wage would he be paid based on the ratio of days worked (3 to 5)?

2. If 23 gallons of gas cost $28.50, what would 12 gallons of gas cost?

3. If the yearly rental cost of a piece of equipment is $4,528, what is the prorated cost for the first three months of the year?

4. If Sam has sold $142,873 worth of goods and this is 3/7 of his annual quota, what is his annual quota?

5. Larry Barnes Chevrolet sold 3/17 of the cars sold in Boise, Idaho during March. If Larry Barnes Chevrolet sold 328 cars, how many cars to the nearest car, were sold in Boise during March?

6. Total current assets were $185,237, and total current liabilities were $42,872 for Marie's Waffle House for 1985. Assuming the same current ratio of assets to liabilities to the nearest dollar, what would the liabilities be in 1986 if assets were $212,803 in 1986?

NOTE: If your calculator will only accept 8 whole numbers, move the decimal place 3 places to the left in each factor. Complete the computations and then move the decimal place in your answer 3 places to the right. For example: $42.872 \times 212.803 \div 185.237 = 49.252$. The same procedure may be needed for problems 7, 8, and 9.

7. If Aoki Fabricators had a net income of $133,513 on net sales of $1,552,841 in 1985, what net sales would be needed 20 years later to have a net income of $1,500,000, assuming the same income-to-sales ratio?

8. If net income was $5,281 last year on net sales of $205,873, what would net income this year be on net sales of $3,807,471, with the same income to sales ratio?

9. If 13 years ago a company had a net income of $31,521 and an owner's equity of $158,487, what should net income be this year if owner's equity is $851,852 to give the same return on investment?

10. If inventory is $285,371 and working capital is $307,802, what is the inventory-to-working capital ratio? State your answer rounded to three places.

Answers: (1) $295.80; (2) $14.87; (3) $1,132.00; (4) $333,370.33; (5) 1,859; (6) $49,252; (7) $17,445,952.83; (8) $97,668.24; (9) $169,422.27; (10) .927

Time Value Concepts

Compound Interest, Present Worth, Annuities, Sinking Fund, and Amortization Using Compound Interest and Annuity Tables

A dollar today does not have the same value as a dollar tomorrow. All sorts of reasons exist for this—inflation, investment opportunities—you may not even be alive tomorrow. A *dollar today is worth more than a dollar tomorrow.* Would you pay one dollar today for a promise to receive one dollar a year from now? Probably not. After all, you could deposit $.94 in a 6% savings account and even at simple interest you would receive one dollar a year from now.

This section looks at how time and money relate to one another. Many problems in the fields of finance, real estate, accounting, banking, insurance, and economics deal with situations in which sums of money that exist in different time periods must be compared. Problem examples are: What will your annual income need to be ten years from now to keep pace with inflation? For an insurance settlement, should you accept a cash amount today or periodic payments over the next ten years? How long will it take the population to double at any given annual growth rate? What is the best rate of return on different investments? What do you need to save each month to accumulate $10,000 in five years? What is $1,000,000, payable in 30 years, worth today, etc.

Time value concepts are used in many business decisions, In actual business calculations, special business calculators or computer programs are usually used instead of compound interest and annuity tables like those in Appendix 5. However, the tables will allow you to easily solve and understand these important time value concepts.

Compound Interest and Present Worth

It is more convenient to use the compound interest and annuity tables found in Appendix 5 when problems have a large number of conversion periods, than to use most calculators. If you wanted to know how much $2,414 invested at 8% compounded annually will amount to in 60 years you could use the method in Chapter 6 and depress the equal key 60 times. You could also turn to Appendix 5, find the first column, on the 8% table "Amount of 1," drop down to the last figure in that column, 60 periods, 101.257064 (rounded to six decimals) and use it. Since the table is worked out on the bases of $1, merely multiply the figure taken from the table by the original principal = $2,414.00 × 101.257064 = $244,434.55.

To find the compound interest only, simply subtract the original principal from the final amount. Thus $244,434.55 − $2,414.00 = $242,020.55, interest compounded annually on $2,414 for 60 years at 8%.

In summary, to find compound interest on a fixed amount (for periods other than one year), simply find the interest rate per period, the number of periods, and look up the appropriate factor in column one, Appendix 5.

Example. Find the amount of $1,827.83 invested for 6 years at 12% compounded quarterly.

Solution: The compound amount of $1 for 24 periods at 3% = 2.032794

$$\$1,827.83 \times 2.032794 = \$3,715.60$$

In the example above the $1,827.83, the present value or present worth today has a future value of $3,715.60, if it is invested for 6 years at 12% compounded quarterly. Businesses sometimes know the future value but need to find the present value. Present value problems are common because businesses often need to make investment decisions in the present, not in the future.

Example. What is the present worth of $3,715.60, if money is worth 12% compounded quarterly?

Solution: From Appendix 5, on the 3% table, column four "Present Worth of 1" for 24 periods is .491934 (rounded to six places).

$$\$3,715.60 \times .491934 = \$1,827.83$$

Look up the growth factor in Appendix 5 and calculate the compound amount for each of the following problems. To match the answers given use six decimals in each growth factor.

Principal	Years	Annual Rate	Frequency of Conversion	Growth Factor	Compound Amount
$490	5	8%	Quarterly	_____ (1)	_____ (2)
1,485	20	12%	Semiannually	_____ (3)	_____ (4)
6,500	8	6%	Annually	_____ (5)	_____ (6)
8,200	30	16%	Semiannually	_____ (7)	_____ (8)
9,540	15	20%	Quarterly	_____ (9)	_____ (10)

Answers: (1) 1.485947; (2) $728.11; (3) 10.285718; (4) $15,274.29; (5) 1.593848; (6) $10,360.01; (7) 101.257064; (8) $830,307.92; (9) 18.679186; (10) $178,199.43

Look up the discount factor and calculate the present worth of the following principal sums. To match the answers given use six decimals in each discount factor.

Principal	Years	Annual Rate	Frequency of Conversion	Discount Factor	Present Worth
$4,520	10	10%	Semiannually	_____ (1)	_____ (2)
7,890	5	20%	Quarterly	_____ (3)	_____ (4)
13,450	18	8%	Annually	_____ (5)	_____ (6)
5,200	4	12%	Monthly	_____ (7)	_____ (8)
10,000	25	12%	Semiannually	_____ (9)	_____ (10)

Answers: (1).376889; (2) $1,703.54; (3) .376889; (4) $2,973.65; (5) .250249; (6) $3,365.85; (7) .620260; (8) $3,225.35; (9) .054288; (10) $542.88

Word Problems

If you deposited $1,200.00 at 12% compounded quarterly what would the value of the deposit be at the end of twelve years?

_____ (1)

What is the present worth of $2,500.00 due in 10 years if money is worth 4% compounded quarterly?

_____ (2)

Glenda Smith wants to send her 5-year-old daughter to college when the daughter reaches age 17. How much money would Glenda need to put aside today in order to have $98,000 when her daughter reaches age 17 if money is worth 8% compounded semiannually?

_____ (3)

What will a deposit of $10,000.00 grow to in 15 years at 8% compounded quarterly?

_____ (4)

In 2001 the value of the gross domestic product of China passed a trillion dollars and was about ten percent of the US GDP of $10 trillion. If the GDP grew at a rate of 8% per year in China and 2% per year in the United States, to the nearest trillion what would the gross domestic products be in both countries 20 years later?

_____ (5)

Answers: (1) $4,958.70 (use 4.132252 × 1,200, i = 3%, n = 48, column one Appendix 5; (2) $1,679.13 (.671653 × $2,500, i = 1%, n = 40, column four, Appendix 5; (3) $38,231.86; (4) $32,810.31; (5) China 5 trillion, the US 15 trillion or in relative terms China's economy would grow from 10% to over 33% of the US economy.

Annuities

Annuities are equal periodic payments with interest compounded at the end of each interval or period. Annuities include installment payments, savings and loan payments, insurance payments, and some insurance settlements.

The amount of an annuity is the accumulated value or amount at the end of the annuity period. The amount includes the sum of the payments plus the accumulated compound interest on the payments.

Example. What will the value of 15 periodic deposits of $250.00 each month be at the end of 15 months if money is worth 12% per year and monthly compounding is used?

Solution: The number of periods is 15, the interest rate per period is 1%, (12% ÷ 12 months in a year). Look up the factor in the second column of Appendix 5, "Amount of 1 per Period," for 15 periods at 1% (16.096896).

$$\$250.00 \times 16.096896 = \$4,024.22$$

The present worth of an annuity is the discounted value of present worth at the beginning of the annuity period. The amount includes the discounted sum of each payment.

Example. What is the present worth of a periodic payment each month of $250.00 for 15 months, if money is worth 12% compounded monthly?

Solution: The number of periods is 15, the interest rate per period is 1%. Look up the factor in the fifth column of Appendix 5, "Present Worth of 1 per Period," for 15 periods at 1% (13.865053).

$$\$250.00 \times 13.865053 = \$3,466.26$$

Look up the growth factor and calculate the compound amount of 1 per period for each of the following investment programs.

Periodic Payment	Annual Rate	Frequency of Conversion	Years	Growth Factor	Compound Amount
$25	12%	Monthly	5	_____ (1)	_____ (2)
175	24%	Monthly	4	_____ (3)	_____ (4)
350	6%	Monthly	2	_____ (5)	_____ (6)
425	12%	Monthly	3	_____ (7)	_____ (8)
635	36%	Monthly	5	_____ (9)	_____ (10)

Answers: (1) 81.669670; (2) $2,041.74; (3) 79.353519; (4) $13,886.87; (5) 25.431955; (6) $8,901.18; (7) 43.076878; (8) $18,307.67; (9) 163.053437; (10) $103,538.93

Look up the discount factor and calculate the present worth of each of the following series of payments.

Periodic Payment	Annual Rate	Frequency of Conversion	Years	Discount Factor	Present Worth
$25.85	6%	Monthly	2	_____ (1)	_____ (2)
183.92	12%	Monthly	1	_____ (3)	_____ (4)
504.50	24%	Monthly	5	_____ (5)	_____ (6)
685.90	36%	Monthly	3	_____ (7)	_____ (8)
755.55	12%	Monthly	4	_____ (9)	_____ (10)

Answers: (1) 22.562866; (2) $583.25; (3) 11.255077; (4) $2,070.03; (5) 34.760887; (6) $17,536.87; (7) 21.832252; (8) $14,974.74; (9) 37.973959; (10) $28,691.22

Word Problems

What is the present worth of 17 monthly payments of $380.00 if money is worth 12% compounded monthly?

_____ (1)

What would the value of your account be at the end of 37 months, if you deposited $217.00 at the end of each month and the account paid 6% interest compounded monthly?

_____ (2)

Your publisher estimates that the latest book you wrote will net $26,000.00 a year for the next ten years. If royalties are paid semi-annually and money is worth 4% compounded semiannually, what is the equivalent cash value of the book today?

_____ (3)

Your investment counselor tells you he can invest the $13,000.00 royalty payments from problem three at 12% compounded semi-annually. If this is true and you invested every payment, what would the value of your investment be at the end of ten years?

_____ (4)

What is the present worth of an annuity that pays $12,500.00 per year for fifty years if money is worth 5% compounded annually?

_____ (5)

Answers: (1) $5,913.66; (2) $8,795.61; (3) $212,568.62; (4) $478,212.68; (5) $228,199.06

Sinking Funds and Amortization

To finance large expenditures businesses sometimes raise money by issuing bonds. The bonds may run for a specified time, such as 10, 20, or 30 years. In order to have funds to pay the bonds at maturity, a sum of money may be set aside from earnings at the end of each year. These funds, when invested at compound interest, will produce an amount equal to the face value of the bonds. This sum of money is termed a sinking fund. Sinking funds can be thought of as the periodic saving necessary to pay off a specific amount in the future. The use of the concept of sinking funds need not be limited to the repayment of bonds.

Example. How much will need to be invested at the end of each year at 8% to pay off a bond issue of $250,000.00 maturing in 20 years?

Solution: The number of periods is 20 and the rate per periods is 8%. Look up the sinking fund factor in the third column of Appendix 5, "Sinking Fund" for 20 periods at 8% (.021852).

$$\$250,000.00 \times .021852 = \$5,463.00$$

Amortization is the method of repaying loans in equal installment payments. Each payment includes interest on the unpaid balance of the loan and a payment on principal.

Example. What is the monthly payment needed to repay a four year loan of $6,127.83 if money is worth 24% compounded monthly?

Solution: The number of periods is 48 and the periodic rate is 2% (24 ÷ 12). Look up the sinking fund factor in the sixth column of Appendix 5, "Partial Payment," for 48 periods at 2%, (.032602).

$$\$6,127.83 \times .032602 = \$199.78$$

Look up the growth factor and calculate the periodic deposit needed for the following sinking fund amounts.

Amount of Sinking Fund	Years	Annual Rate	Frequency of Conversion	Growth Factor	Periodic Deposit
$850,000	30	6%	Semiannually	_____ (1)	_____ (2)
250,000	10	8%	Annually	_____ (3)	_____ (4)
180,000	20	10%	Semiannually	_____ (5)	_____ (6)
12,500	5	20%	Quarterly	_____ (7)	_____ (8)
11,500	3	12%	Monthly	_____ (9)	_____ (10)

Answers: (1) .006133; (2) $5,213.05; (3) .069029; (4) $17,257.25; (5) .008278; (6) $1,490.04; (7) .030243; (8) $378.04; (9) .023214; (10) $266.96

Look up the partial payments for each of the following loans:

Principal	Years	Annual Rate	Frequency of Conversion	Factor	Payment
$24,891	5	6%	Monthly	_____ (1)	_____ (2)
3,827	2	24%	Monthly	_____ (3)	_____ (4)
5,690	3	16%	Quarterly	_____ (5)	_____ (6)
7,825	15	20%	Quarterly	_____ (7)	_____ (8)
13,240	4	12%	Monthly	_____ (9)	_____ (10)

Answers: (1) .019333; (2) $481.22; (3) .052871; (4) $202.34; (5) .106552; (6) $606.28; (7) .052828; (8) $413.38; (9) .026334; (10) $348.66

Word Problems

Betty Zitter purchased a used car today for $6,000. She made a down payment of $2,000 and will play off the balance in 36 equal monthly payments. If money is worth 12% compounded monthly what is the amount of each payment?

_____ (1)

Terry Dewick plans to have a cash fund totaling $200,000.00 when he reaches age 50. If Dewick is 25 years old, how much will he have to deposit in a sinking fund each six months? Assume money is worth 16% compounded semiannually.

_____ (2)

Daniel Haggard took out a business loan for $328,000.00. If the loan is to be amortized with annual payments including 8% interest over 15 years, what would be the amount of each payment?

_____ (3)

What amount would Haggard, in problem three, need to put in a sinking fund each month to accumulate his annual loan payment? Assume the sinking fund earns 12% interest compounded monthly.

_____ (4)

Clark's Storage borrowed $8,959.00 to help purchase a new forklift. If the loan is to be repaid in 12 equal quarterly payments at 20% compounded quarterly what will each payment be?

_____ (5)

Answers: (1) $132.86; (2) $348.60; (3) $38,320.24; (4) $3,021.51; (5) $1,010.80

Review Questions

Nevada had a population of 1,998,257 (the thirty-fifth largest state in the US), in 2000. If the population of Nevada grows by 2% per year for 15 years what will the population be in 2015 to the nearest whole person.

_____ (1)

What is the present worth of one million dollars payable in 15 years, if money is worth 16% compounded quarterly?

_____ (2)

What is the difference in the current value for an insurance settlement of $100,000.00 cash or $2,000.00 per month for five years, if money is worth 12% compounded monthly?

_____ (3)

What would an investment of $1,000.00 per quarter be worth at the end of the 13 years if the investment earned 20% compounded quarterly?

_____ (4)

How much money would need to be deposited each month into a sinking fund that pays 6% monthly to retire a bond issue of $360,000.00 in five years?

_____ (5)

Erma Womac purchased a home with a $192,000 mortgage, with an interest rate of 16% compounded semiannually. If Womac makes semiannual payments on the home, to the nearest thousand dollars how much less would she pay at 6% interest over the 30-year period?

_____ (6)

What is the equivalent cash value of an investment that will give a net income of $20,100.00 per year for 16 years if money is worth 8%.

_____ (7)

If Jim saves $250.00 per month what will the value of his savings be at the end of 4 years if the savings earn 6% compounded monthly.

_____ (8)

How much can Susan borrow for a new car if she can afford to pay $250.00 per month for car payments? She feels the best loan terms she has found are 48 months at 12% interest compounded monthly.

_____ (9)

How long would it take the population of Phoenix, Arizona to double at an annual growth rate of 6%?

_____ (10)

Answers: (1) 2,689,390; (2) $95,060.00; (3) $2,000 per month has a present worth of $89,910.08 which is $10,089.92 less; (4) $232,856.17; (5) $5,159.88; (6) $515,000.00; (7) $177,912.52; (8) $13,524.46; (9) $9,493.49; (10) 12 years, simply look down the first column of the 6% table until you see the factor of 2.012 . . .

Index Numbers

"The dollar is not worth what it used to be" is a saying we have all heard. But, what is worth what it used to be? Sometimes an item is worth more and sometimes it is worth less. For example, a barrel of oil was worth less in both 1985 and 1970 than it was in 1980. We live in a world of constant change. To measure that change we use index numbers. Many indexes, such as the Consumer Price Index, The New York Stock Exchange Composite, and the index of leading economic indicators receive considerable attention on the nightly television news and on the front pages of newspapers. As examples, look at the following *Wall Street Journal* headlines in just three days of May:

> *Consumer Price Index rose 3.2% in the 12 months ending in April. Excluding the food and energy sectors the change was 3.5%.*

The Wilshire 5000 Index representing New York and American stock exchange issues and actively traded over-the-counter stocks was 4,316.12 on April 30. This was down from 4,444.30 on the last trading day in March.

Composite of key indicators of future economic activity fell in March to 152.0% of the 1982 average, from a revised 153.5% in February, the Commerce Department reports.

An index number is a percent that measures the change in price, quantity, value or some other item of interest from one time period to another. The percent sign is usually omitted. However, like the key indicators of future economic activity (152.0%) in the headline above, the percent sign is sometimes shown.

Each index number has a **base.** Until recently the **base period** for most indexes compiled and published by the federal government was 1967. This policy has changed and indexes now have various base periods. The Consumer Price Index currently has a 1982–84 base period. The U.S. import and export price indexes have 1977 as the base period. And the parity ratio or index of prices received and paid by farmers still has a 1910–14 base period.

The **base number** of most indexes is 100.0 and most business and economic indexes are carried out to the nearest tenth of a percent. This makes index numbers easy to interpret. As an example, the consumer price index was 142.6 in March of 1993. This means that consumer prices measured by the index rose 42.6 percent from the 1982–84 base period to March of 1993.

This means if you earned $1,326 per month in the 1982–84 period on the average you would need to earn $1,890.88 ($1,326 × 1.426) to have the same purchasing power in 1993.

The main use of an index number in business is to show the percent change from one time period to another. For example, the average hourly pay of factory workers was $7.27 in 1980 and $11.63 in March of 1993. What is the index of hourly earnings in manufacturing in March of 1993 based on 1980?

Example 1. $\dfrac{\text{Hourly earnings in March of 1993}}{\text{Hourly earnings in March of 1980}} \times 100$

$$= \frac{\$11.63}{\$7.27} \times 100 = 160.$$

An index can also be used to compare one thing with another. For example, the population of Canada in 2000 was 31,002,200 and the population of Mexico was 97,483,400. What was the population of Canada compared with that of Mexico?

Example 2. $\dfrac{\text{Population of Canada}}{\text{Population of Mexico}} \times 100$

$$= \frac{31,002,200}{97,483,400} \times 100 = 31.8$$

This indicates that the population of Canada is 31.8 percent (about one third) of the population of Mexico, or the population of Canada is 68.2 percent less than the population of Mexico (100.0 – 31.8 = 68.2).

Index numbers have been around a long time. An Italian, G.R. Carli, has been credited with originating the first index numbers in 1764. He used them in a report he made about price changes in Europe from 1500 to 1750. The United States started collecting and reporting index numbers in a systematic way about 1900. Today we seldom open a newspaper without seeing some sort of index number.

One of the most important index numbers today is the Consumer Price Index (CPI) which originated in 1913 and has been published regularly since 1921. The CPI serves several major functions. It is an economic indicator of the rate of inflation in the United States. It allows consumers to determine the degree to which their purchasing power is being eroded by price increases. It is a yardstick in revising wages, pensions, and other income payments to keep pace with changes in prices. Here are some changes in the Consumer Price Index one year to the next:

1980	12.5%	1986	1.1%	1992	2.9%	1998	1.6%
1981	8.9%	1987	4.4%	1993	2.7%	1999	2.7%
1982	3.8%	1988	4.4%	1994	2.7%	2000	3.4%
1983	3.8%	1989	4.6%	1995	2.5%	2001	1.6%
1984	3.9%	1990	6.1%	1996	3.3%	2002	2.4%
1985	3.8%	1991	3.1%	1997	1.7%	2003	1.9%
						2004	2.3%

The index includes about many items—including baby cribs, apples, baseballs, lawn mowers, interest rates, dentists' fees and funeral services. Agents collect this data monthly from more than 23,000 retail establishments and 50,000 housing units in 87 urban areas across America. Because prices and consumption patterns are continually changing, there is a need to continually rebase the CPI. The automobile has replaced the horse as a mode of transportation. In 1920, the typical family spent very little on higher education. Today, tuition, books, and personal computers are major segments of the CPI.

There is not just one CPI, there are consumer price indexes for New York City, Chicago, Atlanta, Spokane, and many other cities. There are price indexes for food, apparel, medical care and other items.

In summary, an index number is actually just a percent with the percent sign usually omitted. Each index number has a base period. The index for the base period by definition is 100. Values of an index that are greater than 100 indicates an increase from the base period and values less than 100 indicates that there has been an overall decrease from the base period. An index is an easily understood way of expressing relative changes. Index numbers make it easier to compare the trends in a series of quite different items as well as numbers that have a very different size. The major objective of this unit is to understand that using index numbers is simple.

Yet, we should also be aware that the actual mechanics of computing the producer price index, the quantity index of employment in manufacturing, the value index of construction contracts awarded in the U.S. or the Forbes index might be rather complex.

Example 3. If a gallon of milk cost $2.10 in 1983 and the consumer price index in August of 2002 was 180.7 what would the gallon of milk cost in 2002 if the price of milk increased at the same rate as the consumer price index?

$$\frac{\text{Base price} \times \text{Price index}}{100} = \text{Current price}$$

$$\frac{\$2.10 \times 180.7}{100} = \$3.79$$

Let's solve a few questions using the following Consumer Price index figures for selected years:

Year	CPI	Year	CPI	Year	CPI
1982–84	100.0	1991	136.2	1998	163.9
1985	107.6	1992	141.9	1999	168.3
1986	109.6	1993	145.8	2000	174.0
1987	113.6	1994	149.7	2001	176.1
1988	118.3	1995	153.5	2002	180.7
1989	124.0	1996	158.6	2003	183.7
1990	130.7	1997	161.3	2004	187.2

The price of a Honda was $9,387 in the base period of 1982–84. What would the Honda cost in 2004 if the price increased at the same rate as the CPI?

_____ (1)

If you made \$23,451 in 1988, using an index of 118.3 for 1988 and 193.4 for 2005 how much would you need to make in 2005 to have the same purchasing power?

_____ (2)

Jan made \$4.78 per hour in 1985 and \$5.21 in 1991. In 1991 dollars did she have more or less purchasing power than in 1991? How much?

_____ (3)

If tuition at San Juan College was \$2,381 per quarter in 1985 how much would it have been in 2000 if tuition increased at the same rate that the CPI increased?

_____ (4)

If a new water heater cost \$534.87 in 2004 how much would it have cost in the base year (1982–84) if the price increased at the same rate that the CPI increased?

_____ (5)

Cost of Living Comparisons for U.S. Cities

AVERAGE CITY, U.S.A.	100.0	Idaho		Nebraska		South Dakota	
		Boise	103.7	Lincoln	89.2	Sioux Falls	93.4
				Omaha	91.1		
Alabama		**Illinois**				**Tennessee**	
Birmingham	101.5	Bloomington/ Normal	104.1	**Nevada**		Knoxville	94.9
Huntsville	97.0	Champaign/ Urbana	100.7	Las Vegas	109.3	Memphis	94.2
		Peoria	104.2	Reno/Sparks	109.6	Nashville/ Franklin	92.2
Alaska		Rockford	106.2				
Anchorage	131.7	Schaumburg	121.9	**New Hampshire**		**Texas**	
				Manchester	113.7	Amarillo	86.4
Arizona		**Indiana**				Dallas	103.8
Phoenix	98.7	Indianapolis	95.3	**New Mexico**		EL Paso	97.9
Tucson	106.5	South Bend	92.7	Albuquerque	99.3	Fort Worth	94.5
				Santa Fe	108.7	Houston	99.0
Arkansas		**Iowa**				Lubbock	92.2
Fayetteville	90.2	Des Moines	102.3	**New York**		San Antonio	92.7
Fort Smith	89.1			Albany	112.4		
		Kansas		Binghamton	99.1	**Utah**	
California		Lawrence	94.7	New York City	214.2	Provo/Orem	99.1
Bakersfield	115.8			Syracuse	101.1	Salt Lake City	96.2
Los Angeles/ Long Beach	130.1	**Kentucky** Lexington	99.2	**North Carolina**		**Vermont**	
Palm Springs	120.8	Louisville	91.8	Charlotte	99.6	Montpelier/ Barre	109.6
Riverside City	119.3			Raleigh/ Durham	97.7		
San Diego	132.3	**Louisiana** Baton Rouge	99.0	Winston-Salem	96.1	**Virginia** Prince William	115.2

Colorado		New Orleans 96.8	**North Dakota**
Boulder	105.9		Minot 95.1
Colorado Springs	94.0	**Maryland**	
Denver	103.0	Hagerstown 97.9	**Ohio**
			Cincinnati 103.5
Connecticut		**Massachusetts**	Cleveland 110.1
Hamden	130.2	Boston 136.9	Columbus 107.6
Delaware		**Michigan**	**Oklahoma**
Wilmington	112.5	Benton Harbor/	Oklahoma city 91.1
		St. Joseph 102.8	Tulsa 88.3
District of Columbia		Holland 105.4	
Washington, D.C.	134.7	Lansing 101.4	**Oregon**
			Portland 108.2
Florida		**Minnesota**	Salem 100.0
Jacksonville	95.3	Minneapolis 100.2	
Miami/Dade County	106.5	St. Paul 106.7	**Pennsylvania**
Orlando	98.9		Allentown/
			Bethlehem 108.7
Tampa	95.6	**Missouri**	Harrisburg 104.3
West Palm Beach	110.1	Kansas City 95.5	Lancaster 109.6
		St. Louis 96.6	Philadelphia 131.5
Georgia			**South Carolina**
Atlanta	98.8	**Montana**	Charleston 99.8
		Billings 104.9	

Richmond	105.2
Roanoke	93.4
Washington	
Seattle	117.7
Spokane	102.5
West Virginia	
Charleston	101.7
Berkeley County	92.4
Wisconsin	
Eau Claire	95.6
Green Bay	96.8
La Crosse	98.7
Milwaukee	104.9
Wyoming	
Cheyenne	96.6

We could use the cost of living indexes from the table on the previous page to compare salary offers in different cities.

$$\frac{(\text{City \#1})}{(\text{City \#2})} \quad \frac{\text{Index Number} \times \text{Salary}}{\text{Index Number}} = \$\underline{\hspace{1cm}}$$

How much does a person in Sioux Falls, South Dakota need to earn annually to have the same buying power of someone making $62,000 a year in San Diego, California?

$$\frac{\text{Sioux Falls}}{\text{San Diego}} \quad \frac{93.4 \times \$62,000}{132.3} = \$43,770$$

How much does a person in San Diego need to earn annually to have the same buying power of someone making $35,000 a year in Sioux Falls.

$$\frac{\text{San Diego}}{\text{Sioux Falls}} \quad \frac{132.3 \times \$35,000}{93.4} = \$49,577$$

How much does a person in Washington, D.C. need to earn annually to have the same buying power as someone making $57,500 in Spokane, Washington?

_____ (6)

How much does a person in Nashville, Tennessee need to earn annually to have the same buying power as someone making $47,800 in Boulder, Colorado?

_____ (7)

How much does a person in Billings, Montana need to earn annually to have the same buying power as someone making $102,200 in Anchorage, Alaska?

_____ (8)

In 2000, the median income for women in Manhattan, New York was $45,712 and $51,856 for men. Convert this data to an index number comparing the earnings of women to men.

_____ (9)

The US had a gross domestic product in current dollars of $5,066.5 billion in 1988q2 (q2 is the second quarter of the year) and $10,371.0 billion in 2002q2. Use a consumer price index of 118.3 for 1988 and 180.5 for 2002 to find a growth index of the US GDP from 1988q2 to 2002q2. {HINT: You will need to change GDP to constant (base price) dollars}

_____ (10)

Answers: (1) $17,572.46; (2) $38,338; (3) Less by $.84 per hour; (4) $3850; (5) $285.72; (6) $75,563; (7) $41,616; (8) $81,403; (9) 88.2; (10) $134.2

Statistics

Statistics is the science of collecting, organizing, presenting, analyzing, and interpreting numerical data for the purpose of making more effective decisions. About 100 years ago H. G. Wells noted that "statistical thinking will one day be as necessary for efficient citizenship as the ability to read and write." That day has arrived. Today, we cannot avoid being bombarded with all sorts of numerical data. Statistical techniques are used extensively in almost all career fields—social science, physical science, marketing, accounting, quality control, health science, education, professional sports, and politics to name just a few. This unit introduces and defines the basic measures of central tendency and dispersion that are essential to using and understanding statistical data.

Measures of Central Tendency

Measures of central tendency are often referred to as an **average**. We often need a single number to represent a set of data—one number that can be thought of as being "typical" of all the data. The word average means a single value that represents a set of data. In everyday language average often refers to arithmetic mean, but there are other measures of central tendency or averages. The five most common measures of central tendency are the arithmetic mean, median, mode, weighted mean and geometric mean. Geometric mean, which is used to average such relatives as percents and indexes and to determine the average percent increase from one time period to another, will not be covered in this unit.

✗ Arithmetic Mean =AVERAGE

The arithmetic mean, often called the average, is the most commonly used measure of central tendency. When you add up your examination grades and divide by the number of exams, you have computed the arithmetic mean, or average. The formula for computing the arithmetic mean is

$$\text{Arithmetic mean } = \mu = \frac{\Sigma X}{N} \quad \text{or} \quad \overline{X} = \frac{\Sigma X}{n}$$

add #'s up then divide by how many #'s adding

where the Greek letter sigma (Σ) means "the sum of," x is a variable value, and N is the total number of x values. What follows is an example of how to compute a mean using this formula. During an agonizing quarter, Sam Wise received the following grades on 9 exams in college algebra (arranged in ascending order): 2, 7, 11, 20, 30, 40, 55, 71, and 71. Sam's mean semester grade, then, was (2 + 7 + 11 + 20 + 30 + 40 + 55 + 71 + 71) ÷ 9 = 34.111 or 34, rounded.

#'s!

✗ Median ⇒ Middle

The median is a measurement of position. If you arrange a series of values in either ascending or descending order, then the middle figure in the array of values is called the median. In the case of Sam's grades, the middle or median grade was 30. Both the mean grade of 34 and the median grade of 30 seem to reveal the same thing: Sam was having great difficulty grasping algebra. (He dropped the course and took Basic Business Math and Electronic Calculators to build a strong foundation with basic number skills.) Even if Sam's instructor had thrown out Sam's lowest grade, the median grade would have been halfway between 30 and 40, that is, 35, not much change.

Middle #: Sort in ascending order (lowest to highest)

While Sam's mean grade of 34 differed only slightly from his median grade of 30, it is possible in other cases for the difference between the mean and the median to be substantial, as one of the following examples will show.

✗ Mode ⇒ often

The mode is defined as the most frequently occurring value in a series. In the example of Sam's grades, the mode is 71 (a value that might appeal to Sam, but not his teacher). Although not especially useful in our example, the mode is important to, say, the department store buyer of men's suits who want to order the most popular styles, colors, and sizes.

Find the mean, median, and mode of the following raw data.

6	5	$ 3.57
8	4	8.32
10	2	7.91
10	3	4.50
10	8	9.32
14	2	2.75
15	7	8.32
16	6	75.38
18	2	6.84
	9	

Mean _____ (1) Mean _____ (4) Mean _____ (7)

Median _____ (2) Median _____ (5) Median _____ (8)

Mode _____ (3) Mode _____ (6) Mode _____ (9)

Answers: (1) 11.889; (2) 10; (3) 10; (4) 4.8; (5) 4.5, the middle point after the data are arranged in ascending or descending order; (6) 2; (7) $14.10; (8) $7.91; (9) $8.32

Weighted Mean

Here is an example involving measures of central tendency, weighted mean, where one number is more important or carries more weight than another number.

Miss Julie Smith decides she wants to leave the city and move to a small farm on the Oregon coast, where air and water are clean, the pace is slower, and she can grow strawberries. A realtor tells Julie there are 100 farmers in the area, with an average income of nearly $34,000. Several months later, at a town meeting called to protest a proposed increase in property taxes, someone says that the average income in the area is only about $4,000, too little to pay additional taxes. Julie is confused.

How could the average income have changed so much in a few months? The answer, of course, is that nothing has really changed. Both $34,000 and $4,000 are correct, but there has been a confusion between measures of central tendency. Since the 100 farmers in the area include 99 whose net income is about $4,000 and one lucky farmer whose showplace dairy nets approximately $3,000,000 a year, the mean income for all 100 farmers is

$$\overline{X}_w = \frac{\Sigma(w \cdot X)}{\Sigma w}$$

$$\frac{(99 \times \$4,000) + (1 \times \$3,000,000)}{100} = \$33,960$$

or nearly $34,000. The smaller "average" of $4,000 is not really an average but is the median income as well as the mode, and measures the earnings of the middle and most representative farmers. The $34,000 weighted mean is not a lie in this case, but it is misleading.

The moral of this example? Beware of "averages" that can deceive.

Another example of weighted mean is your grade point average. You already know that it is more important for your GPA that you get an "A" in a five credit class than in a one credit class. What would your GPA for Winter Quarter be if you earned a 4.0 in Macro Economics—a five credit class, a 2.1 in Bowling—a one credit class, a 2.7 in Environmental Science—a five credit class, and a 3.1 in Introduction to Speech—a four credit class?

$$\overline{X}_w = \frac{\Sigma(w \cdot X)}{\Sigma w}$$

$$GPA = \frac{(5 \times 4.0)+(1 \times 2.1)+(5 \times 2.7)+(4 \times 3.1)}{5+1+5+4}$$

$$GPA = \frac{48}{15} = 3.2$$

Measures of Dispersion

If two distributions have the same mean, median, and mode, is there no difference between the distributions? Not necessarily. The distributions below are normal, unimodal, symmetrical, bell (or mound) shaped. They all have the same measures of central tendency, but they are not identical. Distribution A has more spread, a greater dispersion or variability than distribution B.

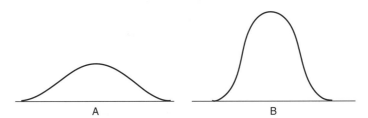

Here is a story that will show the importance of dispersion. Suppose that William Tell, an English teacher at Deer Park High School, is being pressured to coach the track team. William does a little checking and finds that: the four high-jumpers can only clear an average of 4 feet, the three pole vaulters can only manage an average height of 9 feet, and the average runner can only do the mile in 8 minutes. William concludes he does not want to manage such a certain failure and receive verbal abuse of townspeople, colleagues, and students. Is he correct?

Maybe so, but not from the data he collected. Had he checked further, he would have found that one of his four high-jumpers consistently clears 7 feet—good enough to win any competition he might face—while the others can barely manage to stumble over 3-foot heights. In the pole vault, one athlete vaults 15 feet, while the other two can barely explode over a 6-foot bar. The team even has one runner who can break the 4-minute mile. The moral of this tale: averages alone do not give a complete picture without a knowledge of dispersion. (If you have one foot frozen in ice (0 degrees Celsius) and another in almost boiling water (74 degrees Celsius), on the average you should be comfortable because body temperature is 37 degrees Celsius.)

Range

The simplest measure of dispersion is range, which is the difference between the highest and lowest values.

What is the range of the following set of data? 3, 7, 37, 46, 52, 105 _____102_____ (1)

Answer: (1) 102 (105, the highest value, minus 3, the lowest value.)

Quartiles

When an array is divided into quarters the results are called quartiles. (In this unit you will only be asked to find the quartiles of small groups of numbers where "N" is evenly divisible by 4. "N" is usually much larger in real world problems.) The **interquartile range** is the difference between the values of the first and third quartile, indicating the range of the middle fifty percent of the observations. The **quartile deviation** is half the interquartile range. Quartiles are used when there are extremely low or high values in the data and we want to eliminate the lower 25 percent and upper 25 percent. A quartile like the median is a measurement of position.

$$QR = Q_3 - Q_1 \qquad QD = \frac{Q_3 - Q_1}{2}$$

What is the interquartile range and quartile deviation of the following set of data? 4, 12, 7, 2, 5, 9, 3, 67 _____ (1) _____ (2)

Answer:
```
   2
   3 ___ 3.5  1st quartile
   4
   5 ___ 6.0  2nd quartile
   7
   9 ___10.5   3rd quartile
  12
  67
```

(1) $QR = Q_3 - Q_1 = 10.5 - 3.5 = 7$

(2) $QD = \frac{Q_3 - Q_1}{2} = \frac{10.5 - 3.5}{2} = 3.5$

Standard Deviation

The most common statistical measurement of dispersion measured in the same units as the original data is the standard deviation (σ for population data and s for sample data, or expressed another way s is used to approximate σ.) Standard deviation is the positive square root of the **variance.** The variance is the measure of the average squared deviations between each observation and the mean. But what is standard deviation? What does it do, and what does it mean? The above definition really does not tell us much. Perhaps a better way of defining standard deviation is by looking at how it is applied to the many areas where it is useful.

The **empirical rule** as illustrated below is a guideline that states, when a distribution of data is normally distributed or approximately mound-shaped, about 68 percent of the data values fall within one standard deviation of the mean, 95 percent fall within two standard deviations, and almost 100 percent within three standard deviations.

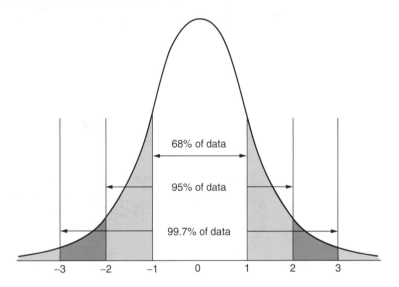

Because many phenomena are distributed approximately in a bell shape, including most human characteristics such as height and weight, the empirical rule is widely used. In the area of quality control, many companies use the mean plus or minus two standard deviations or the mean plus or minus three standard deviations as cutoff points for acceptance or rejection guidelines.

For example, let's say the average fuel consumption rate of automobiles in the United States was 21.2 miles per gallon. If the standard deviation was 5.9 miles per gallon we could use the empirical rule to estimate the distribution of fuel rates of automobiles. About two-thirds of the fuel consumption rates would fall between 15.3 miles per gallon and 27.1 miles per gallon (21.2 plus or minus 5.9). Ninety-five percent of the fuel rates would fall between 9.4 and 33.0 (21.2 plus or minus two times 5.9). And almost all of the automobiles would have fuel rates between 3.5 and 38.9 miles per gallon (21.2 plus or minus three times 5.9).

Understanding standard deviation is important in statistics.

1. It is the most frequently used measure of dispersion. Because of the mathematical properties it possesses, it's more suitable than any other measure of dispersion involving statistical inference procedures.

2. It is affected by the value of every observation in a series. A change in the value of any observation will change the standard deviation value. Its value may be distorted by a relatively few extreme values.

3. It is often used for making control charts, since most control charts are based on the fact that 95 percent of a normal distribution will fall within plus or minus two standard deviations of the mean. Any item in the distribution that is less than two standard deviations from the mean is considered in control. The difference is attributed to sampling error and chance within the process being used. Any time outside the plus or minus two standard deviations is considered out of control. The difference is attributed to some assignable cause that could be corrected.

$$\sigma = \sqrt{\frac{\Sigma(X - \bar{X})^2}{N}} \qquad s = \sqrt{\frac{\Sigma(X - \bar{X})^2}{n - 1}}$$

$$\sigma = \sqrt{\frac{\Sigma X^2}{N} - \left(\frac{\Sigma X}{N}\right)^2} \qquad s = \sqrt{\frac{\Sigma X^2 - \frac{(\Sigma X)^2}{n}}{n - 1}}$$

From a large lecture class 12 students were randomly selected. Their ages were: 29, 23, 43, 22, 21, 45, 20, 21, 27, 29, 39, 29. What is the standard deviation?

Answer:

X	$\bar{X}$	$X - \bar{X}$	$(X - \bar{X})^2$
29	29	0	0
23	29	−6	36
43	29	14	196
22	29	−7	49
21	29	−8	64
45	29	16	256
20	29	−9	81
21	29	−8	64
27	29	−2	4
29	29	0	0
39	29	10	100
29	29	0	0
$\Sigma X = 348$	$\Sigma \bar{X} = 348$	$\Sigma(X - \bar{X}) = 0$	$\Sigma(X - \bar{X})^2 = 850$

$$s = \sqrt{\frac{\Sigma(X - \bar{X})^2}{n - 1}} = \sqrt{\frac{850}{11}} = 8.790$$

Or it may be easier to use this formula:

$$s = \sqrt{\frac{\Sigma X^2 - \frac{(\Sigma X)^2}{n}}{n - 1}} = \sqrt{\frac{10,942 - \frac{(348)^2}{12}}{11}} = 8.790$$

Coefficient of Variation

A measure of relative dispersion, which expresses the standard deviation as a percent of the mean. It is useful in comparing distributions in different units or when values in one set of data are very different than values in another set of data.

The mean salary for administration is $87,527 with a standard deviation of $6,257 and the mean salary for professional employees is $44,563 with a standard deviation of $4,494. Which group has the greatest relative dispersion in salary?

Using population data:

$$C. V. = \frac{\sigma}{\mu}$$

or

Using sample data:

$$C. V. = \frac{s}{\overline{X}}$$

Answer:

Administration $\frac{6,257}{87,527} = 7.1\%$

Professional Employees $\frac{4,494}{44,563} = 10.1\%$

Professional employees have a C. V. of 10.1%, so they have the greatest relative dispersion.

Practice Problems

Find the mean, median, mode, range, quartile deviation, standard deviation, and coefficient of variation for the following sets of prices.

Set 1	Set 2	Set 3
$4.30	$ 47.32	$ 98.09
7.45	33.45	72.10
2.37	18.27	94.20
4.18	12.76	80.35
5.21	35.90	87.48
8.08	29.13	93.72
6.16	86.15	89.09
2.25	44.37	77.54
	654.16	80.35
	12.76	53.13
	33.45	70.40
	11.89	89.09

Mean	_____ (1)	Mean	_____ (8)	Mean	_____ (15)
Median	_____ (2)	Median	_____ (9)	Median	_____ (16)
Mode	_____ (3)	Mode	_____ (10)	Mode	_____ (17)
Range	_____ (4)	Range	_____ (11)	Range	_____ (18)
Q. D.	_____ (5)	Q. D.	_____ (12)	Q. D.	_____ (19)
S. D.	_____ (6)	S. D.	_____ (13)	S. D.	_____ (20)
C. V.	_____ (7)	C. V.	_____ (14)	C. V.	_____ (21)

If the third set of prices in the previous problems is somewhat normally distributed you would expect about 95% of the prices to fall between what two prices?

_____ (22)

What is the grade point average of a student who earns a 3.3 in a five credit class, a 2.9 in a three credit class, a 4.0 in two credit class, a 2.6 in a five credit class and a 3.5 in a one credit class?

_____ (23)

Many companies like McDonalds check the quality of their products by using statistics. If the mean weight of the hamburger in a McDonald's Quarter Pounder is 113.4 grams with standard deviation of 6.2 grams. A weight of 110.0 grams would be acceptable because it would be within the limits expected 95 percent of the time. Using a 95 percent control limit what would the lowest expected weight be?

_____ (24)

Answers: (1) $5.00; (2) $4.76; (3) 0; (4) $5.83; (5) $1.77; (6) $2.16; (7) 43.2%; (8) $84.97; (9) $33.45; (10) $12.76, $33.45; (11) $642.27; (12) $15.17; (13) $180.43; (14) $212.4%; (15) $82.13; (16) $83.92; (17) $80.35, $89.09; (18) $44.96; (19) $8.30; (20) $12.67; (21) 15.4%; (22) $107.47 and $56.79; (23) 3.1; (24) 101.0 grams

Stop

You're now ready to take Pretest X to check your number skills in using a calculator to complete Business Analysis problems. You should be able to complete this test in less than 50 minutes with better than 70 percent accuracy. Unless instructed to do otherwise, turn in your Pretest for correction and review before taking Test X. Be certain you understand each problem on Pretest X before attempting your graded examination.

When you pass Test X you will have proven your ability to use calculators effectively to solve Business Analysis problems.

NAME

DATE

SECTION   PROBLEMS COMPLETED

ERRORS   NUMBER CORRECT

CALCULATOR APPLICATION—BUSINESS ANALYSIS

50 minutes

This test need NOT be worked in sequence. Do the problems you know best first. You need 70 percent correct to pass.

If 9 gallons of gas cost $12.87, what would 7 gallons of gas cost?

_____ (1)

If Jose Fabricators had a net income of $223 thousand on net sales of $2,989 thousand what net sales would be needed 8 years later to have a net income of $750 thousand, assuming the same income-to-sales ratio? (Round your answer to the nearest thousand.)

_____ (2)

Susan spent $1,185 for the airline tickets which was 65% of her vacation budget. What was her vacation budget?

_____ (3)

What is the present worth of a 10% annuity that pays $2,835 semiannually for eleven years?

_____ (4)

What is the present worth of $32,000 due in 5 years, if money is worth 12%, compounded quarterly?

_____ (5)

If you deposited $215 per month in an investment that earned 24% compounded monthly, what would you account be worth at the end of 3 years?

_____ (6)

What would you need to put in a sinking fund each quarter to pay off a debt of $215,000, due in eight years? Assume the sinking fund pays 8% compounded quarterly.

_____ (7)

The population of Jacksonville, Florida in 2000 was 735,617. What would be the population of Jacksonville in 2015, if it grew at a rate of 3% per year? (Round your answer to the nearest thousand.)

_____ (8)

John Johnson purchased a new pickup truck for $15,800. If he finances $9,825 for 36 months at 12% interest compounded monthly, what would Johnson's payments be?

_____ (9)

What is the equivalent cash value of an investment that will give a net income of $51,000 per year for 17 years if money is worth 6%?

_____ (10)

To the nearest year, how long would it take the population of Gilbert, Arizona to double at an annual growth rate of 8%?

_____ (11)

If the Dow Jones Industrial Average is 9,716, what will it be in 14 years if has a semiannual increases of 6%?

_____ (12)

How much does a person living in Roanoke, Virginia need to earn annually to have the same buying power as someone making $43,000 in Des Moines, Iowa? (The cost of living index is 93.4 in Roanoke and 102.3 in Des Moines.)

_____ (13)

The cost for a million personal computer instructions per second (MIPS) continues to decline. Today's cost is only a fraction of the $1,908 in 1990. However, if the index in 1990 was 10.6 using 1981 as a base year, what did a million personal computer instructions per second cost in 1981?

_____ (14)

The consumer price index for food was 179.7 (1982 – 84 = 100) in 2003. To the nearest dollar, what did a typical basket of food cost in the 1982-84 period if it cost $637 in 2003?

_____ (15)

Assuming the consumer price index was 148.7 in 1994 and Jose made $18.95 per hour. How much would he need to make per hour in 2003 to maintain approximately the same purchasing power if the consumer price was 183.7 in 2003?

_____ (16)

If your grades winter quarter were 3.3 in a five credit class, 2.9 in a two credit class, 3.1 in a four credit class and 2.7 in a five credit class, what would your grade point average (GPA) be for winter quarter?

_____ (17)

Three hundred and seven students took the third American History test which had a possible score of 73. If a random sample of 12 scores were 45, 39, 58, 71, 57, 65, 62, 49, 70, 63, 57, and 68, what was the sample:

Mean _____ (18)   Median _____ (19)

Mode _____ (20)   Range _____ (21)

Quartile Deviation _____ (22)   Standard Deviation _____ (23)

Coefficient of Variation _____ (24)

Approximately ninety-five percent of the test scores should fall between what two test scores?

_____ (25)

$$\overline{X} = \frac{\Sigma X}{n} \qquad\qquad s = \sqrt{\frac{\Sigma(X - \overline{X})^2}{n-1}} \qquad\qquad C.\,V. = \frac{s}{\overline{X}}(100)$$

9•

4•51 +

12,121• −

1•32 −

3•25 +

•54 −

Calculator Skill
Development for
Touch Control

Addition with 4, 5, and 6 keys

Work as rapidly as possible while maintaining accuracy. Use correct finger placement. Operate the keys without looking.

(1)	(2)	(3)	(4)	(5)
54	45	56	654	456
55	44	45	544	455
66	65	44	555	664
64	56	54	456	445
56	66	55	565	554
44	55	64	464	666
46	54	56	566	454
45	45	46	655	554
64	64	45	455	654
54	56	56	646	465

(6)	(7)	(8)	(9)	(10)
45	54	65	546	654
44	65	64	645	554
54	55	45	465	655
46	46	46	544	456
54	54	64	546	645
46	65	55	564	445
45	45	45	455	464
54	65	64	646	564
65	64	56	645	654
45	46	45	564	456

(11)	(12)	(13)	(14)	(15)
655	554	645	5 464	6 546
566	465	564	4 565	6 465
465	646	566	5 655	5 465
564	655	465	6 566	4 645
464	645	555	4 564	4 665
656	465	645	5 466	5 465
654	546	465	6 546	4 655
465	456	564	4 554	4 566
645	654	644	5 645	6 645
456	544	564	4 465	4 565

Answer:

(1) 548; (2) 550; (3) 521;(4) 5 560; (5) 5 367; (6) 498; (7) 559; (8) 549; (9) 5 620;
(10) 5 547; (11) 5 590; (12) 5 630; (13) 5 677; (14) 53 490; (15) 53 682

Addition with 1, 2, 3, 4, 5, and 6 keys

Work as rapidly as possible while maintaining accuracy. Use correct finger placement. Operate the keys without looking.

(1)	(2)	(3)	(4)	(5)
54	63	63	321	156
55	45	25	654	432
52	25	41	245	334
41	14	52	364	411
63	63	36	131	256
36	41	14	313	435
14	54	64	253	621
25	52	45	361	642
63	63	36	143	563
52	14	51	231	456

(6)	(7)	(8)	(9)	(10)
24	53	51	624	611
35	63	15	621	522
16	43	25	324	433
53	62	52	351	114
42	26	62	621	224
63	36	26	423	433
14	16	15	315	225
51	53	36	136	336
16	35	63	225	114
42	36	53	633	141

(11)	(12)	(13)	(14)	(15)
213	313	512	5 423	3 223
313	323	315	2 345	4 343
414	516	426	6 123	5 353
151	342	132	2 514	6 363
161	231	231	2 135	1 414
212	145	246	5 124	2 424
233	346	625	3 514	3 434
542	343	613	5 632	4 454
123	526	123	5 236	5 646
342	642	543	5 324	6 565

Answer:

(1) 455; (2) 434; (3) 427; (4) 3 016; (5) 4 306; (6) 356; (7) 423; (8) 398; (9) 4 273; (10) 3 153; (11) 2 704; (12) 3 727; (13) 3 766; (14) 43 370; (15) 43 219

Addition with 4, 5, 6, 7, 8, and 9 keys

Work as rapidly as possible while maintaining accuracy. Use correct finger placement. Operate the keys without looking.

(1)	(2)	(3)	(4)	(5)
54	66	65	654	455
56	55	54	544	654
54	44	45	455	564
45	46	56	466	465
56	56	44	445	645
65	46	66	556	464
66	45	55	564	565
55	55	46	465	545
46	44	54	444	665
54	64	55	566	465

(6)	(7)	(8)	(9)	(10)
74	47	59	747	599
84	48	48	848	488
94	49	67	949	677
57	75	76	789	876
58	85	84	987	549
59	95	48	876	854
76	97	74	796	549
67	76	47	849	947
68	86	95	946	876
69	96	59	875	495

(11)	(12)	(13)	(14)	(15)
454	995	789	8 484	6 868
464	776	864	9 494	7 878
474	945	954	9 696	9 898
848	858	646	4 747	4 949
997	679	789	5 757	5 959
879	876	947	6 767	6 969
798	494	749	8 787	7 979
567	458	875	9 797	8 989
745	749	869	4 848	8 765
856	848	759	5 858	6 789

Answer:

(1) 551; (2) 521; (3) 540; (4) 5 159; (5) 5 487; (6) 706; (7) 754; (8) 657; (9) 8 662; (10) 6 910; (11) 7 082; (12) 7 678; (13) 8 241; (14) 74 235; (15) 75 043

Addition with all keys, including zero

Work as rapidly as possible while maintaining accuracy. Use correct finger placement. Operate the keys without looking.

(1)		(2)		(3)		(4)		(5)	
	10		85		51		509		213
	20		82		64		108		502
	30		20		58		800		122
	40		51		30		409		146
	50		30		96		807		151
	60		83		80		502		426
	70		92		10		113		313
	80		76		37		219		617
	90		90		48		206		900
	21		13		10		780		802

(6)		(7)		(8)		(9)		(10)	
	52		35		43		422		800
	69		51		96		479		213
	31		97		89		588		500
	49		81		27		692		486
	66		20		42		760		752
	29		43		23		657		370
	97		79		64		891		426
	12		26		78		208		895
	10		60		91		696		408
	80		37		10		704		220

(11)		(12)		(13)		(14)		(15)	
	201		449		347		8 040		5 909
	698		821		639		5 090		8 378
	513		219		768		1 080		1 002
	495		578		987		2 170		5 106
	841		436		922		1 409		3 037
	406		420		204		1 007		2 104
	815		680		263		8 602		5 108
	706		207		945		5 806		9 400
	596		621		703		9 007		5 820
	709		433		426		4 100		6 904

Answer:

(1) 471; (2) 622; (3) 484; (4) 4 453; (5) 4 192; (6) 495; (7) 529; (8) 563; (9) 6 097; (10) 5 070; (11) 5 980; (12) 4 864; (13) 6 204; (14) 46 311; (15) 52 768

Adding dollars and cents

Hint

To increase your speed when adding a column of dollars and cents, do not index the decimal. However, if your machine is equipped with an "adding machine" decimal setting, you may to automatically set the decimal at 2 places, without indexing it.

(1)	$3.06	(2)	$7.82	(3)	$7.99	(4)	$6.78	(5)	$3.34
	9.99		4.31		9.88		8.44		5.30
	4.74		4.63		6.03		8.13		6.31
	7.83		4.42		2.14		6.34		4.22
	4.34		8.00		3.76		9.49		5.30
	2.19		2.74		2.74		5.67		6.13
	5.58		1.62		5.75		3.56		9.43
	4.02		2.21		6.50		8.09		7.07
	3.14		2.64		3.14		5.19		1.12
	5.31		3.85		5.99		3.12		2.10

(6)	$6.42	(7)	$9.49	(8)	$7.58	(9)	$1.74	(10)	$1.16
	7.12		5.78		4.62		6.20		2.25
	4.72		8.63		1.94		2.88		3.34
	1.63		4.87		1.22		7.47		4.11
	7.53		7.42		5.92		7.82		4.22
	1.59		3.36		6.09		5.04		3.15
	9.46		9.51		8.43		5.74		6.31
	2.03		2.68		3.04		9.12		5.20
	4.00		4.91		5.94		8.94		9.01
	2.13		6.66		4.16		5.06		2.56

(11)	$62.11	(12)	$25.43	(13)	$29.25	(14)	$265.54	(15)	$358.85
	58.12		24.20		20.96		371.98		655.62
	40.32		68.06		81.13		840.35		140.02
	38.45		79.47		23.94		780.36		430.43
	93.98		43.93		40.55		210.92		321.92
	56.76		83.92		17.92		637.43		972.85
	70.49		34.47		84.79		213.19		406.73
	32.52		19.82		96.88		951.48		275.48
	94.19		58.19		92.36		967.53		343.81
	23.45		84.50		16.74		756.70		152.89

Answer:

(1) $50.20; (2) $42.24; (3) $53.92; (4) $64.81; (5) $50.32; (6) $46.63; (7) $63.31; (8) $48.94; (9) $60.01; (10) $41.31; (11) $570.39; (12) $521.99; (13) $504.52; (14) $5 995.48; (15) $4 058.60

Adding dollars and cents

(1)	$3.45	(2)	$9.86	(3)	$7.36	(4)	$1.57	(5)	$6.89
	6.78		3.45		5.05		2.60		7.98
	9.12		8.36		8.18		6.28		4.35
	3.54		4.73		2.56		1.40		8.36
	6.10		4.17		6.01		2.41		3.45
	3.57		5.28		3.42		4.30		9.21
	1.02		3.96		6.46		9.36		3.58
	5.42		2.19		9.40		7.09		2.06
	6.21		5.38		5.52		5.20		6.91
	4.98		8.73		1.48		2.75		7.48

(6)	$9.47	(7)	$2.17	(8)	$6.10	(9)	$9.51	(10)	$1.99
	4.23		4.91		3.12		8.48		6.30
	1.28		2.46		6.27		5.30		2.48
	2.92		2.21		7.17		3.56		3.15
	5.63		4.93		8.52		5.19		3.82
	7.05		5.36		3.83		6.97		5.75
	2.40		3.07		4.66		2.18		6.43
	7.49		2.13		5.49		4.53		2.81
	3.92		6.04		5.73		2.40		6.32
	1.37		7.82		6.02		9.72		5.05

(11)	$13.24	(12)	$40.35	(13)	$76.41	(14)	$628.81	(15)	$515.73
	57.68		52.13		99.99		140.02		639.27
	91.32		19.82		84.14		756.70		423.40
	10.07		18.47		85.32		201.43		388.32
	14.18		58.22		57.46		915.48		712.84
	21.03		62.54		71.39		639.53		394.02
	76.89		16.92		48.75		213.54		752.91
	24.59		37.96		74.36		161.12		638.50
	16.15		84.13		51.42		132.74		198.71
	33.96		72.14		19.86		938.27		426.03

Answer:

(1) $50.19; (2) $56.11; (3) $55.44; (4) $42.96; (5) $60.27; (6) $45.76; (7) $41.10;
(8) $56.91; (9) $57.84; (10) $44.10; (11) $359.11; (12) $462.68; (13) $669.10;
(14) $4 727.64; (15) $5 089.73

SPECIAL PRACTICE WITH A CALCULATOR
USING 3 DIGIT NUMBERS

	(1)	(2)	(3)	(4)	(5)
4,5,6	446	444	655	456	445
	554	445	455	554	545
	664	456	646	664	565
	666	654	654	544	464
	555	554	455	655	565
	655	466	456	444	646
	654	544	445	656	464

	(6)	(7)	(8)	(9)	(10)
1,2,3,4,5,6	246	153	225	313	616
	336	126	334	626	121
	126	423	633	414	323
	522	116	522	525	434
	423	141	411	424	545
	631	225	422	323	343
	513	411	212	515	246

	(11)	(12)	(13)	(14)	(15)
4,5,6,7,8,9	474	858	776	959	949
	484	959	449	646	454
	969	679	678	858	456
	868	995	749	747	484
	494	949	945	757	786
	767	884	458	659	798
	757	848	545	848	898

	(16)	(17)	(18)	(19)	(20)
all	102	429	881	786	347
	881	596	723	700	922
	704	920	417	362	204
	968	286	284	229	954
	158	407	927	742	806
	760	824	216	616	729
	814	327	880	747	440

Answers:

(1) 4194; (2) 3563; (3) 3766; (4) 3973; (5) 3694; (6) 2797; (7) 1595; (8) 2759; (9) 3140; (10) 2628; (11) 4813; (12) 6172; (13) 4600; (14) 5474; (15) 4825; (16) 4387; (17) 3789; (18) 4328; (19) 4182; (20) 4402

PRACTICE PROBLEMS WITH FOUR DIGIT NUMBERS

	(1)	(2)	(3)	(4)	(5)
4,5,6	5464	5655	4554	4665	4565
	4465	6566	6546	5465	6645
	4565	4564	6465	4655	4654
	5645	5466	5465	4566	5565
	4544	6546	4645	6645	5654

	(6)	(7)	(8)	(9)	(10)
1,2,3,4,5,6	5423	5124	3223	2424	6565
	2345	3514	4343	3434	3223
	6123	5632	5353	4454	5312
	2514	5236	6363	5646	4152
	2135	5324	1414	5656	3216

	(11)	(12)	(13)	(14)	(15)
4,5,6,7,8,9	8484	4858	4564	6789	7769
	9494	6789	4758	8765	9794
	9696	6949	6794	8989	5577
	4747	4958	4794	4474	7685
	7946	8965	8775	5467	7455

	(16)	(17)	(18)	(19)	(20)
all	8040	1786	8378	5189	8001
	1021	6258	1251	4582	2135
	5918	6974	6303	6940	4867
	2171	1459	3037	4225	5237
	4091	9837	2145	6927	4268

	(21)	(22)	(23)	(24)	(25)
all	8594	4098	2131	5269	5909
	8042	5211	5024	3149	8927
	6458	2191	4615	6629	4223
	9637	2064	2462	9712	6478
	4859	7082	3136	3551	9110

Answers:

(1) 24,683; (2) 28,797; (3) 27,675; (4) 25,996; (5) 27,083; (6) 18,540; (7) 24,830; (8) 20,696; (9) 21,614;
(10) 22,468; (11) 40,367; (12) 32,519; (13) 29,685; (14) 34,484; (15) 38,280; (16) 21,241; (17) 26,314;
(18) 21,114; (19) 27,863; (20) 24,508; (21) 37,590; (22) 20,646; (23) 17,368; (24) 28,310; (25) 34,647

SUBTRACTION WITH A CALCULATOR

(1) 8040
     −347

(2) 8378
     −639

(3) 6868
     −263

(4) 8602
     −945

(5) 9222
     −621

(6) 5235
     −513

(7) 6951
     −495

(8) 3197
     −841

(9) 4981
     −406

(10) 6620
     −815

(11) 6620
     −596

(12) 2943
     −449

(13) 5779
     −821

(14) 1037
     −219

(15) 3743
     −433

(16) 5804
     −918

(17) $646.59
     −84.20

(18) $757.18
     −82.66

(19) $238.21
     −75.83

(20) $934.35
     −17.48

(21) $520.34
     −25.99

(22) $828.70
     −36.86

(23) $385.24
     −49.27

(24) $987.86
     −89.92

Answers:

(1) 7693; (2) 7739; (3) 6605; (4) 7657; (5) 8601; (6) 4722; (7) 6456; (8) 2356; (9) 4575; (10) 5805; (11) 6024; (12) 2494; (13) 4958; (14) 818; (15) 3310; (16) 4886; (17) $562.39; (18) $674.52; (19) $162.38; (20) $916.87; (21) $494.35; (22) $791.84; (23) $335.97; (24) $897.94

HORIZONTAL ADDITION AND SUBTRACTION

(1) $213 + 313 - 423 - 110 + 727 =$ _____

(2) $201 - 689 + 513 - 485 - 406 =$ _____

(3) $709 - 596 - 708 + 541 - 811 =$ _____

(4) $219 + 578 - 436 + 410 - 621 =$ _____

(5) $621 - 433 - 347 - 204 + 768 =$ _____

(6) $922 + 703 + 426 - 781 - 589 =$ _____

(7) $426 - 208 + 422 + 479 - 891 =$ _____

(8) $486 + 527 - 380 - 895 + 472 =$ _____

(9) $306 - 910 + 474 - 343 - 162 =$ _____

(10) $782 - 500 - 463 + 988 - 376 =$ _____

(11) $218 + 642 - 712 + 972 - 163 =$ _____

(12) $100 + 990 - 743 - 123 - 286 =$ _____

(13) $946 - 203 - 400 - 312 + 578 =$ _____

(14) $63.325 + 427 - 18044 + 8.47 =$ _____

(15) $8159 + 16.97 - 5.5335 + .2175 =$ _____

(16) $76.45 - 4.137 + 3274 - 2567 =$ _____

(17) $82.767 - 902 + 13421 - 1.94 =$ _____

(18) $1428 + 58.16 - 5.523 + .8761 =$ _____

(19) $45.76 - 1.537 + .8274 - 826.7 =$ _____

Answers:

(1) 720; (2) –866; (3) –865; (4) 150; (5) 405; (6) 681; (7) 228; (8) 210; (9) –635; (10) 431; (11) 957; (12) –62; (13) 609; (14) –17,545.205; (15) 8170.654; (16) 779.313; (17) 12,599.827; (18) 1481.513; (19) –781.650

RANDOM ADDITION WITH TWO DIGIT NUMBERS, WHERE THE ANSWER IS ALWAYS 1000

Work as rapidly as possible while maintaining accuracy. Use correct finger placement. Operate the keys without looking

(1)	(2)	(3)	(4)	(5)
20	78	45	74	53
81	96	93	99	83
77	51	27	36	31
42	74	58	60	98
68	98	76	59	46
95	15	91	28	74
22	80	30	13	87
36	48	88	67	40
89	53	15	18	33
50	96	21	90	81
99	40	67	65	43
11	12	75	52	64
82	93	90	86	22
78	27	52	41	48
44	85	43	83	62
57	43	65	49	59
49	11	64	80	76

(6)	(7)	(8)	(9)	(10)
57	25	97	13	82
93	98	42	57	46
18	47	26	85	55
45	56	38	43	37
89	73	87	35	10
61	80	75	72	93
29	29	12	66	44
10	57	65	50	54
68	41	92	98	32
27	99	43	51	26
83	68	29	23	38
90	42	53	75	87
76	46	89	62	11
85	20	70	48	94
16	55	61	30	70
47	69	13	37	63
86	43	68	86	72
20	52	40	69	86

RANDOM ADDITION WITH THREE DIGIT NUMBERS WHERE THE ANSWER IS ALWAYS 10,000

Work as rapidly as possible while maintaining accuracy. Use correct finger placement. Operate the keys without looking

(1)	(2)	(3)	(4)
565	271	659	964
492	599	875	463
389	867	342	175
742	426	937	852
158	348	423	214
200	761	295	531
374	155	731	378
842	674	517	734
621	931	195	610
934	487	666	542
862	825	283	397
714	321	401	925
275	183	820	486
708	914	379	800
545	700	746	187
259	264	234	731
465	573	598	232
855	701	899	779

(5)	(6)	(7)	(8)
372	851	437	748
901	345	834	621
456	125	513	325
760	630	295	926
536	285	763	123
114	431	396	400
843	706	637	288
278	529	911	549
654	472	152	803
524	728	684	357
359	370	509	432
200	402	360	955
875	584	471	645
432	982	957	782
769	318	175	546
927	842	973	858
609	711	546	179
391	689	341	463

RANDOM ADDITION WHERE THE ANSWER IS ALWAYS 100,000

Work as rapidly as possible while maintaining accuracy. Use correct finger placement. Operate the keys without looking

(1)	5	(2)	8	(3)	3	(4)	7
	23		69		58		91
	489		393		965		520
	3826		8422		5975		9324
	4343		2379		6328		2796
	6421		4053		9850		5371
	9005		3214		2047		6800
	1634		7394		3205		4215
	7851		1991		7793		7183
	2380		9706		1469		1404
	8307		6472		4523		3650
	5993		5419		8961		8942
	8524		8237		1634		6789
	6420		6589		5006		1007
	1457		5054		7632		3275
	3000		3199		4551		7631
	5201		5435		3794		5894
	4319		9762		6206		2763
	9345		2204		8537		9021
	2657		3945		2495		8857
	7259		4035		5906		3004
	1541		2020		3062		1456

(5)	6	(6)	1	(7)	4	(8)	2
	75		83		52		36
	831		435		930		147
	2083		9630		1000		3128
	8210		4712		5311		9564
	5932		3587		7700		6478
	3441		8699		2398		7310
	7860		2854		8964		1234
	4937		7103		3795		5985
	9228		6150		9312		2304
	1543		1234		4628		8961
	6200		5970		7294		4350
	3789		8999		6721		6387
	9543		2482		9567		9500
	7318		5741		2549		2514
	4692		3695		1183		8723
	2875		1846		4106		5194
	1437		7309		3972		1066
	5283		8421		6565		2590
	6794		6002		7860		6183
	4831		3198		2917		3410
	3092		1849		3172		4934

RANDOM ADDITION AND SUBTRACTION, WHERE THE ANSWER IS ALWAYS ZERO

Work as rapidly as possible while maintaining accuracy. Use correct finger placement. Operate the keys without looking

(1)	6	(2)	4	(3)	8	(4)	5
	−9		+1		+9		+7
	−5		−7		−4		−20
	+9		−8		+6		+2
	+8		+3		+2		−13
	−4		+2		−7		+6
	−3		−6		+1		−8
	+8		+5		−5		+15
	−2		−2		+3		−9
	−5		+9		−7		+8
	−3		−1		−6		+7

(5)	3	(6)	9	(7)	65	(8)	73
	−8		−7		−21		−10
	+15		+35		+44		+91
	−20		−19		−92		−64
	−19		−24		−13		+18
	+6		+60		+85		−67
	+17		−77		−49		−23
	−2		+26		−78		+50
	+5		+10		−30		−82
	+9		+65		+61		−34
	−6		−78		+28		+48

(9)	346	(10)	261	(11)	764	(12)	347
	+205		−137		+123		+523
	+710		−589		+529		−709
	−483		+340		−478		+481
	+958		−645		−960		−550
	−500		+723		−838		−927
	−671		−486		+297		+395
	−828		+995		−318		−100
	+132		+604		+603		+253
	+496		−852		−548		−389
	−365		−214		+826		+676

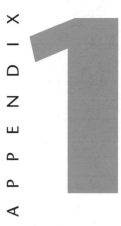

APPENDIX

1

A Review
of Fractions

3rds	4ths	5ths	6ths	8ths	12ths	16ths	32nds	Dec. Eq.
							1/32	.03125
						1/16	2/32	.0625
					1/12			.08333
							3/32	.09375
				1/8		2/16	4/32	.125
							5/32	.15625
			1/6		2/12			.16667
						3/16	6/32	.1875
		1/5						.20000
							7/32	.21875
	1/4			2/8	3/12	4/16	8/32	.25
							9/32	.28125
						5/16	10/32	.3125
1/3			2/6		4/12			.33333
							11/32	.34375
				3/8		6/16	12/32	.375
		2/5						.40000
							13/32	.40625
					5/12			.41667
						7/16	14/32	.4375
							15/32	.46875
	2/4		3/6	4/8	6/12	8/16	16/32	.5
							17/32	.53125
						9/16	18/32	.5625
					7/12			.58333
							19/32	.59375
		3/5						.60000
				5/8		10/16	20/32	.625
							21/32	.65625
2/3			4/6		8/12			.66666
						11/16	22/32	.6875
							23/32	.71875
	3/4			6/8	9/12	12/16	24/32	.75
							25/32	.78125
		4/5						.80000
						13/16	26/32	.8125
			5/6		10/12			.83333
							27/32	.84375
				7/8		14/16	28/32	.875
							29/32	.90625
					11/12			.91666
						15/16	30/32	.9375
							31/32	.96875

Fractions are important in business and as shown in this text are very easy to work with using a calculator. But what if you do not have a calculator? You could convert the fractions to decimals, but that is often cumbersome and inefficient. Better yet, you could work with fractions directly. It is not difficult. Here is a brief review of how to work directly with fractions:

Changing Fractions

Proper fractions are those in which the numerators (top number) are smaller than the denominators (bottom number), such as 1/3, 2/5, or 3/8. **Improper fractions** have larger numerators than denominators, such as 3/1, 5/2, or 8/3. **Mixed numbers**, contain both whole numbers and fractions, such as 5 1/3 or 7 2/5.

To convert improper fractions to mixed numbers divide the numerator by the denominator. For example:

$$\frac{8}{3} = 8 \div 3 = 2\frac{2}{3}$$

Inversely, mixed numbers can be converted to fractions by multiplying the whole number by the denominator, adding the product to the numerator, and writing the result over the denominator of the fraction. For example:

$$2\frac{2}{3} = \frac{(2 \times 3) + 2}{3} = \frac{8}{3}$$

Convert the following improper fractions to mixed numbers:

(1) $\frac{9}{2} =$ (2) $\frac{13}{5} =$ (3) $\frac{25}{7} =$ (4) $\frac{35}{6} =$

Convert the following mixed numbers to improper fractions:

(5) $1\frac{1}{3} =$ (6) $3\frac{3}{8} =$ (7) $7\frac{1}{6} =$ (8) $5\frac{3}{4} =$

Answer: (1) $4\frac{1}{2}$; (2) $2\frac{3}{5}$; (3) $3\frac{4}{7}$; (4) $5\frac{5}{6}$; (5) $\frac{4}{3}$; (6) $\frac{27}{8}$; (7) $\frac{43}{6}$; (8) $\frac{23}{4}$

Reducing Fractions

Fractions should usually be reduced to their lowest terms, such as reducing 4/8 to 1/2. When the numerator and denominator no longer can be divided by a whole number, other than one, the fraction has been reduced to lowest terms. You know when a fraction has been reduced to lowest terms when a **prime number** cannot be evenly divided into the numerator and denominator, the fraction is fully reduced. A prime number is divisible only by itself and by one (1). The smaller prime numbers are: 2, 3, 5, 7, 11, 13.

As illustrated below, four-eighths of a circle is exactly the same as one-half of the circle. To reduce the fraction 4/8 to 1/2, we divide both the 4 (the numerator) and the 8 (the denominator) by 4.

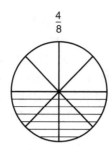

$$\frac{4}{8}$$

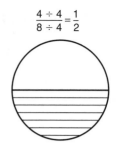

$$\frac{4 \div 4}{8 \div 4} = \frac{1}{2}$$

Reduce the following fractions to lowest terms:

(1) $\dfrac{5}{10} =$ (2) $\dfrac{12}{36} =$ (3) $\dfrac{44}{77} =$ (4) $\dfrac{34}{48} =$

Answer: (1) $\dfrac{1}{2}$; (2) $\dfrac{1}{3}$; (3) $\dfrac{4}{7}$; (4) $\dfrac{17}{24}$

Adding Fractions

Fractions with the same denominator (bottom number) are called **like fractions.** Such fractions have a **common denominator.** For example, 3/8 and 5/8 are like fractions with a common denominator of 8, while 3/7 and 1/4 are not like fractions. Add like fractions by adding the numerators (top number) and then place the result over the common denominator. For example:

$$\frac{3}{7} + \frac{2}{7} + \frac{5}{7} = \frac{3+2+5}{7} = \frac{10}{7}$$ (which should be written as a mixed number reduced to lowest term $= 1\frac{3}{7}$)

Fractions with different denominators, such as 3/8 and 2/5 are **unlike fractions.** Add unlike fractions by first changing the fractions to common denominators. The **least common denominator** (LCD) for two or more fractions is the smallest whole number that can be divided, without remainder, by all the denominators of the fractions. For example, a common denominator can always be found by multiplying the denominators, however, this is not always the LCD. A common denominator for 3/8 and 1/6 can be found by $8 \times 6 = 48$, but the LCD is 24.

Finding the LCD for some fractions can be accomplished by inspection, but what about 2/9, 7/12, 1/3, and 7/60? Continue dividing the denominator by prime numbers until only ones remain. Then multiply the prime numbers to find the LCD as shown below:

5	9	12	3	60
3	9	12	3	12
3	3	4	1	4
2	1	4	1	4
2	1	2	1	2
	1	1	1	1

$$5 \times 3 \times 3 \times 2 \times 2 = 180$$

To add fractions you only need to find a common denominator, a number that can always be found by multiplying the denominators. The advantage of a LCD is that you use smaller numbers. But if by inspection or by multiplication you choose a common denominator that is not the LCD you will still arrive at the correct answer. You should always record your answer in lowest terms however.

Knowing that the LCD is 180 we may add the four fractions.

$$\frac{2}{9} + \frac{7}{12} + \frac{1}{3} + \frac{7}{60}$$

$$= \frac{40 + 105 + 60 + 21}{180}$$

$$= \frac{226}{180} \text{ or } 1\frac{23}{90}$$

The 2/9 was converted to 40/180 by dividing 9 (the denominator) into 180 (the LCD) and then multiplying the answer (20) by 2 (the numerator). For the 7/12, we divided 12 into 180, then multiplied the answer (15) by 7, and so on.

Here is another example:

What does $\dfrac{2}{35} + \dfrac{7}{30} + \dfrac{2}{15} + \dfrac{9}{70}$ equal?

7	35	30	15	70
5	5	30	15	10
3	1	6	3	2
2	1	2	1	2
	1	1	1	1

$$7 \times 5 \times 3 \times 2 = 210$$

$$\frac{2}{35} = \frac{12}{210}$$

$$\frac{7}{30} = \frac{49}{210}$$

$$\frac{2}{15} = \frac{28}{210}$$

$$\frac{9}{70} = \frac{27}{210}$$

$$\frac{116}{210} \text{ or } \frac{58}{105}$$

Combine the following fractions:

(1) $\dfrac{1}{3}+\dfrac{1}{2}=$ (2) $\dfrac{5}{9}+\dfrac{1}{8}=$ (3) $\dfrac{2}{5}+\dfrac{4}{7}=$ (4) $\dfrac{2}{3}+\dfrac{3}{4}=$

(5) $\dfrac{2}{3}+\dfrac{1}{2}+\dfrac{1}{6}=$ (6) $\dfrac{8}{9}+\dfrac{4}{7}+\dfrac{2}{3}=$ (7) $\dfrac{3}{7}+\dfrac{2}{3}+\dfrac{1}{6}=$ (8) $\dfrac{8}{9}+\dfrac{1}{4}+\dfrac{3}{8}=$

(9) $\dfrac{1}{6}+\dfrac{1}{4}+\dfrac{1}{8}+\dfrac{1}{3}+\dfrac{1}{2}=$ (10) $\dfrac{2}{9}+\dfrac{1}{3}+\dfrac{5}{6}+\dfrac{3}{8}+\dfrac{4}{9}=$

(11) $\dfrac{5}{12}+\dfrac{4}{15}+\dfrac{1}{20}+\dfrac{3}{10}+\dfrac{7}{45}=$ (12) $\dfrac{7}{12}+\dfrac{3}{20}+\dfrac{8}{15}+\dfrac{1}{16}+\dfrac{1}{10}=$

Answer: (1) $\dfrac{5}{6}$; (2) $\dfrac{49}{72}$; (3) $\dfrac{34}{35}$; (4) $1\dfrac{5}{12}$; (5) $1\dfrac{1}{3}$; (6) $2\dfrac{8}{63}$; (7) $1\dfrac{11}{42}$; (8) $1\dfrac{37}{72}$;

(9) $1\dfrac{3}{8}$; (10) $2\dfrac{5}{24}$; (11) $1\dfrac{17}{90}$; (12) $1\dfrac{103}{240}$

Subtracting Fractions

Subtracting fractions is similar to adding fractions. To subtract 1/7 from 1/2, find the LCD ($2 \times 7 = 14$) convert the numerators and then subtract. For example:

$$\frac{1}{2}-\frac{1}{7}=\frac{7}{14}-\frac{2}{14}=\frac{5}{14}$$

Here is an example of a mixed number:

$$7\frac{4}{7}-2\frac{3}{4} \quad \text{with LCDs} \quad 7\frac{16}{28}-2\frac{21}{28} \quad \text{or} \quad 6\frac{44}{28}-2\frac{21}{28}=4\frac{23}{28}$$

In this example, it was necessary to borrow a whole number from the 7 because we cannot subtract 21/28 from 16/28 without a negative answer, the borrowed whole number is 28/28, which increases the 16/28 to 44/28. Subtracting 21/28 from 44/28 gives an answer of 23/28.

Find the difference in the following numbers:

(1) $\dfrac{2}{3}-\dfrac{1}{2}=$ (2) $\dfrac{7}{8}-\dfrac{3}{4}=$ (3) $\dfrac{3}{4}-\dfrac{2}{3}=$ (4) $\dfrac{8}{9}-\dfrac{1}{3}=$

(5) $\dfrac{7}{9}-\dfrac{2}{3}=$ (6) $9\dfrac{1}{2}-5\dfrac{3}{8}=$ (7) $5\dfrac{2}{3}-2\dfrac{5}{6}=$

(8) $8\dfrac{5}{8}-4\dfrac{7}{9}=$ (9) $7\dfrac{3}{4}-5\dfrac{2}{3}=$ (10) $9\dfrac{5}{6}-7\dfrac{7}{8}=$

Answer: (1) $\dfrac{1}{6}$; (2) $\dfrac{1}{8}$; (3) $\dfrac{1}{12}$; (4) $\dfrac{5}{9}$; (5) $\dfrac{1}{9}$; (6) $4\dfrac{1}{8}$; (7) $2\dfrac{5}{6}$;

(8) $3\dfrac{61}{72}$; (9) $2\dfrac{1}{12}$; (10) $1\dfrac{23}{24}$

Multiplying Fractions

Multiplying fractions is easy; first reduce the fractions where possible by cancelling and then multiply across as shown below:

$$\dfrac{7}{9}\times\dfrac{5}{6}=\dfrac{35}{54} \qquad \dfrac{\overset{2}{\cancel{6}}}{7}\times\dfrac{\overset{1}{\cancel{3}}}{\underset{1}{\cancel{8}}}\times\dfrac{\overset{1}{\cancel{8}}}{\underset{\underset{1}{\cancel{3}}}{\cancel{9}}}=\dfrac{2}{7} \qquad \dfrac{5}{9}\times\dfrac{\overset{1}{\cancel{7}}}{\underset{2}{\cancel{8}}}\times\dfrac{\overset{1}{\cancel{4}}}{7}=\dfrac{5}{18} \qquad \dfrac{\overset{7}{\cancel{14}}}{15}\times\dfrac{\overset{1}{\cancel{3}}}{\underset{1}{\cancel{7}}}\times\dfrac{\overset{1}{\cancel{7}}}{\underset{\underset{3}{\cancel{6}}}{\cancel{18}}}=\dfrac{7}{45}$$

In the first example since no cancellation is possible, simply multiply across: $7 \times 5 = 35$ and $9 \times 6 = 54$.

In the second example 8 divided by 8 equals 1, the 3 and 9 are reduced to 1 and 3, and the 6 and 3 reduced to 2 and 1. Multiplication of the reduced numbers results in $2 \times 1 \times 1$ over $7 \times 1 \times 1$ which equals 2/7.

Find the products of the following fractions: (Reduce answers to lowest terms)

(1) $\dfrac{6}{7}\times\dfrac{8}{9}=$ (2) $\dfrac{3}{5}\times\dfrac{7}{9}=$ (3) $\dfrac{5}{7}\times\dfrac{3}{4}=$

(4) $\dfrac{7}{9}\times\dfrac{9}{14}\times\dfrac{7}{9}=$ (5) $\dfrac{5}{24}\times\dfrac{3}{14}\times\dfrac{7}{9}=$ (6) $\dfrac{4}{21}\times\dfrac{8}{9}\times\dfrac{7}{16}=$

(7) $\dfrac{7}{9}\times\dfrac{5}{12}\times\dfrac{3}{7}\times\dfrac{1}{8}=$ (8) $\dfrac{7}{9}\times\dfrac{5}{7}\times\dfrac{3}{8}\times\dfrac{8}{9}=$ (9) $\dfrac{9}{14}\times\dfrac{5}{9}\times\dfrac{7}{9}\times\dfrac{3}{7}=$

Answer: (1) $\dfrac{16}{21}$; (2) $\dfrac{7}{15}$; (3) $\dfrac{15}{28}$; (4) $\dfrac{7}{18}$; (5) $\dfrac{5}{144}$; (6) $\dfrac{2}{27}$; (7) $\dfrac{5}{288}$;

(8) $\dfrac{5}{27}$; (9) $\dfrac{5}{42}$;

Dividing Fractions

Since division is the opposite process of multiplication, dividing fractions is almost the same as multiplying them. Simply invert (turn upside down) the divisor and proceed as in multiplication. To divide 1/2 by 3/5, for example just change the 3/5 to 5/3 and multiply:

$$\frac{1}{2} \div \frac{3}{5} = \frac{1}{2} \times \frac{5}{3} = \frac{5}{6}$$

When dividing or multiplying mixed numbers first change the mixed number to an improper fraction as shown below.

$$2\frac{5}{8} \times 3\frac{2}{3} = \frac{21}{8} \times \frac{11}{\cancel{3}_1} = \frac{77}{8} = 9\frac{5}{8}$$

$$4\frac{2}{7} \div 2\frac{1}{4} = \frac{30}{7} \div \frac{9}{4} = \frac{\cancel{30}^{10}}{7} \times \frac{4}{\cancel{9}_3} = \frac{40}{21} = 1\frac{19}{21}$$

Find the quotient of the following fractions:

(1) $\dfrac{4}{7} \div \dfrac{8}{9} =$ (2) $\dfrac{3}{5} \div \dfrac{7}{8} =$ (3) $\dfrac{9}{11} \div \dfrac{4}{5} =$ (4) $\dfrac{6}{7} \div \dfrac{8}{9} =$

(5) $\dfrac{1}{3} \div \dfrac{9}{13} =$ (6) $\dfrac{7}{12} \div \dfrac{9}{10} =$ (7) $\dfrac{2}{5} \div \dfrac{3}{7} =$ (8) $\dfrac{5}{14} \div \dfrac{7}{8} =$

(9) $3\dfrac{3}{8} \times 4\dfrac{2}{3} =$ (10) $2\dfrac{4}{5} \times 5\dfrac{3}{4} =$

(11) $5\dfrac{1}{3} \times 6\dfrac{1}{4} =$ (12) $7\dfrac{5}{7} \times 4\dfrac{2}{21} =$

Answer: (1) $\dfrac{9}{14}$; (2) $\dfrac{24}{35}$; (3) $1\dfrac{1}{44}$; (4) $\dfrac{27}{28}$; (5) $\dfrac{13}{27}$; (6) $\dfrac{35}{54}$; (7) $\dfrac{14}{15}$;

(8) $\dfrac{20}{49}$; (9) $15\dfrac{3}{4}$; (10) $16\dfrac{1}{10}$ (11) $33\dfrac{1}{3}$; (12) $31\dfrac{29}{49}$

Pretest

FRACTIONS

The test must be worked in sequence. Any problems skipped count as errors. To pass, you must answer correctly at least 90 percent of the problems.

Convert the following improper fractions to mixed numbers:

(1) $\dfrac{15}{4}=$ _____   (2) $\dfrac{21}{5}=$ _____   (3) $\dfrac{37}{4}=$ _____   (4) $\dfrac{38}{7}=$ _____

Convert the following mixed numbers to improper fractions:

(5) $3\dfrac{2}{3}=$ _____   (6) $5\dfrac{7}{9}=$ _____   (7) $8\dfrac{2}{5}=$ _____   (8) $5\dfrac{6}{7}=$ _____

Reduce the following fractions to lowest terms:

(9) $\dfrac{14}{26}=$ _____   (10) $\dfrac{18}{72}=$ _____   (11) $\dfrac{55}{77}=$ _____   (12) $\dfrac{38}{64}=$ _____

Addition:

(13) $\dfrac{3}{4}+\dfrac{2}{5}=$ (14) $\dfrac{5}{9}+\dfrac{2}{4}=$ (15) $\dfrac{7}{8}+\dfrac{3}{5}=$ (16) $\dfrac{1}{6}+\dfrac{2}{9}=$

(17) $\dfrac{3}{8}+\dfrac{5}{6}+\dfrac{4}{9}+\dfrac{3}{4}=$ (18) $\dfrac{2}{7}+\dfrac{1}{14}+\dfrac{1}{21}+\dfrac{5}{42}=$

(19) $\dfrac{1}{12}+\dfrac{1}{12}+\dfrac{5}{18}+\dfrac{7}{36}=$ (20) $\dfrac{7}{30}+\dfrac{8}{15}+\dfrac{7}{45}+\dfrac{1}{12}=$

Subtraction:

(21) $\dfrac{2}{3}-\dfrac{1}{2}=$ (22) $\dfrac{7}{8}-\dfrac{2}{5}=$ (23) $\dfrac{4}{9}-\dfrac{1}{3}=$ (24) $\dfrac{7}{9}-\dfrac{1}{2}=$

(25) $\dfrac{11}{15}-\dfrac{3}{5}=$ (26) $\dfrac{11}{34}-\dfrac{4}{17}=$ (27) $\dfrac{19}{45}-\dfrac{11}{30}=$ (28) $\dfrac{23}{51}-\dfrac{5}{12}=$

(29) $5\dfrac{1}{3}-3\dfrac{3}{8}=$ (30) $6\dfrac{1}{8}-5\dfrac{2}{5}=$ (31) $4\dfrac{1}{7}-2\dfrac{2}{9}=$ (32) $8\dfrac{3}{8}-5\dfrac{4}{7}=$

Multiplication:

(33) $\dfrac{3}{4} \times \dfrac{1}{2} =$ _____

(34) $\dfrac{12}{35} \times \dfrac{5}{9} =$ _____

(35) $\dfrac{15}{17} \times \dfrac{2}{45} =$ _____

(36) $\dfrac{21}{52} \times \dfrac{14}{15} =$ _____

(37) $\dfrac{2}{3} \times \dfrac{7}{9} \times \dfrac{9}{14} =$ _____

(38) $\dfrac{5}{17} \times \dfrac{34}{65} \times \dfrac{26}{31} =$ _____

(39) $\dfrac{7}{18} \times \dfrac{3}{14} \times \dfrac{11}{12} =$ _____

Division:

(40) $\dfrac{5}{7} \div \dfrac{2}{3} =$ _____

(41) $\dfrac{7}{8} \div \dfrac{8}{9} =$ _____

(42) $\dfrac{21}{43} \div \dfrac{7}{9} =$ _____

(43) $\dfrac{11}{12} \div \dfrac{11}{24} =$ _____

(44) $\dfrac{2}{7} \div \dfrac{8}{11} =$ _____

(45) $\dfrac{5}{9} \div \dfrac{15}{16} =$ _____

(46) $\dfrac{3}{8} \div \dfrac{6}{7} =$ _____

(47) $\dfrac{14}{15} \div \dfrac{24}{25} =$ _____

Mixed Problems:

(48) $2\dfrac{7}{8} \times 3\dfrac{2}{3} =$ _____

(49) $5\dfrac{7}{9} \div 2\dfrac{1}{4} =$ _____

(50) $2\dfrac{2}{5} \div 6\dfrac{7}{8} =$ _____

APPENDIX 2

Income Tax Withholding Tables

SINGLE Persons—WEEKLY Payroll Period

(For Wages Paid Through December 2004)

If the wages are–		And the number of withholding allowances claimed is—										
At least	But less than	0	1	2	3	4	5	6	7	8	9	10
		The amount of income tax to be withheld is—										
$0	$55	$0	$0	$0	$0	$0	$0	$0	$0	$0	$0	$0
55	60	1	0	0	0	0	0	0	0	0	0	0
60	65	1	0	0	0	0	0	0	0	0	0	0
65	70	2	0	0	0	0	0	0	0	0	0	0
70	75	2	0	0	0	0	0	0	0	0	0	0
75	80	3	0	0	0	0	0	0	0	0	0	0
80	85	3	0	0	0	0	0	0	0	0	0	0
85	90	4	0	0	0	0	0	0	0	0	0	0
90	95	4	0	0	0	0	0	0	0	0	0	0
95	100	5	0	0	0	0	0	0	0	0	0	0
100	105	5	0	0	0	0	0	0	0	0	0	0
105	110	6	0	0	0	0	0	0	0	0	0	0
110	115	6	0	0	0	0	0	0	0	0	0	0
115	120	7	1	0	0	0	0	0	0	0	0	0
120	125	7	1	0	0	0	0	0	0	0	0	0
125	130	8	2	0	0	0	0	0	0	0	0	0
130	135	8	2	0	0	0	0	0	0	0	0	0
135	140	9	3	0	0	0	0	0	0	0	0	0
140	145	9	3	0	0	0	0	0	0	0	0	0
145	150	10	4	0	0	0	0	0	0	0	0	0
150	155	10	4	0	0	0	0	0	0	0	0	0
155	160	11	5	0	0	0	0	0	0	0	0	0
160	165	11	5	0	0	0	0	0	0	0	0	0
165	170	12	6	0	0	0	0	0	0	0	0	0
170	175	12	6	0	0	0	0	0	0	0	0	0
175	180	13	7	1	0	0	0	0	0	0	0	0
180	185	13	7	1	0	0	0	0	0	0	0	0
185	190	14	8	2	0	0	0	0	0	0	0	0
190	195	14	8	2	0	0	0	0	0	0	0	0
195	200	15	9	3	0	0	0	0	0	0	0	0
200	210	16	9	3	0	0	0	0	0	0	0	0
210	220	18	10	4	0	0	0	0	0	0	0	0
220	230	19	11	5	0	0	0	0	0	0	0	0
230	240	21	12	6	1	0	0	0	0	0	0	0
240	250	22	13	7	2	0	0	0	0	0	0	0
250	260	24	15	8	3	0	0	0	0	0	0	0
260	270	25	16	9	4	0	0	0	0	0	0	0
270	280	27	18	10	5	0	0	0	0	0	0	0
280	290	28	19	11	6	0	0	0	0	0	0	0
290	300	30	21	12	7	1	0	0	0	0	0	0
300	310	31	22	13	8	2	0	0	0	0	0	0
310	320	33	24	15	9	3	0	0	0	0	0	0
320	330	34	25	16	10	4	0	0	0	0	0	0
330	340	36	27	18	11	5	0	0	0	0	0	0
340	350	37	28	19	12	6	0	0	0	0	0	0
350	360	39	30	21	13	7	1	0	0	0	0	0
360	370	40	31	22	14	8	2	0	0	0	0	0
370	380	42	33	24	15	9	3	0	0	0	0	0
380	390	43	34	25	17	10	4	0	0	0	0	0
390	400	45	36	27	18	11	5	0	0	0	0	0
400	410	46	37	28	20	12	6	0	0	0	0	0
410	420	48	39	30	21	13	7	1	0	0	0	0
420	430	49	40	31	23	14	8	2	0	0	0	0
430	440	51	42	33	24	15	9	3	0	0	0	0
440	450	52	43	34	26	17	10	4	0	0	0	0
450	460	54	45	36	27	18	11	5	0	0	0	0
460	470	55	46	37	29	20	12	6	0	0	0	0
470	480	57	48	39	30	21	13	7	1	0	0	0
480	490	58	49	40	32	23	14	8	2	0	0	0
490	500	60	51	42	33	24	15	9	3	0	0	0
500	510	61	52	43	35	26	17	10	4	0	0	0
510	520	63	54	45	36	27	18	11	5	0	0	0
520	530	64	55	46	38	29	20	12	6	0	0	0
530	540	66	57	48	39	30	21	13	7	1	0	0
540	550	67	58	49	41	32	23	14	8	2	0	0
550	560	69	60	51	42	33	24	15	9	3	0	0
560	570	70	61	52	44	35	26	17	10	4	0	0
570	580	72	63	54	45	36	27	18	11	5	0	0
580	590	73	64	55	47	38	29	20	12	6	0	0
590	600	75	66	57	48	39	30	21	13	7	1	0

SINGLE Persons—WEEKLY Payroll Period
(For Wages Paid Through December 2004)

If the wages are–		And the number of withholding allowances claimed is—										
At least	But less than	0	1	2	3	4	5	6	7	8	9	10
		The amount of income tax to be withheld is—										
$600	$610	$78	$67	$58	$50	$41	$32	$23	$14	$8	$2	$0
610	620	80	69	60	51	42	33	24	15	9	3	0
620	630	83	70	61	53	44	35	26	17	10	4	0
630	640	85	72	63	54	45	36	27	18	11	5	0
640	650	88	73	64	56	47	38	29	20	12	6	0
650	660	90	75	66	57	48	39	30	21	13	7	1
660	670	93	78	67	59	50	41	32	23	14	8	2
670	680	95	80	59	60	51	42	33	24	15	9	3
680	690	98	83	70	62	53	44	35	26	17	10	4
690	700	100	85	72	63	54	45	36	27	18	11	5
700	710	103	88	73	65	56	47	38	29	20	12	6
710	720	105	90	75	66	57	48	39	30	21	13	7
720	730	108	93	78	68	59	50	41	32	23	14	8
730	740	110	95	80	69	60	51	42	33	24	15	9
740	750	113	98	83	71	62	53	44	35	26	17	10
750	760	115	100	85	72	63	54	45	36	27	18	11
760	770	118	103	88	74	65	56	47	38	29	20	12
770	780	120	105	90	75	66	57	48	39	30	21	13
780	790	123	108	93	78	68	59	50	41	32	23	14
790	800	125	110	95	80	69	60	51	42	33	24	15
800	810	128	113	98	83	71	62	53	44	35	26	17
810	820	130	115	100	85	72	63	54	45	36	27	18
820	830	133	118	103	88	74	65	56	47	38	29	20
830	840	135	120	105	90	75	66	57	48	39	30	21
840	850	138	123	108	93	78	68	59	50	41	32	23
850	860	140	125	110	95	80	69	60	51	42	33	24
860	870	143	128	113	98	83	71	62	53	44	35	26
870	880	145	130	115	100	85	72	63	54	45	36	27
880	890	148	133	118	103	88	74	65	56	47	38	29
890	900	150	135	120	105	90	76	66	57	48	39	30
900	910	153	138	123	108	93	78	68	59	50	41	32
910	920	155	140	125	110	95	81	69	60	51	42	33
920	930	158	143	128	113	98	83	71	62	53	44	35
930	940	160	145	130	115	100	86	72	63	54	45	36
940	950	163	148	133	118	103	88	74	65	56	47	38
950	960	165	150	135	120	105	91	76	66	57	48	39
960	970	168	153	138	123	108	93	78	68	59	50	41
970	980	170	155	140	125	110	96	81	69	60	51	42
980	990	173	158	143	128	113	98	83	71	62	53	44
990	1,000	175	160	145	130	115	101	86	72	63	54	45
1,000	1,010	178	163	148	133	118	103	88	74	65	56	47
1,010	1,020	180	165	150	135	120	106	91	76	66	57	48
1,020	1,030	183	168	153	138	123	108	93	78	68	59	50
1,030	1,040	185	170	155	140	125	111	96	81	69	60	51
1,040	1,050	188	173	158	143	128	113	98	83	71	62	53
1,050	1,060	190	175	160	145	130	116	101	86	72	63	54
1,060	1,070	193	178	163	148	133	118	103	88	74	65	56
1,070	1,080	195	180	165	150	135	121	106	91	76	66	57
1,080	1,090	198	183	168	153	138	123	108	93	78	68	59
1,090	1,100	200	185	170	155	140	126	111	96	81	69	60
1,100	1,110	203	188	173	158	143	128	113	98	83	71	62
1,110	1,120	205	190	175	160	145	131	116	101	86	72	63
1,120	1,130	208	193	178	163	148	133	118	103	88	74	65
1,130	1,140	210	195	180	165	150	136	121	106	91	76	66
1,140	1,150	213	198	183	168	153	138	123	108	93	78	68
1,150	1,160	215	200	185	170	155	141	126	111	96	81	69
1,160	1,170	218	203	188	173	158	143	128	113	98	83	71
1,170	1,180	220	205	190	175	160	146	131	116	101	86	72
1,180	1,190	223	208	193	178	163	148	133	118	103	88	74
1,190	1,200	225	210	195	180	165	151	136	121	106	91	76
1,200	1,210	228	213	198	183	168	153	138	123	108	93	79
1,210	1,220	230	215	200	185	170	156	141	126	111	96	81
1,220	1,230	233	218	203	188	173	158	143	128	113	98	84
1,230	1,240	235	220	205	190	175	161	146	131	116	101	86
1,240	1,250	238	223	208	193	178	163	148	133	118	103	89

$1,250 and over   Use Table 1(a) for a **SINGLE person** on page 35. Also see the instructions on page 33.

MARRIED Persons—WEEKLY Payroll Period
(For Wages Paid Through December 2004)

If the wages are–		And the number of withholding allowances claimed is—										
At least	But less than	0	1	2	3	4	5	6	7	8	9	10
		The amount of income tax to be withheld is—										
$0	$125	$0	$0	$0	$0	$0	$0	$0	$0	$0	$0	$0
125	130	0	0	0	0	0	0	0	0	0	0	0
130	135	0	0	0	0	0	0	0	0	0	0	0
135	140	0	0	0	0	0	0	0	0	0	0	0
140	145	0	0	0	0	0	0	0	0	0	0	0
145	150	0	0	0	0	0	0	0	0	0	0	0
150	155	0	0	0	0	0	0	0	0	0	0	0
155	160	0	0	0	0	0	0	0	0	0	0	0
160	165	1	0	0	0	0	0	0	0	0	0	0
165	170	1	0	0	0	0	0	0	0	0	0	0
170	175	2	0	0	0	0	0	0	0	0	0	0
175	180	2	0	0	0	0	0	0	0	0	0	0
180	185	3	0	0	0	0	0	0	0	0	0	0
185	190	3	0	0	0	0	0	0	0	0	0	0
190	195	4	0	0	0	0	0	0	0	0	0	0
195	200	4	0	0	0	0	0	0	0	0	0	0
200	210	5	0	0	0	0	0	0	0	0	0	0
210	220	6	0	0	0	0	0	0	0	0	0	0
220	230	7	1	0	0	0	0	0	0	0	0	0
230	240	8	2	0	0	0	0	0	0	0	0	0
240	250	9	3	0	0	0	0	0	0	0	0	0
250	260	10	4	0	0	0	0	0	0	0	0	0
260	270	11	5	0	0	0	0	0	0	0	0	0
270	280	12	6	0	0	0	0	0	0	0	0	0
280	290	13	7	1	0	0	0	0	0	0	0	0
290	300	14	8	2	0	0	0	0	0	0	0	0
300	310	15	9	3	0	0	0	0	0	0	0	0
310	320	16	10	4	0	0	0	0	0	0	0	0
320	330	17	11	5	0	0	0	0	0	0	0	0
330	340	18	12	6	0	0	0	0	0	0	0	0
340	350	19	13	7	1	0	0	0	0	0	0	0
350	360	20	14	8	2	0	0	0	0	0	0	0
360	370	21	15	9	3	0	0	0	0	0	0	0
370	380	22	16	10	4	0	0	0	0	0	0	0
380	390	23	17	11	5	0	0	0	0	0	0	0
390	400	24	18	12	6	0	0	0	0	0	0	0
400	410	25	19	13	7	1	0	0	0	0	0	0
410	420	26	20	14	8	2	0	0	0	0	0	0
420	430	27	21	15	9	3	0	0	0	0	0	0
430	440	28	22	16	10	4	0	0	0	0	0	0
440	450	30	23	17	11	5	0	0	0	0	0	0
450	460	31	24	18	12	6	0	0	0	0	0	0
460	470	33	25	19	13	7	1	0	0	0	0	0
470	480	34	26	20	14	8	2	0	0	0	0	0
480	490	36	27	21	15	9	3	0	0	0	0	0
490	500	37	28	22	16	10	4	0	0	0	0	0
500	510	39	30	23	17	11	5	0	0	0	0	0
510	520	40	31	24	18	12	6	0	0	0	0	0
520	530	42	33	25	19	13	7	1	0	0	0	0
530	540	43	34	26	20	14	8	2	0	0	0	0
540	550	45	36	27	21	15	9	3	0	0	0	0
550	560	46	37	29	22	16	10	4	0	0	0	0
560	570	48	39	30	23	17	11	5	0	0	0	0
570	580	49	40	32	24	18	12	6	0	0	0	0
580	590	51	42	33	25	19	13	7	1	0	0	0
590	600	52	43	35	26	20	14	8	2	0	0	0
600	610	54	45	36	27	21	15	9	3	0	0	0
610	620	55	46	38	29	22	16	10	4	0	0	0
620	630	57	48	39	30	23	17	11	5	0	0	0
630	640	58	49	41	32	24	18	12	6	0	0	0
640	650	60	51	42	33	25	19	13	7	1	0	0
650	660	61	52	44	35	26	20	14	8	2	0	0
660	670	63	54	45	36	27	21	15	9	3	0	0
670	680	64	55	47	38	29	22	16	10	4	0	0
680	690	66	57	48	39	30	23	17	11	5	0	0
690	700	67	58	50	41	32	24	18	12	6	0	0
700	710	69	60	51	42	33	25	19	13	7	1	0
710	720	70	61	53	44	35	26	20	14	8	2	0
720	730	72	63	54	45	36	27	21	15	9	3	0
730	740	73	64	56	47	38	29	22	16	10	4	0

MARRIED Persons—WEEKLY Payroll Period
(For Wages Paid Through December 2004)

If the wages are–		And the number of withholding allowances claimed is—										
At least	But less than	0	1	2	3	4	5	6	7	8	9	10
		The amount of income tax to be withheld is—										
$740	$750	$75	$66	$57	$48	$39	$30	$23	$17	$11	$5	$0
750	760	76	67	59	50	41	32	24	18	12	6	1
760	770	78	69	60	51	42	33	25	19	13	7	2
770	780	79	70	62	53	44	35	26	20	14	8	3
780	790	81	72	63	54	45	36	27	21	15	9	4
790	800	82	73	65	56	47	38	29	22	16	10	5
800	810	84	75	66	57	48	39	30	23	17	11	6
810	820	85	76	68	59	50	41	32	24	18	12	7
820	830	87	78	69	60	51	42	33	25	19	13	8
830	840	88	79	71	62	53	44	35	26	20	14	9
840	850	90	81	72	63	54	45	36	27	21	15	10
850	860	91	82	74	65	56	47	38	29	22	16	11
860	870	93	84	75	66	57	48	39	30	23	17	12
870	880	94	85	77	68	59	50	41	32	24	18	13
880	890	96	87	78	69	60	51	42	33	25	19	14
890	900	97	88	80	71	62	53	44	35	26	20	15
900	910	99	90	81	72	63	54	45	36	27	21	16
910	920	100	91	83	74	65	56	47	38	29	22	17
920	930	102	93	84	75	66	57	48	39	30	23	18
930	940	103	94	86	77	68	59	50	41	32	24	19
940	950	105	96	87	78	69	60	51	42	33	25	20
950	960	106	97	89	80	71	62	53	44	35	26	21
960	970	108	99	90	81	72	63	54	45	36	27	22
970	980	109	100	92	83	74	65	56	47	38	29	23
980	990	111	102	93	84	75	66	57	48	39	30	24
990	1,000	112	103	95	86	77	68	59	50	41	32	25
1,000	1,010	114	105	96	87	78	69	60	51	42	33	26
1,010	1,020	115	106	98	89	80	71	62	53	44	35	27
1,020	1,030	117	108	99	90	81	72	63	54	45	36	28
1,030	1,040	118	109	101	92	83	74	65	56	47	38	29
1,040	1,050	120	111	102	93	84	75	66	57	48	39	31
1,050	1,060	121	112	104	95	86	77	68	59	50	41	32
1,060	1,070	123	114	105	96	87	78	69	60	51	42	34
1,070	1,080	124	115	107	98	89	80	71	62	53	44	35
1,080	1,090	126	117	108	99	90	81	72	63	54	45	37
1,090	1,100	127	118	110	101	92	83	74	65	56	47	38
1,100	1,110	129	120	111	102	93	84	75	66	57	48	40
1,110	1,120	130	121	113	104	95	86	77	68	59	50	41
1,120	1,130	132	123	114	105	96	87	78	69	60	51	43
1,130	1,140	133	124	116	107	98	89	80	71	62	53	44
1,140	1,150	135	126	117	108	99	90	81	72	63	54	46
1,150	1,160	136	127	119	110	101	92	83	74	65	56	47
1,160	1,170	138	129	120	111	102	93	84	75	66	57	49
1,170	1,180	139	130	122	113	104	95	86	77	68	59	50
1,180	1,190	141	132	123	114	105	96	87	78	69	60	52
1,190	1,200	142	133	125	116	107	98	89	80	71	62	53
1,200	1,210	144	135	126	117	108	99	90	81	72	63	55
1,210	1,220	145	136	128	119	110	101	92	83	74	65	56
1,220	1,230	147	138	129	120	111	102	93	84	75	66	58
1,230	1,240	148	139	131	122	113	104	95	86	77	68	59
1,240	1,250	150	141	132	123	114	105	96	87	78	69	61
1,250	1,260	152	142	134	125	116	107	98	89	80	71	62
1,260	1,270	155	144	135	126	117	108	99	90	81	72	64
1,270	1,280	157	145	137	128	119	110	101	92	83	74	65
1,280	1,290	160	147	138	129	120	111	102	93	84	75	67
1,290	1,300	162	148	140	131	122	113	104	95	86	77	68
1,300	1,310	165	150	141	132	123	114	105	96	87	78	70
1,310	1,320	167	153	143	134	125	116	107	98	89	80	71
1,320	1,330	170	155	144	135	126	117	108	99	90	81	73
1,330	1,340	172	158	146	137	128	119	110	101	92	83	74
1,340	1,350	175	160	147	138	129	120	111	102	93	84	76
1,350	1,360	177	163	149	140	131	122	113	104	95	86	77
1,360	1,370	180	165	150	141	132	123	114	105	96	87	79
1,370	1,380	182	168	153	143	134	125	116	107	98	89	80
1,380	1,390	185	170	155	144	135	126	117	108	99	90	82
1,390	1,400	187	173	158	146	137	128	119	110	101	92	83

$1,400 and over   Use Table 1(b) for a **MARRIED person** on page 35. Also see the instructions on page 33.

3

Common Metric Conversions

(Accurate to Six Significant Digits)

Symbol	When you know:	Multiply by:	To find:	Symbol
in.	inches	25.4	millimeters	mm
ft	feet	0.3048	meters	m
yd	yards	0.9144	meters	m
mi	miles	1.609 34	kilometers	km
yd^2	square yards	0.836 127	square meters	m^2
ac	acres	0.404 686	hectares	ha
yd^3	cubic yards	0.764 555	cubic meters	m^3
qt	quarts (lq)	0.946 353	liters	l
oz	ounces (avdp)	28.349 5	grams	g
lb	pounds (avdp)	0.453 592	kilograms	kg
°F	degrees Fahrenheit	5/9 (after subtracting 32)	degrees Celsius	°C
mm	millimeters	0.039 370	inches	in.
m	meters	3.280 84	feet	ft
m	meters	1.093 61	yards	yd
km	kilometers	0.621 371	miles	mi
m^2	square meters	1.196 99	square yards	yd^2
ha	hectares	2.471 05	acres	ac
m^3	cubic meters	1.307 95	cubic yards	yd^3
l	liters	1.056 69	quarts (lq)	qt
g	grams	0.035 274	ounces (avdp)	oz
kg	kilograms	2.204 62	pounds (avdp)	lb
°C	degrees Celsius	9/5 (then add 32)	degrees Fahrenheit	°F

Representative
Calendar

This calendar does not necessarily represent the current year. It is provided as a "standard year," for calculation purposes.

S	M	T	W	T	F	S		S	M	T	W	T	F	S		S	M	T	W	T	F	S		S	M	T	W	T	F	S
JANUARY								**FEBRUARY**								**MARCH**								**APRIL**						1
1	2	3	4	5	6	7					1	2	3	4					1	2	3	4		2	3	4	5	6	7	8
8	9	10	11	12	13	14		5	6	7	8	9	10	11		5	6	7	8	9	10	11		9	10	11	12	13	14	15
15	16	17	18	19	20	21		12	13	14	15	16	17	18		12	13	14	15	16	17	18		16	17	18	19	20	21	22
22	23	24	25	26	27	28		19	20	21	22	23	24	25		19	20	21	22	23	24	25		23	24	25	26	27	28	29
29	30	31						26	27	28						26	27	28	29	30	31			30						
MAY								**JUNE**								**JULY**						1		**AUGUST**						
	1	2	3	4	5	6						1	2	3		2	3	4	5	6	7	8			1	2	3	4	5	
7	8	9	10	11	12	13		4	5	6	7	8	9	10		9	10	11	12	13	14	15		6	7	8	9	10	11	12
14	15	16	17	18	19	20		11	12	13	14	15	16	17		16	17	18	19	20	21	22		13	14	15	16	17	18	19
21	22	23	24	25	26	27		18	19	20	21	22	23	24		23	24	25	26	27	28	29		20	21	22	23	24	25	26
28	29	30	31					25	26	27	28	29	30			30	31							27	28	29	30	31		
SEPTEMBER								**OCTOBER**								**NOVEMBER**								**DECEMBER**					1	2
					1	2		1	2	3	4	5	6	7					1	2	3	4		3	4	5	6	7	8	9
3	4	5	6	7	8	9		8	9	10	11	12	13	14		5	6	7	8	9	10	11		10	11	12	13	14	15	16
10	11	12	13	14	15	16		15	16	17	18	19	20	21		12	13	14	15	16	17	18		17	18	19	20	21	22	23
17	18	19	20	21	22	23		22	23	24	25	26	27	28		19	20	21	22	23	24	25		24	25	26	27	28	29	30
24	25	26	27	28	29	30		29	30	31						26	27	28	29	30				31						

APPENDIX 5

Compound
Interest and
Annuity Tables

RATE 1/2% — .005 per period

Compounding (RATE column):
- .005 per period
- ANNUALLY — If compounded *annually* nominal annual rate is 1/2%
- SEMIANNUALLY — If compounded *semiannually* nominal annual rate is 1%
- QUARTERLY — If compounded *quarterly* nominal annual rate is 2%
- MONTHLY — If compounded *monthly* nominal annual rate is 6%

Present Worth Table

n	PRESENT WORTH OF 1 — What $1 due in the future is worth today	PRESENT WORTH OF 1 PER PERIOD — What $1 payable periodically is worth today	PARTIAL PAYMENT — Annuity worth $1 today. Periodic payment necessary to pay off a loan of $1
1	.995 024 8756	.995 024 8756	1.005 000 0000
2	.990 074 5031	1.985 099 3787	.503 753 1172
3	.985 148 7593	2.970 248 1380	.336 672 2084
4	.980 247 5217	3.950 495 6597	.253 132 7930
5	.975 370 6684	4.925 866 3281	.203 009 9750
6	.970 518 0780	5.896 384 4061	.169 595 4556
7	.965 689 6298	6.862 074 0359	.145 728 5355
8	.960 885 2038	7.822 959 2397	.127 828 8649
9	.956 104 6804	8.779 063 9201	.113 907 3606
10	.951 347 9407	9.730 411 8608	.102 770 5727
11	.946 614 8664	10.677 026 7272	.093 659 0331
12	.941 905 3397	11.618 932 0668	.086 066 4297
13	.937 219 2434	12.556 151 3103	.079 642 2387
14	.932 556 4611	13.488 707 7714	.074 136 0860
15	.927 916 8768	14.416 624 6482	.069 364 3640
16	.923 300 3749	15.339 925 0231	.065 189 3669
17	.918 706 8407	16.258 631 8637	.061 505 7902
18	.914 136 1599	17.172 768 0236	.058 231 7305
19	.909 588 2188	18.082 356 2424	.055 302 5273
20	.905 062 9043	18.987 419 1467	.052 666 4520
21	.900 560 1037	19.887 979 2504	.050 281 6293
22	.896 079 7052	20.784 058 9556	.048 113 7973
23	.891 621 5972	21.675 680 5529	.046 134 6530
24	.887 185 6689	22.562 866 2218	.044 320 6103
25	.882 771 8098	23.445 638 0316	.042 651 8570
26	.878 379 9103	24.324 017 9419	.041 111 6289
27	.874 009 8610	25.198 027 8029	.039 685 6456
28	.869 661 5532	26.067 689 3561	.038 361 6663
29	.865 334 8788	26.933 024 2349	.037 129 1390
30	.861 029 7302	27.794 053 9651	.035 978 9184
31	.856 746 0002	28.650 799 9653	.034 903 0394
32	.852 483 5823	29.503 283 5475	.033 894 5324
33	.848 242 2591	30.351 525 1771	.032 947 2727
34	.844 023 1434	31.195 548 9179	.032 055 8560
35	.839 823 3205	32.035 371 3205	.031 215 4958
36	.835 644 9188	32.871 016 2393	.030 421 9375
37	.831 487 4814	33.702 503 7207	.029 671 3861
38	.827 350 7278	34.529 854 4484	.028 960 4464
39	.823 234 5550	35.353 089 0034	.028 286 0714
40	.819 138 8607	36.172 227 8641	.027 645 5186
41	.815 063 5430	36.987 291 4070	.027 036 3133
42	.811 008 5075	37.798 299 9075	.026 456 2163
43	.806 973 6323	38.605 273 5398	.025 903 1969
44	.802 958 8381	39.408 232 3779	.025 375 4086
45	.798 964 0180	40.207 196 3959	.024 871 1696
46	.794 989 0727	41.002 185 4686	.024 388 9439
47	.791 033 9031	41.793 219 3717	.023 927 3264
48	.787 098 4111	42.580 317 7828	.023 485 0290
49	.783 182 4986	43.363 500 2814	.023 060 8690
50	.779 286 0683	44.142 786 3497	.022 653 7580
51	.775 409 0231	44.918 195 3728	.022 262 6931
52	.771 551 2668	45.689 746 6396	.021 886 7486
53	.767 712 7033	46.457 459 3429	.021 525 0686
54	.763 893 2371	47.221 352 5800	.021 176 8606
55	.760 092 7732	47.981 445 3532	.020 841 3897
56	.756 311 2171	48.737 756 5704	.020 517 9735
57	.752 548 4748	49.490 305 0452	.020 205 9777
58	.748 804 4525	50.239 109 4977	.019 904 8114
59	.745 079 0572	50.984 188 5549	.019 613 9240
60	.741 372 1962	51.725 560 7511	.019 332 8015

Formulas: $v^n = \dfrac{1}{(1+i)^n}$ $a_{\overline{n}|} = \dfrac{1-v^n}{i}$ $\dfrac{1}{a_{\overline{n}|}} = \dfrac{i}{1-v^n}$

$i = .005 \quad j_{(2)} = .01 \quad j_{(4)} = .02 \quad j_{(12)} = .06$

Amount / Sinking Fund Table

n	AMOUNT OF 1 — How $1 left at compound interest will grow.	AMOUNT OF 1 PER PERIOD — How $1 deposited periodically will grow.	SINKING FUND — Periodic deposit that will grow to $1 at future date.
1	1.005 000 0000	1.000 000 0000	1.000 000 0000
2	1.010 025 0000	2.005 000 0000	.498 753 1172
3	1.015 075 1250	3.015 025 0000	.331 672 2084
4	1.020 150 5006	4.030 100 1250	.248 132 7930
5	1.025 251 2531	5.050 250 6256	.198 009 9750
6	1.030 377 5094	6.075 501 8788	.164 595 4556
7	1.035 529 3969	7.105 879 3881	.140 728 5355
8	1.040 707 0439	8.141 408 7851	.122 828 8649
9	1.045 910 5791	9.182 115 8290	.108 907 3606
10	1.051 140 1330	10.228 026 4082	.097 770 5727
11	1.056 395 8327	11.279 166 5402	.088 659 0331
12	1.061 677 8119	12.335 562 3729	.081 066 4297
13	1.066 986 2009	13.397 240 1848	.074 642 2387
14	1.072 321 1319	14.464 226 3857	.069 136 0860
15	1.077 682 7376	15.536 547 5176	.064 364 3640
16	1.083 071 1513	16.614 230 2552	.060 189 3669
17	1.088 486 5070	17.697 301 4065	.056 505 7902
18	1.093 928 9396	18.785 787 9135	.053 231 7305
19	1.099 398 5843	19.879 716 8531	.050 302 5273
20	1.104 895 5772	20.979 115 4373	.047 666 4520
21	1.110 420 0551	22.084 011 0145	.045 281 6293
22	1.115 972 1553	23.194 431 0696	.043 113 7973
23	1.121 552 0161	24.310 403 2250	.041 134 6530
24	1.127 159 7762	25.431 955 2411	.039 320 6103
25	1.132 795 5751	26.559 115 0173	.037 651 8570
26	1.138 459 5530	27.691 910 5924	.036 111 6289
27	1.144 151 8507	28.830 370 1453	.034 685 6456
28	1.149 872 6100	29.974 521 9961	.033 361 6663
29	1.155 621 9730	31.124 394 6060	.032 129 1390
30	1.161 400 0829	32.280 016 5791	.030 978 9184
31	1.167 207 0833	33.441 416 6620	.029 903 0394
32	1.173 043 1187	34.608 623 7453	.028 894 5324
33	1.178 908 3343	35.781 666 8640	.027 947 2727
34	1.184 802 8760	36.960 575 1983	.027 055 8560
35	1.190 726 8904	38.145 378 0743	.026 215 4958
36	1.196 680 5248	39.336 104 9647	.025 421 9375
37	1.202 663 9274	40.532 785 4895	.024 671 3861
38	1.208 677 2471	41.735 449 4170	.023 960 4464
39	1.214 720 6333	42.944 126 6640	.023 286 0714
40	1.220 794 2365	44.158 847 2974	.022 645 5186
41	1.226 898 2077	45.379 641 5338	.022 036 3133
42	1.233 032 6987	46.606 539 7415	.021 456 2163
43	1.239 197 8622	47.839 572 4402	.020 903 1969
44	1.245 393 8515	49.078 770 3024	.020 375 4086
45	1.251 620 8208	50.324 164 1539	.019 871 1696
46	1.257 878 9249	51.575 784 9747	.019 388 9439
47	1.264 168 3195	52.833 663 8996	.018 927 3264
48	1.270 489 1611	54.097 832 2191	.018 485 0290
49	1.276 841 6069	55.368 321 3802	.018 060 8690
50	1.283 225 8149	56.645 162 9871	.017 653 7580
51	1.289 641 9440	57.928 388 8020	.017 262 6931
52	1.296 090 1537	59.218 030 7460	.016 886 7486
53	1.302 570 6045	60.514 120 8997	.016 525 0686
54	1.309 083 4575	61.816 691 5042	.016 176 8606
55	1.315 628 8748	63.125 774 9618	.015 841 3897
56	1.322 207 0192	64.441 403 8366	.015 517 9735
57	1.328 818 0543	65.763 610 8858	.015 205 9777
58	1.335 462 1446	67.092 428 9100	.014 904 8114
59	1.342 139 4553	68.427 891 0546	.014 613 9240
60	1.348 850 1525	69.770 030 5099	.014 332 8015

Formulas: $s = (1+i)^n$ $s_{\overline{n}|} = \dfrac{(1+i)^n - 1}{i}$ $\dfrac{1}{s_{\overline{n}|}} = \dfrac{i}{(1+i)^n - 1}$

$i = .005 \quad j_{(2)} = .01 \quad j_{(4)} = .02 \quad j_{(12)} = .06$

Compounding (RATE column): .005 per period; ANNUALLY (nominal annual rate 1/2%); SEMIANNUALLY (1%); QUARTERLY (2%); MONTHLY (6%).

RATE 1%

.01 per period

Section groupings (by period ranges):
- **ANNUALLY** — If compounded *annually* nominal annual rate is **1%** (periods 1–15)
- **SEMIANNUALLY** — If compounded *semiannually* nominal annual rate is **2%** (periods 16–30)
- **QUARTERLY** — If compounded *quarterly* nominal annual rate is **4%** (periods 31–45)
- **MONTHLY** — If compounded *monthly* nominal annual rate is **12%** (periods 46–60)

Table 1 — Compound Interest

n (PERIODS)	AMOUNT OF 1 — How $1 left at compound interest will grow.	AMOUNT OF 1 PER PERIOD — How $1 deposited periodically will grow.	SINKING FUND — Periodic deposit that will grow to $1 at future date.
1	1.010 000 0000	1.000 000 0000	1.000 000 0000
2	1.020 100 0000	2.010 000 0000	.497 512 4378
3	1.030 301 0000	3.030 100 0000	.330 022 1115
4	1.040 604 0100	4.060 401 0000	.246 281 0939
5	1.051 010 0501	5.101 005 0100	.196 039 7996
6	1.061 520 1506	6.152 015 0601	.162 548 3667
7	1.072 135 3521	7.213 535 2107	.138 628 2829
8	1.082 856 7056	8.285 670 5628	.120 690 2920
9	1.093 685 2727	9.368 527 2684	.106 740 3628
10	1.104 622 1254	10.462 212 5411	.095 582 0766
11	1.115 668 3467	11.566 834 6665	.086 454 0757
12	1.126 825 0301	12.682 503 0132	.078 848 7887
13	1.138 093 2804	13.809 328 0433	.072 414 8197
14	1.149 474 2132	14.947 421 3238	.066 901 1717
15	1.160 968 9554	16.096 895 5370	.062 123 7802
16	1.172 578 6449	17.257 864 4924	.057 944 5968
17	1.184 304 4314	18.430 443 1373	.054 258 0551
18	1.196 147 4757	19.614 747 5687	.050 982 0479
19	1.208 108 9504	20.810 895 0444	.048 051 7536
20	1.220 190 0399	22.019 003 9948	.045 415 3149
21	1.232 391 9403	23.239 194 0347	.043 030 7522
22	1.244 715 8598	24.471 585 9751	.040 863 7185
23	1.257 163 0183	25.716 301 8348	.038 885 8401
24	1.269 734 6485	26.973 464 8532	.037 073 4722
25	1.282 431 9950	28.243 199 5017	.035 406 7534
26	1.295 256 3150	29.525 631 4967	.033 868 8776
27	1.308 208 8781	30.820 887 8117	.032 445 5287
28	1.321 290 9669	32.129 096 6898	.031 124 4356
29	1.334 503 8766	33.450 387 6567	.029 895 0198
30	1.347 848 9153	34.784 891 5333	.028 748 1132
31	1.361 327 4045	36.132 740 4486	.027 675 7309
32	1.374 940 6785	37.494 067 8531	.026 670 8857
33	1.388 690 0853	38.869 008 5316	.025 727 4378
34	1.402 576 9862	40.257 698 6170	.024 839 9694
35	1.416 602 7560	41.660 275 6031	.024 003 6818
36	1.430 768 7836	43.076 878 3592	.023 214 3098
37	1.445 076 4714	44.507 647 1427	.022 468 9006
38	1.459 527 2361	45.952 723 6142	.021 761 4958
39	1.474 122 5085	47.412 250 8503	.021 091 5951
40	1.488 863 7336	48.886 373 3588	.020 455 5980
41	1.503 752 3709	50.375 237 0924	.019 851 0232
42	1.518 789 8946	51.878 989 4633	.019 275 6260
43	1.533 977 7936	53.397 779 3580	.018 727 3705
44	1.549 317 5715	54.931 757 1515	.018 204 4058
45	1.564 810 7472	56.481 074 7231	.017 705 0455
46	1.580 458 8547	58.045 885 4703	.017 227 7499
47	1.596 263 4432	59.626 344 3250	.016 771 1103
48	1.612 226 0776	61.222 607 7682	.016 333 8354
49	1.628 348 3385	62.834 833 8459	.015 914 7393
50	1.644 631 8218	64.463 182 1844	.015 512 7309
51	1.661 078 1401	66.107 814 0062	.015 126 8048
52	1.677 688 9215	67.768 892 1463	.014 756 0329
53	1.694 465 8107	69.446 581 0678	.014 399 5570
54	1.711 410 4688	71.141 046 8784	.014 056 5826
55	1.728 524 5735	72.852 457 3472	.013 726 3730
56	1.745 809 8192	74.580 981 9207	.013 408 2440
57	1.763 267 9174	76.326 791 7399	.013 101 5595
58	1.780 900 5966	78.090 059 6573	.012 805 7272
59	1.798 709 6025	79.870 960 2539	.012 520 1950
60	1.816 696 6986	81.669 669 8564	.012 244 4477

Formulas:
$$s = (1+i)^n \qquad s_{\overline{n}|} = \frac{(1+i)^n - 1}{i} \qquad \frac{1}{s_{\overline{n}|}} = \frac{i}{(1+i)^n - 1}$$

$i = .01 \qquad i_{(2)} = .02 \qquad i_{(4)} = .04 \qquad i_{(12)} = .12$

Table 2 — Present Worth

n (PERIODS)	PARTIAL PAYMENT — Annuity worth $1 today. Periodic payment necessary to pay off a loan of $1.	PRESENT WORTH OF 1 PER PERIOD — What $1 payable periodically is worth today.	PRESENT WORTH OF 1 — What $1 due in the future is worth today.
1	1.010 000 0000	.990 099 0099	.990 099 0099
2	.507 512 4378	1.970 395 0593	.980 296 0494
3	.340 022 1115	2.940 985 2072	.970 590 1479
4	.256 281 0939	3.901 965 5517	.960 980 3445
5	.206 039 7996	4.853 431 2393	.951 465 6876
6	.172 548 3667	5.795 476 4746	.942 045 2353
7	.148 628 2829	6.728 194 5293	.932 718 0547
8	.130 690 2920	7.651 677 7518	.923 483 2225
9	.116 740 3628	8.566 017 5760	.914 339 8242
10	.105 582 0766	9.471 304 5307	.905 286 9547
11	.096 454 0757	10.367 628 2482	.896 323 7175
12	.088 848 7887	11.255 077 0182	.887 449 2253
13	.082 414 8197	12.133 740 0728	.878 662 5993
14	.076 901 1717	13.003 703 0423	.869 962 9696
15	.072 123 7802	13.865 052 5172	.861 349 4748
16	.067 944 5968	14.717 873 7794	.852 821 2622
17	.064 258 0551	15.562 251 2667	.844 377 4873
18	.060 982 0479	16.398 268 5809	.836 017 3142
19	.058 051 7536	17.226 005 4959	.827 739 9150
20	.055 415 3149	18.045 552 5663	.819 544 4703
21	.053 030 7522	18.856 983 1349	.811 430 1687
22	.050 863 7185	19.660 379 3415	.803 396 2066
23	.048 885 8401	20.455 821 1302	.795 441 7887
24	.047 073 4722	21.243 387 2576	.787 566 1274
25	.045 406 7534	22.023 155 7006	.779 768 4430
26	.043 868 8776	22.795 203 6640	.772 047 9634
27	.042 445 5287	23.559 607 5881	.764 403 9241
28	.041 124 4356	24.316 443 1565	.756 835 5684
29	.039 895 0198	25.065 785 3035	.749 342 1470
30	.038 748 1132	25.807 708 2213	.741 922 9178
31	.037 675 7309	26.542 285 3676	.734 577 1463
32	.036 670 8857	27.269 589 4729	.727 304 1053
33	.035 727 4378	27.989 692 5474	.720 103 0745
34	.034 839 9694	28.702 665 8885	.712 973 3411
35	.034 003 6818	29.408 580 0876	.705 914 1991
36	.033 214 3098	30.107 505 0373	.698 924 9496
37	.032 468 9006	30.799 509 9379	.692 004 9006
38	.031 761 4958	31.484 663 3048	.685 153 3670
39	.031 091 5951	32.163 032 9751	.678 369 6702
40	.030 455 5980	32.834 686 1140	.671 653 1389
41	.029 851 0232	33.499 689 2217	.665 003 1078
42	.029 275 6260	34.158 108 1403	.658 418 9186
43	.028 727 3705	34.810 008 0597	.651 899 9194
44	.028 204 4058	35.455 445 4648	.645 445 4648
45	.027 705 0455	36.094 508 4401	.639 054 9156
46	.027 227 7499	36.727 236 0793	.632 727 6392
47	.026 771 1103	37.353 463 0091	.626 463 0091
48	.026 333 8354	37.973 959 4935	.620 260 4051
49	.025 914 7393	38.588 078 7064	.614 119 2129
50	.025 512 7309	39.196 117 5311	.608 038 8247
51	.025 126 8048	39.798 136 1694	.602 018 6383
52	.024 756 0329	40.394 194 2271	.596 058 0577
53	.024 399 5570	40.984 196 7199	.590 156 4928
54	.024 056 5826	41.568 664 0791	.584 313 3592
55	.023 726 3730	42.147 192 1576	.578 528 0784
56	.023 408 2440	42.719 992 2352	.572 800 0776
57	.023 101 5595	43.287 121 0250	.567 128 7898
58	.022 805 7272	43.848 634 6782	.561 513 6532
59	.022 520 1950	44.404 588 7903	.555 954 1121
60	.022 244 4477	44.955 038 4062	.550 449 6159

Formulas:
$$\frac{1}{a_{\overline{n}|}} = \frac{i}{1-v^n} \qquad a_{\overline{n}|} = \frac{1-v^n}{i} \qquad v^n = \frac{1}{(1+i)^n}$$

RATE 2%

.02 per period

ANNUALLY — If compounded *annually* nominal annual rate is **2%**

SEMIANNUALLY — If compounded *semiannually* nominal annual rate is **4%**

QUARTERLY — If compounded *quarterly* nominal annual rate is **8%**

MONTHLY — If compounded *monthly* nominal annual rate is **24%**

$i = .02 \quad i^{(2)} = .04 \quad i^{(4)} = .08 \quad i^{(12)} = .24$

PERIODS	PRESENT WORTH OF 1 — *What $1 due in the future is worth today.*	PRESENT WORTH OF 1 PER PERIOD — *What $1 payable periodically is worth today.*	PARTIAL PAYMENT — *Annuity worth $1 today. Periodic payment necessary to pay off a loan of $1.*
1	.980 392 1569	.980 392 1569	1.020 000 0000
2	.961 168 7812	1.941 560 9381	.515 049 5050
3	.942 322 3345	2.883 883 2726	.346 754 6726
4	.923 845 4260	3.807 728 6987	.262 623 7527
5	.905 730 8098	4.713 459 5085	.212 158 3941
6	.887 971 3822	5.601 430 8907	.178 525 8123
7	.870 560 1786	6.471 991 0693	.154 511 9561
8	.853 490 3712	7.325 481 4405	.136 509 7991
9	.836 755 2659	8.162 236 7064	.122 515 4374
10	.820 348 2999	8.982 585 0062	.111 326 5279
11	.804 263 0391	9.786 848 0453	.102 177 9428
12	.788 493 1756	10.575 341 2209	.094 559 5966
13	.773 032 5251	11.348 373 7460	.088 118 3527
14	.757 875 0246	12.106 248 7706	.082 601 9702
15	.743 014 7300	12.849 263 5006	.077 825 4723
16	.728 445 8137	13.577 709 3143	.073 650 1259
17	.714 162 5625	14.291 871 8768	.069 969 8408
18	.700 159 3750	14.992 031 2517	.066 702 1022
19	.686 430 7663	15.678 462 0115	.063 781 7663
20	.672 971 3331	16.351 433 3446	.061 156 7181
21	.659 775 8168	17.011 209 1614	.058 784 7689
22	.646 839 0361	17.658 048 1974	.056 631 4005
23	.634 155 9177	18.292 204 1151	.054 668 0976
24	.621 721 4879	18.913 925 6031	.052 871 0973
25	.609 530 8705	19.523 456 4384	.051 220 4384
26	.597 579 2848	20.121 035 7584	.049 699 2308
27	.585 862 0440	20.706 897 8024	.048 293 0862
28	.574 374 5529	21.281 272 3553	.046 989 6716
29	.563 112 3068	21.844 384 6620	.045 778 3552
30	.552 070 8890	22.396 455 5510	.044 649 9223
31	.541 245 9696	22.937 701 5206	.043 596 3472
32	.530 633 3035	23.468 334 8241	.042 610 6073
33	.520 228 7289	23.988 563 5530	.041 686 5311
34	.510 028 1656	24.498 591 7187	.040 818 6728
35	.500 027 6134	24.998 619 3320	.040 002 2092
36	.490 223 1504	25.488 842 4824	.039 232 8526
37	.480 610 9317	25.969 453 4141	.038 506 7789
38	.471 187 1880	26.440 640 6021	.037 820 5663
39	.461 948 2225	26.902 588 8256	.037 171 1439
40	.452 890 4152	27.355 479 2407	.036 555 7478
41	.444 010 2110	27.799 489 4517	.035 971 8836
42	.435 304 1284	28.234 793 5801	.035 417 2945
43	.426 768 7533	28.661 562 3334	.034 889 9334
44	.418 400 7386	29.079 963 0720	.034 387 9391
45	.410 196 8025	29.490 159 8745	.033 909 6161
46	.402 153 7280	29.892 313 6025	.033 453 4159
47	.394 268 3607	30.286 581 9632	.033 017 9220
48	.386 537 6086	30.673 119 5718	.032 601 8355
49	.378 958 4398	31.052 078 0115	.032 203 9639
50	.371 527 8821	31.423 605 8937	.031 823 2097
51	.364 243 0217	31.787 848 9153	.031 458 5615
52	.357 101 0017	32.144 949 9170	.031 109 0856
53	.350 099 0212	32.495 048 9382	.030 773 9189
54	.343 234 3345	32.838 283 2728	.030 452 2618
55	.336 504 2496	33.174 787 5223	.030 143 3732
56	.329 906 1270	33.504 693 6494	.029 846 5645
57	.323 437 3794	33.828 131 0288	.029 561 1957
58	.317 095 4700	34.145 226 4988	.029 286 6706
59	.310 877 9118	34.456 104 4106	.029 022 4335
60	.304 782 2665	34.760 886 6770	.028 767 9658
n	$v^n = \dfrac{1}{(1+i)^n}$	$a_{\overline{n}|} = \dfrac{1-v^n}{i}$	$\dfrac{1}{a_{\overline{n}|}}$

RATE 2%

.02 per period

ANNUALLY — If compounded *annually* nominal annual rate is **2%**

SEMIANNUALLY — If compounded *semiannually* nominal annual rate is **4%**

QUARTERLY — If compounded *quarterly* nominal annual rate is **8%**

MONTHLY — If compounded *monthly* nominal annual rate is **24%**

$i = .02 \quad i^{(2)} = .04 \quad i^{(4)} = .08 \quad i^{(12)} = .24$

n	AMOUNT OF 1 — *How $1 left at compound interest will grow.*	AMOUNT OF 1 PER PERIOD — *How $1 deposited periodically will grow.*	SINKING FUND — *Periodic deposit that will grow to $1 at future date.*
1	1.020 000 0000	1.000 000 0000	1.000 000 0000
2	1.040 400 0000	2.020 000 0000	.495 049 5050
3	1.061 208 0000	3.060 400 0000	.326 754 6726
4	1.082 432 1600	4.121 608 0000	.242 623 7527
5	1.104 080 8032	5.204 040 1600	.192 158 3941
6	1.126 162 4193	6.308 120 9632	.158 525 8123
7	1.148 685 6676	7.434 283 3825	.134 511 9561
8	1.171 659 3810	8.582 969 0501	.116 509 7991
9	1.195 092 5686	9.754 628 4311	.102 515 4374
10	1.218 994 4200	10.949 720 9997	.091 326 5279
11	1.243 374 3084	12.168 715 4197	.082 177 9428
12	1.268 241 7946	13.412 089 7281	.074 559 5966
13	1.293 606 6305	14.680 331 5227	.068 118 3527
14	1.319 478 7631	15.973 938 1531	.062 601 9702
15	1.345 868 3383	17.293 416 9162	.057 825 4723
16	1.372 785 7051	18.639 285 2545	.053 650 1259
17	1.400 241 4192	20.012 070 9596	.049 969 8408
18	1.428 246 2476	21.412 312 3788	.046 702 1022
19	1.456 811 1725	22.840 558 6264	.043 781 7663
20	1.485 947 3960	24.297 369 7989	.041 156 7181
21	1.515 666 3439	25.783 317 1949	.038 784 7689
22	1.545 979 6708	27.298 983 5388	.036 631 4005
23	1.576 899 2642	28.844 963 2096	.034 668 0976
24	1.608 437 2495	30.421 862 4738	.032 871 0973
25	1.640 605 9945	32.030 299 7232	.031 220 4384
26	1.673 418 1144	33.670 905 7177	.029 699 2308
27	1.706 886 4766	35.344 323 8321	.028 293 0862
28	1.741 024 2062	37.051 210 3087	.026 989 6716
29	1.775 844 6903	38.792 234 5149	.025 778 3552
30	1.811 361 5841	40.568 079 2052	.024 649 9223
31	1.847 588 8158	42.379 440 7893	.023 596 3472
32	1.884 540 5921	44.227 029 6051	.022 610 6073
33	1.922 231 4039	46.111 570 1972	.021 686 5311
34	1.960 676 0320	48.033 801 6011	.020 818 6728
35	1.999 889 5527	49.994 477 6331	.020 002 2092
36	2.039 887 3437	51.994 367 1858	.019 232 8526
37	2.080 685 0906	54.034 254 5295	.018 506 7789
38	2.122 298 7924	56.114 939 6201	.017 820 5663
39	2.164 744 7682	58.237 238 4125	.017 171 1439
40	2.208 039 6636	60.401 983 1807	.016 555 7478
41	2.252 200 4569	62.610 022 8444	.015 971 8836
42	2.297 244 4660	64.862 223 3012	.015 417 2945
43	2.343 189 3553	67.159 467 7673	.014 889 9334
44	2.390 053 1425	69.502 657 1226	.014 387 9391
45	2.437 854 2053	71.892 710 2651	.013 909 6161
46	2.486 611 2894	74.330 564 4704	.013 453 4159
47	2.536 343 5152	76.817 175 7598	.013 017 9220
48	2.587 070 3855	79.353 519 2750	.012 601 8355
49	2.638 811 7932	81.940 589 6605	.012 203 9639
50	2.691 588 0291	84.579 401 4537	.011 823 2097
51	2.745 419 7897	87.270 989 4828	.011 458 5615
52	2.800 328 1854	90.016 409 2724	.011 109 0856
53	2.856 334 7492	92.816 737 4579	.010 773 9189
54	2.913 461 4441	95.673 072 2070	.010 452 2618
55	2.971 730 6730	98.586 533 6512	.010 143 3732
56	3.031 165 2865	101.558 264 3242	.009 846 5645
57	3.091 788 5922	104.589 429 6107	.009 561 1957
58	3.153 624 3641	107.681 218 2029	.009 286 6706
59	3.216 696 8513	110.834 842 5669	.009 022 4335
60	3.281 030 7884	114.051 539 4183	.008 767 9658
n	$s = (1+i)^n$	$s_{\overline{n}|} = \dfrac{(1+i)^n - 1}{i}$	$\dfrac{1}{s_{\overline{n}|}} = \dfrac{i}{(1+i)^n - 1}$

RATE 3% · .03 per period

Top Table

Formulas:
- PARTIAL PAYMENT: Annuity worth $1 today. Periodic payment necessary to pay off a loan of $1. — $\dfrac{1}{a_{\overline{n}|}}$
- PRESENT WORTH OF 1 PER PERIOD: What $1 payable periodically is worth today. — $a_{\overline{n}|} = \dfrac{1-v^n}{i}$
- PRESENT WORTH OF 1: What $1 due in the future is worth today. — $v^n = (1+i)^{-n}$

PERIODS	PARTIAL PAYMENT	PRESENT WORTH OF 1 PER PERIOD	PRESENT WORTH OF 1
1	1.030 000 0000	.970 873 7864	.970 873 7864
2	.522 610 8374	1.913 469 6955	.942 595 9091
3	.353 530 3633	2.828 611 3549	.915 141 6594
4	.269 027 0452	3.717 098 4028	.888 487 0479
5	.218 354 5714	4.579 707 1872	.862 608 7844
6	.184 597 5005	5.417 191 4439	.837 484 2567
7	.160 506 3538	6.230 282 9552	.813 091 5113
8	.142 455 8888	7.019 692 1895	.789 409 2343
9	.128 433 8570	7.786 108 9219	.766 416 7323
10	.117 230 5066	8.530 202 8368	.744 093 9149
11	.108 077 4478	9.252 624 1134	.722 421 2766
12	.100 462 0855	9.954 003 9936	.701 379 8802
13	.094 029 5440	10.634 955 3336	.680 951 3400
14	.088 526 3390	11.296 073 1394	.661 117 8058
15	.083 766 5805	11.937 935 0868	.641 861 9474
16	.079 610 8493	12.561 102 0260	.623 166 9392
17	.075 952 5294	13.166 118 4718	.605 016 4458
18	.072 708 6959	13.753 513 0795	.587 394 6076
19	.069 813 9027	14.323 799 1063	.570 286 0268
20	.067 215 7076	14.877 474 8605	.553 675 7542
21	.064 871 7765	15.415 024 1364	.537 549 2759
22	.062 747 3948	15.936 916 6372	.521 892 5009
23	.060 813 9027	16.443 608 3857	.506 691 7484
24	.059 047 4159	16.935 542 1220	.491 933 7363
25	.057 427 8710	17.413 147 6913	.477 605 5693
26	.055 938 2903	17.876 842 4187	.463 694 7274
27	.054 564 2103	18.327 031 4745	.450 189 0558
28	.053 293 2334	18.764 108 2277	.437 076 7532
29	.052 114 6711	19.188 454 5900	.424 346 3623
30	.051 019 2593	19.600 441 3495	.411 986 7595
31	.049 998 9288	20.000 428 4946	.399 987 1452
32	.049 046 6183	20.388 765 5288	.388 337 0361
33	.048 156 1219	20.765 791 7755	.377 026 2467
34	.047 321 9633	21.131 836 6752	.366 044 8997
35	.046 539 2916	21.487 220 0731	.355 383 3978
36	.045 803 7942	21.832 252 4981	.345 032 4251
37	.045 111 6244	22.167 235 4351	.334 982 9369
38	.044 459 3401	22.492 461 5874	.325 226 1524
39	.043 843 8516	22.808 215 1334	.315 753 5460
40	.043 262 3779	23.114 771 9742	.306 556 8408
41	.042 712 4089	23.412 399 9750	.297 628 0008
42	.042 191 6731	23.701 359 1990	.288 959 2240
43	.041 698 1103	23.981 902 1349	.280 542 9360
44	.041 229 8469	24.254 273 9174	.272 371 7825
45	.040 785 1757	24.518 712 5412	.264 438 6238
46	.040 362 5378	24.775 449 0691	.256 736 5279
47	.039 960 5065	25.024 706 8341	.249 258 7650
48	.039 577 7738	25.266 706 6350	.241 998 8009
49	.039 213 1383	25.501 656 9272	.234 950 2922
50	.038 865 4944	25.729 764 0070	.228 107 0798
51	.038 533 8232	25.951 227 1913	.221 463 1843
52	.038 217 1837	26.166 239 9915	.215 012 8003
53	.037 914 7059	26.374 990 2830	.208 750 2915
54	.037 625 5841	26.577 660 4690	.202 670 1859
55	.037 349 0710	26.774 427 6398	.196 767 1708
56	.037 084 4726	26.965 463 7279	.191 036 0882
57	.036 831 1432	27.150 935 6582	.185 471 9303
58	.036 588 4819	27.331 005 4934	.180 069 8352
59	.036 355 9281	27.505 830 5761	.174 825 0827
60	.036 132 9587	27.675 563 6661	.169 733 0900

Compounding notes (top table):
- ANNUALLY — If compounded annually nominal annual rate is **3%**
- SEMIANNUALLY — If compounded semiannually nominal annual rate is **6%**
- QUARTERLY — If compounded quarterly nominal annual rate is **12%**
- MONTHLY — If compounded monthly nominal annual rate is **36%**
- $i = .03$, $i_{(2)} = .06$, $i_{(4)} = .12$, $i_{(12)} = .36$

Bottom Table

RATE 3% · .03 per period

Formulas:
- AMOUNT OF 1: How $1 left at compound interest will grow. — $s = (1+i)^n$
- AMOUNT OF 1 PER PERIOD: How $1 deposited periodically will grow. — $s_{\overline{n}|} = \dfrac{(1+i)^n - 1}{i}$
- SINKING FUND: Periodic deposit that will grow to $1 at future date. — $\dfrac{1}{s_{\overline{n}|}} = \dfrac{i}{(1+i)^n - 1}$

n	AMOUNT OF 1	AMOUNT OF 1 PER PERIOD	SINKING FUND
1	1.030 000 0000	1.000 000 0000	1.000 000 0000
2	1.060 900 0000	2.030 000 0000	.492 610 8374
3	1.092 727 0000	3.090 900 0000	.323 530 3633
4	1.125 508 8100	4.183 627 0000	.239 027 0452
5	1.159 274 0743	5.309 135 8100	.188 354 5714
6	1.194 052 2965	6.468 409 8843	.154 597 5005
7	1.229 873 8654	7.662 462 1808	.130 506 3538
8	1.266 770 0814	8.892 336 0463	.112 455 8888
9	1.304 773 1838	10.159 106 1276	.098 433 8570
10	1.343 916 3793	11.463 879 3115	.087 230 5066
11	1.384 233 8707	12.807 795 6908	.078 077 4478
12	1.425 760 8868	14.192 029 5615	.070 462 0855
13	1.468 533 7135	15.617 790 4484	.064 029 5440
14	1.512 589 7249	17.086 324 1618	.058 526 3390
15	1.557 967 4166	18.598 913 8867	.053 766 5805
16	1.604 706 4391	20.156 881 3033	.049 610 8493
17	1.652 847 6323	21.761 587 7424	.045 952 5294
18	1.702 433 0612	23.414 435 3747	.042 708 6959
19	1.753 506 0531	25.116 868 4359	.039 813 9027
20	1.806 111 2347	26.870 374 4890	.037 215 7076
21	1.860 294 5717	28.676 485 7236	.034 871 7765
22	1.916 103 4089	30.536 780 2954	.032 747 3948
23	1.973 586 5111	32.452 883 7042	.030 813 9027
24	2.032 794 1065	34.426 470 2153	.029 047 4159
25	2.093 777 9297	36.459 264 3218	.027 427 8710
26	2.156 591 2675	38.553 042 2515	.025 938 2903
27	2.221 289 0056	40.709 633 5190	.024 564 2103
28	2.287 927 6757	42.930 922 5246	.023 293 2334
29	2.356 565 5060	45.218 850 2003	.022 114 6711
30	2.427 262 4712	47.575 415 7063	.021 019 2593
31	2.500 080 3453	50.002 678 1775	.019 998 9288
32	2.575 082 7557	52.502 758 5228	.019 046 6183
33	2.652 335 2384	55.077 841 2785	.018 156 1219
34	2.731 905 2955	57.730 176 5169	.017 321 9633
35	2.813 862 4544	60.462 081 8124	.016 539 2916
36	2.898 278 3280	63.275 944 2668	.015 803 7942
37	2.985 226 6778	66.174 222 5948	.015 111 6244
38	3.074 783 4782	69.159 449 2726	.014 459 3401
39	3.167 026 9825	72.234 232 7505	.013 843 8516
40	3.262 037 7920	75.401 259 7333	.013 262 3779
41	3.359 898 9258	78.663 297 5253	.012 712 4089
42	3.460 695 8935	82.023 196 4511	.012 191 6731
43	3.564 516 7703	85.483 892 3446	.011 698 1103
44	3.671 452 2734	89.048 409 1149	.011 229 8469
45	3.781 595 8417	92.719 861 3884	.010 785 1757
46	3.895 043 7169	96.501 457 2300	.010 362 5378
47	4.011 895 0284	100.396 500 9469	.009 960 5065
48	4.132 251 8793	104.408 395 9753	.009 577 7738
49	4.256 219 4356	108.540 647 8546	.009 213 1383
50	4.383 906 0187	112.796 867 2892	.008 865 4944
51	4.515 423 1993	117.180 773 3089	.008 533 8232
52	4.650 885 8952	121.696 196 5082	.008 217 1837
53	4.790 412 4721	126.347 082 4035	.007 914 7059
54	4.934 124 8463	131.137 494 8756	.007 625 5841
55	5.082 148 5917	136.071 619 7218	.007 349 0710
56	5.234 613 0494	141.153 768 3135	.007 084 4726
57	5.391 651 4409	146.388 381 3629	.006 831 1432
58	5.553 400 9841	151.780 032 8038	.006 588 4819
59	5.720 003 0136	157.333 433 7879	.006 355 9281
60	5.891 603 1040	163.053 436 8015	.006 132 9587

Compounding notes (bottom table):
- ANNUALLY — If compounded annually nominal annual rate is **3%**
- SEMIANNUALLY — If compounded semiannually nominal annual rate is **6%**
- QUARTERLY — If compounded quarterly nominal annual rate is **12%**
- MONTHLY — If compounded monthly nominal annual rate is **36%**
- $i = .03$, $i_{(2)} = .06$, $i_{(4)} = .12$, $i_{(12)} = .36$

RATE 4%

.04 *per period*

ANNUALLY — If compounded *annually* nominal annual rate is **4%**

SEMIANNUALLY — If compounded *semiannually* nominal annual rate is **8%**

QUARTERLY — If compounded *quarterly* nominal annual rate is **16%**

MONTHLY — If compounded *monthly* nominal annual rate is **48%**

$i = .04$
$j_{(2)} = .08$
$j_{(4)} = .16$
$j_{(12)} = .48$

PERIODS	AMOUNT OF 1 *How $1 left at compound interest will grow.*	AMOUNT OF 1 PER PERIOD *How $1 deposited periodically will grow.*	SINKING FUND *Periodic deposit that will grow to $1 at future date.*
1	1.040 000 0000	1.000 000 0000	1.000 000 0000
2	1.081 600 0000	2.040 000 0000	.490 196 0784
3	1.124 864 0000	3.121 600 0000	.320 348 5392
4	1.169 858 5600	4.246 464 0000	.235 490 0454
5	1.216 652 9024	5.416 322 5600	.184 627 1135
6	1.265 319 0185	6.632 975 4624	.150 761 9025
7	1.315 931 7792	7.898 294 4809	.126 609 6120
8	1.368 569 0504	9.214 226 2601	.108 527 8320
9	1.423 311 8124	10.582 795 3105	.094 492 9927
10	1.480 244 2849	12.006 107 1230	.083 290 9443
11	1.539 454 0563	13.486 351 4079	.074 149 0393
12	1.601 032 2186	15.025 805 4642	.066 552 1727
13	1.665 073 5073	16.626 837 6828	.060 143 7278
14	1.731 676 4476	18.291 911 1901	.054 668 9731
15	1.800 943 5055	20.023 587 6377	.049 941 1004
16	1.872 981 2457	21.824 531 1432	.045 819 9992
17	1.947 900 4956	23.697 512 3889	.042 198 5221
18	2.025 816 5154	25.645 412 8845	.038 993 3281
19	2.106 849 1760	27.671 229 3998	.036 138 6184
20	2.191 123 1430	29.778 078 5758	.033 581 7503
21	2.278 768 0688	31.969 201 7189	.031 280 1054
22	2.369 918 7915	34.247 969 7876	.029 198 8111
23	2.464 715 5432	36.617 888 5791	.027 309 0568
24	2.563 304 1649	39.082 604 1223	.025 586 8313
25	2.665 836 3315	41.645 908 2872	.024 011 9628
26	2.772 469 7847	44.311 744 6187	.022 567 3805
27	2.883 368 5761	47.084 214 4034	.021 238 5406
28	2.998 703 3192	49.967 582 9796	.020 012 9752
29	3.118 651 4519	52.966 286 2987	.018 879 9342
30	3.243 397 5100	56.084 937 7507	.017 830 0991
31	3.373 133 4104	59.328 335 2607	.016 855 3524
32	3.508 058 7468	62.701 468 6711	.015 948 5897
33	3.648 381 0967	66.209 527 4180	.015 103 5665
34	3.794 316 3406	69.857 908 5147	.014 314 7715
35	3.946 088 9942	73.652 224 8553	.013 577 3224
36	4.103 932 5540	77.598 313 8495	.012 886 8780
37	4.268 089 8561	81.702 246 4035	.012 239 5655
38	4.438 813 4504	85.970 336 2596	.011 631 9191
39	4.616 365 9884	90.409 149 7100	.011 060 8274
40	4.801 020 6279	95.025 515 6984	.010 523 4893
41	4.993 061 4531	99.826 536 3264	.010 017 3765
42	5.192 783 9112	104.819 597 7794	.009 540 2007
43	5.400 495 2676	110.012 381 6906	.009 089 8859
44	5.616 515 0783	115.412 876 9582	.008 664 5444
45	5.841 175 6815	121.029 392 0365	.008 262 4558
46	6.074 822 7087	126.870 567 7180	.007 882 0488
47	6.317 815 6171	132.945 390 4267	.007 521 8855
48	6.570 528 2418	139.263 206 0438	.007 180 6476
49	6.833 349 3714	145.833 734 2855	.006 857 1240
50	7.106 683 3463	152.667 083 6570	.006 550 2004
51	7.390 950 6801	159.773 767 0032	.006 258 8497
52	7.686 588 7073	167.164 717 6834	.005 982 1236
53	7.994 052 2556	174.851 306 3907	.005 719 1451
54	8.313 814 3459	182.845 358 6463	.005 469 1025
55	8.646 366 9197	191.159 172 9922	.005 231 2426
56	8.992 221 5965	199.805 539 9119	.005 004 8662
57	9.351 910 4603	208.797 761 5083	.004 789 3234
58	9.725 986 8787	218.149 671 9687	.004 584 0087
59	10.115 026 3539	227.875 658 8474	.004 388 3581
60	10.519 627 4081	237.990 685 2013	.004 201 8451
n	$s=(1+i)^n$	$s_{\overline{n}\vert}=\frac{(1+i)^n-1}{i}$	$\frac{1}{s_{\overline{n}\vert}}=\frac{i}{(1+i)^n-1}$

RATE 4%

.04 *per period*

ANNUALLY — If compounded *annually* nominal annual rate is **4%**

SEMIANNUALLY — If compounded *semiannually* nominal annual rate is **8%**

QUARTERLY — If compounded *quarterly* nominal annual rate is **16%**

MONTHLY — If compounded *monthly* nominal annual rate is **48%**

$i = .04$
$j_{(2)} = .08$
$j_{(4)} = .16$
$j_{(12)} = .48$

PRESENT WORTH OF 1 *What $1 due in the future is worth today.*	PRESENT WORTH OF 1 PER PERIOD *What $1 payable periodically is worth today.*	PARTIAL PAYMENT *Annuity worth $1 today. Periodic payment necessary to pay off a loan of $1.*	PERIODS
.961 538 4615	.961 538 4615	1.040 000 0000	1
.924 556 2130	1.886 094 6746	.530 196 0784	2
.888 996 3587	2.775 091 0332	.360 348 5392	3
.854 804 1910	3.629 895 2243	.275 490 0454	4
.821 927 1068	4.451 822 3310	.224 627 1135	5
.790 314 5257	5.242 136 8567	.190 761 9025	6
.759 917 8132	6.002 054 6699	.166 609 6120	7
.730 690 2050	6.732 744 8750	.148 527 8320	8
.702 586 7356	7.435 331 6105	.134 492 9927	9
.675 564 1688	8.110 895 7794	.123 290 9443	10
.649 580 9316	8.760 476 7109	.114 149 0393	11
.624 597 0496	9.385 073 7605	.106 552 1727	12
.600 574 0861	9.985 647 8466	.100 143 7278	13
.577 475 0828	10.563 122 9295	.094 668 9731	14
.555 264 5027	11.118 387 4322	.089 941 1004	15
.533 908 1757	11.652 295 6079	.085 819 9992	16
.513 373 2459	12.165 668 8537	.082 198 5221	17
.493 628 1210	12.659 296 9747	.078 993 3281	18
.474 642 4240	13.133 939 3988	.076 138 6184	19
.456 386 9462	13.590 326 3450	.073 581 7503	20
.438 833 6021	14.029 159 9471	.071 280 1054	21
.421 955 3867	14.451 115 3337	.069 198 8111	22
.405 726 3333	14.856 841 6671	.067 309 0568	23
.390 121 4743	15.246 963 1414	.065 586 8313	24
.375 116 8023	15.622 079 9437	.064 011 9628	25
.360 689 2329	15.982 769 1766	.062 567 3805	26
.346 816 5701	16.329 585 7467	.061 238 5406	27
.333 477 4713	16.663 063 2180	.060 012 9752	28
.320 651 4147	16.983 714 6327	.058 879 9342	29
.308 318 6680	17.292 033 3007	.057 830 0991	30
.296 460 2577	17.588 493 5583	.056 855 3524	31
.285 057 9401	17.873 551 4984	.055 948 5897	32
.274 094 1731	18.147 645 6715	.055 103 5665	33
.263 552 0896	18.411 197 7611	.054 314 7715	34
.253 415 4707	18.664 613 2318	.053 577 3224	35
.243 668 7219	18.908 281 9537	.052 886 8780	36
.234 296 8479	19.142 578 8016	.052 239 5655	37
.225 285 4307	19.367 864 2323	.051 631 9191	38
.216 620 6064	19.584 484 8388	.051 060 8274	39
.208 289 0447	19.792 773 8834	.050 523 4893	40
.200 277 9276	19.993 051 8110	.050 017 3765	41
.192 574 9303	20.185 626 7413	.049 540 2007	42
.185 168 2023	20.370 794 9436	.049 089 8859	43
.178 046 3483	20.548 841 2919	.048 664 5444	44
.171 198 4118	20.720 039 7038	.048 262 4558	45
.164 613 8575	20.884 653 5613	.047 882 0488	46
.158 282 5553	21.042 936 1166	.047 521 8855	47
.152 194 7647	21.195 130 8814	.047 180 6476	48
.146 341 1199	21.341 472 0013	.046 857 1240	49
.140 712 6153	21.482 184 6167	.046 550 2004	50
.135 300 5917	21.617 485 2083	.046 258 8497	51
.130 096 7228	21.747 581 9311	.045 982 1236	52
.125 093 0027	21.872 674 9337	.045 719 1451	53
.120 281 7333	21.992 956 6671	.045 469 1025	54
.115 655 5128	22.108 612 1799	.045 231 2426	55
.111 207 2239	22.219 819 4037	.045 004 8662	56
.106 930 0229	22.326 749 4267	.044 789 3234	57
.102 817 3297	22.429 566 7564	.044 584 0087	58
.098 862 8171	22.528 429 5735	.044 388 3581	59
.095 060 4010	22.623 489 9745	.044 201 8451	60
$v^n=\frac{1}{(1+i)^n}$	$a_{\overline{n}\vert}=\frac{1-v^n}{i}$	$\frac{1}{a_{\overline{n}\vert}}=\frac{i}{1-v^n}$	n

RATE 5%

.05 per period

ANNUALLY — If compounded *annually*, nominal annual rate is **5%**
SEMIANNUALLY — If compounded *semiannually*, nominal annual rate is **10%**
QUARTERLY — If compounded *quarterly*, nominal annual rate is **20%**
MONTHLY — If compounded *monthly*, nominal annual rate is **60%**

$i = .05 \qquad j_{(2)} = .1 \qquad j_{(4)} = .2 \qquad j_{(12)} = .6$

Amount of 1 / Amount of 1 per period / Sinking Fund

n	AMOUNT OF 1 — How $1 left at compound interest will grow. $s=(1+i)^n$	AMOUNT OF 1 PER PERIOD — How $1 deposited periodically will grow. $s_{\overline{n}|}=\dfrac{(1+i)^n-1}{i}$	SINKING FUND — Periodic deposit that will grow to $1 at future date. $\dfrac{1}{s_{\overline{n}|}}=\dfrac{i}{(1+i)^n-1}$
1	1.050 000 0000	1.000 000 0000	1.000 000 0000
2	1.102 500 0000	2.050 000 0000	.487 804 8780
3	1.157 625 0000	3.152 500 0000	.317 208 0294
4	1.215 506 2500	4.310 125 0000	.232 011 8326
5	1.276 281 5625	5.525 631 2500	.180 974 7981
6	1.340 095 6406	6.801 912 8125	.147 017 4681
7	1.407 100 4227	8.142 008 4531	.122 819 8184
8	1.477 455 4438	9.549 108 8758	.104 721 8136
9	1.551 328 2160	11.026 564 3196	.090 690 0800
10	1.628 894 6268	12.577 892 5355	.079 504 5750
11	1.710 339 3581	14.206 787 1623	.070 388 8915
12	1.795 856 3260	15.917 126 5204	.062 825 4100
13	1.885 649 1423	17.712 982 8465	.056 455 7652
14	1.979 931 5994	19.598 631 9888	.051 023 9695
15	2.078 928 1794	21.578 563 5882	.046 342 2876
16	2.182 874 5884	23.657 491 7676	.042 269 9080
17	2.292 018 3178	25.840 366 3560	.038 699 1417
18	2.406 619 2337	28.132 384 6738	.035 546 2223
19	2.526 950 1954	30.539 003 9075	.032 745 0104
20	2.653 297 7051	33.065 954 1029	.030 242 5872
21	2.785 962 5904	35.719 251 8080	.027 996 1071
22	2.925 260 7199	38.505 214 3984	.025 970 5086
23	3.071 523 7559	41.430 475 1182	.024 136 8219
24	3.225 099 9437	44.501 998 8743	.022 470 9008
25	3.386 354 9409	47.727 098 8180	.020 952 4573
26	3.555 672 6879	51.113 453 7589	.019 564 3207
27	3.733 456 3223	54.669 126 4468	.018 291 8599
28	3.920 129 1385	58.402 582 7692	.017 122 5304
29	4.116 135 5954	62.322 711 9076	.016 045 5149
30	4.321 942 3752	66.438 847 5030	.015 051 4351
31	4.538 039 4939	70.760 789 8782	.014 132 1204
32	4.764 941 4686	75.298 829 3721	.013 280 4189
33	5.003 188 5420	80.063 770 8407	.012 490 0437
34	5.253 347 9691	85.066 959 3827	.011 755 4454
35	5.516 015 3676	90.320 307 3518	.011 071 7072
36	5.791 816 1360	95.836 322 7194	.010 434 4571
37	6.081 406 9428	101.628 138 8554	.009 839 7945
38	6.385 477 2899	107.709 545 7982	.009 284 2282
39	6.704 751 1544	114.095 023 0881	.008 764 6242
40	7.039 988 7121	120.799 774 2425	.008 278 1612
41	7.391 988 1477	127.839 762 9546	.007 822 2924
42	7.761 587 5551	135.231 751 1023	.007 394 7131
43	8.149 666 9329	142.993 338 6575	.006 993 3328
44	8.557 150 2795	151.143 005 5903	.006 616 2506
45	8.985 007 7935	159.700 155 8699	.006 261 7347
46	9.434 258 1832	168.685 163 6633	.005 928 2036
47	9.905 971 0923	178.119 421 8465	.005 614 2109
48	10.401 269 6469	188.025 392 9388	.005 318 4306
49	10.921 333 1293	198.426 662 5858	.005 039 6453
50	11.467 007 7858	209.347 995 7151	.004 776 7355
51	12.040 769 7750	220.815 395 5008	.004 528 6697
52	12.642 808 2638	232.856 165 2759	.004 294 9660
53	13.274 948 6770	245.498 973 5397	.004 073 3368
54	13.938 696 1108	258.773 922 2166	.003 864 3770
55	14.635 630 9164	272.712 618 3275	.003 666 8637
56	15.367 412 4622	287.348 249 2439	.003 480 0978
57	16.135 783 0853	302.715 661 7060	.003 303 4300
58	16.942 572 2396	318.851 444 7913	.003 136 2568
59	17.789 700 8515	335.794 017 0309	.002 978 0161
60	18.679 185 8941	353.583 717 8825	.002 828 1845

Present Worth of 1 / Present Worth of 1 per period / Partial Payment

PRESENT WORTH OF 1 — What $1 due in the future is worth today. $v^n=\dfrac{1}{(1+i)^n}$	PRESENT WORTH OF 1 PER PERIOD — What $1 payable periodically is worth today. $a_{\overline{n}|}=\dfrac{1-v^n}{i}$	PARTIAL PAYMENT — Annuity worth $1 today. Periodic payment necessary to pay off a loan of $1. $\dfrac{1}{a_{\overline{n}|}}=\dfrac{i}{1-v^n}$	PERIODS
.952 380 9524	.952 380 9524	1.050 000 0000	1
.907 029 4785	1.859 410 4308	.537 804 8780	2
.863 837 5985	2.723 248 0294	.367 208 0294	3
.822 702 4748	3.545 950 5042	.282 011 8326	4
.783 526 1665	4.329 476 6706	.230 974 7981	5
.746 215 3966	5.075 692 0673	.197 017 4681	6
.710 681 3301	5.786 373 3974	.172 819 8184	7
.676 839 3620	6.463 212 7594	.154 721 8136	8
.644 608 9162	7.107 821 6756	.140 690 0800	9
.613 913 2535	7.721 734 9292	.129 504 5750	10
.584 679 2891	8.306 414 2183	.120 388 8915	11
.556 837 4182	8.863 251 6364	.112 825 4100	12
.530 321 3506	9.393 572 9871	.106 455 7652	13
.505 067 9530	9.898 640 9401	.101 023 9695	14
.481 017 0981	10.379 658 0382	.096 342 2876	15
.458 111 5220	10.837 769 5602	.092 269 9080	16
.436 296 6876	11.274 066 2478	.088 699 1417	17
.415 520 6549	11.689 586 9027	.085 546 2223	18
.395 733 9570	12.085 320 8597	.082 745 0104	19
.376 889 4829	12.462 210 3425	.080 242 5872	20
.358 942 3646	12.821 152 7072	.077 996 1071	21
.341 849 8711	13.163 002 5783	.075 970 5086	22
.325 571 3058	13.488 573 8841	.074 136 8219	23
.310 067 9103	13.798 641 7943	.072 470 9008	24
.295 302 7717	14.093 944 5660	.070 952 4573	25
.281 240 7350	14.375 185 3010	.069 564 3207	26
.267 848 3190	14.643 033 6200	.068 291 8599	27
.255 093 6371	14.898 127 2571	.067 122 5304	28
.242 946 3221	15.141 073 5782	.066 045 5149	29
.231 377 4487	15.372 451 0269	.065 051 4351	30
.220 359 4749	15.592 810 5018	.064 132 1204	31
.209 866 1666	15.802 676 6684	.063 280 4189	32
.199 872 5396	16.002 549 2080	.062 490 0437	33
.190 354 7996	16.192 904 0076	.061 755 4454	34
.181 290 2854	16.374 194 2929	.061 071 7072	35
.172 657 4146	16.546 851 7076	.060 434 4571	36
.164 435 6330	16.711 287 3405	.059 839 7945	37
.156 605 3647	16.867 892 7053	.059 284 2282	38
.149 147 0040	17.017 040 6717	.058 764 6242	39
.142 045 6823	17.159 086 3540	.058 278 1612	40
.135 281 6022	17.294 367 9562	.057 822 2924	41
.128 839 6211	17.423 207 5773	.057 394 7131	42
.122 704 4011	17.545 911 9784	.056 993 3328	43
.116 861 3344	17.662 773 3128	.056 616 2506	44
.111 296 5089	17.774 069 8217	.056 261 7347	45
.105 996 6752	17.880 066 4968	.055 928 2036	46
.100 949 2144	17.981 015 7113	.055 614 2109	47
.096 142 1090	18.077 157 8203	.055 318 4306	48
.091 563 9133	18.168 721 7336	.055 039 6453	49
.087 203 7270	18.255 925 4606	.054 776 7355	50
.083 051 1685	18.338 976 6291	.054 528 6697	51
.079 096 3510	18.418 072 9801	.054 294 9660	52
.075 329 8581	18.493 402 8382	.054 073 3368	53
.071 742 7220	18.565 145 5602	.053 864 3770	54
.068 326 4019	18.633 471 9621	.053 666 8637	55
.065 072 7637	18.698 544 7258	.053 480 0978	56
.061 974 0607	18.760 518 7865	.053 303 4300	57
.059 022 9149	18.819 541 7014	.053 136 2568	58
.056 212 2999	18.875 754 0013	.052 978 0161	59
.053 535 5237	18.929 289 5251	.052 828 1845	60

RATE 6%

Right-hand table

PERIODS (n)	PRESENT WORTH OF 1 — What $1 due in the future is worth today.	PRESENT WORTH OF 1 PER PERIOD — What $1 payable periodically is worth today.	PARTIAL PAYMENT — Annuity worth $1 today. Periodic payment necessary to pay off a loan of $1.
1	.943 396 2264	.943 396 2264	1.060 000 0000
2	.889 996 4400	1.833 392 6664	.545 436 8932
3	.839 619 2830	2.673 011 9495	.374 109 8128
4	.792 093 6632	3.465 105 6127	.288 591 4924
5	.747 258 1729	4.212 363 7856	.237 396 4004
6	.704 960 5404	4.917 324 3260	.203 362 6285
7	.665 057 1136	5.582 381 4396	.179 135 0181
8	.627 412 3713	6.209 793 8110	.161 035 9426
9	.591 898 4635	6.801 692 2745	.147 022 2350
10	.558 394 7769	7.360 087 0514	.135 867 9582
11	.526 787 5254	7.886 874 5768	.126 792 9381
12	.496 969 3636	8.383 843 9404	.119 277 0294
13	.468 839 0222	8.852 682 9626	.112 960 1053
14	.442 300 9644	9.294 983 9270	.107 584 9090
15	.417 265 0607	9.712 248 9877	.102 962 7640
16	.393 646 2837	10.105 895 2715	.098 952 1436
17	.371 364 4186	10.477 259 6901	.095 444 8042
18	.350 343 7911	10.827 603 4812	.092 356 5406
19	.330 513 0105	11.158 116 4917	.089 620 8604
20	.311 804 7269	11.469 921 2186	.087 184 5570
21	.294 155 4027	11.764 076 6213	.085 004 5467
22	.277 505 0969	12.041 581 7182	.083 045 6885
23	.261 797 2612	12.303 378 9794	.081 278 4847
24	.246 978 5483	12.550 357 5278	.079 679 0050
25	.232 998 6305	12.783 356 1583	.078 226 7182
26	.219 810 0288	13.003 166 1870	.076 904 3467
27	.207 367 9517	13.210 534 1387	.075 697 1663
28	.195 630 1431	13.406 164 2818	.074 592 5515
29	.184 556 7388	13.590 721 0206	.073 579 6135
30	.174 110 1309	13.764 831 1515	.072 648 9115
31	.164 254 8405	13.929 085 9920	.071 792 2196
32	.154 957 3967	14.084 043 3887	.071 002 3374
33	.146 186 2233	14.230 229 6119	.070 272 9350
34	.137 911 5314	14.368 141 1433	.069 598 4254
35	.130 105 2183	14.498 246 3616	.068 973 8590
36	.122 740 7720	14.620 987 1336	.068 394 8348
37	.115 793 1811	14.736 780 3147	.067 857 4274
38	.109 238 8501	14.846 019 1648	.067 358 1240
39	.103 055 5190	14.949 074 6838	.066 893 7724
40	.097 222 1877	15.046 296 8715	.066 461 5359
41	.091 719 0450	15.138 015 9165	.066 058 8551
42	.086 527 4010	15.224 543 3175	.065 683 4152
43	.081 629 6235	15.306 172 9410	.065 333 1178
44	.077 009 0788	15.383 182 0198	.065 006 0565
45	.072 650 0743	15.455 832 0942	.064 700 4958
46	.068 537 8060	15.524 369 9002	.064 414 8527
47	.064 658 3075	15.589 028 2077	.064 147 6805
48	.060 998 4033	15.650 026 6110	.063 897 6549
49	.057 545 6635	15.707 572 2746	.063 663 5619
50	.054 288 3618	15.761 860 6364	.063 444 2864
51	.051 215 4357	15.813 076 0721	.063 238 8028
52	.048 316 4488	15.861 392 5208	.063 046 1669
53	.045 581 5554	15.906 974 0762	.062 865 5076
54	.043 001 4674	15.949 975 5436	.062 696 0209
55	.040 567 4221	15.990 542 9657	.062 536 9634
56	.038 271 1529	16.028 814 1186	.062 387 6472
57	.036 104 8612	16.064 918 9798	.062 247 4350
58	.034 061 1898	16.098 980 1696	.062 115 7359
59	.032 133 1979	16.131 113 3676	.061 992 0012
60	.030 314 3377	16.161 427 7052	.061 875 7215

$$v^n=\frac{1}{(1+i)^n} \qquad a_{\overline{n}|}=\frac{1-v^n}{i} \qquad \frac{1}{a_{\overline{n}|}}=\frac{i}{1-v^n}$$

- **ANNUALLY** — If compounded *annually* nominal annual rate is **6%** (PERIODS 1–10)
- **SEMIANNUALLY** — If compounded *semiannually* nominal annual rate is **12%** (PERIODS 11–30)
- **QUARTERLY** — If compounded *quarterly* nominal annual rate is **24%** (PERIODS 31–45)
- **MONTHLY** — If compounded *monthly* nominal annual rate is **72%** (PERIODS 46–60)

$i = .06 \quad j_{(2)} = .12 \quad j_{(4)} = .24 \quad j_{(12)} = .72$

.06 per period

Left-hand table

n	AMOUNT OF 1 — How $1 left at compound interest will grow.	AMOUNT OF 1 PER PERIOD — If you $1 deposited periodically will grow.	SINKING FUND — Periodic deposit that will grow to $1 at future date.
1	1.060 000 0000	1.000 000 0000	1.000 000 0000
2	1.123 600 0000	2.060 000 0000	.485 436 8932
3	1.191 016 0000	3.183 600 0000	.314 109 8128
4	1.262 476 9600	4.374 616 0000	.228 591 4924
5	1.338 225 5776	5.637 092 9600	.177 396 4004
6	1.418 519 1123	6.975 318 5376	.143 362 6285
7	1.503 630 2590	8.393 837 6499	.119 135 0181
8	1.593 848 0745	9.897 467 9088	.101 035 9426
9	1.689 478 9590	11.491 315 9834	.087 022 2350
10	1.790 847 6965	13.180 794 9424	.075 867 9582
11	1.898 298 5583	14.971 642 6389	.066 792 9381
12	2.012 196 4718	16.869 941 1973	.059 277 0294
13	2.132 928 2601	18.882 137 6691	.052 960 1053
14	2.260 903 9558	21.015 065 9292	.047 584 9090
15	2.396 558 1931	23.275 969 8850	.042 962 7640
16	2.540 351 6847	25.672 528 0781	.038 952 1436
17	2.692 772 7858	28.212 879 7628	.035 444 8042
18	2.854 339 1529	30.905 652 5485	.032 356 5406
19	3.025 599 5021	33.759 591 7015	.029 620 8604
20	3.207 135 4722	36.785 591 2035	.027 184 5570
21	3.399 563 6005	39.992 726 6758	.025 004 5467
22	3.603 537 4166	43.392 290 2763	.023 045 6885
23	3.819 749 6616	46.995 827 6929	.021 278 4847
24	4.048 934 6413	50.815 577 3545	.019 679 0050
25	4.291 870 7197	54.864 511 9957	.018 226 7182
26	4.549 382 9629	59.156 382 7155	.016 904 3467
27	4.822 345 9407	63.705 765 6784	.015 697 1663
28	5.111 686 6971	68.528 111 6191	.014 592 5515
29	5.418 387 8990	73.639 798 3162	.013 579 6135
30	5.743 491 1729	79.058 186 2152	.012 648 9115
31	6.088 100 6433	84.801 677 3881	.011 792 2196
32	6.453 386 6819	90.889 778 0314	.011 002 3374
33	6.840 589 8828	97.343 164 7133	.010 272 9350
34	7.251 871 2758	104.183 754 5961	.009 598 4254
35	7.686 086 7923	111.434 779 8719	.008 973 8590
36	8.147 251 9999	119.120 866 6642	.008 394 8348
37	8.636 087 1198	127.268 118 6640	.007 857 4274
38	9.154 252 3470	135.904 205 7839	.007 358 1240
39	9.703 507 4879	145.058 458 1309	.006 893 7724
40	10.285 717 9371	154.761 965 6188	.006 461 5359
41	10.902 861 0134	165.047 683 5559	.006 058 8551
42	11.557 032 6742	175.950 544 5692	.005 683 4152
43	12.250 454 6346	187.507 577 2434	.005 333 1178
44	12.985 481 9127	199.758 031 8780	.005 006 0565
45	13.764 610 8274	212.743 513 7907	.004 700 4958
46	14.590 487 4771	226.508 124 6181	.004 414 8527
47	15.465 916 7257	241.098 612 0952	.004 147 6805
48	16.393 871 7293	256.564 528 8209	.003 897 6549
49	17.377 504 0330	272.958 400 5502	.003 663 5619
50	18.420 154 2750	290.335 904 5832	.003 444 2864
51	19.525 363 5315	308.756 058 8582	.003 238 8028
52	20.696 885 3434	328.281 422 3897	.003 046 1669
53	21.938 698 4640	348.978 307 7331	.002 865 5076
54	23.255 020 3718	370.917 006 1970	.002 696 0209
55	24.650 321 5941	394.172 026 5689	.002 536 9634
56	26.129 340 8898	418.822 348 1630	.002 387 6472
57	27.697 101 3432	444.951 689 0528	.002 247 4350
58	29.358 927 4238	472.648 790 3959	.002 115 7359
59	31.120 463 0692	502.007 717 8197	.001 992 0012
60	32.987 690 8553	533.128 180 8889	.001 875 7215

$$s=(1+i)^n \qquad s_{\overline{n}|}=\frac{(1+i)^n-1}{i} \qquad \frac{1}{s_{\overline{n}|}}=\frac{i}{(1+i)^n-1}$$

RATE 6% — .06 per period

- **ANNUALLY** — If compounded *annually* nominal annual rate is **6%**
- **SEMIANNUALLY** — If compounded *semiannually* nominal annual rate is **12%**
- **QUARTERLY** — If compounded *quarterly* nominal annual rate is **24%**
- **MONTHLY** — If compounded *monthly* nominal annual rate is **72%**

$i = .06 \quad j_{(2)} = .12 \quad j_{(4)} = .24 \quad j_{(12)} = .72$

RATE 8%

.08 per period

ANNUALLY — If compounded *annually* nominal annual rate is 8%
SEMIANNUALLY — If compounded *semiannually* nominal annual rate is 16%
QUARTERLY — If compounded *quarterly* nominal annual rate is 32%
MONTHLY — If compounded *monthly* nominal annual rate is 96%
i = .08   i₍₂₎ = .16   i₍₄₎ = .32   i₍₁₂₎ = .96

Right-hand table (Present Worth / Partial Payment)

PERIODS n	PARTIAL PAYMENT — Annuity worth $1 today. Periodic payment necessary to pay off a loan of $1.	PRESENT WORTH OF 1 PER PERIOD — What $1 payable periodically is worth today.	PRESENT WORTH OF 1 — What $1 due in the future is worth today.
1	1.080 000 0000	.925 925 9259	.925 925 9259
2	.560 769 2308	1.783 264 7462	.857 338 8203
3	.388 033 5140	2.577 096 9872	.793 832 2410
4	.301 920 8045	3.312 126 8400	.735 029 8528
5	.250 456 4546	3.992 710 0371	.680 583 1970
6	.216 315 3862	4.622 879 6640	.630 169 6269
7	.192 072 4014	5.206 370 0592	.583 490 3953
8	.174 014 7606	5.746 638 9437	.540 268 8845
9	.160 079 7092	6.246 887 9109	.500 248 9671
10	.149 029 4887	6.710 081 3989	.463 193 4881
11	.140 076 3421	7.138 964 2583	.428 882 8593
12	.132 695 0169	7.536 078 0169	.397 113 7586
13	.126 521 8052	7.903 775 9416	.367 697 9247
14	.121 296 8528	8.244 236 9830	.340 461 0414
15	.116 829 5449	8.559 478 6879	.315 241 7050
16	.112 976 8720	8.851 369 1555	.291 890 4676
17	.109 629 4315	9.121 638 1069	.270 268 9514
18	.106 702 0959	9.371 887 1360	.250 249 0291
19	.104 127 6275	9.603 599 2000	.231 712 0640
20	.101 852 2088	9.818 147 4074	.214 548 2074
21	.099 832 2503	10.016 803 1550	.198 655 7476
22	.098 032 0684	10.200 743 6621	.183 940 5070
23	.096 422 1692	10.371 058 9464	.170 315 2843
24	.094 977 9616	10.528 758 2837	.157 699 3373
25	.093 678 7791	10.674 776 1886	.146 017 9049
26	.092 507 1267	10.809 977 9524	.135 201 7638
27	.091 448 0962	10.935 164 7707	.125 186 8183
28	.090 488 9057	11.051 078 4914	.115 913 7207
29	.089 618 5350	11.158 406 0106	.107 327 5192
30	.088 827 4334	11.257 783 3431	.099 377 3325
31	.088 107 2841	11.349 799 3918	.092 016 0487
32	.087 450 8132	11.434 999 4368	.085 200 0451
33	.086 851 6324	11.513 888 3674	.078 888 9306
34	.086 304 1101	11.586 933 6736	.073 045 3061
35	.085 803 2646	11.654 568 2163	.067 634 5427
36	.085 344 6741	11.717 192 7928	.062 624 5766
37	.084 924 4025	11.775 178 5119	.057 985 7190
38	.084 538 1370	11.828 868 9925	.053 690 4806
39	.084 185 1297	11.878 582 6736	.049 713 4080
40	.083 860 1615	11.924 613 3337	.046 030 9333
41	.083 561 4940	11.967 234 5683	.042 621 6345
42	.083 286 8407	12.006 698 6743	.039 464 4061
43	.083 034 1370	12.043 239 5133	.036 540 2339
44	.082 801 5156	12.077 073 6234	.033 834 4101
45	.082 587 2845	12.108 401 5032	.031 327 8797
46	.082 389 9085	12.137 408 7992	.029 007 2961
47	.082 207 9922	12.164 267 4067	.026 858 6075
48	.082 040 2660	12.189 136 4877	.024 869 0810
49	.081 885 5731	12.212 163 4345	.023 026 9268
50	.081 742 8582	12.233 484 6431	.021 321 2286
51	.081 611 1575	12.253 226 5214	.019 741 8783
52	.081 489 5903	12.271 506 0383	.018 279 5169
53	.081 377 3506	12.288 431 5169	.016 925 4786
54	.081 273 7003	12.304 103 2564	.015 671 7395
55	.081 177 9629	12.318 614 1263	.014 510 8699
56	.081 089 5180	12.332 050 1170	.013 435 9906
57	.081 007 7963	12.344 490 8490	.012 440 7321
58	.080 932 2748	12.356 010 0454	.011 519 1984
59	.080 862 4729	12.366 675 9680	.010 665 9226
60	.080 797 9488	12.376 551 8222	.009 875 8542

Formulas:
$$\frac{1}{a_{\overline{n}|}} \qquad a_{\overline{n}|} = \frac{1 - v^n}{i} \qquad v^n = \frac{1}{(1+i)^n}$$

Left-hand table (Amount of 1 / Sinking Fund)

SINKING FUND — Periodic deposit that will grow to $1 at future date.	AMOUNT OF 1 PER PERIOD — How $1 deposited periodically will grow.	AMOUNT OF 1 — How $1 left at compound interest will grow.	PERIODS n
1.000 000 0000	1.000 000 0000	1.080 000 0000	1
.480 769 2308	2.080 000 0000	1.166 400 0000	2
.308 033 5140	3.246 400 0000	1.259 712 0000	3
.221 920 8045	4.506 112 0000	1.360 488 9600	4
.170 456 4546	5.866 600 9600	1.469 328 0768	5
.136 315 3862	7.335 929 0368	1.586 874 3229	6
.112 072 4014	8.922 803 3597	1.713 824 2688	7
.094 014 7606	10.636 627 6285	1.850 930 2103	8
.080 079 7092	12.487 557 8388	1.999 004 6271	9
.069 029 4887	14.486 562 4659	2.158 924 9973	10
.060 076 3421	16.645 487 4632	2.331 638 9971	11
.052 695 0169	18.977 126 4602	2.518 170 1168	12
.046 521 8052	21.495 296 5771	2.719 623 7262	13
.041 296 8528	24.214 920 3032	2.937 193 7243	14
.036 829 5449	27.152 113 9275	3.172 169 1142	15
.032 976 8720	30.324 283 0417	3.425 942 6433	16
.029 629 4315	33.750 225 6850	3.700 018 0548	17
.026 702 0959	37.450 243 7398	3.996 019 4992	18
.024 127 6275	41.446 263 2390	4.315 701 0591	19
.021 852 2088	45.761 964 2981	4.660 957 1438	20
.019 832 2503	50.422 921 4420	5.033 833 7154	21
.018 032 0684	55.456 755 1573	5.436 540 4126	22
.016 422 1692	60.893 295 5699	5.871 463 6456	23
.014 977 9616	66.764 759 2155	6.341 180 7372	24
.013 678 7791	73.105 939 9527	6.848 475 1962	25
.012 507 1267	79.954 415 1490	7.396 353 2119	26
.011 448 0962	87.350 768 3609	7.988 061 4689	27
.010 488 9057	95.338 829 8297	8.627 106 3864	28
.009 618 5350	103.965 936 2161	9.317 274 8973	29
.008 827 4334	113.283 211 1134	10.062 656 8891	30
.008 107 2841	123.345 868 0025	10.867 669 4402	31
.007 450 8132	134.213 537 4427	11.737 082 9954	32
.006 851 6324	145.950 620 4381	12.676 049 6350	33
.006 304 1101	158.626 670 0732	13.690 133 6059	34
.005 803 2646	172.316 803 6790	14.785 344 2943	35
.005 344 6741	187.102 147 9733	15.968 171 8379	36
.004 924 4025	203.070 319 8112	17.245 625 5849	37
.004 538 1370	220.315 945 3961	18.625 275 6317	38
.004 185 1297	238.941 221 0278	20.115 297 6822	39
.003 860 1615	259.056 518 7100	21.724 521 4968	40
.003 561 4940	280.781 040 2068	23.462 483 2165	41
.003 286 8407	304.243 523 4233	25.339 481 8739	42
.003 034 1370	329.583 005 2972	27.366 640 4238	43
.002 801 5156	356.949 645 7210	29.555 971 6577	44
.002 587 2845	386.505 617 3787	31.920 449 3903	45
.002 389 9085	418.426 066 7690	34.474 085 3415	46
.002 207 9922	452.900 152 1105	37.232 012 1688	47
.002 040 2660	490.132 164 2793	40.210 573 1423	48
.001 885 5731	530.342 737 4217	43.427 418 9937	49
.001 742 8582	573.770 156 4154	46.901 612 5132	50
.001 611 1575	620.671 768 9286	50.653 741 5143	51
.001 489 5903	671.325 510 4429	54.706 040 8354	52
.001 377 3506	726.031 551 2783	59.082 524 1023	53
.001 273 7003	785.114 075 3806	63.809 126 0304	54
.001 177 9629	848.923 201 4111	68.913 856 1129	55
.001 089 5180	917.837 057 5239	74.426 964 6019	56
.001 007 7963	992.264 022 1259	80.381 121 7701	57
.000 932 2748	1072.645 143 8959	86.811 611 5117	58
.000 862 4729	1159.456 755 4076	93.756 540 4326	59
.000 797 9488	1253.213 295 8402	101.257 063 6672	60

Formulas:
$$\frac{1}{s_{\overline{n}|}} = \frac{i}{(1+i)^n - 1} \qquad s_{\overline{n}|} = \frac{(1+i)^n - 1}{i} \qquad s = (1+i)^n$$

RATE 8%

.08 per period

ANNUALLY — If compounded *annually* nominal annual rate is 8%
SEMIANNUALLY — If compounded *semiannually* nominal annual rate is 16%
QUARTERLY — If compounded *quarterly* nominal annual rate is 32%
MONTHLY — If compounded *monthly* nominal annual rate is 96%

i = .08   i₍₂₎ = .16   i₍₄₎ = .32   i₍₁₂₎ = .96

Glossary of Common Business Terms

Account	A business record showing amounts paid and owed.
Accounts payable	Bills owed to others.
Accounts receivable	Total bills to be collected from others.
Accrue	To grow, to be added to, to mature.
Accumulative multiplication	The sum of one or more products and a previously known number.
Adjust	Put in order, regulate, or make a settlement.
Adjusted balance	Actual amount available in a checking account at a particular point in time.
Aggregate	Total sum, quantity, or number of anything.
Algorithm	A fixed, step-by-step procedure designed to lead to the solution of a problem.
Allocate	Assign or allot.
Allotment	A share, part, or portion, granted or distributed.
Amortizing	Paying off a loan in monthly payments.
Analysis	Careful study of a problem, or the method of finding a solution or a better way.
Annual	Yearly, coming every year.
Annual Percentage Rate (APR)	The annual rate of interest based on total finance charges including interest, carrying charges, insurance, and special fees. The Federal Truth In Lending Act requires the APR be given by creditors to make consumers aware of the true cost of credit.
Annuity	A sum paid to another party for a period of years; an equal period payment.
Approximate	Come close to; not exact; about.
Ascertain	Find out by trial, examination, or experiment, so as to know for certain; determine.
Assessment	Value put on property for tax purposes.
Assets	Possessions of value; all things a business owns or owed to it.
Audit	Examine or check records, inventory, or other data.
Bad debts	Money owed by a customer unwilling or unable to pay.
Balance	Makes things equal.

Balance due	Amount owed.
Balance sheet	A financial report presenting a complete picture of the financial condition of a business on a particular date.
Base	Basis of comparison, 100%, the number of which so many hundredths is taken.
Beneficiary	Person or organization that will receive the financial benefits of a life insurance policy.
Bias	The design of a study is biased if it systematically favors certain outcomes.
Bill of lading	A receipt issued by a transport company, with copies going to sender of goods and to receiver.
Bill of sale	A document transferring title of personal property from seller to buyer.
Bills	Statements of money owed for work done, things supplied, or service provided.
Bond	A certificate of debt (usually in units of $1,000) guaranteeing payment of the original investment plus interest (usually paid semi-annually) by a specified future date.
Book value	Estimated worth of a fixed asset, adjusted for depreciation. Different from actual or marketable value.
Budget	An estimate of expected income and expense, or of operating results, for a given period in the future.
Budget deficit	The amount by which expenditures exceed revenue in any one period, usually a year.
Cancel	With fractions, eliminating a common divisor from numerator and denominator; removing equivalent values from both sides of an equation.
Cash	Currency, checks, money orders.
Cash discount	A reduction in the price of merchandise offered to a buyer for early payment; A reduction in price for not using a credit card.
Census	A process of gathering data from the whole population for a measurement of interest.
Chain discount	A method of price adjustment based on a series of discounts, each discount being taken on the net price after the preceding discount has been deducted.
Check	A written order instructing a banker to pay a certain amount of money out of a particular account.
Chip	In a calculator the integrated electronic circuitry that transforms what is entered on a keyboard into a displayed answer. A chip is very small and does the job of what formerly took many thousands of transistors.
Coefficient of Variation	The ratio of the standard deviation to the mean expressed in percentage.
Co-insurance	Policy holder and insurance company share the financial loss of property damage.

Commission	A sum of money allowed an agent for services rendered.
Common carrier	A transportation firm authorized by the federal government to carry freight over established routes on established schedules and at approved rates.
Compensation	Something given or received as an equivalent for services, debt, loss, suffering; an indemnity.
Complement	Difference between a number and the next higher power of ten.
Complex fraction	A fraction with a mixed number in the numerator or denominator or both.
Compound interest	Interest that is earned on interest and redeposited or credited to an account at the end of a conversion period.
Computation	Reaching a solution by adding, subtracting, dividing, or multiplying.
Computer	A machine that accepts instructions and information and which follows the instructions to perform operations on the information.
Constant	A numerical value that remains unchanged during a given period or during a series of calculations.
Constant function	On a calculator, a device for locking in a number used in successive calculations, to avoid re-entering the number each time it is used. Most constant functions work for both multiplication and division.
Consumer sovereignty	Determination by consumers of the types and quantities of goods and services that are produced from the scarce resources of the economy.
Contract carrier	An independent transport firm that has negotiable rates, schedules, and routes.
Control chart	A graph containing an upper control limit and lower control limit, that is often set at plus or minus two standard deviations from the mean or centerline so that 95% of the data should fall within the control limits; used in quality control.
Correlation	A measure of the degree of relatedness of two or more variables.
Cost	Amount owed for a good or service provided.
Credit	Payment over time for goods or services sold on trust; the balance in a person's favor in an account. In customer accounts, a reduction.
Credit balance	Total result of over-subtracting; a negative balance.
Credit memorandum	A paper showing credit on account.
Creditor	Person or company to whom money is owed.
Cross-footing	Adding a column or columns vertically, after computing horizontally; provides a check of calculation accuracy.
CWT	Hundred weight, or 100 pounds; indicates that a weight given is in units of 100 pounds.

Database	Usually a computerized collection of information arranged for ease and speed of retrieval.
Debit	In customer accounts, a charge.
Debtor	Person or company owing money.
Decimal equivalent	Number in decimal from resulting from the division of the numerator of a fraction by the denominator.
Decimal point, floating and fixed	A floating decimal point in an electronic calculator automatically moves the decimal to the correct position in an answer. If set to a fixed decimal position, the calculator drops all but the significant decimal digits; if it has automatic round-off, the calculator rounds the displayed answer.
Denominator	The part of a common fraction written below the line; indicates the number of equal parts into which the whole has been divided.
Depreciation	A decrease in value due to wear, decay, age, or obsolescence.
Digit	Any of the integers from 0 through 9.
Discount	A deduction allowed from the face amount of an invoice for a certain consideration, such as cash payment or quantity purchase; interest deducted in advance from the proceeds of a loan.
Discounting	Purchase of a negotiable note due in the future, for a sum smaller than the face value of the note.
Dividend	Number that is to be divided by another.
Dividends	Profits distributed to shareholder-owners or a corporation.
Divisor	Number by which to divide.
Double multiplication	Machine multiplication of two numbers by another number to give two products simultaneously.
Endorsement	Signature of the payee on the back of a check.
Entrepreneurial ability	The human resource which combines the other resources to produce a product, makes non-routine decisions, innovates, and bears risks.
Escrow account	An account kept by a lending institution into which a borrower pays in order to accumulate enough money to pay property taxes and property insurance when they come due.
Exemptions	For income tax purposes, the legal dependents and employee claimed by an employee to reduce the amount of tax withheld.
Exports	Goods and services produced in a nation and sold to customers in other nations.
Extension	The product of multiplying two factors, as in extending an invoice. Quantity times price equals extension.
F.O.B. (Free on Board)	When merchandise is placed on a transport vehicle free of charge.
Face value	Original amount of a loan or bond.

Flowchart	A graphic representation of a computer program in which symbols represent operations.
Fraction	A way of expressing division or a ratio, in which one number (numerator) is above a line, and another number (denominator) is below the line. See also **Complex fraction, Improper fraction, Mixed number**, and **Proper fraction**.
Gross	Twelve dozen (or 144) items; overall total before deductions.
Gross earnings	Amount earned by an employee in a pay period before deductions.
Gross domestic product (GDP)	The total market value of all find goods and services produced annually within the boundaries of the United States, whether by American or foreign-supplied resources.
Gross national product (GNP)	The total market value of all final goods and services produced annually by land, labor, capital, and entrepreneurial talent supplied by American residents, whether these resources are located in the United States or abroad.
Imports	Spending by individuals, firms, and governments of an economy for goods and services produced in foreign nations.
Improper fraction	A fraction in which the numerator is larger than the denominator; value is always greater than one.
Income statement	A report showing the financial activity of a firm over a period of time.
Inflation	A general increase in the prices of most goods and services.
Installment	A partial payment.
Interest	Any payment made for the use of capital.
Inventory	A detailed list of assets with numbers of and value of each.
Invoice	An itemized bill sent to a buyer, containing the prices that comprise the total charge.
Itemize	Make a list of items.
Liabilities	Things of value that a business owes to others; debts.
Liquidate	Discharge, pay off, convert into cash by selling.
List price	Price shown in a catalog, often subject to trade discounts.
Lowest common denominator (LCD)	Smallest whole number that is divisible, without a remainder, by all the denominators in a series of fractions. Addition or subtraction of fractions having different denominators is simplified by converting each fraction to its equivalent in terms of the LCD.
Margin	Difference between cost and selling price.
Mark down	Lowering the prices on overstocked or out-of-style goods in order to sell them faster.

Mark up	Adding to the price of goods an amount to cover costs and profit. Cost plus mark up equals retail selling price.
Maturity	Due date of a loan.
Maturity value	Loan principal plus interest.
Mean	Sum of the variables divided by number of variables.
Median	Middle-ranked value of a data set.
Merchandise	Goods bought for resale.
Mill	Monetary value equal to 1/1,000 of a dollar.
Minuend	A number from which another is to be subtracted.
Mixed number	A fraction consisting of a whole number and a proper fraction.
Mode	Most frequently occurring value in a data set.
Monopoly	A market in which the number of sellers is so small that each seller is able to influence the total supply and the price of the good or service.
Multiplicand	A number being multiplied by another number.
Multiplier	A number by which one multiplies.
Nanosecond	One thousandth of a millionth of a second.
Negative multiplication	Subtraction of one product from another or from any previous known number.
Negotiable instrument	A written paper, signed by a maker or drawer, containing a promise or order to pay a sum of money, which is transferable.
Net	That which remains after deducting all charges, outlay, or loss.
Net earnings	Amount earned by an employee in a pay period after deductions.
Net income	Profit after all expenses and taxes.
Net purchases	Total amount of purchases less than amount of returned goods.
Net sales	Total amount of sales minus discount allowance and net returns.
Net worth	Total value of a business after all debts have been deducted.
Note	A written promise to pay a definite sum of money on demand or at a specified time.
Numerator	That part of a proper fraction written above the line, indicating the number of equal parts of the whole represented by the fraction.
Overhead	Expenses of managing a business.
Overtime	Time worked by an employee in addition to regular work time.
Payee	Person to whom a check is payable.
Payment	Money given to discharge a debt.
Percent	Literally, parts of 100.
Percentile	A number that corresponds to one of 100 equal divisions.
Policy	A contractual document explaining the financial commitment of an insurance company to a policy holder.

Premium	A payment amount for insurance protection.
Present value	Amount which, when compounded at a given rate per period, will total a desired sum at a future date.
Price index	An index number which shows the average price of a "market basket" of goods changes through time.
Principal	Quantity of money borrowed or invested on which interest is calculated.
Proceeds	The amount received when merchandize or a negotiable instrument is exchanged for cash.
Product	Result of multiplication.
Program	A set of computer instructions.
Proper fraction	A fraction in which the numerator is smaller than the denominator; value is always less than one.
Prorate	To divide or distribute proportionately.
Quartile	The value of the boundary at the 25th, 50th, or 75, percentiles of a frequency distribution divided into four parts, each containing a quarter of the populations.
Quartile deviation	The difference between the first and third quartiles.
Quotient	Result of division.
Range	The difference between the largest and smallest numbers in a set of numbers.
Rate	Percent or parts of 100, applied against a base amount or figure.
Ratio	A relationship expressed in numbers. Examples: 2 to 1, or 2:1, or 2/1.
Reciprocal	Quotient resulting from dividing 1 by a given number.
Remit	Give or send payment.
Remittance	Payment of an amount due.
Sales allowance	Adjustments made in the price of merchandise to compensate the buyer for keeping the damaged or wrong merchandise.
Service charge	A charge to a depositor by a bank for use of an account, for imprinting of checks, or for other services.
Simulation	Using a computer program as a model of a real-life situation.
Sinking fund	The accumulation of payments in an interest-paying investment to reach a desired amount at a future date.
Software	A computer's programs, plus the procedure for their use.
Spreadsheets	Computer programs to speed and simplify the many arithmetic and accounting steps performed in a business.
Standard deviation	The square root of the average of the squared deviations about the arithmetic mean for a set of numbers.
Statistic	A descriptive measure of a sample.

Statistics	A science dealing with the collection, analysis, interpretation, and presentation of numerical data.
Stock	Shares in a corporation entitling the holder to dividends and to other ownership rights.
Subroutine	A computer program called for as part of a larger program.
Subtrahend	A number to be subtracted from another number.
Sum	The result of adding two or more numbers.
Tare	Allowance made for the weight of a merchandise container; weight of a vehicle without its load.
Term of note	Number of days between the date of a note and its due date.
Trade discount	A reduction from list price for quantity purchase or for the assumption of marketing functions by the buyer.
Turnover	Number of times the average inventory is solid. A measure of success for the retailer.
Variable	A value that changes with each problem. The opposite of a variable is a constant.
Verify	Prove as true.

Index